T0380713

# THE
# PLIGHT
## AND
# TRAVELS
## OF THE
# HEBREWS

### According to Vance: History, Science, and Scripture

## Anthony J. Vance

**BALBOA**.PRESS
A DIVISION OF HAY HOUSE

Copyright © 2021 Anthony J. Vance.

All rights reserved. No part of this book may be used or reproduced by any means, graphic, electronic, or mechanical, including photocopying, recording, taping or by any information storage retrieval system without the written permission of the author except in the case of brief quotations embodied in critical articles and reviews.

Balboa Press books may be ordered through booksellers or by contacting:

Balboa Press
A Division of Hay House
1663 Liberty Drive
Bloomington, IN 47403
www.balboapress.com
844-682-1282

Because of the dynamic nature of the Internet, any web addresses or links contained in this book may have changed since publication and may no longer be valid. The views expressed in this work are solely those of the author and do not necessarily reflect the views of the publisher, and the publisher hereby disclaims any responsibility for them.

The author of this book does not dispense medical advice or prescribe the use of any technique as a form of treatment for physical, emotional, or medical problems without the advice of a physician, either directly or indirectly. The intent of the author is only to offer information of a general nature to help you in your quest for emotional and spiritual well-being. In the event you use any of the information in this book for yourself, which is your constitutional right, the author and the publisher assume no responsibility for your actions.

Any people depicted in stock imagery provided by Getty Images are models, and such images are being used for illustrative purposes only. Certain stock imagery © Getty Images.

The Authorized (King James) Version of the Bible ('the KJV'), the rights in which are vested in the Crown in the United Kingdom, is reproduced here by permission of the Crown's patentee, Cambridge University Press.

The Cambridge KJV text including paragraphing, is reproduced here by permission of Cambridge University Press.

The Orthodox Jewish Bible fourth edition, OJB. Copyright 2002,2003,2008,2010, 2011 by Artists for Israel International. All rights reserved.

Print information available on the last page.

ISBN: 978-1-9822-6436-9 (sc)
ISBN: 978-1-9822-6486-4 (hc)
ISBN: 978-1-9822-6437-6 (e)

Balboa Press rev. date: 02/22/2021

# CONTENTS

Introduction .................................................................... ix

Foreword ......................................................................... xv

The Beginning Of Beginnings To Never Ending: The
Bereshis/Genesis ............................................................... 1

The Plight And Travels Begin With Mitzrayim (Egypt) ................. 93

The Laws To Govern The People ........................................ 143

History Of The English Language Bible ............................... 151

Combining The Canons That Discuss Reproduction ............... 167

Covering Most Of Devarim/Deuteronomy ........................... 183

The Prophet ................................................................... 251

The War Between Yehuwdah And Yisra'el (Ephraim) ............ 275

The Hebrew And Christianity ........................................... 289

The Book In Review ....................................................... 331

References ..................................................................... 337

*Thesis Statement:*

*How does religion influence an individual or group behavior, and their character as being of good or evil countenance?*

*Has humanity existed more than six thousand (6,000) years? Has there been more than one (1) creation? Who is Lilith, and was she created before Chavvah (Eve)? What has Science revealed to us by way of Carbon Testing? What occurred in the Triassic Period? What actually happened in the Garden of Eden? Can Malachs (Angels) and Humans reproduce? Was the Messenger hung on a cross? Who brings salvation to humanity? Where are the Biblical Hebrews today? What value does history and science add to Scripture?*

# INTRODUCTION

This book has taken years of Study and Research to compile before reaching its time for publication. It is my hope that the writings of this book will be an enlightenment of world events, events of ancient days, to the recent past, unto present time. Hopefully, this book will shine some light on topics of the Scriptures, and World History that otherwise has been kept hidden from the general population for many millennia.

This book is a compilation of writings from the *Authorized King James Bible, The Book of Enoch, The Cabala/Talmud, The Septuagint, The Book of Yashar, The Orthodox Jewish Bible, History Manuals, Science Manuals*, and various World Institutions, such as: *The U.S. Geological Service; National Geographic; The Smithsonian; The Vatican; The British Museum; The Russian Museum; Archaeological Museums, and in Artifacts Museums of Ancient Mitzrayim (Egypt)*.

In taking a panoramic view of history, science, and Scripture, a more clear overstanding of true history is formed. In opening the pages of this book, the stories of the creations will begin to come into focus in your thought processes. The time before time will be thoroughly discussed, meaning: The *Triassic Period* involves different eras of the land of the earth forming and reforming, and the land's movement. The Triassic Period is comprised of: The *Mesozoic, Permian, Tertiary, and Cenozoic* eras, and can be viewed as different creations. Time long ago, the earth was vastly different than it appears today. In the Triassic Era all land was one large landmass. That time period is known as: *Pangaea/Pangea*. During that time all of *Africa, Australia, Madagascar, Antarctica, India*, and all of the countries below the equator, including *South America, are referred to as: Gondwanaland/Gondwana*.

In bringing multiple sources together, to explore what occurred in *Shamayim* (heaven), and in the Garden of Eden many millennia ago, one will discover secrets of those time periods long ago. In only reading from one source, that is not a compilation work, the reader will not have the necessary information to form a thorough overstanding of history. Some books which help to fill-in gaps in history have been labeled as *pseudepigraphon* (false), or they have been called *mythology*. Those reference books fill-in gaps about the history of the *homo erectus*, who are *Pre-Aw-dawnic* (Adam) creatures, thought to be more like an animal than a human. Those books also tell us about Lilith, thought to be the first woman, created before *Chavvah* (Eve). Additionally, books such as, *The Book of Yashar* help to explain the *Nephilim* (giants) in the Bereshis/Genesis story.

We will also examine the travels of humanity in *The African Diaspora*, and the many millennia it took humanity to cover the earth, including lands disconnected by seas and oceans; such as, *The Strait of Gibraltar* and *The Iberian Peninsula*. In the people branching out farther apart, humanity would begin to be different families, with different languages. We will explore which families lived in the different geographical regions of the earth.

Using historical data, *deoxyribonucleic acid* (DNA) tests, and geography, we will examine characteristic traits of the four races of people: The Negroid, The Caucasoid, The Mongoloid, and the Hamitic people of Africa. Included in that research we will examine the *Peniel* gland, and how the sun has an effect on the Peniel gland, and the Peniel gland's regulation of body functions; such as, *melanin* production.

From the historical perspective, we will look at information from the *Arab Slave Trade, The Trans Atlantic Slave Trade, The Babylonian Exile*, and the history of the *Biblical Hebrews*. Included in the history will be U.S. and British History, along with, in part, Jewish History, Nigerian and Egyptian History. The history of all of these nations is necessary to tell the story of the Twelve Tribes of Yisra'el. There are numerous *epithets* (titles) that have been used for the name Yisra'el. But even so, in word *etymology* there are other names for Yisra'el that supersede the epithet Yisra'el, and moreover, epithets that provide a better idea of who Yisra'el is. The following names are all synonymous with Yisra'el because these names relate to the forefather of Yisra'el: *Ibrahim, Hebrew, Iberia, Eber, Ibrim, Ibriyyim,* and all of them trace back to the name *Abraham.*

In doing research which involves the history of language, it is necessary that root findings of specific words are overstood in origin of words and their usage. Here we will see the history of what is referred to as: *"Lingua Franca".* The Lingua Franca is a combination language of the following languages: *Italian, French, Arabic, Spanish, and Greek.* The Lingua Franca led to the development of the English language. Therefore, of necessity, we will also examine the development of the English language Bible from the historical perspective.

In looking at the laws written to rule over the people, the Scriptures say, we are to follow the laws of those in leadership, and the Laws of Scripture. There is a problem in some laws when those laws are written to benefit some, while simultaneously written to oppress others. We will examine the *Thirteenth Amendment,* and compare its content to that of Scripture. In doing so, we will be able to overstand that, while people of good countenance are the same people, and that those of evil countenance are also one people. With that said, regardless of skin color, there are only two kinds of people: The *hatov* (good), and the *harah* (evil).

In deep study of the Scriptures, from various books, topics such as sexuality should not be taboo to discuss. Sexuality is written of in the Scriptures going all the way back to the beginning of humanity. The Scriptures speak to prostitution, bestiality, pregnancy, homosexuality, and love. The Scriptures tell us when sexual activity is allowed and when it is restricted. The fact of Scripture tells us that the story of Sodom and Gohmorrah was sexual deviancy, and that what occurred in the Garden of Eden was also sexual deviancy, causing the fall of humanity.

There are many aspects of Scripture that are difficult to overstand because of the language used to present the information. Therefore, we will discuss parts of speech from the English language perspective. In view of the English language, we will define parts of speech such as, *pleonasm,* and *dative.* We will also examine the history of certain invaluable words; such as: *God, Lord, Holy, and Savior.* With better overstanding of word usage, and how changing one word in a sentence, can and does change the entire meaning of the original statement. As part of the segment dealing with the pleonasm and the dative, we will examine why some words, when a book is written in another language, how certain words cannot be *translated* into the full contextual value of the original writing. Across all languages there are words that have no qualifying word of equal value in another language. Therefore, such words should be *transliterated* into the *Lexicon* of the receiving language.

In history, all people have used a form of capital punishment for criminal offenses in their provinces. Here we will use multiple Scriptures to overstand the sentence of death by hanging. There is a very heinous implication behind such punishment. Hanging is the worst death sentence any person can ever receive. It is the most vicious torture, humiliation, and astonishment anyone could witness. We will see the wickedness behind carrying-out such a demoralizing death sentence.

Another very important aspect in reading any book has to be this: Who wrote the material, and what is their goal in writing it? Therefore, it is imperative for the writer to leave personal bias out of their work. With that said, true *Historians*, and *Theologians* will present the information as it truly was or is, regardless of whether it shows a negative result on their own race. Those, who write with bias, will use what is referred to as *Iconography* to distort the characteristics of true history. We will see how portions of Scripture have been *iconized* to hide the true identity of the characters of the *Original Hebrew Scrolls*.

In order to gain better overstanding of Scripture there is another aspect to history that has to be overstood, and that is: What is the origin of the different religions? We will briefly visit *Hinduism* and *Buddhism*. We will also look at some of the gods of religion, such as: *Anubis, Hermes, Baal, and Molech* from circa 6000-3150 BCE (Before Common Era).

There can be no true history books written on Scripture or World History without looking at U.S. History. With that said, in addition to discussing what is contained in the *Thirteenth Amendment*, we will briefly discuss *Jim Crow and Sundown Laws*; laws that applied strictly to the Negroes in the Southern States of the United States of America.

In looking at the history of the United States, formerly known as *Turtle Island*, a phenomenal transformation occurred over many decades. Those changes affected both the indigenous people of the land, and the Europeans, who arrived long after other people had lived in the land for millennia. The U.S. is a vast land that lies between the *Gulf of Mexico, the Atlantic Ocean, and the Pacific Ocean*. In this segment of reading is detailed how *amalgamation*, and *acculturation* has a devastating effect on the indigenous people of the land. This section of reading will be extensive in its presentation.

# FOREWORD

Most people living today are not in the truth of history for several reasons: 1. People have been given a partial history or 2. People have been provided a false version of history; and 3. There are outright invented stories of history that never occurred, stories from the minds of people whose only desire is to control the riches of the world. One of the best measures to find true history is in the world of *Science*. When it comes to science, the problem of inferior education becomes in and of itself a problem. Science is the true tests of history and Scripture. With science there can be no distortions of history or religion on humanity. Many people have little interest in science because it involves dissecting animals, worms, birds, or human corpses. Science has complicated mathematical computations that require long hours to resolve. The study of science for many is too complicated, and filled with words of more than 2-3 syllables. The words alone are enough to keep most people away from science because most people only read on the elementary level. When it comes to the Scriptures there are many valuable Scripture verses that are never discussed in the *ekklesia* (church) setting today. Many of those verses have hidden meaning that only the most studied and *ruach* (spirit) filled persons will ever grasp an *overstanding*, and will remain in *understanding* of the depth involved in the creation of the *Shamayim* (Heaven), and of the *Eretz* (Earth). Science tells us how creation has begun multiple times in the *eons*, millions to billions of years in human time have passed. The Scriptures provide information, to those of a discerning *ruach* (spirit), that many *millennia* ago the first recorded history was written by the people, who Elohim decided to call HIS Own, the *Hebrews*. Science too, has given us proof that what is recorded in the Scriptures, as related to length of humanity, far exceeds the common belief that humanity is only six thousand (6,000) years in existence. By science, and the development of *carbon testing* we have the means to measure time in millions of years in time. History books provide information going back six thousand years or so. However, the problem with history books is this: The oldest books have been confiscated by an *Elite Class* of people, who have made sure the books, and the information in those books has been hidden from the general population of the world for centuries. Rather than the information being shared, it was hidden, and new narratives written for public consumption, while locking away the original writings that only the *Elite Class* could access. Since the time of the earliest written records, most of what was recorded then, has passed away. Today, we must incorporate the history of modern times with the history of those first *Scrolls* (Books) in order to paint a clear picture of what occurred eons ago, and of that which is yet to come to fruition. The First Scrolls written contain information that some preachers will not delve into because it is filled with sexual content; and therefore, is viewed as off limits to discuss. That attitude in and of itself is *antithetical*. There is nothing written in the Scriptures too obscene, or vulgar, or dirty to teach. Without discussing those acts of sexuality, there can be no true *overstanding*, not understanding, of how the earliest of humanity divided into different races of people. Furthermore, the Scriptures also reveal to us, there were other creatures prior to humankind, and how later in creation those creatures invaded humanity by mating with humans (Bereshis/Gen. 6:4). Those Scripture verses tell us that: In *Ancient Days*, there was lewd and wild sexual activity. Those sexual acts were included in the Scriptures for a reason and a purpose: To inform us of what actually transpired many eons before the *Garden of Eden*. *Science, Paleontology, Astronomy,* and *Geology* inform us on how the *Eretz* (Earth) itself has undergone multiple changes in what is referred to as the *Triassic Era*. Humanity, as we know it today, is not what humanity was millions of years ago. In fact, *Science* and *Paleontology* reveals to us that the people living millennium ago were not completely human, but were rather more of the animal world, those creatures are referred to as: *Homo Erectus*, more like an ape than a human. The history books that have been hidden provide us invaluable information about early human travel leading up to the *African Diaspora*, forward to modern times.

Note: The *African Diaspora* is the moving away of the people from the ancestral homeland, the land first occupied by humanity.

*Geological* and *Paleontological Sciences* (The studies of earth's formation; and skeletal remains of creatures that lived eons ago that have been excavated) provide information of who early people were; where they lived; the routes of early travel, and how the *Eretz* (Earth) formed, and reformed from a *Supercontinent* in *Pangaea/Pangea* to the seven continent theory taught in schools today. The Scripture verses contained in the books of *Enoch, The Septuagint, The Talmud,* and many other books, tell us that there was lewd, and wild sexual activity eons ago. In this book, you will find openly explicit, but not vulgar discussion of sex, violence, rape, love, homosexuality, and prostitution. Open sexual discussion does not mean vulgarity; it is simply expressing the <u>truth</u> of the story. There is nothing too taboo to discuss in the Scriptures. Additionally, we will examine the time before humanity when the *dinosaurs* roamed the earth, and the time when giant <u>hybrid</u> humans were on the earth. All of the topics contained in this book should be discussed with our children, who are of an age old enough to comprehend matters of life. There were a multitude of events in ancient days that preceded man as we are today. This book will cover the stories of the *Torah/Law: Bereshis/Genesis; Shemot/Exodus; VaYikra/Leviticus; Bamidbar/Numbers;* and *Devarim/Deuteronomy.* Moreover, this book will discuss why *Hisgalus/Revelation,* and *Ioudas/Yude* should be the introduction to the *Book of Bereshis/Gen..* Moreover, this book is composed of information stored in world renown institutions that correspond directly to Scripture, and true historical documents that parallel the Scriptures, and how Science partners the two together.

The primary focus of this book is to open up our minds about what is written in history books, and science books that relates to Scripture. Information which helps to bind the stories together that are scattered in the Scriptures, pulling the parts of the stories together into one place for clarity of the story. In pulling all of those parts of stories into one place, the reader will gain a greater overstanding of true history.

In example: Part of the *Bereshis/Genesis* story is actually found in the Books of *Ioudas/Yude* and *Hisgalus/Revelation,* the last two books in the bible. In fact, these two books should be the first books of the Scriptures because they provide us with information on: *The War In Shamayim* (Heaven). The Book of *Bereshis/Gen.,* tells us nothing about *The War in Shamayim.* When we look at the Scriptural, and geological historical facts, it becomes apparently clear that, there is much more to history than what is recorded in the bible. But even so, the gaps in the bible are not gaps in the least; but rather, those seeming gaps are cleverly written phrases, written that way by the Elite Class to prevent the regular class away from the truth. However, those of a discerning *ruach* (spirit) will see and overstand there is more hidden in the words than appears as written.

This book contains many Scripture verses; however, let me state from the onset of this book: This is not a book of religion. The main points of all that is contained in these pages have to do with history, the history of *Shamayim* (Heaven), *HaAretz* (The Earth), the life that existed before humanity, and very importantly, humanity itself.

Note: There will be limited use of words in this book such as: God, Lord, and Holy Spirit. When those words do appear in the text, their use will be to make specific observations; otherwise, those words will not be completely spelled-out. What you will find in this writing are the names used in antiquity: *Elohim* (HASHEM); *Hashem/Ha Mashiach* (The Messenger); *Ruach Hakodesh* (Sacred Spirit), and *Hashilush Hakadosh* (Sacred Trinity).

# THE BEGINNING OF BEGINNINGS TO NEVER ENDING: THE BERESHIS/GENESIS

There is something present in the Scriptures that most people have no comprehension thereof, and that is: There is no beginning of beginnings. The HASHEM (L-RD) has told us: For I, the HASHEM, the Elohim of all existence always was, is now, and will forever be, for that which was made was already made in the spirit before it was manifested in the physical. All that is, and all that shall ever be, at MY Command, when *I AM THAT I AM* shall speak, it will appear. Let no one fool you into believing that creation can be contained in a book. I, the HASHEM have created and built more than any book can contain.

I, the HASHEM, has began the worlds, and ended the worlds as I have chosen to do. I, the HASHEM have revealed to MY Chosen Vessels, specified accounts of human time to be recorded in *ruach* (spirit) and in truth, certain acts that I have done for the sake of humanity. I have given to each of MY Chosen Vessels a proscribed amount of knowledge to be recorded for all of human time. A knowledge to allow those, who are willing to see Who I AM; for I AM that which I AM. I AM from always to always will be.

In the first accounts of human time, *I AM THAT I AM*, have given knowledge to male, and female Chosen Vessels, to record the creation of *Shamayim* and of *HaAretz* (The Earth). Those recorded creations were written in a style that leads many to no overstanding of Who I AM, for the deception of *Hasatan* (Satan) over many millennia crept into the writings, using language which cloaks, and causes the truth of the writings to be concealed. The workers of iniquity, by way of subtility, have endeavored to hide that which has actually transpired in all of human history, and the eons of man years that have passed, and are yet to pass. But I, the HASHEM, have sent those, who are unknown, to undo the influence of Hasatan upon the writings to reveal MY truths. I AM the HASHEM, and I know no time.

From Eternality, *I AM THAT I AM* have always been, as is the *Ruach Hakodesh* (Sacred Spirit), and the Son, *Ha Mashiach* (The Messenger of Elohim), Whom I, in human time eventually sent among men to bring MY messages for the people; messages of hope to bring their *ruachs* (spirits) into MY realm of Eternality. I AM the Architect of everything that is; and MY Son is the builder of the worlds:

Y'hochanan/Jn. 21:25 (AKJV):

*'And there are also many other things which Ha Mashiach did, the which, if they should be written every one, I suppose that even the world itself could not contain the books that should be written.'*

In the beginning was Elohim, before anything was, was The Most High Elohim, the Maker and Creator of everything that now is. With The *Abba* (Father) was *Ha Mashiach*; in Him would come all of the *Shamayim* (Heaven), and *HaAretz* (The Earth). Also from the beginning with The Abba, and *Ha Mashiach* (The Messenger), was the *Ruach Hakodesh* (Sacred Spirit). By The Ruach Hakodesh is the ability to see and to hear in the realm of *spirituality*. From The Abba is the blueprint for all of creation. By Ha Mashiach was all of the works of the blueprint constructed. By the Ruach Hakodesh is all safety, guidance, and direction for the Chosen People of Elohim.

At the first was the *Hashilush Hakadosh* (Abba, Ruach, and Son). The Architect of all there is, is the Abba (Bereshis/Gen. 1:1). After Abba completed all of HIS designs, HE gave them over to *Ha Mashiach* (The Messenger), the Builder of all things designed by the Abba (Y'hochanan/Jn. 1:1-3). After Elohim completed the designs; and Mashiach completed the work, Elohim sent the Ruach Hakodesh to teach all who are willing to learn the Ways of The Most High Elohim (Y'hochanan 14:26).

Many hundreds of thousands to millions of years ago, The Most

High Elohim created life in the *ruach* (spirit). Those spiritual Beings existed since the beginning of time. In the beginning the *Malachs* (Angels) were with Elohim; free to travel in all that Mashiach had made; infinity was theirs. The Malachs, were free to travel wheresoever they would. But even so, there is a place strictly reserved for the most Sacred of Sacred, and the most Sacred of all existence dwell there: the Abba, the Ruach, and the Son (Psalm 113:4; Isa. 6:1; Throne/Seat; 2 Thes. 2:4). Also in the most Sacred of Sacred, is a mighty *Malach* (Angel), whose *epithet* (title) is *Archangel*. This Malach is the Chief of all of the Malachs; his name is *Michael the Archangel* (Ioudas 9), a mighty warrior.

Over many millennia the *Shamayim* (Heavens) and *HaAretz* (The Earth) were completed, which includes the Archangel Michael, the Chief of *Malachs* (Angels), along with *Gabriel* the *Malach of Vision*, and all of the Malachs, to include *Lucifer*, who would cause the downfall of the *Goyim* (Nations; Isaiah/Yeshayahu 14:12).

The construction of creation is in the beginning building process, it will be eons before The Most High's plan would be completed by Ha Mashiach, and declared finished by the Abba, leading to the *Day of Rest: The Shabbath Day*. The creation is an ongoing constructive process from the beginning to the ending of endings. Elohim alone knows when HE will say: The End (Mat.24:36). The ongoing constructive process of creation is not the rotation of the *Sun* orbiting around *HaAretz* (The Earth) on a twenty four hour clock. The creation of the *Shamayim* precedes any time-clock, for the Elohim of all existence is timeless. Elohim knows no time, time is set for humankind; insomuch, the *ish* (man), and the *isha* (woman) has not yet been made, and does not come into existence until the last construction phase of creation, the *Sixth Day*. Though the *Sun* and the *Moon* have not been constructed, and everything is in *Darkness,* Elohim brought *Light* from the *Darkness* (Bereshis/Gen. 1:3), which began *Night* and *Day* (Ber. 1:3-4). However, the time from *Night* to *Day* has <u>no</u> time, and could be anywhere from a second to millennia. But even so, Elohim said, That was the *First Day of Creation* (Ber. 1:5). Night and Day are living entities from Elohim, whose names are *Night* and *Day*. After the coming of Night and Day, the *Firmament,* a great ocean without end, which preceded Night and Day was opened. With the opening of the *Firmament,* a space, a great *dome* was created as the place to house the Sun and the Moon, and all of the *Planetary* life to come. This great *expanse* or *dome* is the place for all of the physical structures that will come into existence (Ber. 1:6). In opening the *Firmament,* Elohim called it the *Second Day* (Ber. 1:8).

The *Eretz* (Earth/Land) is now under the *dome* surrounded by water in all directions, and yet, Eretz is under the water (Ber. 1:9). The water is one, but not so. The water of the Firmament is that of a gas or more porous consistency; the water of the eretz is more dense or solid. Then Elohim Commanded the water, and the water moved all to "*one place*", and the Eretz came out of the water as <u>one</u> large landmass. In looking at a <u>True World Map</u>, it is easy to see how the pieces of Eretz fit together like a puzzle. *HaAretz* (The Earth) was not stable, the moving of the plates caused *earthquakes, volcanoes, tsunamis,* and many kinds of natural disasters. All of those natural events, especially the earthquakes and volcanoes, caused all of the islands to form. Islands, simply put, are the tops of volcanoes. The waters of the Eretz, Elohim called Seas. Now the trees, and the grass, and all green plants will spring forth from the ground. The plants all have the capability to reproduce from within themselves; no mating is required (Bereshis/Gen. 1:9-12).

There is something else in these verses that most people reading the creation story don't grasp; there is a *cognitive dissonance* in all of the water moving to one place, and what that really means. It means that all of the land is also in one place. Without great study and research, one will not easily recognize: All land millions of years ago was one *contiguous* landmass. In fact, all land is one landmass unto this day, the difference being, most of the land is submerged under the water. The following information will shed some light on this great mass of land.

"Some 200 million years ago, *Antarctica* was joined to *South America, Africa, India, and Australia* in a single large continent called *Gondwanaland.* There was no ice sheet, and trees and large animals flourished. Today, only geological formations, coal beds, and fossils remain as clues to Antarctica's warm past."

nsf.gov/geo/opp/support/gondwana.jsp

Do you see the picture of what transpired in ancient times? In *Pangaea,* all of the land above the equator was warm to hot land, and because of that, when humanity would be brought forth from Mother Eretz, the inhabitants will be people of melanin, made from the *melanized* Eretz. All of the land below the equator would not be inhabited for many millennia to come, as that region would be unstable, with a more harsh climate. Over millions of years the earths plates separated more and more until there were four (4) continents as we have today, there were never seven (7) continents. In pulling up the map from *pubs.usgs.gov/publications/text/historical.html*, published by *nsf.gov/geo/opp/support/gondwana.jsp*, you will see the directional information of the globe. As the earth's shifts occurred, the narrow land-bridge at the *Tethys Sea* is the route that would eventually be the route from *Gondwanaland* to *Laurasia* in the *African Diaspora*. That land-bridge being part of *Mitzrayim* (Egypt), and *Yisra'el* (Israel) of today. It would take many *millennia* before those crossing into the hostile land of *Laurasia* (Asia and Europe) would lose the melanin from their skin, and take on physical changes in body structure (hair texture, eye color, facial features) in the cold, harsh conditions of the land. I hope you overstand what all of this information tells us: All of the land was a single landmass as the Scriptures tell us in Bereshis/Gen. 1:9. In addition, this information tells us all of the people of the eretz were people of melanin skin. Unto this day, nature itself verifies that all of the brown skin people live in the warmest regions of the eretz, and those of non-melanin skin live below the equatorial line. The word *below* the equatorial line is not in error. We have all been taught wrong by the Elite Class, who have concealed the history of the true map. Thankfully today, electronic transmission of data has opened the door of hidden information, making information available with the push of a button on a cellphone.

There are multiple sources online featuring the eretz drawn in reverse orientation to what we have been taught (*www.flourish.org/upsidedownmap*). The commentaries on those maps tell us straightforwardly, and without hesitation, we have all been defrauded by those, who have presented the map upside down to make the land they occupy as the top of the world, as in showing them superior to the melanized peoples of the North. Speaking matter-of-factually, it makes absolutely no sense at all, that the areas of the eretz farther away from the sun, or at the bottom of the globe, when it comes to spatial orientation to the sun, would be the hottest.

Let us now continue with the unfolding of events in the days of the creation. The waters have been parted: separating the *Upper Firmament* (waters of the air; vapor) from the *Lower Firmament* (waters of the land; dense), creating a place for HaAretz to live in its own space in the <u>never</u> ending Shamayim. This portion of the construction phase is monumentally important to overstand: The Firmament existed before the creation of the Sun, the Moon, and every Star. The Stars are different Beings from the Sun and the Moon. The Sun and the Moon rule the nightlight and the daylight. The Stars give us direction for navigation; however, the Stars have something else of great value in the <u>creations stories</u>, there is gold and silver in Stars.

> *"It's long been known that earthly metals like <u>gold</u> and <u>silver</u> were forged in supernova explosions"*

> Andrew Fazekas, For National Geographic News; Sep 9, 2012

The significant information of the stars containing precious metals will be discussed as we follow the history of the creations. After Elohim separated the Firmament from the Firmament, and the dry land appeared, Abba brought forth all of the plant life. All of creation is phenomenal, but there is something special with the plant life: the plants of all life to come can reproduce of themselves. This is the end of the Third Day of Creation (Bereshis 1:7-12).

See, hear, and overstand the Word of the Abba. The *Light* was already created before the Sun and the Moon were created. The Light is a <u>life-form</u> that Elohim created prior to giving us the Sun and the Moon to rule time for humanity that is yet to come (v.1:4). This is the end of the Fourth Day of the creation (Bereshis 1:14-19).

We must now look at a great deal of information about the eretz, in a time period that ended long before man was created from the melanized ground. The time period of the eretz before man is known as the *Triassic Period*:

> "**_Triassic_**: *of, relating to, or being the earliest period of the* **_Mesozoic Era_** *or the corresponding system of rocks marked by the first appearance of the* **_dinosaurs_**"

> **_Mesozoic Era_**: *of, relating to, or being an era of* **_geological history_** *comprising the interval between the* **_Permian_** *and the* **_Tertiary_** *or the corresponding system of rocks that was marked by the presence of* **_dinosaurs, marine and flying reptiles_**, *ammonites, ferns, and gymnosperms and the appearance of angiosperms,* **_mammals_**, *and birds*

> **_Permian_**: *of, relating to, or being the last period of the Paleozoic Era or the corresponding system of* **_rocks_**

> **_Tertiary_**: *capitalized : of, relating to, or being the first period of the* **_Cenozoic_** *Era or the corresponding system of rocks marked by the* **_formation of high mountains_** *(such as the Alps,* **_Caucasus_**, *and Himalayas) and the dominance of mammals on land*

> **_Cenozoic_**: *of, relating to, or being an era of* **_geological history_** *that extends from the beginning of the Tertiary period to the present time*"

Merriam-Webster.com

The information about the *Triassic Period* correlates to the Scriptures equivocally. Stop believing this planet has only been in existence six thousand (6,000) years. And do not continue to believe dinosaurs did not exist. In the Triassic Period, the earth (dry land) was being formed by the Almighty Elohim. This can be directly associated with *'let the dry land appear'* (Ber. 1:9). The planet (earth) was very unstable at that time because Abba was forming it until HE decided it was the shape HE desired, that which is pleasing to HIM. It is the equivalent to: The Potter molding the clay. The process of time involved in shaping the eretz is unspecified eons, before the land would evolve into anything close to what the eretz is today. The Triassic Period involves different eras of the land of the earth forming, and its movement. The *Mesozoic, Permian, Tertiary, and Cenozoic* eras can be viewed as different creations. Each of these creations were like the Potter molding the clay. The Worker of the clay molding the shapes, and remolding the shapes of the land until satisfied with the works. *Scholars* and *Government Agencies* know the truth of Ancient History. The *Elite Class* too know this information. If you are not of the Elite Class or a study of *Geology,* this information may be new to you, or may have been briefly presented to you as *pseudoscience* in school. Those, who control this planet, know the truth.

The following information is directly related to the *Cenozoic Era.* This information tells us how Elohim initially formed the land after bringing the land out of the water. *Gondwanaland/Gondwana: Pangaea/ Pangea,* is in plain language, a time long ago when all of the land was connected with the Northern hemisphere being the area of a warm climate. The Southern hemisphere was ice covered.

In studying maps of today, making a comparison to the map of ancient Gondwanaland, one can see Gondwanaland consist of *Africa, Australia, Madagascar, Antarctica, India,* and all of the countries below the equator, including *South America.*

Do you see the picture of what transpired in ancient times? In *Pangaea,* the time when all the land was one large landmass, all of the land above the equator had a warm to hot climate. All of the land below the equator were ice capped. The entirety of the land was not stable, with a more harsh climate below the equator. Over millions of years the earth's *tectonic* plates separated more and more until there were four (4) continents as we have today. As the earth's shifts occurred, the narrow land-bridge at the *Tethys Sea* and the *Atlantic Ocean* is the land that would eventually be the travel route from *Gondwanaland* to *Laurasia* as Elohim continues to build and mold the land into what HE desires the land to be.

There is something very phenomenal in the Triassic Period also: *Mesozoic, Permian, Tertiary, and Cenozoic,* all mention the formation of rocks. As improbable as this may sound, during that time, even the rocks were growing. In fact, rocks are still growing today. Depending on where you live, you may be able to find the evidence of such growth right under your feet. In digging into the ground, as you dig deeper into the eretz you will see the dirt change over to a mix of dirt and clay. You will then come to clay with a few rocks. As you continue to dig you will see clay that is becoming more solid or compressed. Going down deeper, eventually you will hit solid rock. In close observation of the clay/rock part of the dig, you will see the clay is transforming into rock. As the rocks form they expand or grow. In the Triassic Period that growth occurred over unspecified millennia, those rocks became one mass above the water level. That one large landmass is referred to as *Pangaea/Pangea*. During Pangaea, the eretz, because of the shifts in the solid portions was very unstable. Those movements caused earthquakes, volcanoes, *tsunamis*, and all manner of natural disasters. Because of those natural phenomenon the eretz was not yet suitable for life of any kind, not even plants (Bereshis 1:11). The seemingly gaps in the Scriptures are not gaps at all. What happened is, there is such a vast amount of history that no book can give you all of that information. We must see pass the words written on the page in order to receive the message(s) contained in the words.

> "*Non-bird dinosaurs lived between about 245 and 66 million years ago, in a time known as the **Mesozoic Era**. This was many millions of years before the first modern humans, Homo sapiens, appeared.*

*Scientists divide the **Mesozoic Era** into three periods: the **Triassic, Jurassic and Cretaceous**. During this era, the <u>land gradually split</u> from one huge continent into smaller ones. The associated changes in the climate and vegetation affected how dinosaurs evolved.*" (Natural Science Museum)

nhm.ac.uk/discover/when -did-dinosaurs

After many millennia, Elohim went into the 5<sup>th</sup> Day of the construction phrase of the creations. Day 5 of the creation would bring about the first life with blood running in its veins. Those life forms would be diverse creatures from the smallest insects to many species of mammoth size animals (Ber. 1:24-25). Those creatures would roam all of Gondwanaland, Eurasia remained ice capped at that time. The different species that lived at that time were reptiles that walked upon the land, some were capable of flying, some were creatures of the water, and some were amphibian. All that occurred in those time periods comes under the heading of the *Triassic Period*. All of the dinosaur-like creatures, no matter what they were, they existed eons before there was a man. The era of the dinosaurs extinction is a creation story that ended millions of years ago. The proof of dinosaurs existence are the remains of those animals excavated, studied, and time dated by paleontologists, and scientists using *carbon testing*. Whatever caused the extinction of those animals is not as important as, it was a creation that no longer exists, and in the next creation would come even more revelations that only one creation in all of time is a fallacy.

The era of the *Jurassic* and *Cretaceous Periods* ended, thus meaning another creation was yet to come. After the time of the *Jurassic* and *Cretaceous Periods*, there would be the creation of different animals to be brought forth by Elohim. The proof of the dinosaurs of the *Jurassic Period* are the unearthed remains still being discovered today. Those periods would be followed by the animal kingdom of lions, tigers, and bears, and elephants, and rhinoceros, and the pre-human creatures called *homo-erectus* that would come into existence on Day 5 of the creation. This is verified in the Scriptures because those creatures came before humanity arrived on Day 6 of creation. There is another phenomenon that occurred in the post Jurassic Period: The fallen malachs had already been thrown out of Shamayim, and imprisoned or confined to the earthly realm (Isaiah 14:12; Hisgalus/Rev. 12:7-9). The fallen malachs were sexual creatures, who possessed or retained the knowledge they had in Shamayim. The malachs were mating with the dinosaurs, and other animals, and creatures of the sea. That all occurred in the *Mesozoic Period* millions of years ago. I will not speculate or guess what happened to end the creation period of the dinosaurs and other giant reptiles that roamed the earth. What I know is, that creation and all of the creations before that ended. The malachs had contaminated all of the lifeforms because the malachs were knowledgeable, and corrupt Beings.

The malachs had knowledge in Shamayim, and retained all of that knowledge in confinement on ha'aretz. The following information comes from a discredited source, labeled as *pseudepigraphical* or false by the Elite Class. All I can say on that is: The *Book of Enoch* was discredited by the workers of Hasatan, because it presents a clear picture of who the real enemy of Elohim is: The descendants of the fallen angels.

Enoch 9:5:

> "5 You have seen what **Azazyel** has done, how he has taught **every species** of iniquity upon earth, and has disclosed to the world **all the secret things** which are done in the heavens."

Though the dinosaurs were extinct well before humanity came into existence, in the day of the dinosaurs the fallen malachs did all manner of sexual acts with the animals. Not to get ahead of Day 6 of the creations, but after humanity was formed, the malachs showed humankind what things they had done with animals, and the result is this:

Midrash Rabbah 1:292-293:

> "*Ham sodomized a dog on board Noah's Ark*"

*Bestiality* is nothing new, and neither is homosexuality. Some people are so religious, they refuse to see the truth of Scripture; and moreover, most religions don't use books beyond that of the most used bible in the world: The AKJV of Scripture. In fact, most people have no clue that other ancient writings even exist. Beyond that, the general population has been under-educated to the point that even when reading Scripture, they are unable to comprehend what they have read. But even greater than that is, because of false teaching over decades from the time they were in diapers, most people fail to recognize the meaning of the words in the story: It is a mental condition referred to as *Cognitive Dissonance*. Ham was into sex with animals. Ham is the focus of more discussions to come as we build line and precept.

All of the creation Days we have looked at so far actually cover millennia to millions of years in reference to human years. There are seemingly gaps in the Scriptures as related to time gone by; however, in clear overstanding, not understanding of what has actually transpired, there is no gap. The first thing to overstand is this: time did not start until Elohim created the Sun and the Moon. Nothing that occurred prior to the Sun and the Moon was time stamped, all of those events happened in the existence of the Elohim of Eternality, the realm of no beginning to no ending. Simply put it means, there is no number of years that can be applied to any of those events from Day 1 through Day 5. Now let us look at Day 6 of the creation. In examining Day 6 of the creation, one has to keep in mind that the malachs have been on eretz through all of the creations periods, eretz is their habitation. Therefore, before we get into Day 6, let us examine the Scriptures in a line and precept consistency, pulling the parts together from *Ioudas*/Yude, Isaiah, and *Hisgalus*/Revelation. These Canons provide us considerable background into what is thought to be gaps in the texts of the Bereshis stories.

*Ioudas* is one of the most revealing books of the Sacred Scriptures with regard to Biblical History and of that which is yet to come.

Ioudas, verse 6 (AKJV):

*'And the Malachs (__Angels__) which __kept not their first estate__,
but left their __own habitation__, He hath reserved in everlasting
chains under confinement unto the sentencing of the great day.'*

The malachs, who lived with Elohim in Shamayim, one third of
them, listened to Lucifer in the first lie ever told, convincing them that
he, Lucifer, is more powerful than Elohim. Overstand this: The malachs
are powerful Beings, in Shamayim, and in *HaAretz* (The Earth). Their
problem came in believing they were equal to or of superior power to
Elohim. In fact, there were other Malachs more powerful than Lucifer.
Lucifer plotted a coup against The Most High Elohim to dethrone
Abba, which would make Lucifer the king, so he believed. Lucifer and
the malachs, who followed him are being held in the prison, which
prison is the *eretz* (earth), waiting for the day of their sentencing before
the Throne of Abba.

Ioudas has told us that Lucifer has been imprisoned for the attempted
coup. Now watch this: line and precept.

Isaiah 14:12 (AKJV):

*'How are you __fallen from Shamayim, O Lucifer__, son of
the morning! How are you __cut down to the ground__, who
continues to __weaken the nations__!'*

*Lucifer* (Hasatan) had a great desire for power, something in his
personality caused him to become vain, and filled with greed and
superiority. What Lucifer did not recognize is that, Elohim had other
Malachs in the *Mamlachah* (Kingdom) more powerful than Lucifer.
Lucifer has been thrown out of Shamayim, now his home is the eretz.
Do you get it? The eretz is a prison, the place where all, who rebel against
Elohim are confined. We will expound upon earth as a prison, line and
precept as we continue our reading.

Now let us gain more credence about the malachs being exiled from

Shamayim, and how Ioudas describes the rouge malachs, who lost their *First Estate*.

Ioudas, verse 13 (AKJV):

'*Raging waves of the sea, foaming out their own shame;* ***wandering stars****, to whom is **reserved the gloominess of obscurity for ever**.*'

The above verse represents empty, void, uselessness, worthless, and of no value. The malachs, who left "***their First Estate***" are the "***wandering stars***". In the Fourth Day of the Creation the Stars were created; however, something happened that caused a problem between Elohim and some of the Stars. Line upon line and precept upon precept, let us pull this story more together with information from the Book of Hisgalus/Revelation. Here is the tie-end to the Malachs of the *Mamlachah* (Kingdom).

Hisgalus 12:7-9 (AKJV):

'*And there was **war in Shamayim**: **Michael** and his **Malachs** (Angels) fought against the **dragon** (angel); and the dragon fought and his malachs, 8 and prevailed **not; neither was their place found any more in Shamayim**. 9 And the great dragon was **cast out**, that old serpent, called the **Devil**, and **Hasatan**, who would **deceive the whole world**: he was **cast out into the earth**, and his malachs were cast out with him.*'

The Scriptures are cleverly, deceitfully written. Pulling all of the parts together provides for a greater overstanding of Ancient History. The *Malachs* and the *Stars* are one entity. These particular malachs, under the leadership of Lucifer, have been kicked out of Shamayim by Michael, the Archangel. Listen-up closely to the Word of the HASHEM, the messages in these verses is multifaceted: *Lucifer* (Hasatan) has been kicked-out of Shamayim; other malachs like *Azazyel* have also been kicked-out of Shamayim. Michael has won the battle against Lucifer;

Michael and his Malachs have confined Lucifer and his malachs to eretz. Here is the Word of the HASHEM: There is a war that has taken place in Shamayim, Michael and his army against Lucifer and his army. Here is the point: Many thousands to millions, if not billions of years have passed in human time, and yet humanity of Day 6, has not yet been created. Because of the failed coup attempt of Lucifer against the Almighty Elohim, the eretz is now a prison for the malachs, who committed evil against the Abba.

The fallen malachs made a conscious decision to coup against Elohim. That attempt led to their ouster from Shamayim, and their confinement on the eretz. This all occurred before the animals of any kind were created. The animals were created before humanity. We have gone through the *Triassic Period* to the creation of the dinosaurs, and on to the lions, tigers, bears, rhinoceros, and all of the animal kingdom. Almost everything Elohim created became contaminated by the evil fallen malachs. Many creations have come and gone over many millennia, and yet, there is no man. This is the end of the Fifth Day of the creation (Bereshis 1:20-25).

Let us continue to pull the creations stories together with Geological data and some Scripture verses from one source that some have labeled as *pseudepigraphical* (false). We have already discussed somewhat the *Triassic Period*; however, there is more that must be brought to our attention about that era. Over millions of years the earth's *tectonic plates* separated more and more until there were four (4) continents as we have today. These points are valuable in that, the seeming gaps in Scripture are not gaps at all. More what occurred is that: There were many eons that passed, and in those times the malachs, who are forever *ruachs* (spirits), have been sexual with the creatures called *homo erectus*. Those creatures, homo erectus, and the malachs produced at times giant offspring. That is where in *mythology*, you were taught of creatures by names such as, *Triton* and *Poseidon*. Those Beings were before man existed, and they were part malach and part animal, or fish, or fowl.

*I AM THAT I AM*, gave us some of the secrets of Shamayim by way of Enoch:

Enoch 8:1:

*'1 Moreover **Azazyel** taught men to make swords, knives, shields, breastplates, the fabrication of mirrors, and the workmanship of bracelets and ornaments, the use of paint, the **beautifying of the eyebrows**, the use of stones of every valuable and select kind, and all sorts of dyes, **so that the world became altered**.'*

*Azazyel* was one of the leaders of the fallen malachs, he gave many secrets of Shamayim to humanity after the HASHEM brought humanity forth from the *eretz* (Ber./Gen. 2:7). Did you catch what is hidden in this verse? This verse tells us that: make-up and certain ornamental body decorations is knowledge that was never meant to be on eretz. Those things were meant for Shamayim only, and were not forbidden to use in Shamayim. However, when the fallen malach, Azazyel, brought that knowledge to eretz, its use became evil knowledge. When humanity would be brought forth on Day 6, Azazyel would teach that knowledge to the people, changing the very nature of good knowledge to that of evil knowledge, for the purpose of seduction, by which the eretz would be corrupted.

Enoch 63:1:

*'1 I saw also other **countenances** (unspecified Beings, likely of those in the Garden of Eden) in that **secret place**. I heard the voice of an angel, saying, These are the angels who have descended from heaven to earth, and have **revealed secrets** to the sons of men, and have **seduced the sons of men** to the commission of sin.'*

Enoch 63:1 is very important to comprehend. Though this verse tells us that the fallen malachs taught men many secrets of things done in Shamayim, prior to humanity being created, many secrets of Shamayim were given to the homo erectus, who were extinct before man came into existence. Those evil fallen malachs were having sex with animals, fishes, and fowls. The fallen malachs have an insatiable appetite for sex, and they have no preference of the gender.

Enoch 64:10:

'They have **discovered secrets**, and they are those who have been prosecuted; **but not you my son**. The HASHEM of spirits knows that you are pure and good, free from the reproach of **discovering secret**.'

There are many things done in Shamayim that if it had not been for the fallen malachs, that humanity would not have been exposed to, possibly ever. That is why *I AM THAT I AM* Commanded Aw-dawn and Chavvah to never touch the *tree* (creature) in the middle of the Garden (Bereshis/Gen. 3:3). That creature was most likely one of the fallen angels or other countenance, who had Aw-dawn and Chavvah not engaged in conversation, may never have known what sex is or anything about reproduction. I have drawn this conclusion based completely on the Scriptures: Aw-dawn and Chavvah did not even know they were naked (Bereshis/Gen. 2:25; 3:7; 3:10; 3:11). Most people have no overstanding of Bereshis, Chapters 1 and 2. In the creation story of Chapter 1, the humans are told to reproduce (1:28). In Chapter 2, clearly expression of reproduction does not come into action until the man and the woman have been seduced by the creature(s) they were instructed to keep therefrom. Watch this!

Enoch, Chapter 68, provides us the names of the **Watchers**, the leaders of the fallen malachs, **Kesabel** and **Gadrel** who brought sex to humanity:

Enoch 68:5-7:

'The name of the second is **Kesabel**, who pointed out evil counsel to the sons of the sacred angels, and induced them to **corrupt their bodies by generating mankind**. 6 The name of the third is **Gadrel**: he discovered every stroke of death to the children of men. 7 **He seduced Eve**; and discovered to the

17

*children of men the instruments of death, the coat of mail, the shield, and the sword for slaughter; every instrument of death to the children of men.'*

The AKJV of Scripture, while it excludes this valuable information, the KJ does not leave out the story of what happened to Chavvah. The KJ simply cloaks the story in wording that most people do not comprehend what is hidden in the words. One must see pass the words written on the page, and look into the message in the words. The fallen malachs brought sexual knowledge to earth, and with that knowledge, caused the tragedy that would follow: The very nature of the plants would be altered (Ber./Gen. 3-18); pain and sorrow for women in childbirth (Ber./Gen. 3:15-16); and very importantly, **hatred** (enmity) between the offspring of Hasatan and Chavvah (Ber./Gen. 3:15).

There is another element contained in the above verses, watch this: Enoch 63:1 is a combination of physical and spiritual nature, while Enoch 64:10 is purely about the spirit. This is a very important point because there are too many people today focusing on the physical: what to eat or not to eat; circumcision; attending an *ekklesia* (church); tithes of money, and so on. Those things don't amount to anything in the presence of TMH Elohim. *I AM THAT I AM* is a Spiritual Being, Who has given us, humanity, the choice for our life: To be a good *ruach* (spirit), dedicated to HIM, or to attach ourselves to the forces of evil, the fallen malachs. The physical acts we commit are not intrinsically linked to us returning to Shamayim, it is our spiritual connection to the Abba which assures our return to Shamayim.

Another important aspect of Enoch 68:5-7 is, the fallen malachs taught humanity how to make weapons to kill. It was that knowledge that allowed those of devious intent, those of superior mindedness, to overcome other peoples as time moved forward. The descendants of the Annunaki, as were the Annunaki, are filled with hate and superiority. The same mind-set that caused the War in Shamayim, is the same mind-set present in their offspring today: wealth, power, and superiority. In time the children or offspring of the Annunaki would gain control and power over many nations of people as time moves forward.

Let us now take a look at Day 6 of creation. In the beginning the malachs were with Elohim; free to travel in all that *Ha Mashiach* (The Messenger) had made; infinity was theirs, except the upper levels of *Shamayim* (Heaven). The upper levels were only accessible to Elohim, Ha Mashiach, the Ruach Hakodesh, and Special Envoys to The Most High Elohim; such as, Michael and Gabriel.

At some point in Eternality, eons ago, some of the angels decided they wanted access to the highest level of Shamayim, where the Throne of Elohim is located. The malachs having power granted to them by Elohim, were free to go wheresoever they wanted to go, except the *Seventh Shamayim* (Psalm 11:4; His./Rev. 4:4). Then something happened that would change everything from that time forward. Lucifer and his army decided they wanted to overthrow the *Mamlachah* (Kingdom) of Shamayim (Ioudas 9). Lucifer was defeated in the War of Shamayim, and thrown out of Shamayim. Lucifer and his followers are now confined to the *eretz* (earth), expelled from Shamayim forever. Lucifer has been transformed by The Most High Elohim, to an evil demon of wickedness. Lucifer's name has also been changed to Hasatan. Hasatan is a deceptive, cunning, slickstor, of high intelligence. Hasatan and other creatures were in the Garden of Eden before Aw-dawn and Chavvah were created. After Aw-dawn and Chavvah were created, one day when Aw-dawn was not in the presence of Chavvah, Hasatan made his approach to Chavvah. At the time Hasatan approached Chavvah, Chavvah had no knowledge beyond the Command The Most High Elohim had given to Aw-dawn and Chavvah, not to touch the tree of good and evil, and of knowledge. Here is the point, Hasatan is that **tree** of good and evil, and knowledge. Hasatan took advantage of the naive Chavvah, using his good looks, physical prowess, and intelligence to seduce Chavvah (Bereshis 3:6), who had no knowledge of sex. Chavvah, before Hasatan showed her the pleasure of sex, did not even know she was naked (Bereshis 3:7). Chavvah then taught Aw-dawn about sex, which caused his eyes to open to good and evil, and knowledge. Aw-dawn before having sex with Chavvah did not realize she was naked (3:11). Here is something that is a must overstand: NOT ONLY DID CHAVVAH HAVE DIRECT CONTACT WITH CREATURE IN

THE MIDDLE OF THE GARDEN, AW-DAWN HAD CONTACT WITH THAT SAME CREATURE, THIS IS WHAT THE VERSE SAYS: "... *SHE TOOK OF THE FRUIT THEREOF, AND <u>DID EAT</u>, AND GAVE ALSO UNTO HER HUSBAND <u>WITH HER</u>; AND HE <u>DID EAT</u>* (Ber./Gen. 3:6)". Did you catch it? Aw-dawn and Chavvah committed the same act, they were together but Chavvah committed the act first, and Ad-dawn committed the same violation with the creature. This verse is a prime example of the *cognitive dissonance* many people suffer therefrom, and the cleverly deceptive way the Scriptures are written.

Of Note: There is no specific verse that reads Seventh Shamayim. The levels of Shamayim have been determined by the use of seven/seventh throughout Scriptures representing seven as: the end, completion, nothing more to follow.

Listen-up: There are many topics in the KJ bible pertaining to sex, more than many people realize. However, the KJ does not go into detail about many of the acts from time eons ago. The KJ is written in code to prevent most people reading it from comprehending what it is telling us. The *Elite Class*, the descendants of the Annunaki; however, are fully aware of the secrets embedded in the writings. Here is the thing: There are other books that have been kept hidden, secret, or that have been labeled by the Elite Class to be *pseudepigraphon*. But today with the advent of technology more information is available and accessible for anyone to access. To find concurring information of what is hidden in Bereshis, Chapters 1-3, go online, do an engine search for: *Caligastia* and *Daligastia*. This source will provide you information that will cause you to view everything you have been taught about the Garden of Eden in a whole new light. The writings on Caligastia and Daligastia go into great detail about Lucifer, Hasatan, and how existence is hundreds of thousands of years old.

The creation of the homo erectus and the animal kingdom, and the creation of humans are two (2) separate creations that did not exist at the same time. Lets examine some scriptural data, to pull this all together. Elohim is continuing to provide Ha Mashiach, HIS Son, with instructions for the next phase of construction. Now every creature that The Most High Elohim desired to make will come forth from the <u>waters</u>: the <u>birds</u>, the animals, and the fishes, all manner of bugs, and creeping things. All of these creatures Elohim brought forth from the waters of the deep, including the <u>fowls</u>. HASHEM gave humans a Commandment: *"Be fruitful and multiply"* (v.1:22). There is something in those words that eludes most people reading those words, and that is: the creatures have all been instructed to have sex to reproduce their own species; whereas, the plants have the innate capability to procreate, and or rather to innately reproduce. This is very important because of what will occur in the *Garden of Eden*. One other very crucial point about the Commandment for the plants and the animals to procreate is this: That Command tells us one of the secrets of Shamayim: there is sex in the *Mamlachah* (Kingdom) of Elohim.

Here is something that must be <u>overstood</u>: the *Annunaki* (fallen angels) contaminated the *Pre-Aw-dawnics*, and other animals with their wild and extreme sexual prowess. Those *Pre-Aw-dawnic* creatures were not completely human; they were a cross between the animal world, and the humans yet to come; those creatures are referred to as *homo erectus*. *Homo erectus* is a species more resembling an *ape*, than a human. Here is the thing: those creatures have been presented to the whole world as fabled stories. Not fable folks! *Mythology* were real, and by *deoxyribonucleic acid* (DNA) manipulation, and sexual reproduction of the homo erectus with the Annunaki, there were millions of them. Here is knowledge that when combined with true history of Creations Stories, will paint the story of a preceding creation in vivid color. Prior to the fall of humanity in the *Garden of Eden*, at least one creation had already ended due to the corrupt, evil influence of the Annunaki. The greatest proof we have of previous creations are the *pyramids* themselves. According to some sources the pyramids were built 250,000 years ago. How could any man/woman of normal size, as we know humanity today, have built the pyramids? Moreover, the pyramids pre-date man by thousands of millennia. This has been scientifically proven through *carbon testing (mariobuildreps.com)*. Those structures were built by a previous set of giants, not the giants of Bereshis 6:4, who went extinct before humanity came into existence in the era of Aw-dawn. I cannot emphasize strongly enough, Aw-dawn and Chavvah were having conversations in the Garden of Eden, they were talking to creatures that were in existence before Elohim created the two of them. The following information comes from the *Orthodox Jewish Bible*; hopefully, it will lend more credence to multiple creations:

Isaiah. 34:14:

*"The **tziyyim** (martens) shall also encounter **iyyim** (wild cats), and a **sa'ir** (wild goat) calls to its companion, and **lilit** (night creature) dwells there and finds for itself a **mano'ach** (place of rest)."*

Orthodox Jewish Bible (OJB)

The OJB tells us briefly of the existence of *Lilith*. Lilith was the first recorded female on the eretz. She was under the influence of the fallen malachs. Though Lilith is not mentioned by name in the Authorized King James Version (AKJV) of Scripture, she is present in the Scriptures in (Bereshis/Gen. 1:27). Additionally, Lilith is also recorded in the *Arslan Tash*, which is kept in a museum in *Aleppo, Syria*.

There are many documents/books that contain hidden history of antiquity. Another such book is the *Babylonian Talmud*. Here is what the Talmud says about Lilith.

Shabbat 151a:

*"It is forbidden for a man to **sleep alone** in a house, **lest Lilith get hold of him**."*

The Babylonian Talmud

What has to be taken into consideration about the Scriptures is this: It does not matter which source you read there is almost never full discloser of the story, the books are written in code so that only the very well educated or the *ruach* (spirit) filled person can come to full overstanding of what is deceitfully written in the Scriptures. Case in point: In the AKJV of Scripture, without clear recognition, one will never see that Bereshis 1:27, is not represented by the same people in Bereshis 2:21-23. In Bereshis 1:27, the man and the woman are simultaneous creations. In Bereshis 2:21-23, the woman is made from the man after the man had already been alive for many years.

The use of the word *"Replenish"* in Bereshis/Gen. 1:28 is not by mistake, it is in all likelihood in reference to the time of Lilith. Lilith is mentioned in many ancient writings, not only bibles. Lilith preceded Chavvah, and according to many sources, Lilith had children. Let this sink in: Lilith was a very sexual creature; Lilith raped men with the intention to become pregnant, producing demon *seed* (offspring, children); Lilith was a spiritual creature of wickedness. Here is something that is a must comprehend: The story of Lilith is written of in the *Orthodox Jewish Bible, The Babylonian Talmud,* and many other documents; however, there is not one word written about Lilith in the *Authorized King James Version of Scripture.* Whether that is an oversight on the part of the *Council of Nicea* at *Rome,* or the transcribers of the AKJ Bible, *England,* or an intentional omission, I cannot say. The point being the story of Lilith is crucial information that helps to bring clarity to the creations stories. The information available on the history of Lilith from multiple sources is the type of *intersectionalism* required to bring overstanding of what is fact, from that of fiction.

It is errant for anyone teaching on the creations stories, and the giants not to include Lilith. Not only were the Annunaki responsible for the production of the giant *Nephilim,* many *homo erectus* were also giants. To obtain or grasp what is actually contained in the Scriptures, one has to be in the ruach, studying what is written. The casual reading of the Scriptures will yield an empty basket. You must read the entire creations stories with your eyes wide open, and you will see the hidden information of Scripture; use your spiritual eye to see the truth.

Let us look at what occurred in the mixing of Spiritual Beings with the Physical Beings:

Bereshis/Gen. 6:1-5 (OJB):

*'And it came to pass, when **Ha Aw-dawn** (The Men) began to multiply on the face of **ha'adamah** (the earth), and **banot** (daughters) were born unto them, 2 That the **bnei** (sons) HaElohim saw the **banot** (daughters) Ha Aw-dawn that they were **tovot** (beautiful); and they took them **nashim** (wives) of all which they chose. 3 And HASHEM said, MY Ruach Hakodesh shall not always strive with **Aw-dawn** (Man), for that he also is **basar** (flesh): yet his **yamim** (days) shall be a hundred and twenty **shanah** (years). 4 **Ha Nefilim** (The Nephilim or giants) were on **ha'aretz** (the earth) in those **yamim** (days); **and also after that**, when the **bnei** (sons) HaElohim came in unto the **banot** (daughters) **Ha Aw-dawn** (The Men), and **they bore children to them**, the same became **gibborim** (mighty men) which were of **old**, men of **renown**. 5 And HASHEM saw that the wickedness of **Ha Aw-dawn** (The Men) was great in **ha'aretz** (the earth) and that every **yetzer** (inclination) of the **machshevot** (thoughts) of his **lev** (heart) was only **rah** (evil) continually.'*

Those reading these verses with their spiritual eyes wide open will see, the spirit world *intermingled* (produced offspring) with the physical world. The Beings that came from Shamayim invaded the physical world causing a gross form of posterity, some of giant proportion. Overstand this: the products of that mating are not the creation of Elohim. As the Annunaki made bodies for themselves, they also found a method on how to walk among humans from generation to generation, changing bodies when the body of the invaded person dies. The Annunaki are among us unto this day, and they are the powers of this world, the *Elite Class.* As unbelievable as this sounds, the Scriptures themselves tell us: Hasatan is on eretz going here, and there seeking someone to take control thereof (Yob 1-3; 1 Pet. 5:8). The children of Elohim and the children of the Annunaki are not the same people but are the same species, closely enough related in *deoxyribonucleic acid* (DNA) to mate, and through *interbreeding*, reproduce offspring. <u>Once the</u>

Annunaki invaded humanity, producing offspring, those offspring are not of Elohim, and those offspring serve and worship their gods, the Annunaki. The children of Elohim possess the ruach of Elohim, and the children of the Annunaki possess the spirit of the Annunaki. The children of Elohim have been sent to eretz to choose their direction for life on this planet, good or evil, to determine where their final travel will take them. In other words, after the children of Elohim die the death of the flesh, the fate of their ruach then hinges on one act only: Did that ruach remain in obedience to the Abba or did that spirit go the way of the fallen malachs? Inasmuch, the children of the Annunaki also have to make a choice: To renounce their gods, the Annunaki, which would remove the spirit of *rah* (evil) from their physical bodies. Do you overstand? The children of the fallen malachs are in demon possession. Those under the influence of the Annunaki are possessed with the spirit of *rah* (evil) occupying their physical bodies. It is only the fallen malachs, who have no choice, those creatures are forever banned from returning to Shamayim. The children of Elohim praying for healing of the children of the Annunaki are praying in vain, those creatures cannot be redeemed by the children of Elohim praying for them. Those possessed by the Annunaki must renounce their gods, and pray to Elohim of their own free will. In addition, the child of Elohim praying for the enemy, is most likely, although unknowingly, praying to those Annunaki gods. Listen-up: The fallen malachs, who have directly invaded humans; such as, in the case of Ham, those people are of superior mind-set, they are the most powerful, and wealthy people on this planet. Do you overstand? It is the Elite Class, who cause all of the division between the races. Those of the Elite Class use brainwashing tactics on their people, making them to see themselves as superior to others. That superior mind-set in particular, is directed toward the children of Elohim, the Hebrews. Now get this: To assure their people are of superior mind-set, the Annunaki reward their people with the best rewards: gold, silver, expensive cars, mansions, and lots of money.

Now let us return to the malachs falling from greatness. Ioudas/Yude is one of the most revealing books of the Sacred Texts about Biblical

History, and of the future. Many things will come into existence before the New World to come will occur.

Ioudas/Yude 6 (AKJV):

*'And the angels which kept **not their first estate**, but left their **own habitation**, HE hath reserved in everlasting chains under darkness unto the sentencing of the great day.'*

*Ioudas* tells us specifically that the malachs who were in Shamayim, by self-default, left their own dwelling place. Though this verse reads as if the malachs had a choice to remain in Shamayim, or to leave Shamayim, they had no choice, they were kicked out of the *Mamlachah* (Kingdom) for their violations, their attempted coup of Shamayim. On the eretz those malachs are going to and from seeking out humans they can influence, and then connect with in the spirit world. Once the fallen spirit enters the person, that person then has to make a choice: To remain under the influence of the fallen malach or to free their-self from that spirit by allowing the *Ruach Hakodesh* of Elohim to enter interceding on their behalf, pushing out the spirit of the evil one. In obedience to Elohim, that person is then free. If that person does not renounce the evil spirit their fate will be the same punishment as the evil spirit(s). The tie-in to Bereshis/Gen. 6:1-5, and Ioudas 6 is this: The malachs who rebelled against The Most High Elohim are spiritual Beings, who are among us today in physical bodies. Also know this, good agents of Elohim are also among us performing duties assigned to them by The Most High Elohim. History and science have given us a better view of what the Scriptures tell us in the first 5 days of the creations stories.

I, Elohim, *I AM THAT I AM*, have laid out the construction plans for the worlds, and I, Elohim, have given those plans to MY Son, Ha Mashiach, Who has in obedience to ME, carried out MY instructions with honor and respect to ME. However, this next phase of the construction will be a family decision from ME, The Elohim; and of the Ruach Hakodesh; and of MY Son, *Ha Mashiach* (The Messenger).

And Elohim called a meeting with the Ruach Hakodesh, and Ha Mashiach. With that commenced the 6th and final Day of the creations, prior to the final creation to come (Isa. 65:17; His./Rev. 21:5).

Elohim said to the Ruach and to the Son:

Bereshis/Gen. 1:26-28 (AKJV):

*'Let Us make **man** in Our image, after Our likeness ... 27 So Elohim created man in HIS image, in the image of Elohim created HE him; male and female created HE them. 28 And Elohim blessed them, and Elohim said unto them, Be fruitful, and multiply, and **REPLENISH** the eretz, and subdue it: and have dominion over the fish of the sea, and over the fowl of the air, and over every living thing that moves upon the earth.'*

Thus, when Elohim created the first man and woman, the *Annunaki* having knowledge of sexual procreation, had intercourse with the men and women Elohim created. The Annunaki had already mated with the animals producing all manner of strange offspring. The proof of such creatures and their prehistoric existence comes from *geological* and *paleontological* finds of remains of such creatures embedded in rock from millions of years past. This information is readily available online by many *Scientific Research Centers*, simply do a word search: *Fossils embedded in rock*. I know someone is shaking their head about the statement of the fallen malachs having sexual relations with the men, and the women. Watch this! In *The Cabala/Talmud* is the following: *'Ham is told by his outraged father that: "Because you have **abused** me (**sodomized**/buggered me) in the darkness of the night,* (Midrash Rabbah 1:292)'. This is also referenced in the AKJV of Scripture Bereshis/Gen. 9:21-22. The question is: How did Ham learn such behavior? He was possessed with the spirit of the Annunaki. We will discuss this in more detail line and precept, as we continue to pull the Scriptures together. I know this goes against your understanding of Scripture, but the facts of Scripture are the facts. Cleverly written verses have left most people unknowingly in ignorance of what is embedded in the writings. In example: In the story of Benoni, some of the men of that Shevet (Tribe) were homosexuals (Yudges 19:22). This is a line upon line and precept upon precept moment in Scripture.

The first point of these verses it this: "*man*" is humankind, not a single man or woman; man is a species, made in the flesh that covers the ruach inside of an otherwise lump of clay (Isa. 64:8; Yob 10:9-33:6). Man is, when he or she is connected in the ruach to the Ruach Hakodesh the express "*image*" and "*likeness*" of the Creators. Hear clearly now what the Scriptures have revealed to us: Everything that was made, was made before the man was made; the malachs and the animals, and all non-human life, the vegetation, and the sea life. The malachs had already rebelled against The Most High Elohim, and have been cast-down to the eretz, their place of confinement (eretz/prison), before humanity was created. The fallen angels are knowledgeable Beings, who retain the power they had in Shamayim. The fallen angels are almost *omniscient*, in almost all things; and get this, though they are not *omnipotent*, their power well supersedes that of humanity. The fallen angels were aware of the Commandment Elohim gave to the animals to *procreate* (Bereshis/Gen. 1:22). Having the knowledge of sex, the fallen angels were mating with the animals, the fish, and the fowls, and humans (Enoch 10:10-18). What Ham did to the dog, that is, having sex with the dog is found in, *Midrash Rabbah* 1:292-293; and what Ham did to Noah is found in Bereshis/Gen. 9:24. When Abba created humanity, there was from the animal world creatures referred to as *Pre-Aw-dawnics*. The fallen angels mated with those creatures, the fallen angels becoming the gods of those Pre-Aw-dawnic creatures.

Think on this, and it will make sense, I hope: *Aw-dawn* (Adam), and *Chavvah* (Eve) encountered Hasatan or some other evil Being in the Garden of Eden. Hasatan and other Beings were already there along with other life forms before Aw-dawn and Chavvah were taken from Mother Eretz (Ber./Gen. 3:1). With that said, let us move forward to the 6th Day of creation. In examining Day 6 of the creation, one has to keep in mind that the malachs have been on eretz through all of the creations periods, the eretz is their habitation. The forerunner to humanity are the creatures called *homo erectus*. Those creatures were more like an ape than a human.

Homo erectus:

*"an extinct large-brained hominid of the genus Homo (H. erectus) that is known from __fossil remains__ in Africa, Europe, and Asia, is estimated to have flourished from __1.6 million years ago to 250,000 years ago__, is thought to be the first hominid to master fire and inhabit caves, and is believed to be the immediate __ancestor__ of modern man"*

Merriam-Webster.com

Do you see the picture of what transpired in ancient times? Stop believing the lie that this earth and the people are only 6,000 years in existence. The homo erectus species is a man or woman but a rather crude form of what we are today. Elohim made those creatures but they were not made in HIS express likeness and image.

In recognition of the method used in writing the JK bible: its clever, deceitful rhetoric, let us examine writing from another source that is labeled as *pseudepigraphical,* by the Elite Class because the writings of this book uncloak what is hidden in the AKJV of Scripture with regard to sexual intercourse.

### THE CABALA/TALMUD:

*'She (Miriam) who was the descendant of princes and governors __played harlot with carpenters__' (Sanhedrin 106a) ... __All gentile children are animals__ (Yebamoth 98a) ... __Adam had sexual intercourse__ with all the __animals in the Garden of Eden__ (Yebamoth 63a) ... __Hasatan had sexual intercourse with Chavvah in the Garden and Cain was their issue__ (offspring); therefore, all of humanity is basically demonic/evil __EXCEPT the Hebrews__ whom became purified when Mosheh went to the Mountain (Mount Sinai).'*

In order to make sense of Scripture, writings from multiple books have to be included. The books of *Enoch, The Babylonian Talmud, The Cabala Talmud,* and many other books bring the picture into clear focus.

Books such as the Talmud tell the stories of antiquity with a more open approach to the events that transpired in comparison to what is recorded in the KJ bible. The reasons the KJ bible is the most popular bible in the world are several: 1. Everywhere those in possession of the KJ bible traveled, they presented that book to the indigenous people of that land; 2. The possessors of the KJ bible used *iconography* in that bible to paint themselves as the characters of the original Hebrew Scrolls; and most importantly: 3. The writers of that bible forced the content of that bible upon the other peoples in the most heinous, and brutal methodology in the history of the world. The above verses from the Talmud lend credence to the story-line in Bereshis, Chapter 3; the sexual acts of Hasatan, Aw-dawn, and Chavvah. The information in the KJ bible, and the Talmud, combined with what is written in Enoch, Chapter 68, and the *Orthodox Jewish Bible*, Isaiah Chapter 34, are conclusively telling us: There was sexual intercourse in the Garden of Eden. It was by sexual intercourse that the enemies of Elohim entered into humanity. The fallen malachs brought the secrets of Shamayim to eretz. Those secrets involved all manner of sex. Hear me well in this: The War in Shamayim was fought over power, wealth, and superiority. There is not one book written about the War in Shamayim that points to any other behavior than sex as causing the fall of man, and or what is called sin. From the time of the fall there are many behaviors today that the Scriptures refer to as sin. Those sins are all listed for us in the *Torah*. The First Ten (10) Commandments must be adhered thereto but none more important than the First Four (4) Commandments (She./Exo. 20:2-17). To violate the First Four (4) Commandments results in soul death, if the person does not recovery in <u>repentance</u> and <u>obedience</u>. The Cabala Talmud tells us of a certainty: The Scriptures are written to the children of Elohim. All other people are condemned unless they follow the guidelines given to the Hebrews. Moreover, those hybrid creatures have no redemption to come, they are the Annunaki, they are soulless creatures, capable of the most brutal torture tactics possible to keep their first place status in the world: the power, wealth, and superiority mindset. The posterity of the Annunaki however, can achieve redemption by denouncing their gods, the fallen malachs, and coming under the Laws given to the Hebrews.

Overstand this: The Annunaki are forever spirits, as are all spirits. When the host body of the Annunaki dies, they transfer to another body. With that said, do not believe that all of the people of a particular race are the same, they are not. The Annunaki are possessors of people from the darkest skin hues, to those of almost absent melanin in their skin. The Hebrew people are the stand alone people of The Most High Elohim. The Scriptures have presented this to us as matter-of-fact, not hypothesis or boasting, the Hebrews were separated from all other people to serve and worship Elohim only (Ber./Gen. 17:5-8).

I, Elohim have shaped and reshaped the workings of MY hands. MY Son has built, and I, Elohim have approved or disapproved, making changes as I desired to do so. I, your Elohim, have ended creations, and began new creations in MY timeless Eternality. Now, I, Elohim will make a new creation, from the eretz, and form it into that which pleases ME.

The use of *"creations stories"* is not a typo; the homo erectus is a creation story; Aw-dawn is a creation story, and when you get to Seth in the Scriptures, is another creation story. Here is something that is a must overstand: Bereshis 1:27: '*created male and female*' simultaneously, is not the same creation as Bereshis 2:22: '*made from the rib of the man*'. These are two separate births or *genesis*. Listen-up: Your pastor will tell you Chapter 1 of Bereshis, is an overview of the chapters to follow, that is absolutely false. That explanation is many pastor's way of trying to explain the seemingly errors and or gaps of Scripture. The Scriptures are not in error: IT IS TWO SEPARATE CREATIONS. The pastors with overstanding have to sway the Scriptures in understanding, and illogical rhetoric to keep their parishioners believing a false narrative in a false religion. The pastors know that most people don't possess what it takes to fully grasp the content, the depth involved in the Scriptures. With regard to creations stories, what no one has been able to determine is, how many creations there have been? Read the creation story of Aw-dawn again; pay attention to one key word that people reading the story do not comprehend, and that word is "**_Replenish_**". Look this word up for yourself; once you have the meaning of this word, your outlook on the creation will change. Furthermore, if you believe the Scriptures, there is yet another creation to come; a *New Shamayim* (Heaven) and a *New Eretz* (Earth; Isaiah 66:22).

Before we get into all of the events of Day Six of the creation there is vital information to be considered. Let us do a short review of the information we have looked at thus far, and of the creations already gone by. According to the *U.S. Geological Institute*, and other geological institutions, this planet is at minimum 200 million years old. Prior to the eretz was Shamayim, and all of the heavenly bodies, including the Malachs. We have viewed information proof positive that the pyramids pre-date man by thousands of millennia, before there is any modern man as we are today. *Gondwanaland* was a time that all of the eretz was one large mass. During the *Triassic Period, Mesozoic Era*, were all of the dinosaurs, and other giant creatures that were gone prior to *homo erectus*. Changes in the landmass in *Pangaea* resulted in the end of several creations, the *Jurassic Period* being one of those creations. We have also seen in the Scriptures that *Lilith* is written of in some Bibles by name, while she is only eluded to in other bibles. Now, let us look at what Elohim created in Day Six.

*I AM THAT I AM*, have made a creation to test the *celestial* Beings of Shamayim that I, Elohim have already created, to prove their worthiness to remain in Shamayim. Those celestial Beings will have to travel from Shamayim to eretz to be tested for their worthiness to return to Shamayim or their permanent banning from Shamayim. The Malachs that were with ME in Shamayim rebelled against MY Supreme **Mamlachah** (Kingdom), and MY Servant, Michael and his army tossed them from the Mamlachah. Now, *I AM THAT I AM*, will cause the **ruachs** (spirits) that I have already made to go through a test to prove their loyalty to ME. The test for them is one: to possess a ruach of good or a ruach of evil. The ruachs, who go the way of the malachs that rebelled against ME will suffer the same fate as the fallen ones. Each ruach will go about on the eretz in a body made from the eretz. At the end of their earthly travel, the ruachs of good countenance will return to Shamayim, and the ruachs of evil, will remain on Eretz, the prison until the day of sentencing.

Now let us look at the first creation story for man.

Bereshis/Gen. 1:26-27 (AKJV):

*'And Elohim said, Let **us** make man in our **image**, after our **likeness**: and let them have dominion over the fish of the sea, and over the fowl of the air, and over the cattle, and over all the earth, and over every creeping thing that creeps upon the earth. 27 So Elohim created man in his own image, in the image of Elohim created he him; **male and female** created he them.'*

Here, the first true humans, *male* and *female,* have been created in the image of Elohim, but with the likeness of the Ruach Hakodesh, and the Son, Ha Mashiach. These two have been given the duty of naming all of the creatures Elohim designed, constructed by Ha Mashiach. What follows these unnamed persons comes in:

Bereshis/Gen. 1:28-29 (AKJV):

*'And Elohim blessed them, and Elohim said unto them, **Be fruitful, and multiply**, and **replenish** the earth, and subdue it: and have **dominion** over the fish of the sea, and over the fowl of the air, and over every living thing that moves upon the earth. 29 And Elohim said, Behold, I have given you every herb bearing **seed**, which is upon the face of **all the earth**, and every tree, in the which is the fruit of a tree yielding seed; to you it shall be for meat.'*

What you have in these verses is very cleverly written. Most people reading this have no clue what it is actually saying. The <u>man</u> and the <u>woman</u> have been given the responsibility for everything on the earth. These two are equal partners; these two have no name; these two have been Commanded to procreate to replace (**replenish**) the creatures that came before them, the homo erectus who no longer exist. What is also absent in these verses is that these two people are not given the status of a *living soul.* When additional information from other sources are assessed along with the above verses, it can be recognized that Lilith is possibly the woman in the verse. The unnamed male and Lilith produced a lot of offspring. However, because Lilith colluded with the fallen malachs, all of those creatures were destroyed. This is information not contained in your AKJV of Scripture but is contained in other books; such as, Shabbat 151a- in the *Babylonian Talmud*. Do you get it? It is these two people that are having conversations with the contaminated *Annunaki* or fallen malachs in the garden. The malachs had full knowledge of all things involving power, wealth, superiority, and sexual pleasure. Those malachs showed the humans:

Enoch 63:1:

"... and have **revealed secrets** to the sons of men, and have **seduced the sons of men** to the commission of sin."

What the malachs showed to Lilith, and the unnamed male was not supposed to be on the eretz. You don't believe the word **seduced** is representative of sex? It certainly is a sexual reference! Those malachs were having sex with both the males and females of Chapter 1 of the Bereshis. Listen-up: even supposing seduced in the verse is not representative of sexual intercourse, it is still an at of *sedition* because it is disobedience to Elohim. And it is possible, these people were promised the knowledge of Shamayim in exchange for their sex. But again, even so, it was forbidden and disloyal to Elohim. Man, woman, male, female represents multiples of people, not a singularity.

I, Elohim, *I AM THAT I AM*, have heard the report of what the malachs have done on the eretz; therefore, I will destroy all of the contaminated people and animals of the eretz. *I AM THAT I AM*, will bring forth a man which is pleasing to ME.

Watch this! There is a big difference in the verses of Bereshis, Chapter 1, and the following verses of Chapter 2:

Bereshis 2:4-7:

'These are the generations of the heavens and of the earth when they were created, in the day that the Hashem Elohim made the earth and the heavens, 5 and **every plant** of the field **before** it was in the earth, and every herb of the field **before** it grew: for *the Hashem Elohim had not caused it to rain upon the earth, and there **was not a man** to till the ground. 6 But there went up a mist from the earth, and watered the whole face of the ground. 7 And the Hashem Elohim **formed** man of the dust of the ground, and breathed into his nostrils the breath of life; and man became a **living soul**.'*

Word usage is vital in overstanding the hidden information in the Scriptures. Clearly here, *I AM THAT I AM* has told us, the vegetation was already made before HE put it on the eretz. Had you ever thought on that before? Undoubtedly, most people have not. Most people being in a state of *cognitive dissonance* because of false teaching. Now let us do a comparison of Bereshis, Chapters 1 and 2. In Chapter 1, the male and female were created simultaneously. In Chapter 2, initially there is only the man. In Chapter 1, the man and woman are equal partners, given the same responsibilities to govern over the animals, and all of the eretz. In Chapter 2, the man has already been tasked with caring for the eretz without a partner. In Chapter 1, the people are alive, and yet, not so. Here is the difference: In Chapter 1, the people are only fashioned in the "***image***" and "***likeness***" of Elohim, but in Chapter 2, the man is a "***living soul***". There is also another big difference, the male and female are comprised of a spoken existence, while the man of Chapter 2 is fashioned by Elohim from the innocent eretz. Do not allow anyone to continue to tell you Bereshis Chapter 1, is an overview of the first 5 chapters of Bereshis, that is simply not true.

Here is something that has to be overstood about the Scriptures, the Scriptures are not, in my opinion, in sequential order. Parts of a story may be found in different chapters of a book; and moreover, parts of the same story may be in several different books throughout different *Canons*. Now let us look at the creation of the woman in Bereshis, Chapter 2.

*I AM THAT I AM*, has destroyed the animals, and the people of Chapter 1. HE has made a new man because the first man and woman became infected by the evil *Annunaki*. Elohim has now made a new man and animals. This is important because Lilith (Isa. 34:14 OJB),

35

in Bereshis, Chapter 1, was influenced by the Annunaki to commit evil. Lilith and her unnamed companion were given the secrets of Shamayim by **_Azazyel_** (Enoch 8:1; 9:5; 10:12-13). Lilith then shared with her partner what the Annunaki had shared with her. The acts they committed involved sexual pleasure, whether of fowl, fish, animal, and same sex. Briefly for the doubters of what is presented here, let us look at:

Enoch 10:13:

'*To Gabriel also the HASHEM said, Go to the biters, to the **reprobates,** to the children of **fornication**; and destroy the children of **fornication**, the **offspring** of the **Watchers**, from among men; bring them forth, and excite them one against another. Let them perish by mutual slaughter; for length of days shall not be theirs.*'

The most significant words in the verse are **_fornication_** and **_reprobates_**. Elohim sent Gabriel to destroy the offspring produced by the fallen malachs, and whatsoever creatures there were on the eretz, with whom they had mated. Don't allow yourself to be fooled any longer, believing that the Book of Enoch is a false book. Enoch tells us what happened in antiquity; whereas, the AKJV of Scripture is authored by the offspring of the Annunaki, who have not allowed the truth to be clearly spelled out in their book, because the truth tells who they are. The writers of the KJ bible, left out at minimum 14 books that came before the KJ bible was even a thought. Enoch 10:13 is all about the sexual prowess of the fallen ones and their offspring. Listen-up: the story in Bereshis, Chapter 1 is vague, written that way intentionally. What is written in Enoch is verification of Bereshis. Enoch has been labeled as *pseudepigraphical* (false) because Enoch tells who the offspring of the fallen malachs are today. The fornication and production of vile offspring came to humanity by way of Lilith. It is because of the acts of the Annunaki and Lilith that the creation period for Lilith ended. It is because of Lilith that Elohim in Bereshis, Chapter 2, made the man without a coequal female partner. Watch this!

Bereshis 2:21-22 (AKJV):

*'And the HASHEM Elohim caused a deep sleep to fall upon Aw-dawn, and he slept: and HE took one of his ribs, and closed up the flesh instead thereof; 22 and the rib, which the HASHEM Elohim had* **taken from man, made HE a woman,** *and brought her unto the man.'*

In the creation story of Lilith and the man, Bereshis, Chapter 1, they were created simultaneously. Those two people however, were soulless. In the next creation the man was created without the woman, and the man has a soul but he is alone. All of the animals can mate but the man has no mate. Elohim decided this time, HE would bring the woman from the man; thereby, she too would be a living soul. It was the woman in Chapter 1 that caused sin to come upon humanity, now perhaps, the woman having a soul, she will not listen to or fall victim to the voice of the Annunaki. However, being brought from the male, she was not as strong as the male being a replica, and humanity would not do well once again. There is another important point in the creations stories of Bereshis, Chapters 1 and 2: the first record of humanity, in Chapter 1, there is no mention of the Garden of Eden, those people were not confined or restricted in travel, and were free to go wheresoever they would. When Elohim decided to bring back humanity, HE put them in a specified place, a little bit of heaven on earth; a place called the *Garden of Eden*.

This is a great break-in place to insert some great information that has been most likely deliberately left out of the AKJV of Scripture. Afterward, we will resume the Creations Stories. As we have already seen above, the Book of Enoch has been labeled by those of power to be *pseudepigraphical*. Here is one reason why the Book of Enoch has been discredited:

Enoch, Chapters 86:1-3; 87:1-5:

*"86:1 Again I perceived them, when they began to strike and to swallow each other; and the earth cried out. Then I raised my*

*eyes a second time towards heaven, and saw in a vision, that, behold, there came forth from heaven as it were the likeness of **white men**. One came forth from thence, and three with him. 2 Those three, who came forth last, seized me by my hand; and raising me up from the generations of the earth, elevated me to a high station. 3 Then they showed me a **lofty tower** on the earth, while **every hill became diminished**. And they said, Remain here, until you perceive what shall come upon those elephants, camels, and asses, upon the stars, and upon all the cows. ... 87:1 Then I looked at that one of the four **white men**, who came forth first. 2 He seized the first star which fell down from heaven. 3 And, binding it hand and foot, he cast it into a valley; a valley narrow, deep, stupendous, and gloomy. 4 Then one of them drew his sword, and gave it to the elephants, camels, and asses, who began to strike each other. **And the whole earth shook on account of them**. 5 And when I looked in the vision, behold, one of those **four angels**, who came forth, **hurled from heaven**, collected together, and took all the great stars, whose form partly resembles that of horses; and binding them all hand and foot, cast them into the cavities of the earth."*

First I have to say this: If you are a person of non-melanin skin writing a book, seeing what is represented in these verses, and you are of a superiority mind-set, would you allow that into the book you are writing? Undoubtedly the answer is: No. The point is this: The malachs, the fallen angels were turned white by The Most High Elohim. They were tossed out of Shamayim to eretz. The eretz is the prison for the rebellious, and simultaneously, a proving ground for the inhabitants of Shamayim, who must now come to eretz in human form to make the choice of life: the Elohim side or the side of the fallen ones, the *Annunaki*. The Annunaki are the **Watchers** who were supposed to keep observance of what the fallen malachs were doing upon the eretz. However, even some of the Watchers went to the Hasatan side. In the hierarchy of Shamayim, the following *Archangels* remained loyal to Elohim, and the following are their names, and their observations of what the evil ones did on the eretz:

Enoch 9:1-4:

'Then **Michael** and **Gabriel**, **Raphael**, **Suryal**, and **Uriel**, _looked down from heaven_, and saw the quantity of blood which was shed on earth, and _all the iniquity_ which was done upon it, and said one to another, It is the voice of their cries; 2 The earth deprived of her children has cried even to the gate of heaven. 3 And now to you, O You sacred One of heaven, the souls of men complain, saying, _Obtain equity for us with The Most High_. Then they said to their Hashem, the King, You are Hashem of lords, Elohim of gods, King of kings. The throne of Your glory is for ever and ever, and for ever and ever is Your name sanctified and glorified. You are blessed and glorified. 4 You have made all things; You possess power over all things; and all things are open and manifest before You. You behold all things, and nothing can be concealed from You.'

The loyal Watchers observed what the fallen malachs had done on the eretz: all of the chaos; all of the destruction, and killing, and oppression, and forbidden sexual prowess. The people were able to communicate with the good Watchers, and called out to them. The Watchers then reported to Elohim what they had observed, which is as follows:

Enoch 9:5:

'You have seen what **Azazyel** has done, how he has taught **every species** of iniquity upon earth, and has disclosed to the world **all the secret things** which are done in the heavens.'

Listen-up: This is vitally important to digest, not only did the fallen malachs teach humans the secrets of things done in Shamayim, the fallen malachs committed all manner of crime to: **'every species'** of the earth. Do you comprehend the inclusiveness of the wording? Every species includes: fowl, fish, reptiles, and humans. The things done in Shamayim were never supposed to come to humanity. This too is related to the great flood, and why the innocent animals were slaughtered along with the people.

What these verses tell us is: There will come a day that a dominant race of people will emerge, from the bloodline of the fallen watchers, who will terrorize and brutalize much of the world, and bring all manner of forbidden pleasures to eretz. The acts done in Shamayim were never supposed to be shared with humanity, and even more so, forced upon the non-human life as well. The books of *Enoch, The Babylonian Talmud, The Orthodox Jewish Bible*, and *The Cabala/Talmud*, fill-in much of what is missing from the KJ bible. It is for that very reason that the writers of the KJ bible would exclude such writings, and label them as *pseudepigraphon*. Moreover, these verses make it specifically known what the outer appearance of these men will be, and who these people are: "***white men***". Anyone taking offense in what these verses are saying, it is because the truth is harder to accept than a lie. This has to be overstood: these white men are the powers of the world, the men of wealth, the men who believe in and promote white supremacy. These white men are not representative of all none melanized people, they are representative of who they are: The Annunaki in a human body. These Annunaki gods have always had one goal and intent, to overthrow the Will of The Most High Elohim. Let me make this expressly clear: All white people **are not**, I repeat, **are not** the enemy to people of color. The Annunaki gods have stoked division among the people by race, using skin color to coerce anarchy. The best way to carryout such plans, is to feed the people of white skin rhetoric of their supremacy, and to give them wealth to support their agenda. In particular, the Annunaki gods work diligently to destroy the Chosen, Set-apart people of Elohim, the Hebrews. As we continue to inform what the Scriptures are telling us, we will see how these Annunaki gods have tormented the world because they are angry about being forever banned from returning to Shamayim. Enoch, Chapters 86:1-3; 87:1-5 is simply a forecast of what the outer appearance of those hybrid creatures will be on eretz. Also observe in Enoch 86:3, the "***lofty tower***". That is in reference to the Tower of Babel. The tower was very high at the time before its destruction, it was higher than the peaks of the mountains. We will look at that in detail as we follow the flow of the Scriptures.

Now let us look at who was in the Garden of Eden, and what happened in the Garden.

Bereshis (OJB) 3:1-7:

'Now the **serpent** (Hasatan or other evil spirit) was more **subtil** (cunning, clever, deceitful) than any beast of the field which the HASHEM Elohim had made. And he said unto the woman, Yea, has Elohim said, You shall not **eat** (become wise) of every tree (man) of the garden? 2 And the woman said unto the serpent, **We** (Aw-dawn and Chavvah) may **eat** (become wise) of the **fruit** (reward) of the **trees** (people) of the garden: 3 but of the fruit of the **tree** (person/creature) which in the middle of the garden, Elohim has said, You shall not eat of it (undetermined sex), neither shall you touch it, less you die. 4 And the **serpent** said unto the woman, You shall not surely die: 5 for Elohim does know that in the day you eat thereof, then your eyes shall be opened, and you shall be as gods, knowing good and evil. 6 And when the woman saw that the tree (man) was **good** (handsome) for **food** (wisdom), and that **it** (penis) was pleasant to the eyes, and a **tree** (man) to be desired to make one **wise** (desire), she took of the **fruit** (reward) thereof, and did **eat** (became sexually wise), and **gave** (withdrew from Elohim) also unto her husband with her; and he did eat (became sexually wise). 7 And the eyes of them both were opened, and they knew that they were **naked** (took bad advice); and they sewed fig leaves together, and made themselves aprons.'

*Eat* (akal): burn up, consume, devour, wise (398)
*Food* (ma'akal: flesh, fruit (3978), of *akal* (398), to become wise.
*Fruit* (periy): reward (6529)
*Serpent* (nachash): snake, hiss (5175), of (5172): divine enchanter, to learn by experience, to diligently observe.
*Gave* (nathan): prime root word of multiple applications; withdraw, +would to God, and yield (5414)

41

*Good* (towb): men or women, beautiful, pleasure (2896)
*Tree* (Anuwb): borne (6086), from *enab*: to bear fruit (6025)
*Eyes* (ayin): affliction (5869)
*Wise* (sakal): intelligent, instruct, teach, cause to make or act (7919)
*Naked* (eyrom): nudity (5903) from 6191: bare, deal subtilly, to take crafty counsel (Source- Strong's Exhaustive Concordance of the Bible)
*It*: a person or animal whose sex is unknown or disregarded (Merriam-Webster.com).

Folks, do not allow *cognitive dissonance* to continue to dictate what you have been taught, above that which you have read with your own eyes. Let the synapses of your mind fully open for you to achieve the reality of Scripture. Allow me to pull some of the most important word definitions above together in graph-form to make it easier to follow: *Wise= intelligent or knowledge or teach an act; fruit= reward or gift; tree= seed or offspring; serpent= snake deceiver with experience; gave= withdraw or remove or disobedience; good= a beautiful person or pleasure; eyes= punishment; naked= nude by trickery.* Hopefully, this breakdown of the words draws a clear picture of what Hasatan did to Chavvah in the Garden of Eden: It was sex! Chavvah then encouraged Aw-dawn to also partake of the same act(s), with the same *creature* (tree), she had gained knowledge therefrom.

Conclude what you will about the above Scriptures, and specific word meaning in the Scriptures. One thing that must be pointed out is something that is evasive to most readers of the Garden of Eden story; and that is: there was more than Aw-dawn, Chavvah, and Hasatan in the Garden. The Bible uses the word *tree* in many instances to represent a person or persons (Yudges 9:8-15; Teh./Psl. 1:3; 37:35; Pro. 3:18; Shel./Sol. 2:3; 7:7; Isa. 14:8). Clearly these verses say- paraphrasing: Aw-dawn and Chavvah are free to interact with all of the ***trees***, except the ***tree*** in the middle of the Garden (3:3): "***We*** *may **eat** of the **fruit** of the **trees** of the garden* (3:2)". Aw-dawn and Chavvah were only restricted from that one tree, the tree of evil seed. Was that tree Hasatan or other fallen malach or the product of Hasatan? There is no clear Scripture which says, directly the tree is Hasatan. Chavvah was already in contact with Hasatan meaning, she was in communication with him. Listen-up: It was not in having a conversation with Hasatan that caused the <u>disobedience</u>, it was the physical act Chavvah did with Hasatan, and then having Aw-dawn to do the same. But whatsoever transpired between the three of them, the communication all centered on that one *tree* in the middle of the Garden.

We have come to the point of Aw-dawn and Chavvah being in sin. Before we examine what is yet to come because of the sin committed in the Garden, we have to revisit somewhat *Gondwanaland* and *Pangaea*. We must also look at what happened in the *African Diaspora*. Over some 200-250 million years ago in human time, Elohim formed the *eretz* (earth). All of the land was one large mass. All of the eretz was water, dirt, and rock, nothing else had been formed by Elohim at that time. Elohim then decided to change the eretz into land masses bringing about Pangaea, separating the land into continents. In the time from Gondwanaland to Pangaea are untold creations stories because Elohim designed and redesigned the eretz until it was acceptable to HIM. The times of *Triassic: Mesozoic; Permian; Tertiary; and Cenozoic* are different creations stories that came and went. After Elohim separated the land, HE decided on where HE would put the animals, and eventually the humans yet to come. The first animals included dinosaurs, and other mammoth size creatures. Those creatures would eventually be polluted by the Annunaki, and because many of them were *carnivorous* (meat eaters), they were incompatible with the humans that will be formed by Elohim. The creation period for the dinosaurs (Mesozoic Era, 200-250 million years ago) ended many eons before humanity would come into existence. In Gondwanaland all of the creatures lived above the equatorial line, the climate above the equator was warm; whereas, the land below the equator was ice covered. In Pangaea, as Elohim moved the land where HE chose to put it, the wildlife on the moved sections of eretz became specific to that region, lending credence to why some animals can only be found in specific areas of the earth. When Elohim decided to bring humanity about, the foul, evil Annunaki, who had polluted the wildlife, also polluted Lilith and her mate. Those Pre-Aw-dawnic creatures were then destroyed by Elohim, ending another creation. In the next creation of humanity, Elohim decided to make a garden to place the man, and instructed the man on his duties in the Garden. After the man completed his tasks, Elohim decided to give the man a partner. Listen-up: There were other creatures in the Garden of Eden other than Aw-dawn and Chavvah. Those creatures were in full contact with Aw-dawn and Chavvah; however, the creature that was confined to the middle of the Garden, Aw-dawn and Chavvah were forbidden to interact therewith. The <u>disobedience</u> that occurred in the Garden led to the spreading out of the people outward from the Garden. We can postulate from the countries mentioned in the location of the Garden of Eden that the Garden was in Africa. The countries listed in the Scriptures are *Assyria, Ethiopia and Havilah*. Havilah can be directly connected to *Iraq and Mitzrayim* (Egypt). Don't continue to believe there is a continent called, the *Middle East*, it is all Africa. The Garden of Eden was quite large. This brings us to the *African Diaspora*.

After the time of Lilith, and then the time of Aw-dawn and Chavvah, the evil of the Annunaki will continue in humanity, and exacerbate as time moves forward, and the population increases. We have all read the Creation Story in Bereshis, Chapters 1-2, but really don't give thought to what is actually contained in the Scriptures. Let us look at some specific events, that most people lend no credence to at all. The people of that day were all people of melanin, and additionally many people of that time were giants.

In *Pangaea,* the time when all the land was one large landmass, all of the land above the equator was inhabited by people of melanin skin: It only makes sense! The man was taken from Mother Eretz, the eretz is pigmented from brown, to red, to black. Overstand this: From 60,000 BC years ago, until 2,000 AD or so, is the time approximation of any Europeans arriving in any lands above the equator. When Elohim put Aw-dawn and Chavvah, and every creature out of the garden, the people began to spread out, away from the garden. That spreading out is referred to as, *The African Diaspora*. We know the people were melanized as fact because even today, all of the lands above the equator are still inhabited by people of melanin skin. When Europeans came to lands above the equator, it was many millennia after they had left Africa, and essentially, their return was a re-return to Africa. In other words, when the melanized people left Gondwanaland traveling into Laurasia, into the frigid Southwest, many millennia later, after their skin lost its melanin, they began to travel back into the land their ancestors originated therefrom. However, without the melanin which controls our physical appearance, mental stability, and overall health, those returning were no longer the same people. The most obvious differences being eye color, hair texture, and facial features. The greatest change of all being, their skin has faded to what we of today call white.

The following is what the experts say concerning the land and the people.

> "*__Prior to the Europeans__ arriving there had been Aboriginal people here for possibly 60,000 years! There were something like 250–500 Aboriginal languages so the country probably had a multitude of names.*"

quora.com

The above information is in reference to Gondwanaland, now divided into *Africa, North America, India, Madagascar, Australia*, and all of the land above the equator. According to many studied men and women of geology, and of governments, including the *U.S. Geological Service*, people have been here at least 60,000 years. However, those of white skin lost their skin color due to climate. Let us now look at information about the *African Diaspora*, not to point to bias of any type, but rather to see the flow of what happened when Elohim closed the Garden of Eden.

> "*40,000 – 10,000 BC Late Stone Age; Rise of __brown-skinned__ Homo Sapiens, spreading to __all major regions__ of the world and adapting to variations in __climate and environment__; Development of bow and arrow; evidence of rock paintings;*

*Hunter gathering lifestyle; Arrival of the <u>Grimaldian Negroid</u> <u>in Europe</u>"*

African Diaspora II International Migration; NEGRO HEBREW HERITAGE AND ENSLAVEMENT, page 244; Anthony J. Vance; Dorrance Publishing, 585 Alpha Dive, Pittsburgh, PA 15238 ISBN: 978-1-4809-5794-7

Mind you, all of the events of the Garden of Eden occurred many millennia after Gondwanaland. Many creations have come and gone since the time of Gondwanaland. What the above data tells us is that, the warm climate above the equator, and the man being formed from the brown eretz, that all of humanity was of melanized skin. Let me pull this all together: All of the land below the equator, *Laurasia*, was not inhabited, and was not stable, with a more harsh climate. By the time we get to The Garden of Eden, many changes had occurred in all of nature. As the people moved west out of Africa, changes in skin color would be a normal process as the people lived in areas with cooler to cold temperatures. By the time the people began to reverse travel, not habitation, many millennia had passed. When those people returned to areas their ancestors had lived, they did not resemble their ancestors. The hair, eyes, noses, and skin color had all changed. The people traveling back to Africa are now referred to as Europeans. Listen-up: Europeans have only existed some 6,000 years or so. What should standout in this information is this: Six thousand years is the time period the children of Hasatan have convinced the world that humanity has only existed 6,000 years. It is trickery to fool the world into believing there was no human life prior to that point, and that they have always been in control. It is the Elites way of keeping their identities hidden.

Before Aw-dawn and Chavvah came into existence, many creations had passed. At some time, most likely, the time of Lilith, because of the evil influence of the Annunaki, and the sexual interactions between the *homo erectus* and the Annunaki, a breed of offspring was produced, with varying stature, some of which were giants. This refers back to our discussion of the fossil remains of the *hominids*, who lived "*1.6 million years ago to 250,000 years ago,"* Moving forward, we know from the Scriptures, the Annunaki did indeed produce offspring with humans. This is what the Scriptures tell us:

Bereshis/Gen. 6:4 (AKJV):

'*There were **giants** in the earth in those days; and also after that, when the **sons of Elohim** came in unto the daughters of men, and they **bare children** to them, the same became **mighty men** which were of **old**, men of **renown**.'*

Let us examine the words of this verse and define the significant, specific words that detail what is going on in this verse. All of the definitions of the words below come from the *Strong's Exhaustive Concordance of the Bible.*

*Giants (5303):* is a bully or tyrant, from the prime root word *naphal (5307),* which is fall, cast-down, out, fugitive, be judged, overthrow, mistake.

These giants were of ruinous character being the products of human and fallen malach. Their very nature was that of bully, and tyrant. The point that must be made about these giant people is this: Though they are primitive creatures, they have the guidance of the fallen malachs. It was those giant humans who built the pyramids. Think on this: The pyramids date back from the time of the Cenozoic Period, a time before modern day man.

*Sons (1121):* of the word *ben (1122),* has many meanings; some of the defining words for sons in this text are: rebel, tumultuous, very fruitful, in the wildest sense of relationship, **Ammon**, nation, and much, much more.

These sons are recalcitrant (difficult to handle), involve themselves in chaos, lewd and lascivious behavior, live a wild lifestyle, and engage in sexual intercourse often, with many different partners. There is something about **Ammon** that will be a continual, recurring theme when we get to the historical data of who the Hebrews are, and who their adversaries are.

> *Mighty (1368):* from the word *gibbor* (1397) means, powerful, tyrant, warrior, chief.

Being of large stature, these men possessed great strength, and could easily brutalize those of normal statue; and therefore, made excellent fighters. Inasmuch, they became the chiefs over the people by force.

> *Men (120):* of the Hebrew word *enowsh (582)*, is to be a hypocrite, low, species, mean, low degree; and get this, in the flower of their age. Otherwise stated, excited, youthful hormonal influence.

These were scandalous, mean, disrespectful men. They were hypocrites, doing and saying one thing, and dictating to others what they could and could not do and say, committing acts that demeaned others for their own pleasures.

> *Old (5769):* from the word *olam (5769)*, is equal to the word old, which is: eternity, always, long time, perpetual, beginning of the world.

These figures were of ancient times, they had been around for a long time. They were of a time that apparently existed for eons. All of the words used to define *"Old"* in this text are words that mean from the beginning, the bereshis/genesis. They have existed as long as Shamayim has existed.

> *Renown (8034):* shame, from the prime root word *shem (8034)* which means, name, individual, through the idea of definite and conspicuous position, report. It is an appellation or description, <u>which is to appoint and set apart for a special purpose.</u>

These men brought about a high level of shame to themselves. They spread false reports to those around them. They each, had a specific role and position in their original place of habitation. They had never-ending positions in Eternality, positions of authority and an open, and obviously renowned status in that habitation, which habitation is Shamayim. *Shem* is a very interesting word in that, its hidden use will be specified when we come to the section of this study discussing genealogy. However, as a precursor, the word Hebrew is a synonym derived from Shem.

Let us now turn back to Bereshis/Gen. 3:15, which reads:

> 'And I will put **enmity** between Hasatan and the woman, and
> between **your seed and her seed**; it shall bruise your head, and
> you shall **bruise** his heel.'

*Enmity (342):* from *eybah (340)*, is hatred and hostility.

This is plain, simple and to the point. Elohim is very displeased with Hasatan and the woman. HE is causing a great separation between the two of them and between her children and his children. Again, let me emphasize the word *"seed"*. It is referring to propagation (reproduction) of the species in every use of the word that appears in the Old Testament.

*Seed (2233):* from *zera (2232)* means, carnally, posterity, conceive.

The seed are the posterity or children, grandchildren, the product(s) of sexual intercourse, the conception for life by mating. It includes all species of life whether of fowl, fish, or mammal.

*Bruise 7779):* of the Hebrew prime root word *shumph (7779)* is to: gape, cover, overwhelm.

The bruise is a predetermined promise from Elohim that in the time of the end, evil will not win. The head will be rend off of the evil doer(s), by the followers of Elohim. All evil will be cast-down and destroyed, never to rear its ugly head again.

My Scripture believing friends, when we put all of these verses together, they become all inclusive in the interpretation thereof. The meanings of these words, and the specificity of the words used in Bereshis/Gen., Chapters 1-8, provide us with a chronological view of the events that unfolded. The fallen malachs, *"sons of Elohim"* were mating with the daughters of men (Ber./Gen. 6:4). The combination of those fallen malachs with the human Beings made an abnormal size person to come about. Those sons of Elohim had been cast-down from their original place of habitation. The children they produced with the women were mean spirited and power hungry. They kept turmoil and chaos going. They like to take power and be in control at all times. These mighty, renown men have apparently been around from the beginning of creation. In their original estate, they did something so terrible; they lost the very positions they were created to do for all of their existence.

We must examine the word *"seed"* closer before going on in this portion of our study. The word seed is used over 200 times in the Old Testament, in each and every case it means the same thing, of the word *zera*: from the prime root word *zara*: fruit, plant, sowing-time, posterity, carnally, child, fruitful, seed-time. This word seed without exception is used to describe a form of reproduction, whether of fowl, fish, animals, or of human Beings. In human Beings, we call the seed, *spermatozoa*, of men and *ova*, of women.

Many say the Bible is all *allegory* and or *metaphor,* sometimes those tools are valuable to tell the story without being considered obscene. With that said, the story is not fictional allegory or metaphor, and nor is it *mythological.* Let us build upon what happened in the Garden by looking at more Scripture.

Bereshis 3:14-16 (OJB):

*'And the HASHEM Elohim said unto the serpent, <u>Because you have done this</u>, you are cursed above all cattle, and above every beast of the field; upon your belly shall you go, and dust shall you eat all the days of your life: 15 and I will put **enmity** (hatred) between you and the woman, and between <u>your **seed** (children)</u>*

*and her **seed** (children); it shall bruise your **head** (you were
first), and you shall bruise his **heel** (Ha Mashiach will step on
your head). 16 Unto the woman HE said, I will greatly multiply
your sorrow and your **conception**; in sorrow you shall bring
forth children; and your **desire** (sexual wantonness) shall be to
your husband, and he shall rule over you.'*

These verses provide us a multitude of valuable data. Elohim was
handing out the punishment to all parties for violating HIS rules. Here
is the thing, the entire punishment for Chavvah had to do with child
bearing, conception, desire for her husband, and the woman being
relegated to unequal, secondary status to Aw-dawn. Listen up and think
on this: Why would Elohim *'put **enmity** (hatred) between you and the
woman, and between your **seed** (children) and her **seed** (children); (3:15)'*?
The **seed** is a child or children (**zera**: child, fruit, posterity, carnally:
Strong's 2233). The answer to the question is one: what Hasatan or the
serpent showed to or did to Chavvah was sexual.

In the Book of Enoch is part of the story that is not in the KJ Bible.

Enoch 10:18-20:

*'Destroy all the souls addicted to **dalliance**, (15) and the
**offspring** of the **Watchers**, for they have tyrannized over
mankind.
(15) Dalliance. Or, "lust" (Knibb, p. 90; cp. Charles, p. 76).
19 Let every oppressor perish from the face of the earth;
20 Let every **evil** work be destroyed;'*

These verses, not allowed into the KJ bible tell us without a doubt,
that the fallen malachs bore children with humans. To exclude this
information from the KJ bible is another tactic used by the Elite Class
to keep the general population from the truth. In order to obtain
full overstanding of the Scriptures, all of the parts have to be pulled
together from within the KJ bible, and other bibles as well. Clearly,
these verses tell us that: the Watchers/Annunaki/Fallen Malachs, were
indeed having sexual relations with humans and producing offspring.

Don't continue to allow your mind to be dulled by those teaching spirits and flesh cannot mingle. That is far from the truth. If you don't believe flesh and spirit can come together to produce offspring, then you cannot possibly believe Miriam was impregnated by the Ruach Hakodesh. *Dalliance* is not a commonly used or well-known word. It is imperative in reading Scripture to study words you are not familiar with; otherwise, the importance of what is written remains hidden. The children of the Watchers know this information; those offspring are the Elite Class of the earth. The main target of the Watchers, to destroy, to rule over, and to enslave are the Hebrews, because the Hebrews are the pure people of the earth, created by Elohim to serve and worship HIM only (She./Exo. 33:16).

When The Most High approached Aw-dawn, Aw-dawn tried to hide from TMH, and Elohim asked Aw-dawn: Why are you hiding from ME (Ber./Gen. 3:10)? Aw-dawn answered and said: Because I am naked. Elohim then had a conversation with Chavvah, and she confessed to Abba, that she had indeed been touched by the creature/person in the middle of the Garden, the one creature/person she was instructed not to touch (3:13). The Most High then had a conversation with Hasatan, who was already cursed and banned from Shamayim, informing Hasatan that he is now cursed more than any other creature of the eretz. Here is where the punishment comes into play: There will be *enmity* (hatred) between the seed (children) of Chavvah, and the seed (children) of Hasatan (3:15); and in childbirth for Chavvah, her pain will be great (3:16). Here is the cleverness of the Scriptures: Chavvah told us that Hasatan had sex with her; however, the Scripture writers chose not to fully describe what happened with words that may be offensive to some; therefore, rather than saying sex, they wrote "***beguiled me***" (3:13). The word beguiled has several meanings, some of those meanings are: carnally, child, seduce, and posterity to name a few.

The Scripture also tells us something that most people don't catch, and that is: "*enmity between thee and the woman, and between **thy seed and her seed***" (3:15). In looking pass the words on the paper, one will see the truth of Scripture. As Chavvah will produce children (seed) so will Hasatan produce children (seed). The Scriptures are scattered line upon line, and precept upon precept. As the Scriptures continue to build we will see the presentation of the first child of Hasatan.

Aw-dawn, Chavvah, and Hasatan were all put out of the Garden of Eden, and *Cherubims* placed at the gate to prevent anyone from entering the Garden ever again. Chavvah and Aw-dawn begin to have children, twin boys: Cain and Abel. As young adults the boys made tribute to TMH; Cain's tribute, of the eretz, was not honored by TMH; whereas, Abel's tribute was accepted of Elohim. Then something happened that will begin to explain the contents of Bereshis 3:13: "***beguiled me***" and "***thy seed and her seed***" (3:15). Because Cain's offering was taken from the cursed ground (3:17), it was not considered by Elohim to be clean; and Elohim already knew Cain might not do good, potentially leading to Cain doing evil (4:7). The Scriptures make it perfectly clear when read with overstanding: Since the War in Shamayim, one is either on the Elohim side or the Hasatan side; the choice is personal. Cain went to the side of evil in murdering his brother Abel. Abba spoke with Cain, who denied knowing where he buried Abel or that he killed Abel. Abba knew what Cain did and after having a conversation with Cain, Elohim cursed Cain (4:11-12).

Follow the route of the Scriptures: At least 130 years have passed since Cain slew Abel. Aw-dawn and Chavvah have had many children in those years. Chavvah has conceived again, and gives birth to Seth. Look at this! The Scriptures weave and curve all over the place, making good overstanding of the Scriptures difficult. Look at all of the people born in Bereshis 4:16-24; and yet, in verses 4:25-26, it reads, Aw-dawn had impregnated Chavvah for the third time. Chavvah says: She had been given a replacement for Abel. Then in verses 5:1-3, is the same wording that is found in Bereshis 1:26: Elohim made Aw-dawn in HIS Own "***likeness***" and "***image***", and now Aw-dawn has made a man in his own likeness and image. Here is what is not easily recognizable in the Scriptures: Cain has his own family-line, not of the family-line of Aw-dawn; and now Aw-dawn has created another family that is to carry-out the Will of TMH Elohim. Seth was the product of Aw-dawn and Chavvah; Aw-dawn's first born child was murdered by Cain. From Seth and his descendants would eventually come Enoch. Enoch was of such character that Elohim took him up to heaven without Enoch dying the death of the flesh (5:24). <u>The Scriptures that Enoch wrote were not allowed into many of the bibles available today, and has been discredited by many as being false.</u> The fact of the matter is, The Book of Enoch, has scathing information against Hasatan, and who the children of Hasatan are unto this day. The Hebrew family-line goes from Enoch to Lamech, to Methuselah, to Noah. I know this is not completely clear to you, we are getting closer to overstanding fully what Chapters 4 and 5 of Bereshis are leading up to.

In Bereshis, Chapter 6, is where we find the first 5 chapters of Bereshis coming together. Let us look at "***the daughters of men***", and "***the sons of Elohim*** (6:2)". Follow this! The sons of Elohim bear children by the daughters of men; and many of their offspring became giants (6:4). In the time between the murder of Abel and the birth of Seth, at least 130 years have passed. Chavvah has produced children, who have themselves produced children; male and female. However, there is a problem: the curse of Hasatan (3:14) and the curse of Cain (4:11) are in full effect. Cain the child of Hasatan, has mated with one or more of the women. Chapter 4 gives us the family-line of Cain (4:16-24). Then when we get to Chapter 5, we come to a new beginning of the family-line of Aw-dawn. The first child of Aw-dawn was murdered by Cain, now in Seth is a renewal or purity established in the seed of Aw-dawn (4:25). Chapter 5 gives us the pure family-line and genealogy of Aw-dawn to Seth, all the way to Noah, Shem, Yepheth, and Ham. It is with Noah's three sons another creation story will emerge. Hear this well: Because Hasatan retained all of the knowledge he had in Shamayim, he knew that The Most High was planning to destroy the family-line of Cain with the great flood. Hear this well: The evil corruption that plagued the earth came from Hasatan's child in the production of Cain. The children of Elohim became infected by the same spirit that produced Cain. That evil spirit contaminated everything causing the women who were impregnated by the fallen malachs, some of their offspring became giants (6:4). Moreover, the destruction to come in the flood was multi-faceted: The seed of Hasatan and the fallen malachs were having sexual intercourse with all of the other creatures: fowl, fish, and animals (6:12). Make no mistake about it, verse 6:12 is the story of why the flood would be brought upon the earth. The word "**_corrupted_**" has many derogatory meanings, of which are *social engineering* (Cambridge English Dictionary); *sexual indulgence* (Merriam-Webster); immorality, against nature, and much more.

Before going forward in the creations stories, allow me to present a medical fact that most people have never been taught: There is a medical term for a woman impregnated by two different men at the same time: *Hetero-paternal super-fecundation.* Chavvah was made pregnant by Hasatan, and Aw-dawn at the same time. When she gave birth to Cain and Able, Cain was the product of Hasatan, not Aw-dawn. Cain was born a corrupt seed, and was then cursed not because he was the seed of Hasatan but rather because he killed Able (4:11).

In returning to the creations stories, Hasatan came up with his own plan on how to come back after the flood. Hasatan and his followers went into the spirit realm, and in the spirit, connected their spirits to the spirit of Ham. This information is only partially available in the KJ bible. After the flood those evil spirits would emerge from Ham to begin their destructive ways again. For now we will leave this specific topic, and continue to follow the Scriptures in the order written.

The reason Noah was chosen as the progenitor to begin humanity again is not because he was perfect; but rather, because his blood was not contaminated by the evil spirits of the fallen angels (the Annunaki). Here is the important information about what was going on in the world. The fallen angels had corrupted almost everything on the earth: they were lewd creatures with a sexual appetite for anything with blood in its veins (6:12). The result of the fallen angels having sex with all types of creatures resulted in the most hideous hybrid offspring imaginable. Let no one convince you these stories are *mythological,* which means the stories are not true: the dinosaurs and the giants were real. The biggest dinosaurs died in a previous creation; but creatures such as, *Titan* and *Poseidon,* are of the giants spoken of in Bereshis 6:4. Those giants were the result of contamination, the fallen ones mating with the other creatures Elohim had made. Therefore, Elohim decided to destroy all of the life except the animals Noah was to gather and put on the ship;

and Noah's wife, his sons, and his sons wives. I have to say this also: Stop listening to stories from sources telling you that Noah collected all of the animals to load onto the Ark two by two. That is simply not the truth. The animals were sent to Noah (7:15), and the clean animals were matched in pairs of seven (7) each (7:2). Before the flood waters rose, the animals gathered and came onto the ship: seven couples each of the clean animals; and of the dirty animals one couple each (7:2-3). It is taught in the churches that all life was destroyed except Noah and his family, and the animals on the ship. That is not of Scripture; clearly you can see in the Scriptures that is false teaching, the creatures of the deep were not destroyed (7:22-23).

After the day of the great flood, time reset and the date was the year 601 B.C.; day 1; month 1; that date coinciding with the waters drying up and the age of Noah; and Noah and all on the ship could leave the ship and begin to rebuild everything (8:13). In this beginning creation, as is in previous creations, the green plants are already fully grown trees, grasses, fruits, and vegetables. This is important for all of the creatures to have food to eat. Which also means that, even carnivorous animals initially ate plants also; otherwise, the carnivorous beasts would have surely eaten many of the other animals, potentially wiping out the creatures that had been preserved on the Ark.

In the beginning creation under Noah, Elohim tells Noah and his family to "***REPLENISH***" (9:1) the Eretz. Elohim also gives them further Commands not to eat any bloody meat, and that HE has given them "***Every moving thing that liveth shall be meat for you;*** (9:3)"; and that every creature on eretz is under the dominion of man (9:2); Elohim also tells them not to kill (9:6). In the creation story of the sons of Elohim mating with the women (6:2), and that creation ending, there is still the spirits of the fallen angels (Annunaki) to deal with; they are ready to emerge from their hiding place. Many years have passed since the water receded into its place. The families of men and animals have multiplied; Ham, has a particular son by the name of Canaan. Noah was not perfect as in sinless, Noah was uncontaminated by evil spirits. One night Noah lay in a drunken stupor, so much so, he was in a coma. Having lost all control of consciousness, the evil spirits of Ham were free to do whatsoever they wanted to Noah. Noah was out cold, seriously unaware of anything, as he lay in the tent stalk naked (9:22), Ham entered his father's tent and "***saw***" that his dad was naked. Ham left the tent and told his brothers Shem and Yepheth that he saw his dad naked in the tent. Shem and Yepheth then took a cover and put it on Noah to cover him up. As likely, as is the case most nights with men, Noah had an erection. So Shem and Yepheth not wanting to see Noah in that state went in backward so they would not see their dad's erect penis. In the morning when Noah awoke he "***knew***" what Ham had "***done***" (9:24); and Noah placed a curse on Canaan, Ham's son, Noah's grandson (9:25). There are two points here: First, there is no way someone in a comatose state could ever kno*(e)*w someone saw them asleep. How does one see when asleep that someone saw them asleep? That is an oxymoron! And as preposterous as the comatose person seeing who saw them asleep while in a drunken coma is, to know who saw him asleep is even more preposterous. Second, the language in v.9:22 does not match the language of v.9:24. The reason Noah knew something happened to him is, there was physical evidence: there was either pain Noah was experiencing or there was body fluid of some sort from another person on Noah's body that Noah "***knew***" what happened to him. The part of the entire ordeal that is not clear is this: Was it Ham or Canaan that committed the offense of raping Noah? In view of the flow of the verses, it is more reasonable to believe it was Canaan, who raped Noah, as the curse was put on Canaan. However, the *Cabala/ Talmud* states emphatically that it was Ham, who "*sodomized*" Noah.

## "THE CABALA/TALMUD

*Ham is told by his outraged father that: "Because you have **abused** me (**sodomized**/buggered me) in the darkness of the night, your children shall be born black and ugly... because you have twisted your head to cause me embarrassment, they shall have kinky hair and red eyes...because your lips 'mocked' at my exposure, theirs shall swell... and because you neglected my nakedness, they shall go naked with their shamefully elongated male members exposed to all to see..."*

Midrash Rabbah 1:292-293

In order to draw a clear picture of biblical history, one must read from all of the books containing information on a particular topic. Clearly in only reading from the AKJ bible, it is difficult for those without discernment to comprehend the complexity of the story. The Cabala/Talmud indeed fills in what is cloaked in the King James. Listen-up: homosexual activity is as old as humanity. As taught in seminary schools across continents, **_Laws_** are enacted when something in the community becomes so widespread that rules are made to control that particular circumstance; thus came the *Law* for man not to have sex with man, as he does with a woman (VaYikra/Lev. 18:22).

In the beginning, the order to multiply is in full account: Ham has fathered Canaan, and Canaan fathered *Sidon*, a giant. All of the family-lines of the giants after the flood came from cursed Ham and his son Canaan (10:15-18). In *mythology*, Sidon is presented as a fictional character, and not a real person. The truth of Scripture is: Sidon was real, as were the giants; mythology would have you to believe the stories of Sidon and the giants are fiction. The record of the Scriptures tells us the giants did exist. Furthermore, excavated bones of giant humanoids and dinosaurs bare out this fact. There is another element of Canaan to come in bringing together parts of stories scattered in the Scriptures. Watch this! Line upon line, and precept upon precept.

In the beginning Yepheth fathered the *Goyim* (Nations) of the Gentiles (10:5). This too will be a precept moment.

Bereshis 10:1-10 (AKJV):

'Now these are the generations of the sons of **_Noah, Shem, Ham, and Yepheth_**: and unto them were sons born after the flood. 2 The sons of Yepheth; Gomer, and Magog, and Madai, and Yavan, and Tubal, and Meshech, and Tiras. 3 And the sons of Gomer; **_Ashkenaz,_** and Riphath, and Togarmah. 4 And the sons of Yavan; Elishah, and Tarshish, Kittim, and Dodanim. 5 By these were the isles of the **_Gentiles_** divided in their lands; every one after his tongue, after their families, in their nations.

*6 And the sons of **Ham; Cush**, and Mizraim, and Phut, and **Canaan**. 7 And the sons of Cush; Seba, and Havilah, and Sabtah, and Raamah, and Sabtecha: and the sons of Raamah; Sheba, and Dedan. 8 And **Cush begat Nimrod**: he began to be a mighty one in the earth. 9 He was a mighty hunter before the Hashem: wherefore it is said, Even as Nimrod the mighty hunter before the Hashem. 10 And the beginning of his kingdom was **Babel**, and Erech, and Accad, and Calneh, in the land of Shinar.'*

The elemental fact of Scripture that many don't overstand is this: The land of Canaan is the same land that will be become the *Promised Land*. This is very important information because from Noah, Shem, Yepheth, and Ham will come all of the people living today. From these four men will come the four races of the earth unto this day. The Negroid, Hamites, Mongoloids, and Caucasoids are the only races of people, but there are many branches on that tree. The land of Canaan is where the Hebrews, who are the Negroes will eventually inhabit but their plight and travel will be arduous. The human race is basically made up of four groups, and even in mixing races, and producing offspring, the four race factor does not change: the offspring are the race of the father, period. There are however, many ethnicities and cultures; in example, a Chinese, and a Japanese are the same people, who over the centuries developed their own identities, but both are Mongoloids. Those groups derive from the customs of their family, and the region of the world they live in. There is something else very important in the above verses that will be discussed in the line and precept model as we continue to pull the Scriptures together, and that is the name **Ashkenaz**. I would be remiss in proceeding from this point without making a specific point about Ham, because rather ignorantly, many people believe the Negro and the Hamite are the same people. The following comes from an authoritative source:

> "**Ham** (ham, persons, hot). 1. The youngest son of Noah, born probably about 96 years before the Flood; and one of eight persons to live through the Flood. He became the *progenitor of the **dark***

> *races; **not the Negroes**, but the <u>Egyptians, Etiopians, Libyans</u>*
> *<u>and Canaanites (Gen. 10:6-20).</u> His indecency, when his father*
> *lay drunken brought a curse upon Canaan (Gen.9:25)"*

Zondervan Bible Dictionary

In reading Scripture, one must incorporate science along with history, and other credentialed literary works to achieve greater overstanding of Scripture. The picture laid-out in the story of Noah is much greater than most people realize. Here is the association of Shem, the Hebrews, and the Negroes. In the beginning Shem fathered all the family-line of *Eber* (Ber./Gen. 10:21). After many generations this family-line begins to take on more of what Elohim created man to do; to serve and worship HIM only. This family-line brings us to Abram (11:27), who will become the *Patriarch Abraham*, the first to be called Hebrew. Abram was told by TMH Elohim to separate his family from the rest of the family (12:1) to establish his own *Goyim* (Nation) (12:2). In <u>obedience</u> to Abba, Abram will be blessed and all who follow his lead will be blessed; but those who oppose Abram will be doomed (12:3).

Note: Shem became the Hebrews. The family-line of Shem, to Aram, to Arphaxad, to <u>Eber</u> (synonym: *Iberia*). The name Eber is the <u>etymological</u> name from which came the name Hebrew (etymonline. com). This too is a line upon line, and precept upon precept moment when we get into the *Book of Devarim/Deuteronomy*.

During the early life of Abram, there was famine in the land, and Abram took his family into *Mitzrayim* (Egypt) to avoid the famine (12:10). Abram knew the reputation of the Egyptians, and how a beautiful woman could be unwillingly taken for a *nashim* (wife) for the Pharaoh. Even a married woman could be taken, and Pharaoh having the husband executed to gain access to the *nashim* (wife). Therefore, Abram told his beautiful nashim to say: She is Abram's sister (12:13). As Abram suspected, Pharaoh tried to take Sarai for his own nashim, and Pharaoh gave Abram many gifts for Sarai (12:16). However, Elohim was not going to allow that to happen, and Elohim brought a plague on the house of Pharaoh as a warning to Pharaoh, not to take another man's nashim into his bed. Pharaoh cried foul to Abram, and ordered Abram, Abram's family and all of Abram's riches out of Mitzrayim (12:20). Abram was very rich with many herds of animals; and also with Abram was his nephew *Lot*, who also had gained much wealth in Mitzrayim (13:2;7). After being expelled from Mitzrayim, Abram and Lot continued to live together, and the substance of their wealth grew too large for the land. They decided to go separate ways: Lot went to the west toward Yarden, near to Sodom, and Abram went toward Canaan. Lot had no idea what was going on in Sodom: there was all manner of evil going on there (13:13). After Abram settled in *Canaan* (Yisra'el), Elohim spoke to Abram telling him: All the land you see, I (Elohim) will give to you and your children **forever** (13:14-16). Abba is not mocked: HE gave HIS Word to Abram, and HIS Word does not come back void. However, there is a problem with the land of Canaan that will have to be cleaned-up before the land would be called Yisra'el. There is something in the above verses that must be pointed out: Canaan, the man is cursed by Noah; Canaan is a land; Canaan is the same land as Yisra'el; and yet, Canaan/Yisra'el is the *Promised Land*. Ironic for sure.

Elohim created Aw-dawn to be a counter to the Pre-Aw-dawnic, homo erectus the Annunaki contaminated with *deoxyribonucleic acid* (DNA) manipulation; and that creation ended in Bereshis, Chapter 1. Elohim then made Aw-dawn in Bereshis, Chapter 2, for a, *in the beginning act*, as a pure human line of existence; and later making the woman to be Aw-dawn's companion, as all of the other creations were Commanded to reproduce. However, the time had not come for Aw-dawn and Chavvah to have sex; therefore, Elohim did not give them the knowledge of many things that were yet to come. Howbeit, that evil fallen angel, who is very powerful and retained all of the knowledge he had in *Shamayim* (Heaven), caused the contamination of both the homo erectus animals, and eventually Aw-dawn and Chavvah. The contamination of the homo erectus by the Annunaki led to the end of that creation.

Non one knows how many times creation has restarted ; therefore, if the creations are numbered, it is for better overstanding that the unnamed characters in Bereshis, Chapter 1, are different from the named characters in Bereshis, Chapter 2. The most important point in this is: The first people were not completely human, they were ape-like creatures, who served their gods, the Annunaki. Those creatures, and all of the creatures on the earth were used by the Annunaki for manual labor and sexual pleasure. The Annunaki possess great sexual prowess, and the offspring they produced also became gods to the Pre-Aw-dawnic homo erectus: *Enki, Heru, Osiris, Poseidon, Zeus, Hades,* and all of the giants. Sex is the one element of life that can actually transfer the *ruach* (spirit) of one person into another person's ruach. With that said: Aw-dawn was going to be the vessel by which the *Ruach hakodesh* (Sacred Spirit) of the Most High Elohim would eventually come down to *eretz* (earth) by the Ruach hakodesh, in the human form of *Ha Mashiach* (The Messenger). But before that plan would be put into action, there had to be a cleansing process by which the contamination of the Annunaki had to be removed for a pure line of Elohim's people to emerge. Abba sent HIS people into the land of the enemy, *Mitzrayim* (Egypt), to test them or to prove them worthy of serving HIM <u>only</u> (12:10). Abram passed the test with flying colors, thereby receiving the *brocha* (blessing) of The Most High Elohim.

After Abram was expelled from Mitzrayim, Elohim made a *Promise* to Abram that Abram's family-line would have the land west of Mitzrayim to the great river Euphrates (15:18). The life of Abram would be a test that would take several generations for Abba to be satisfied that the Annunaki were not in that bloodline. Abram was put to the paces by Sarai, Hagar the Egyptian, and Ishmael, Abram's first son, the son of the Egyptian woman Hagar (16:10-12). The reason Abba gave Abram an Egyptian wife, producing Abram's first child was another test to prove Abram worthy, and of the mind-set to serve and worship The Most High Only. There is no greater test than: Will Abram remain with TMH, or come under the influence of the religious practices of an Egyptian wife, and half Egyptian son? (There is truly no half race person, the race of the child is determined by the race of the father). Also the role of Ishmael is very important to comprehend: Ishmael will be an antagonist to the world, and the world an antagonist to Ishmael (16:12). Let me be expressly clear in this: Abram has not been spiritually transformed into a new man at the time he fathered Ishmael; therefore, Abram is not yet what he will become. Here is the point: When Abram received his *Commission,* he became *Abraham* (Ber./Gen. 17:5). Therefore, Ishmael being born before Abram was transformed with the *Promise* of Elohim, Ishmael is not Hebrew. The family-line of Ishmael are the Arabs of today. It is because of Ishmael being fathered by Abram that many *Arab States* today also claim Abraham as their father; but even so, they do not claim the status of being Hebrew. The Arab people overstand this information better than most Westerners; they overstand that Abram was an idolater until his transformation, as was his father *Terah.* This too will be a line upon line, and precept upon precept event as we continue in this study.

In the Covenant between Elohim and Abram, Abram had to fulfill one physical act to begin his legacy in becoming the *Patriarch* of a *New People* to come: Abram had to be circumcised, and all of the males of the camp (Ber./Gen. 17:all). After all of the men had been circumcised, three *Malachs* (Angels) visited Abram, and Abram immediately knew they were Malachs in a physical body. Abram offered them food, and water to cleanse themselves. The three Malachs had come to visit Abram for several reasons: To deliver the news that Abram and Sarai in their old age will have a child. From Canaan the Malachs would travel on to Sodom and Gomorrah to see what was going on in the land. Abram received a message from Elohim that Sodom and Gomorrah were going to be destroyed. Abram pleaded with Abba to spare the cities for the sake of any righteous people living there. Abram had gained the respect of Abba by complying with everything Abba had asked him to do. In being compliant to Elohim, that gave Abram, whose name is now Abraham (Ber./Gen.17:5), permission to speak directly to Elohim. Howbeit, Abraham's request could not be fulfilled because there were not ten righteous found in the two cities (18:32). The two Malachs then proceeded on to Sodom and Gomorrah where they were met by Lot. Lot took the Malachs into his home, offering them the same hospitality Abram previously showed. Then the men of the city pressed upon Lot to send the Malachs out so they could have sex with them (19:5). Hear me well in this: This story is more about rape than male on male sex.

Lot offered the men of the city his daughters rather than them wanting to rape the Malachs (19:8). The men refused to leave the Malachs along, causing the destruction to come upon Sodom and Gomorrah. Here is a line upon line, and precept upon precept moment of the Scriptures: Bereshis/Gen. 9:24, tells us about the rape of Noah; now we have the offspring of the Annunaki wanting to get down with the Malachs sent from Elohim. Here is what has to be overstood: As the Annunaki are very sexual, and don't care what they have sex with, fowl, fish, animal, or human, so are their offspring. Look, in keeping it real, homosexuality and bestiality has been ongoing for eons. What these verses also tell us is, the angels can and do take on human form. For those who doubt or don't believe the Annunaki, spiritual Beings, could take flesh and blood wives, and impregnate a female, as Hasatan did to Chavvah, you cannot possibly believe the Ruach Hakodesh entered into Miriam to impregnate her with Ha Mashiach. Moreover, Chavvah was pregnant with twins: Cain by Hasatan, and Abel by Aw-dawn. When a woman is pregnant with twins by two different men it is called: *hetero-paternal super-fecundation*. These are your line upon line, and precept upon precept moments of Scriptural History. What also has to be considered about sex is this: Lot offered up his own daughters to the men. So again the story-line is not about sex; otherwise, Lot was contributing to what would be considered immorality. The men wanted to have sex with unwilling participants, which is rape.

The Patriarch of the Hebrew family, Abraham, has another *epithet* (title) that is revealed in Ber./Gen. 20:7: Abraham is also a *Prophet*. There are many today in a state of self-proclamation of being a prophet; a <u>True Prophet</u> is Commissioned by The Most High Elohim, and is a *Seer*; someone who can see what is yet to come to fruition. When Abram and his family went into Mitzrayim to escape the famine, Abram told Sarai to say, she is his sister (12:9-13). Abram and Sarai are now in *Gerar,* which is east of Canaan; a land filled with the worshipers of demigods, and not the Elohim of Abraham. In Gerar, Abraham tells Sarah the same thing, for the same reason he stated to her about Mitzrayim: Tell them you are my sister (20:12). King Abimelech took Sarah into his palace to be his *nashim* (wife); however, the king never had the opportunity to take his pleasure with Sarah because The Almighty Elohim blocked him from touching her (20:6). Elohim appeared to Abimelech in a dream and revealed to him the true marital status of Sarah, and warned him to release her or face death (20:7). Abimelech was deeply disturbed by the dream and summoned Abraham, asking him: What have you done to me (20:9)? Elohim had blocked or closed the wombs of all the women in Abimelech's Kingdom (20:18). Abimelech and his people worshiped their gods, but yet, Abimelech knew his gods were no match for the Almighty Elohim, and Abimelech feared Elohim (20:9;11).

After Abimelech released Abraham and Sarah, Elohim restored Abimelech's people: the wombs of the women opened, as did the womb of Sarah, and she conceived in her old age. Abraham is going into another phase of life that will show he is true to The Most High Elohim, and that whatsoever Elohim commands him to do, that will he do. Sarah is now with child, and does not want Hagar and Ishmael around anymore (21:9-10). Sarah told Abraham to send Hagar and Ishmael away, which thing bothered Abraham tremendously. Elohim spoke to Abraham and instructed him to do as Sarah requested of him, but not to worry, because Elohim will take care of them in the wilderness (Ber./Gen.21:20). Ishmael, the son of Abraham will become a multitude of people. Line upon line and precept upon precept; we will see who Ishmael becomes as a people.

Abraham's only son, Ishmael, has been sent away, with the promise of Elohim that Ishmael will be protected from harm, and will be multiplied *Goyim* (Nations). Sarah is now pregnant and will bring forth a second son for Abraham; this son will be full-blood Hebrew. This is very important because the *Ha Mashiach* (The Messenger) will come from this bloodline. In times past, Abraham has been obedient to Elohim, and offered sacrifice to Elohim. Now Abraham is about to undergo the greatest act of obedience of his life to Elohim: Abraham must offer up his son for a burnt sacrifice (Ber./Gen. 22:1-3). Obedient Abraham follows the instructions of Elohim, and takes his travel into the mountains where the sacrifice is to take place. As Abraham had made all of the preparations for the sacrifice, taking the knife in hand to slay *Yitzhaq* (Isaac: 22:9-10), the *Malach* (Angel) of Elohim called out to Abraham from *Shamayim* (Heaven), telling him: Do no harm to the child (22:11-12). Abraham had passed the test; there are two points here: First of all, those teaching Elohim does not tempt people are surely rebuffed by verse 22:1; and secondly, obedience to Elohim has to be of the highest importance in our lives; in obedience is life. With that said, obedience to Elohim means never allowing any demigod worship or idolatry into your life; it does not mean you are sinless, none of us are sinless.

The testing of the obedience of Abraham in this story is crucial: it reveals to us what Elohim has in mind down the road, a people separated from all other people to serve and worship HIM only. So far in our reading, we have seen there is more than one creation; translating to: STOP PUTTING ELOHIM IN A BOX; ELOHIM CAN DO WHATSOEVER HE CHOOSES TO DO WHEN HE CHOOSES TO DO IT. This story of Abraham is the foretelling of Ha Mashiach to come, and what Elohim will allow to happen to HIS Son, in the flesh. Don't listen to those who will tell you this story is pure *allegory* (fiction); and even more importantly, let no one tell you that Elohim cannot create, destroy, begin again, make new plans, or change plans mid-stream. I am simply telling you, the most Powerful Force in all of Eternality can do whatsoever HE chooses, whensoever HE chooses: Period.

The obedience of Abraham to Elohim resulted in Elohim making a *brocha* (blessing) over Abraham: the children of Abraham will become a multitude of people. Moreover, all of the *Goyim* (Nations) of the *eretz* (earth) who will follow the Hebrews will be blessed in the children of Abraham. As blessings come from obedience; curses come from disobedience; this too will become a line upon line, and precept upon precept moment of the Scriptures.

Sarah has died and has been buried. Now in old age, Abraham is nearing to death. Elohim has promised Abraham that the land of Canaan (Same land called Yisra'el today) shall be the land that Abraham's posterity will possess (Ber./Gen. 24:7). However, at this time, Abraham, though he is very wealthy, he has not become a nation. Abraham realizing he is living in the land of heathens, summons his servant, and makes the servant vow, that the servant will go to Abraham's brother *Nahor,* to take a wife for his son *Yitzhaq* (Isaac), born to him by Sarah. It is absolutely imperative that Yitzhaq's wife is from the pure bloodline of Aw-dawn. Rebekah is Abraham's niece, who became the wife of Yitzhaq. Before moving forward in the Bereshis/ Gen., it is important to insert some genealogy at this point because the Scriptures are scattered, making them hard to follow and difficult to overstand. This will be a brief genealogy for specificity of the bloodline of *Shem,* and will not include all of the names written in the text. The brothers: Abraham; Haran; and Nahor (11:27; 22:20): of Haran came Lot: of Nahor came Bethuel, the father of Rebekah (22:23): of Abraham came Yitzhaq (Isaac; 25:22). Yitzhaq and Rebekah are cousins of the bloodline of *Shem.*

The genealogy insertion was very necessary because the Scriptures are scattered, and require much time to decipher. With that said, let us look at what happened to Rebekah and her being pregnant with Ya'aqov and Esau. Abraham knew his time on *HaAretz* (The Earth) was coming to a close; to assure that *Yitzhaq* (Isaac) maintained the purity of the bloodline, Abraham made sure that Yitzhaq married a Hebrew woman. The story-line becomes somewhat blurred because Rebekah and Yitzhaq are both full-blood Hebrew, but even so, something very strange happens in Rebekah's womb: Ya'aqov and Esau, who are twins, are two different *Goyim* (Nations; Ber./Gen. 25:23): One is Hebrew, and the other is Syrian (25:23). That brings us to a struggle that will continue between the brothers for all generations to come. Here is what must be overstood in these verses: ABRAHAM, OBEDIENT ABRAHAM ONLY, IS OF THE PROMISE OF ELOHIM, not his brothers Haran, and Nahor. Abraham's brothers become whole other people and *Goyim* (Nations).

In the womb, Ya'aqov and Esau begin their struggle (Ber./Gen. 25:23). Esau should have been the head of the Hebrews, because he was the first born child (25:25). However, Elohim never intended for Esau to lead the Hebrew people (25:23). Esau brought offense upon himself, and offended Elohim by selling his birthright to Ya'aqov (25:31). At that time Yitzhaq and his family lived in the land of the *Philistines* (26:1);

and Elohim spoke to Yitzhaq, reminding him of the Promise HE made to Abraham because Abraham was obedient to all that Elohim asked of Abraham (26:4-5). Now Esau has become a man and is ready to marry; Esau chooses *nashim* (wives) from the Gentiles, which was not approved of by his parents (26:34-35).

There is important information about the Philistines that must be inserted here. DNA plays a large part in determining who a group was in antiquity. Bones of some Philistine remains were discovered in the *Mediterranean Region,* as were some of the pottery used by the Philistines. DNA showed the Philistines to be from the: *"Land of Caphtor" (modern-day Crete) before taking control of the coastal region of what is now southern Israel and the Gaza Strip".* Additionally, the pottery had writing on it that closely matched that of ancient *Greece.* It was the Greeks, who first translated the Hebrew Scrolls. This Scientific and Historical data, comports to what is written in the Scriptures, the Philistines are adversary to the Hebrews because the Philistines are of the bloodline of Cain and Esau, who both are tainted with the evil spirit of the fallen malachs. Yeshua 13:3 and Yudges 3:3, tell us precisely who the Philistines are: They are part of the family-line of the giants; such as, Goliath (1 Sam. 17:4). More details of this can be found online at: *nationalgeographic.com/culture/2019/07/ancient-dna-reveal-philistine-origins/#close.*

Though Esau had screwed-up several times, he was very much loved by Yitzhaq. The story of *brocha* (blessing) Esau and Ya'aqov is quite lengthy, the brief of the story is this: Yitzhaq was an old man, and wanted to brocha his sons before his death. He summoned Esau, his first born child to brocha him above any brocha he would place on Ya'aqov because of tradition, the older child gets the greater brocha. However, Rebekah loved Ya'aqov more than Esau, and she wanted Ya'aqov to get the greater brocha. Rebekah then schemed up a plan on how to steal the brocha from Esau, which her scheme worked (Ber./Gen. 27:6-7; 24-30). Ya'aqov received the brocha, and when Esau realized what had transpired, Esau went to his dad requesting a brocha for his life. Esau is sad and angry that Ya'aqov has gotten the better of him twice (27:34-36). Yitzhaq had already given the best brocha to Ya'aqov, and does not have much left to brocha to Esau. Howbeit, what he did bless Esau with, would become a curse to Esau, and physical suffrage for Ya'aqov. The brocha Yitzhaq placed upon Esau was for Esau to eventually rise up stronger and more powerful than Ya'aqov (27:40). Esau would become a sword yielding, dominating force of destruction, who would pierce Ya'aqov through repeatedly (27:40-41). What Yitzhaq did in brocha Esau with those words, went against what Elohim had already spoken in verse 25:23; the elder child is to serve the younger child. Esau and Ya'aqov have been enemies before coming forth from their mother's womb (25:22).

Esau is the <u>enemy</u> of The Most High Elohim and of the Hebrews. Esau is the antagonist to the world, and especially so toward anyone who stands with The Most High Elohim. Here is the thing: Yitzhaq has now become an enemy, per se, of Esau because Yitzhaq gave the greater brocha to Ya'aqov, and in an act of rebellion or defiance, Esau to the displeasure of Yitzhaq took wives of the Gentile Nation of Ishmael (28:8-9).

Some time after Ya'aqov received the brocha from Yitzhaq, he was in travel to the city of Haran. Ya'aqov decided he had traveled far enough for the day, and that he would camp where he was for the night. As Ya'aqov lay asleep something mysterious began to happen: he was dreaming a dream, where he saw the *Malachs* (Angels) of Elohim using a figurative ladder to come and go from *Shamayim* (Heaven) to *HaAretz* (the Earth) (Ber./Gen. 28:12). This is a line upon line, and precept upon precept moment: Where in the creation stories or anywhere in the Scriptures, do you find the creation of the *Malach* (angels)? The answer: No where in the Scriptures will you find that; but suddenly in Bereshis, Chapter 3, verse 1, is the appearance of the "**serpent**"; the fallen angel, Hasatan. Then in Bereshis 6:2 '**The sons of Elohim**' appear, indicating there are many Malachs. The first mention of or use of the word "**angel**" is found in Bereshis 16:7. What Ya'aqov is experiencing in this dream is revelation knowledge of the good Malachs opening the pathway from Shamayim to HaAretz (The Earth) for Ya'aqov to receive a direct communication from The Most High Elohim. The message being: By Abraham, and by Yitzhaq, came the Covenants that

I (Elohim) have Chosen this family-line as MY people; and now, by you Ya'aqov, will come the fulfillment of the Covenants. In Ya'aqov will come the Children that will spread all over the world, and their duty is to bring ME (Elohim), to every person of HaAretz (28:12-15). Let me be perfectly clear here: this does not include anyone with the spirit of Esau. *Esau* (Edom: 25:30) is the spirit of antagonism, brutality, terror, persecution, and hate; Esau/Edom is not a race of people; Esau is the spirit of evil. After Ya'aqov received the information in the dream, the *Promise,* Ya'aqov did that which is right before Elohim: he gave honor to Elohim by building an altar and anointing the altar with oil (28:18). Ya'aqov believed The Most High, and vowed a vow to give back the tenth of all that Elohim gives to him (28:22). Now don't get the wrong takeaway that some crooked ministers will put on this: THIS IS NOT COMMANDED BY ELOHIM, it is a freewill gift, a vow between Ya'aqov and Elohim. Line and precept, this is a great place to insert one of the most misused verses in all of Scripture:

Malachi 3:8 (AKJV):

'Will a man rob Elohim? Yet you have robbed ME. But you say, Wherein have we robbed YOU? **In tithes and offerings**.'

Given the fact that the tithe has always been foodstuffs, let us take up a collection of fruits, vegetables, oil, and wine, and bring it to the **Ekklesia** (Church), as Commanded by TMH Elohim. The point I'm trying to convey is: the tithe was a welfare system set-up by TMH to assure everyone in the village was taken care of; not a means to gather riches for the *Kohen* (Priests). In reading Malachi, Chapter 2, you will see why the question of: "*Will a man rob Elohim?*" was asked to begin with, and why TMH said to the *Kohen* (Priests), HE will "*spread dung upon your faces*" (Mal. 2:3). The Kohen robbed Elohim by taking the best of the herds, fruits, and vegetables for themselves, rather than using the best of the best in offering or sacrifice to Elohim. That is how they robbed Elohim. What the saying, "*spread dung upon your faces*" tells us is: Elohim telling the Kohen: You and the despicable acts you have committed against ME, are fit for nothing but to be cast-out, you are polluted, and need to be buried under the dirt. Now we will return to our story of Ya'aqov: The plight and travel of the Hebrews continues.

After resting and sleeping, Ya'aqov made his way to the city of Haran. Haran is named after Abraham's brother, Haran. Cities were normally named after the leader of the tribe. Ya'aqov located his family in Haran, and his mission there was to find a wife to begin the Promise Elohim had made in Ber./Gen. 28:13-14, that Ya'aqov's children will spread upon all the earth. Ya'aqov does get his *nashim* (wives) from his cousin Laban. Those unions will lead to genealogies, which can be very difficult to follow. Therefore, the focus here is the pure Hebrew genealogies only: Leah = Reuben (29:32), Simeon (v. 33), Levi (v. 34), Yehuwdah (v. 35), Issachar (30:16-18), Zebulun (30:20), and a daughter whose name is Dinah (30:21). Rachel = Yosef (30:24), and Benoni (35:17-18). That means eight (8) of Ya'aqov's children are from his cousins: Leah and Rachel. In order for Ya'aqov to marry the cousins, he had to work for Laban for many years. Ya'aqov decided it was time for him to take his family away from Haran (30:30), and he spoke to Laban about leaving. The two of them reached an agreement for the division of property, that is the animals. Ya'aqov used the *apothecary* (natural medicine) to cause his cattle to multiply more than the cattle of Laban (30:37-39). After some time had passed, Ya'aqov decided the time to leave was at hand because Laban was not dealing fairly with him (31:7-8). Now this entire chapter is about to take on an entirely different revelation. If you recall the *Promise* was made to Abraham because Abraham was obedient to all Elohim asked of Abraham (26:4-5). Let's put this line upon line, precept together:

Abraham was the First to be called Hebrew (Bereshis/Gen. 14:13). Nahor, Abraham's brother became the *Syrians* (29:5); the Syrians and all of the people of the Middle World are Mongoloid. Now we see in verse 31:20 that Laban is also Syrian. Laban and Rebekah are siblings (25:20). Here is what is missing in how Abraham is Hebrew, and his brother a Syrian: It all has to do with the *Promise* of the *Covenants* with Abraham, Yitzhaq, and Ya'aqov; they three, each received a different Promise. Abraham's family branching off into other *Goyim* (Nations) is futuristic and will take many years to complete. Additionally, there will be many events to come that will play a part in the development of new nations; those events include geographical areas people will live in, and the climate of those regions of the planet.

The different nations to come from the Promises given to Abraham, Yitzhaq, Ya'aqov, Ishmael, and others will eventually lead to problems and division in the *Shevets* (Tribes) of Yisra'el. In explanation of this, we have to visit 1 Kings. Afterward, we will return to Ya'aqov breaking away from Laban.

Melachim Alef/1 Kings 12:21 (OJB):

> 'And when Rechav'am was come to **Yerushalayim**, he assembled all the <u>Bais (House) Yehuwdah</u>, with the <u>Shevet Benoni</u>, an hundred and fourscore thousand **bachur oseh milchamah** (chosen men of war), to fight against the Bais (House) Yisra'el, to regain the kingdom for Rechav'am **Ben** (Son of) Shelomoh.'

Did you catch what is hidden in plain sight in the above verse? You see, the *"Bais Yehuwdah"*, and the *"Bais Yisra'el"*, are clearly shown in the verse to be separate *Goyim*. This is very important to grasp because, as time moves forward, Yisra'el will split into the *Northern* and *Southern Kingdoms*. Yehuwdah and Benoni the Southern Kingdom, and Ephraim, the other 10 Shevets, the Northern Kingdom. The Hebrew Yisra'elites are comprised of Yehuwdah, Ephraim, and Levi'im, **kol** (all) of which are separate Goyim, with separate roles to administer in <u>spirituality</u>, and yet, they are all one family. This point has to be overstood: There can be no freedom, royal status, or leadership for Yisra'el until **kol** (all) of Yisra'el comes back together as a family with Yehuwdah in its Elohim appointed position as the head of the family (Ber./Gen. 49:8-12), and Yisra'el being obedient to TMH Elohim. Overstand this: There can only be one leader over a household, and Yehuwdah if forever the head of Yisra'el. We will see why this is so important because if the family is divided, it leads to fractures in the family with serious consequences such as war.

Now we will return to the story of Ya'aqov. Ya'aqov did break away from Laban without letting Laban know he was leaving (31:20). Ya'aqov was in route to Padanaram in Canaan, back home to Yitzhaq, his father (31:18). In Ya'aqov having his family to pack-up their belongings to begin their travel, Rachel took some items that belonged to her dad Laban (31:19). Laban after realizing his idols were gone (31:30) set-out to catch-up to Ya'aqov to retrieve the items, and to confront Ya'aqov for leaving without telling him. However, Elohim had spoken to Laban telling him that: In confronting Ya'aqov, do not cause any harm to Ya'aqov (31:24). Laban caught-up to Ya'aqov and asked him to return his idol gods (31:30). Ya'aqov was not aware the idols had been taken; and therefore, he said to Laban: Search us, and if you find your idols, let the offender die (31:32). Rachel had taken the idols, but she was clever with her words to avoid discovery: Rachel told her dad that, she was on her period and could not rise-up for the search (31:35). Ya'aqov became angry with Laban when the idols were not found and blasted Laban in verse 31:42 telling him: If it was not for Elohim protecting Ya'aqov that surely Laban would have caused him harm. Elohim was protecting Ya'aqov, as HE did Abraham, and all who serve the True Elohim only. Also Laban feared Yitzhaq, Ya'aqov's dad. After talking the two men reached an agreement and parted ways (31:49).

Ya'aqov continued in his travel toward Canaan, and was met by two *Malachs* (Angels; Ber./Gen. 32:1). Ya'aqov knew that the presence of the Malachs had meaning, though the meaning may not be revealed immediately. What Ya'aqov did is what we all should do: he called upon Elohim, the Elohim of Abraham and Yitzhaq, Ya'aqov's granddad, and dad (32:9). Ya'aqov knew the presence of the Malachs was a message, and he took the following action: As Ya'aqov came closer to Canaan, he sent messengers to Esau, who is the head of Canaan (32:3). When the men returned, they reported to Ya'aqov that, Esau was on his way to meet him with 400 men (32:6). That caused Ya'aqov to fear that Esau, the antagonist, was coming to engage war against him. Ya'aqov had to develop a strategy for the war, he decided to divide the family into two sections, and to put distance between the two sections of the family. If Esau attacked the one group, the other group could escape

(32:7-8). After Ya'aqov prayed a beautiful prayer to Elohim (32:9-12), he continued to strategize how to deal with Esau. Ya'aqov sent presents to Esau (32:13-16), and he also sent his family away from the rest of the groups (32:22-23). Bereshis 32:24 transitions the topic of the chapter from the family as a whole to Ya'aqov only.

Ya'aqov was alone when he was met by the Malach of The Most High Elohim. Ya'aqov and the Malach engaged in a struggle: Stop right there! You have missed some valuable information right there: Bereshis 32:24, is telling you that the spiritual Being, the Malach, is in physical form, encased in a flesh and blood body. You still don't get it! Malachs, whether good or evil, can and do take on physical form; in other words, they are capable of shape-shifting. In wrestling with the Malach of Elohim, Ya'aqov gained advantage over the Malach in the struggle, so the Malach disabled Ya'aqov by causing trauma to Ya'aqov's thigh. Ya'aqov refused to give in to the Malach until the Malach blessed him (32:24-26). Ya'aqov and the Malach had a conversation, and in that conversation, the Malach tells Ya'aqov, his name will NO LONGER BE YA'AQOV BUT **YISRA'EL** (32:26-29).

In Bereshis 32:30, the word **_Peniel_** is used. This word is very important for the following reason: Because this place is the establishment of Ya'aqov becoming Yisra'el. Because Ya'aqov was victorious in the struggle against the Malach, he named the place the event occurred _Peniel_. As Ya'aqov travels on from Peniel, the trauma to Ya'aqov's thigh caused him to struggle in walking. That trouble in walking is the indication that, Ya'aqov will have a struggle with those of <u>demonic influence in the future but the **_sun_** will be with Ya'aqov</u>. The Word SUN, of the Hebrew word _shemesh_ means: brilliant; battlement; toward the west. Sun is also of the Hebrew word _Beyth Shemesh_, and is _house of._ Furthermore, the word Peniel, of the Hebrew word _penuw'el_ and _penit'el_ means: Face of Elohim. These two words are also related to _paniyn_ and mean: a pearl or ruby. In combination, all of these words represent the Special Status the Hebrew family has with The Most High Elohim. The purpose of this Special People is one: to serve TMH Elohim <u>only</u>, and to stand against Hasatan and his army of demons; that is: the teachers and followers of religion. Furthermore, there is something else hidden in the word *Shemesh*. Did you catch it? *House of; battlement; pearl and ruby*: these are all attributes of the family-line of *Shem*, more specifically, the Shevet of *Yehuwdah* (Ber./Gen. 49:8-12); meaning, this Shevet is the Shevet of special status: this Shevet is the head of the family Yisra'el, the Shevet of Yehuwdah, the Shevet from which Ha Mashiach will eventually be born therefrom; this Shevet is the Hebrews, the Negroes. This too will be a line and precept moment of the Scriptures.

The result in the meanings of all the Hebrew words derived from the word *Peniel* concludes that, Elohim is with the family-line of the Hebrew Yisra'elites, as HIS Chosen Vessels to lead the world in the True Spirituality of The Most High Elohim. The Hebrew Yisra'elites hold great esteem and value (pearl, ruby) to Elohim. Having such status means that <u>all</u> of the other races of the earth will be <u>adversary</u> to the Hebrew Yisra'elites, especially to the ***<u>Shevet</u>*** (Tribe) of Yehuwdah. Moreover, it also means that Yisra'el will be, at times, adversary to Yehuwdah. Thus the struggle in Ya'aqov's walk is the burden the Hebrew Yisra'elites will have; but and yet, the Hebrews will be victorious, as long as the Hebrews continue to honor and worship The One and Only True and Living Elohim.

Now let us look at the word Peniel from the scientific perspective. The *Pineal Gland* in our brain has many functions, and is as follows:

> "***<u>Melanin</u>*** *is important because it's the **<u>most primitive</u> <u>and universal pigment in living organisms</u>**. Melanin is produced in the **<u>pineal gland</u>**. Abundantly found in primitive organisms such as fungi, as well as advanced primates. Furthermore, within each living organism, melanin appears to be located in the major functional sites. For example, in vertebrates, melanin is not only present in the **<u>skin, eyes, ears, central nervous system, it can also be found in the pineal gland, pituitary gland, thyroid gland, thymus gland, adrenal gland, and the barathary gland</u>**. Melanin is abundantly present in the viscera, including the heart, liver, arteries, and the gastrointestinal tract; thus, within each and every living organ which aids the human body melanin appears. Regardless of what color your skin appears to be **<u>all genes in all</u>***

> *creatures on this planet are black because they are coated* *with melanin*. ... *So, what is so important about melanin?* *Melanin controls all mental and physical body activities*. *Melanin is an extremely stable molecule, and highly resistant to* *the digestion by most acids and bases, and is one of the hardest* *molecule to ever be analyzed. If you do not purify your melanin* *molecule, you will* ***not heal your body of diseases***."

sankofa.ch/Melanin.htm

Here is the point: *Peniel* is the same as *Pineal*, with a different spelling. When Ya'aqov got the victory over the Malach, and having been blessed by the Malach, Ya'aqov named the place *Peniel*. The tie-in is this: Ya'aqov, whose name is now Yisra'el, was wounded in wrestling with the Malach; though wounded, and now walking with a limp, Ya'aqov is already healed. His healing comes in the transformation of his mind, thought processes, and his personal contact with Elohim. Though Ya'aqov will walk with a limp for the rest of his life, he is already healed; thus the name *Peniel* is equivalent to healed or new. The *Pineal* gland plays a huge role in our healing; this signifies that Ya'aqov was created to heal the world by bringing the truth of The Most High Elohim to the Gentiles, who follow religion: Kemet; Christianity; Catholicism; Hindi, or any other religion; <u>all</u> religions are <u>evil</u>. The Malach that wounded Ya'aqov, made Ya'aqov whole in that Ya'aqov, who already had the favor of Elohim, is a new man by the name of Yisra'el. From this new man, will come a new people: THE HEBREW YISRA'ELITES. Listen-up: Here is the importance of the ***Sun***; the sun is the best developer or promoter of *Melanin* production in the skin for stimulation of the Pineal gland. Furthermore, it is symbolic of Ha Mashiach being with Yisra'el, to give Yisra'el the victory in the battle against the enemy (Mal. 4:2-3).

When *Ya'aqov* (Yisra'el) was in travel back to his homeland, as he neared Esau, Ya'aqov arranged the *nashim* (wives) and the *banim* (children) in a specific order: the handmaids, and their banim in front; followed by Leah and her banim; with Rachel and her banim in the rear (33:2). This presents as if Ya'aqov does not value the handmaids and their banim equal to Leah; Leah and her banim even less importantly than Rachel and her banim. The reality of the Scripture is this: no harm was going to come to the family because Elohim was with them. The fact of the arrangement is that, if danger was a possibility, Yosef would need to be the most secure of all the banim. This too will become a line upon line, and precept upon precept moment, when we come to the Scriptures showing the important role Yosef plays in the history of Hebrew Scripture. Ya'aqov and Esau had an amicable conversation, and no violence came about when they came together. Ya'aqov took his family to the part of the land named *Succoth*; there Ya'aqov built an altar unto The Most High Elohim, and he named it: El-el-o-he-Yis-ra-el: meaning Elohim, the Elohim of Yisra'el (33:20). Did you catch it? The Elohim of Yisra'el is the Elohim of Yisra'el only, no other people. However, that does not exclude anyone who will renounce their gods, and follow the Commandments given to Yisra'el (Devarim/Deu., 23:2-8).

Also living in the land of Canaan were Gentiles. One day Leah's only daughter Dinah, was out in the community checking out their new homeland. One of the Gentiles by the name of Shechem, saw Dinah and was immediately infatuated with her. Shechem did an awful thing, he raped Dinah (Ber./Gen. 34:2); but because he had developed an immediate liking for Dinah, he wanted to marry her. The discussion of the marriage went on between both dads: Dinah's and Shechem's, and the sons of Ya'aqov. They reached an agreement for the marriage (34:3-12). However, Dinah's brothers were angry that Shechem had raped Dinah, and were not willing to let Shechem get away with defiling Dinah. Simeon and Levi came up with a plan on how to avenge their sister, Dinah. The men of Shechem would all have to be circumcised before marriage would be allowed between the two groups. The men of Shechem all consented and were circumcised. On the third day after the circumcisions, when the men were very sore, Simeon and Levi came into their camp, and finding the men incapacitated killed all of the men (34:25). When Ya'aqov found out what Simeon and Levi did, he was not pleased with them, and neither was Elohim (35:1). This too will become a line and precept matter that will build in the scattering of the tribes segment of our reading.

In overstanding what is contained in the Scriptures, old teaching has to be thrown out in order for clarity to flow into one's mind. I have prefaced this segment because there are things in the Scriptures that go against what we have been led to believe about the Scriptures. Before getting into Bereshis, Chapter 35:2-7: Elohim had spoken to Ya'aqov in verse 35:1, and instructed him on what to do because of the murders committed by Simeon and Levi. In the instructions from Elohim, Ya'aqov is to go into the land of Bethel to build an altar there for Elohim. Here is the part most people don't grasp: the Hebrews had idol gods in their possession, and it was no secret to Ya'aqov. Ya'aqov tells the people to remove the idols and prepare to go through a purging process to honor The Most High Elohim (35:2). You did not catch the depth of the verse? Some of the Hebrews were practicing idolatry, and yet, they believe Elohim is the Supreme Elohim of gods. You still did not catch it: there are other gods, but the Hebrews are to have no other god before Elohim, the Supreme Creator. Elohim is very aware of the other gods, HE created them, as HE created us. Without going into depth at this point, let me say this: the *First Commandment* tells us to have 'no other gods before Elohim (Shemot/Exo. 20:3)'. Let that sink into your brain, and stop allowing uneducated people to feed you what the Scriptures don't say. Read that again! It does not say to have no other god, it says, 'no other gods before Elohim'. Did you catch it? There are other gods, they are the gods of the Gentiles, not the Hebrews. The Hebrews are not to have reverence for any god but Elohim, WHO created the Hebrews to serve and worship HIM only (She./Exo. 23:13; Dev./Deu. 12:30, 6:14, 8:19, 28:14; 2 Kings 17:35; Psalm 81:9); and many more verses. The Hebrews are not even to speak the names of other gods. Do you get it? The Hebrews are created for the express purpose of serving Elohim only. No one else has that special status but the Hebrews only.

When Ya'aqov told the people to purge the idols in there possession, the people were seemingly cheerful and excited to pay homage to The Most High Elohim. The people took away their idol gods, and removed the golden earrings from their ears (Ber./Gen. 35:4). So the people traveled from Shechem to Bethel; Ya'aqov built the altar, and named the place El-beth-el: Elohim of Bethel. After the altar was completed Elohim appeared to Ya'aqov, as HE had done in that place before (35:7). Elohim has appeared to Ya'aqov three times, and each time Ya'aqov received a *brocha* (blessing; 35:1, 7, and 9). Elohim is getting ready to do something that will change who Ya'aqov is as a person, a spiritual transformation. Ya'aqov, as did Abraham and Yitzhaq, always paid honor to TMH, and remained obedient to HIS Commands. Now an extraordinary event is about to happen, Ya'aqov will no longer be called Ya'aqov, but **Yisra'el** (35:10). TMH had already made a Promise to Abraham and Yitzhaq, now HE is telling Yisra'el that he is the finality of the Promise; and that in him, the Hebrew Yisra'elite family will become a Goyim (Nation; 35:11-12).

Many believe Esau is the white man; I do not ascribe to that belief because the Scriptures do not support that position. Esau is Edom, and he took his wives from the Canaanite family (36:1-2); which are the descendants of Ham (Ber./Gen. 9:22). Esau being Edom is reiterated in verses 36:6-9, and throughout Chapter 36 of the Bereshis. Listen-up: If you believe that Esau is only the white man, you are a racist; and furthermore, you have completely ignored the fact that: the family-line of Ham, the Hamites, are the darkest hue people on the entire earth. With that said, there are white skin Hamites/Canaanites, due to the change in environment. Many Edomites moved into the mountains, Mt. Seir. The point of Esau being Edom is reiterated again in the final verse of chapter 36. This is an important issue in Scripture because Esau is the enemy of Elohim. The redundancy of repeating who Esau is, is to make it clear that Esau is the problem for this earth: Esau is the hatred, the greed, the power hungry, the warrior, the religious leadership, the conqueror, and the destroyer. Esau is every skin color on the earth; anyone of evil countenance; anyone, who stands against the Chosen People of Elohim, the Hebrews.

There are people born into this world with one purpose in life: to be a True Servant of Elohim. These True Servants are sometimes targeted, abandoned, lied on, and may appear at times a pitiful *nefesh* (soul) to some because they are different than most people. The True Servant's special status makes them oftentimes seem unlikable or unfriendly, or haughty. Yosef is one of those Special people. Yosef had a dream, and he shared the dream with his family; as a result of the dream, Yosef was hated by his siblings (Bereshis 37:4-5). Yosef became the envy of the family because of his Elohim appointed gifts. Listen-up: Yosef has a gift that few people ever have: Yosef is a *Seer*. The *Seer* is one of the Special Prophets TMH uses to bring the Truth of what has been, and what is yet to come; the Seer is a True Servant of TMH. Yosef's brothers hated him because Yisra'el showed more favor to Yosef than he did to them. Yosef dreamed a dream showing the family paying tribute to him. Yosef shared that dream with the family, and his siblings hated him the more (37:7-8). Yosef dreamed yet another dream showing him as the head of the family, which none of the family appreciated the dream, and Yosef's perceived arrogance (37:9-10). Yisra'el knew in his **ruach** (spirit) there was something special with Yosef, though Yisra'el might not have known exactly why Yosef was different; he felt there could be something to the dreams (37:11). When the young siblings were in the field feeding and watering the animals, Yosef came to the field to check on them. When they saw him coming, they began to plot on how to kill Yosef (37:18-20). Reuben, the eldest son was listening to them and was opposed to what they planned to do to Yosef, and came up with his own plan on how to save Yosef from death (37:22-23). Reuben told his brothers not to harm Yosef, so they put Yosef in a hole in the ground, and stripped him of his coat of many colors. The intent was to present the coat to Yisra'el as evidence that Yosef had been eaten by a wild beast (37:23). Then Yehuwdah came up with another plan, rather than to kill Yosef, let us sell him to the Ishmeelites (37:26-28). Reuben was away from his brothers when they sold Yosef to *Ishmael,* and upon Reuben returning to the hole, because he had planned to recover Yosef from harm, Reuben, seeing Yosef was not there, Reuben became distraught and tore his own clothing. The rest of Yosef's brothers then killed a goat and put blood on the coat of many colors to present to Yisra'el, as proof that Yosef had been eaten by some wild beast (37:33). The Ishmeelites sold Yosef to the Egyptians, which meant now the brothers had no idea where Yosef was or if he was still alive.

A point of history, a must need at this point of our study is this: Many have been presented with distorted, and limited information about the *Trans Atlantic Slave Trade*. Folks, the selling of Hebrews into slavery was something done many times in the history of the Hebrews for one reason only: The Hebrews are a stiffnecked, stubborn, and disobedient people. The reason for this insertion is this: Many people have no overstanding that it was *Ishmael*, who enslaved the Hebrews many years before the Europeans arrived on the scene. What Ishmael did to the Hebrews is referred to as: *The Arab Slave Trade*. When the Europeans came to Africa, they came searching out the Hebrews, making allegiance with the *Hamites*, seeking information on where to find the Hebrews. Let me make this expressly clear, the Hamites did not sell the Hebrews to the Europeans, the Hamites rather pointed out to the Europeans where the Hebrews lived. In fact, many Hamites after coming to the realization of what was actually going on tried to stop the Europeans; however, the Europeans had guns and other weapons the Hamites did not have. Many years before Europeans arrived in Africa seeking the Hebrews, the last recorded invasion of the Hebrews was done by the *Babylonians*. Many Hebrews escaped Yisra'el in the *Babylonian Exile* by sea to the Americas, *Turtle Island*, and to the *Iberian Peninsula*, and had been there for centuries before being invaded, first by the *Spanish*. Many of the Hebrews escaped on foot landing in places like: *South Africa, Nigeria, and other East African Countries*. Here is what is imperative to overstand: <u>Everywhere in Africa, and in the Eastern Hemisphere</u> the Hebrews had escaped to, the Europeans came seeking out the Hebrews, and the outcome for the Hebrews was the same each time: *enslavement, colonization, Apartheid, oppression, and torture*. What happened to the Hebrews was the direct result of the Hebrews <u>disobedience</u> to Elohim, bringing to fruition the curses of Devarim/ Deu 28.

Sometimes people put the leaders of groups, or communities, or countries, and especially churches, above every one else, expecting them to be perfect. That type of thinking is very much flawed because all of us have problems. But even so, whether you are a leader or a follower, self-respect and honor is what we must all possess; the old saying goes something like this: '*Discretion is the better part of valor*'. In other words, keep one's private life, private. One of the most well known bible characters is Yehuwdah; Yehuwdah had children by the family-line of Ham, a Canaanitish woman (Ber./Gen. 38:1-5). Elohim was not pleased with two of the children, and HE slew them (Ber./Gen. 38:7-9) because they were <u>evil</u>, and or <u>disobedient</u>. After the death of Er, who did evil, Yehuwdah told the second son Onan, to go in to Tamar, the widow of Er, Yehuwdah's daughter-in-law, to have sex with her to impregnate her. Onan went in, did his thing, and reached climax; however, he spilled his sperm onto the ground, and not inside of Tamar. For that act of <u>disobedience</u>, TMH killed Onan (38:7-10). Yehuwdah then instructed Tamar to remain a widow until Yehuwdah's third son Shelah, was of age, and that she should have children by Shelah (38:11). Tamar had something else in mind for her life, she came up with a plan on how to defraud Yehuwdah. Tamar covered herself, hiding her identity from Yehuwdah, and played the role of a prostitute (38:15-16). Yehuwdah was tempted and went in to Tamar; she sold herself to Yehuwdah for a goat, which Yehuwdah agreed to pay. Howbeit, he did not have a goat with him, and Tamar made sure he would keep his word by requesting from Yehuwdah a surety: his signet, bracelets, and staff (38:16-18). This is the thing that most people don't know about what is contained in these verses: If you have sex with a prostitute, you must pay for the pleasure; not to do so is shameful for the offender (38:23). When Yehuwdah found out that Tamar had played the whore, and was pregnant, he ordered her to be put to death (38:24). Here is the thing: Yehuwdah was operating under a double standard; he too was guilty of prostitution, but ordered Tamar to be put to death. However, Tamar had the signet, and Yehuwdah's other belongings, and presented them as proof that Yehuwdah was the man she slept with, and is pregnant with Yehuwdah's child (38:25).

Tamar was actually pregnant with twins, and their names were Pharez and Zarah. Zarah should have been born first, but went backward in the womb after showing his hand, and Pharez came out first (38:27-30). Here is a line upon line, and precept upon precept moment: Pharez was meant to come out first because Pharez is the family-line of Ha

Mashiach. Tamar is actually full-blood Hebrew, who in the *Babylonian Exile* was separated from the Hebrew family (Ezr. 2:53). It was <u>never</u> meant to be for Er, Onan, or Shelah, to have offspring with Tamar, as they were all half Canaanite, of the polluted family-line of Ham, and evil Esau. The Hebrew family-line is, Yehuwdah to Pharez; and Pharez to Hezron (1Chr. 2:5), and to, and to, and to Ha Mashiach. The name Pharez means: *breach or breakthrough.* Therefore, the bottom line is this: from this family-line will come the Power that will break the neck of the evil, that has plagued humanity from the beginning of beginnings. The fallen *malachs* (angels) will be defeated in the Hebrew family-line, the pure family-line of Abraham, Yitzhaq, and Yisra'el, the Progenitors. Now we will shift back to Yosef and the role for his life.

In *Mitzrayim* (Egypt) Yosef was imprisoned without cause, ostracized, and disrespected. Yosef, the True Servant of Elohim, the son of **Ya'aqov** (Yisra'el) is next in line to lead the Hebrews. Yosef went through the fire many times; and yet, only once, because Elohim was burning the rust off of him to prepare him for the leadership role he was to fulfill. The favor of The Most High was upon Yosef before he was birthed from his mother's womb. Yosef's brothers meant him harm because of the dreams he had about becoming the leader of the family; and yet, he was being protected by Reuben, the eldest son, at the same time. Even in captivity Yosef was successful and prospered because The Most High was with him. Then came Hasatan to bring wrath upon Yosef; you see:

Bereshis/Gen. 39:6 (OJB):

*"... Yosef was yafeh to'ar (well built) and yafeh mareh (good looking)".*

What Hasatan had to do was to find the best way to tempt Yosef into <u>disobedience</u> to The Most High Elohim. Hasatan thought to set Yosef up by having him to sleep with a married woman. I can imagine Hasatan saying to himself, I got this; I have set the perfect trap that will cause the Appointee of Elohim to fall into disfavor; thereby, foiling the plan HASHEM has to make Yosef of the most powerful in all the land of *Mitzrayim* (Egypt). Hear me well in this: Hasatan is very clever and skilled in evil deeds, and he knows exactly where to strike to get the best results. Hasatan had Pharaoh's wife to approach Yosef to give her sex (39:7). I imagine the queen was a strikingly beautiful and well-built woman. Her approach to Yosef was refused (39:8), and she became a scorned woman; the saying goes *'Hades hath no fury as a woman scorned'*. Pharaoh's wife was furious that Yosef refused her advances, and immediately came up with the plan on how to have Yosef imprisoned or put to death. Yosef was put into the prison and Hasatan thought he had won the battle; even though, Yosef did not have sex with Pharaoh's wife. Hasatan believed that because Yosef was in prison there is no way he could possibly become a mighty leader in Mitzrayim. HASHEM is burning the rust and heavy metals off of Yosef, preparing him for greatness. In prison, Yosef gained immediate favor from the warden, and became a leader in the prison (39:21-23); Elohim was with Yosef.

In the prison, the cup-bearer and the chief baker had dreams that Yosef interpreted for them. After Yosef had interpreted the dreams of the cup-bearer and the chief baker (40:18-23), and Pharaoh having a dream that none of his people could interpret (41:8), word came to Pharaoh that Yosef was an interpreter of dreams. The story unfolds as follows: Pharaoh summoned many of the ***Kemetic*** (Egyptian) Sciences (diviners; soothsayers; magicians; and so forth) to interpret his dream, and none of them were able to interpret the dream. Elohim, believe me, was in full control; HE was about to bring HIS Servant into the place HASHEM intended for Yosef to be in. Yosef had to have the rust and heavy metals burned off of him for this purpose: HASHEM sent Yosef into Mitzrayim to insure that HIS Chosen People, would survive the famine to come. In addition, there is another purpose for Yosef being in Mitzrayim, rising to great status in Mitzrayim: The Hebrew Yisra'elites will gain wealth while in the land of Mitzrayim. There is a lot to this story! The Yisra'elites will have to also go through the fire to burn the rust and heavy metals off of them in order to become the world leaders of *Spirituality;* and after they have gone through the fire, and freed from their captivity in Mitzrayim, they will need that wealth to build the **_Ohel Mo'ed_** (The Tabernacle of the Congregation). Moreover, the Yisra'elites, and the *Kemetians* (Egyptians) will see the <u>power</u> of The Most High by the plagues that will come upon Mitzrayim. The plagues will show the Hebrews that in <u>obedience</u> to TMH, no one nor anything can stand against the Hebrews.

In Yosef remaining obedient to Elohim, Elohim will bring Yosef to power in Mitzrayim. After Pharaoh received the interpretation of the dream from Yosef, Pharaoh determined the following: Pharaoh has placed Yosef in charge of "**_all the land of Egypt_** (41:41)". This is very important because Mitzrayim is the land of the enemy of Elohim. Because Yosef was able to interpret Pharaoh's dream, Pharaoh promoted Yosef to the second highest rank in the land (41:40, and gave him a wife; Pharaoh loved and respected Yosef because of his gifts as a *Seer*.

Yosef having gained the favor of Pharaoh, Pharaoh gave Yosef a wife whose name was *Asenath* (41:45). Asenath bore Yosef two sons, Ephraim and Manasseh (Ber./Gen. 41:51-52). Here is the line and precept moment of this information: TEN (10) of the *Shevet* (Tribes) of **_Yisra'el_** (Ya'aqov) came from Yisra'el; the other Two (2) Shevet came from Yosef. This is very important because as time moves forward, the *Mamlachah* (Kingdom) <u>of Yisra'el will split into the Northern and Southern Kingdoms</u>. Manasseh and Ephraim, in particular Ephraim, will fight against Yehuwdah many times before all of the shevets are overrun and defeated by the Babylonians. LOOK, LISTEN, HEAR: Manasseh and Ephraim are half Hebrew, and half Egyptian (There is no such thing as half race people, the race of the offspring is determined by the father (Bamidbar/Num 1:3-4). Did Yosef break the Commandment? No, the Commandment does not come into effect until their exodus from Mitzrayim (Shemot/ Exo. 12:37). The Law is found in Dev./Deu. 7:3-4. We will discuss that in our breakdown of Devarim.

The dream that Pharaoh had was about seven years of plenty, followed by seven years of drought and famine (41:26-31). Because Yosef was able to interpret the dream, Pharaoh put Yosef in charge of the kingdom. Yosef ordered the grains in the seven years of plenty to be stored in great bins. When the time of drought came, there was sufficient grain stored up to last the seven years of drought. The regions roundabout Mitzrayim were all running short of grains, and the people were all coming to Mitzrayim to buy food (41:57). Yisra'el told his sons to go to Mitzrayim to buy food, but that *Benoni* could not go with them (42:1-4). While in Mitzrayim, the brothers had to appear before Yosef to make the purchase. Yosef immediately recognized his brothers, and hid his identity from them (42:7). Chapter 42 of Bereshis is a very lengthy story, that will be presented in summary. Yosef inquired of his brothers about the status of their family: Did they have a dad? In receiving the information they have a living dad, Yosef asked them the state of their father's health, and they reported Yisra'el to be in good health. In telling the family history the information came out they also have another brother. Yosef used that information to his advantage because he wanted to see all of his family. So Yosef devised a plan on how to accomplish getting his family to Mitzrayim. The plan involved charging the brothers with being spies (42:9). The deal was this: You must prove to me that you are not spies, and the proof needed is for you to travel back to your home, and then return to Mitzrayim with your younger brother. As assurance that you will return, one of you will be imprisoned here until the rest of you return with your brother. Reuben, the elder son, who had tried to protect Yosef from his brothers previously, was again grieved by this turn of events, and he reminded his brothers why this evil has fallen upon them (42:21-24). To be sure the brothers fully overstood the severity of Yosef's words, Yosef ordered Simeon to be bound before their very eyes (42:24).

The brothers purchased the food, and started on their travel back to Canaan/Yisra'el. On the trip back to Canaan, they stopped to rest and to feed the animals; when they opened their food sacks to eat, the money they used to make the purchase was in their sacks (42:27). The brothers continued on to Canaan, and reported to their dad all that they had encountered. Yisra'el was distressed: Yosef gone, and now Simeon imprisoned; and you request now to take Benoni to Mitzrayim (42:36). Yisra'el refused fearing that he will also lose his youngest son. However, as time moved forward, the food began to deplete again, and Yisra'el told Yehuwdah to go to Mitzrayim to purchase food again. Yehuwdah reminded Yisra'el of Yosef's demand; Yisra'el had no choice but to let

Benoni go with them if they were going to survive the famine. Here is the thing: There is a message hidden in plain sight in verse 42:38: It is out of the natural order for the children to decease before the parents; Yisra'el is letting them know that, if something happens to Benoni, it will cause him such anguish, that he will age and languish unto death.

Yehuwdah persuaded Yisra'el to allow Benoni to travel to Mitzrayim to obtain more food; however, Yisra'el had some words for Yehuwdah that we should all observe: "... *Wherefore dealt ye so ill with me, as to tell the man whether ye had yet a brother*"? (Ber./Gen. 43:6). In other words, DON'T BE TELLING ALL OF YOUR BUSINESS. All of the brothers went to Mitzrayim, including Benoni, to buy the food; Yehuwdah giving his word to Yisra'el that he would protect Benoni. Yosef's plan is still in the works as for getting his family to safety in Mitzrayim. The brothers obtain the food, and leave Mitzrayim, heading back to Canaan with the food. Now comes the next part of Yosef's plan to bring the family to safety in Mitzrayim; Yosef had his men to put all of the money for the food into the grain sacks of the brothers again, but this time they were instructed to put Yosef's silver cup into Benoni's sack. As the brothers were in travel from Mitzrayim, Yosef sent his steward after them with this message: Why have you stolen from my master (44:5)? Of course, the brothers did not know what the steward was talking about, so they made a pledge that, whomsoever the cup is found, let him be put to death (44:9). The cup was found in Benoni's sack; the brothers were in anguish, and tore their clothes (44:12-13). Yehuwdah makes the case that, if you hurt the child, it will kill their father; and pleaded to take the punishment, and to let Benoni go free.

Yosef's plan is about to take form; really it is the plan of The Most High Elohim, being directed by HIS Servant, Yosef. The brothers are brought back to Mitzrayim. Yosef was ready to reveal his identity to his brothers. Before revealing himself to them, being emotionally in glee of happiness, Yosef had to take a moment to compose himself. Yosef in a forceful voice ordered all of the Egyptians out of his presence. When the Egyptians cleared the room, Yosef sobbed so loudly the Egyptians could hear him crying (45:2). Yosef then revealed himself to his siblings, and they were in fear because of selling him to the Ishmeelites. Yosef told his brothers to come near to him (45:3-5). This is the part of the story that every child of Elohim has to overstand: There are *Special Servants* of The Most High Elohim, whose entire existence is to carryout specific works, as Commissioned by the HASHEM. Yosef was sent ahead of the family into Mitzrayim to prepare a place for HIS people, the Hebrews to live and to thrive (45:5-8). However, this would only be a temporary homeland for the Hebrews, and their purpose for being in Mitzrayim will be revealed in this line and precept reading.

After Yosef revealed himself to his brothers, he embraced Benoni with his arms around his neck. Benoni and Yosef weeping; and they both wept upon one another (45:14). Benoni was the first brother Yosef hugged and kissed because they have the same mother, Rebekah. Afterward, Yosef hugged and kissed all of his brothers (45:15).

The story of Yosef is the *In The Beginning Story* of the Hebrews in Mitzrayim. Pharaoh heard the news of Yosef's brothers being there; Pharaoh told Yosef they are welcome in Mitzrayim, and Pharaoh made provision for the entire family to live in Mitzrayim. Elohim came to Yisra'el in a vision, telling him that in Mitzrayim, his family will grow into a multitude, and for Yisra'el not to fear going into a strange land (46:2-3). The sum total of persons of Hebrew blood coming into Mitzrayim is seventy (70) *nefesh* (souls; 46:27). The Hebrews brought all of their possessions, and all of their livestock from Canaan into Mitzrayim. The Hebrews were given the land of *Goshen* to live in peace in the land (47:6).

Yosef is to become the fulfilling of the Twelve *Shevet* (Tribes) of Yisra'el. **Ya'aqov** (Yisra'el) brought into existence Ten *Shevet* (Tribes), but Yosef would be the ***progenitor*** (beginning) of the fulfillment for Twelve Shevet total. Let me paint a picture for you because I know it is difficult to overstand the Twelve Shevet situation because of the Scriptures being so scattered. The best way I know to draw out the True History is to put all of the names together in a breakdown format:

THE CHILDREN OF YA'AQOV: Reuben, Simeon, Levi, Yehuwdah, Dan, Naphtali, Gad, Asher, Issachar, Zebulun, Yosef, and Benoni: that totals 12 children (Bereshis/Gen. 29:32 to 30:6-24; 35:18).

THE CHILDREN OF YOSEF: Manasseh and Ephraim: 2 children

(Bereshis/Gen. 41:51-52). There are a total of 14 children between Ya'aqov and Yosef, but the 12 tribes are not all from Ya'aqov. Lets break this down:

The Twelve Shevet are the children of Yisra'el, and Yosef combined: Reuben, Simeon, Yehuwdah, <u>Dan</u>, Naphtali, Gad, Asher, Issachar, Zebulun, <u>Yosef</u>, Ephraim, and Manasseh (Bamidbar/Num. 2:2-32).

Did you catch it? <u>Levi</u> is not listed as a Shevet of Yisra'el because the Shevet of Levi were set-apart to become the *Levitical Priesthood* (Bamidbar/Num. 2:33). <u>Dan</u> is on the list, but tragedy shall befall Dan because of a great blasphemy that shevet committed. The doom of Dan is foretold by Yisra'el in Bereshis/Gen. 49:16-17.

The final Twelve Tribe list is found in Hisgalus/Revelation 7:5-8, and is: Yehuwdah, Reuben, Gad, Asher, Naphtali, Manasseh, Simeon, <u>Levi</u>, Issachar, Zebulun, Yosef, and Benoni. Because of the evil Dan committed in creating another god to worship, the Shevet of <u>Dan</u>, that shevet was wiped out and <u>Levi</u> was restored to the Twelve Shevet. Dan took a god of their own, and not the Elohim of Yisra'el, which broke the First Three Commandments (Amos 8:14). Amos 9:1-4, tells us of the wrath HASHEM brought upon Dan.

In addition to the stories of Levi not being part of the Twelve Shevet, and then being re-inserted into the Twelve Shevet; and Dan being killed off is this: Manasseh and Ephraim were brought into the Twelve Shevets, though not the sons of Yisra'el for a specific purpose. Yisra'el made a declaration prior to his death that Manasseh and Ephraim will be counted as his children, and that anyone soever that came to Yosef after those two children, would be counted the children of Yosef (Ber./Gen. 48:5-7). Yisra'el then goes on to bless Ephraim and Manasseh, but Yisra'el blesses the younger son Ephraim, above that of the oldest son, Manasseh. Yosef was not pleased with that, and his dad explained to Yosef why it must be that way (48:18-20). The reasoning behind Ephraim being blessed above the oldest son, Manasseh, will be made apparent when we get to the section dealing with the *Mamlachah* (Kingdom) splitting into the *Northern and Southern Kingdoms*. But briefly, the Yisra'elites as a whole have to go through trial and tribulation to purge out the impurities in them, in order for the Hebrews to finally serve and worship Elohim <u>only</u>. Yisra'el gives us a brief glimpse of why it is necessary for Ephraim to be above Manasseh:

Bereshis/Gen48:17 (AKJV):

'The **_Malach_** (Angel) which <u>_redeemed me from_ **_all_** _evil_</u>, bless the lads; and let my name be named on them, and the name of my fathers <u>Abraham</u> and <u>Yitzhaq</u>; and let them grow into a multitude in the middle of the earth.'

Abraham, Yitzhaq, and Ya'aqov all had to go through a purging, and yet, evil still remained among the Twelve Shevets of Yisra'el. The Hebrews time in Mitzrayim has a purpose that we will discuss in great detail as line and precept intersections of Scripture.

Yisra'el goes into detail and prophesy for all of his children, and provides us much valuable information about the disbursement of Yisra'el today. We will look at the four main groups of Yisra'el: Mind you, all of the groups are important, but the condition of these four groups tells us why the Twelve Shevet changed over the centuries. LEVI: There is a reason why we don't truly know who Levi is today, Levi and Simeon did an awful thing, they killed all of the men of Shechem (Ber./Gen. 34:25). The Prophet, Yisra'el, tells us outright, Levi, who is the Priesthood, will be scattered into all of the shevets, and that is why we don't know who the Levites are today (49:5-7). There is another point I have to insert here, and that is: Don't believe that through _Deoxyribonucleic Acid_ (DNA), they have traced the heritage of anyone living today to Levi, it is a lie from the pit of fire. Yisra'el put a <u>curse</u> upon Levi, scattering them into all of the shevets. YEHUWDAH: The Strength of <u>all</u> Yisra'el comes from the Shevet of Yehuwdah. Yehuwdah is the Shevet of Ha Mashiach, and is for everlasting redemption for the world. Yehuwdah is the PROTECTOR, THE LAW GIVER, THE BINDING FORCE; it is the duty of Yehuwdah to teach the <u>truth</u> of Ha Mashiach to those who are willing to see and hear the truth (49:8-12). DAN: The disrupter was evil, taking on another god as the Elohim of life. Because of what Dan did this group became adversary to Yehuwdah. Dan struck down the teaching of Yehuwdah, biting the heels of the horse (Ber./Gen. 49:15-17). The horse is Yehuwdah: the *foal* (v.11) is the horse in verse 17. Some will say Dan was not destroyed, but Amos 8:14-9:1-4, brings the scattered line and precept aspects of what happened to Dan all together; they were wiped out for evil, Dan broke the First Three Commandments, and paid the price. YOSEF: The shevet that is to bring all of the shevets back together from wheresoever they have traveled. Yosef in bringing the foal together fulfills their role, so Yehuwdah can do its duty as the head of the family. The work of Yosef surpasses the work of Abraham and Yitzhaq, the PROGENITORS (49:26).

In the blessings Ya'aqov placed upon the Twelve Shevets of Yisra'el, there is one other topic that has to be pointed out, and will be greatly discussed when we get to Benoni, and the wickedness committed by the men of Benoni. Benoni is a destructive shevet, who will go to war against the other shevets of Yisra'el, and their great battle strength is revealed in Bereshis/Gen. 49:27. Benoni will come under the influence of the evil spirits of the fallen malachs, and will commit the same acts as that of the story of Sodom and Gomorrah.

The final chapter of Bereshis tells us why Yosef was placed in Mitzrayim from before the beginning of Yosef's trouble of any kind; Yosef was to bring the Promise of Abraham and Yitzhaq to fruition (50:20). Furthermore, the example Yosef is for us is the attitude of forgiveness. All of you hate mongers out there, your day will come by The Most High Elohim. The enemies of the HASHEM, are the haters of HIS people.

To closeout the ending stories of the beginning to no ending, the creation in which Elohim created: **male and female created HE** them (1:1-27), was a creation of itself that likely existed for eons; and the unnamed male and female were commanded to reproduce, which means they were having sex. There is a period of time left out of the KJ bible that does not tell us why that creation ended, but even so: **formed the man** from the ground, **breathed into him** making him a **living soul** (2:7), and **made the woman** from the **rib of the man** (2:22) are separate creations stories. In the creation where the man and the woman were created at the same time, there are other writings that fill-in what is missing from the story: the man and the woman in that story became corrupted and went over to the Hasatan side, the woman's name was Lilith, and the man's name was Aw-dawn. Look at the contradictions in the writing: created vs. made; created HE them vs. formed man, followed later by the woman being made from the bone of the man. Then we come to Seth, a new beginning of beginnings to continue the second uncontaminated era after the death of Able. In the ending of that creation, which was also many millennia, it too became corrupted by the evil of Hasatan; the ending of that creation was the great flood. From the great flood to present is another creation, and it too shall explode into oblivion, it has to for the New Shamayim and New Eretz to come into play (Isaiah 65:17; 66:22: Hisgalus/Rev. 3:12; 21:1).

Something that is line upon line, and precept upon precept in the Bereshis is this: Yehuwdah is the Head of all Yisra'el. Yehuwdah actually means *Promise*, and Yehuwdah is the fourth in line from the First Covenant given to Abraham, meaning: Yehuwdah is the ending of the beginning of the Promise, and will lead Yisra'el forever. Four or fourth in Bible Numerology means: complete or completion. When Yosef's brothers conspired to kill him, it was the leader of the group, Yehuwdah, who advised against causing physical trauma to the lad (Ber./Gen. 37:26). In the time of the famine, when the food was running low again, and Yisra'el told his sons to return to Mitzrayim to obtain more food, it was Yehuwdah who spoke up to Yisra'el, telling him: They could not return unless Benoni was with them (43:3; 8-9). After returning to Mitzrayim, and Yosef's plan still unfolding, it was Yehuwdah who spoke up pleading for the life of Benoni to be spared (44:18-34). In the move to Mitzrayim, it was Yehuwdah who was appointed to guide the Hebrews to the land of Goshen (46:28). In the *brocha* (blessings) and or curses of Yisra'el upon his children, he tells us that Yehuwdah is the <u>lion and pride</u> of Yisra'el, the Protectors of the family (49:8-10). Yehuwdah is the Spokesmen for all the *Shevets* (Tribes) of Yisra'el; the Leaders.

Now that the creations, at least for now, are completed, and the Twelve **_Shevets_** (Tribes) of Yisra'el have been established, let us venture into the early years of Yisra'el in Mitzrayim; and what transpired with Yisra'el unto the day of the Shemot/Exodus.

# THE PLIGHT AND TRAVELS BEGIN WITH MITZRAYIM (EGYPT)

Let us begin this segment of our reading by making a bold statement of fact about the time Yisra'el was in Mitzrayim: YISRA'EL WAS NOT IN SLAVERY 430 YEARS IN MITZRAYIM, THAT IS SIMPLY NOT TRUE, AND COMES FROM THE MOUTH OF UNLEARNED TREACHERS (teachers/preachers), who don't overstand Scriptures as well as they should. The Yisra'elites were in Mitzrayim 400-430 years total; howbeit, the enslavement the Hebrews suffered there was for 80-120 years are so, and was not the suffrage described in Devarim/Deuteronomy 28. We will see from the Shemot/Exodus, the foolery of teaching that time period as the time period prophesied in Devarim/Deuteronomy, Chapter 28. Before opening Shemot, think about this: In the time of Hebrew enslavement in Mitzrayim, what had the Hebrews done to come under such punishment from Elohim? What were the rules the Hebrews broke at that time? Had they forsaken the Elohim of **_Shamayim_** (Heaven) at that time? The answers to the questions is: NOTHING! The Hebrews had done absolutely nothing at that time for such devastating punishment. Hear, see, and open up your mind to gain a clear overstanding of Scripture by allowing the **_Ruach Hakodesh_** (Sacred Spirit) to teach you. It is an impossibility for the Hebrews time in Mitzrayim to be the 400 years of enslavement for the Hebrews to come as Prophesied in Devarim 28. There can be no Prophesy going backward in time; Prophesy is what is to come. Let us have a look at the first years of Yisra'el in Mitzrayim.

Pharaoh and Yosef have both died. Remember, Pharaoh and Yosef were friends, and the Hebrews lived in peace in the city of *Goshen*. The Hebrews have been in Mitzrayim from Yosef's youth, teens to early twenties. Yosef at the age of his death was 110 years old (Bereshis 50:26). That indicates the Hebrews at the time of Yosef's death have already lived free in Mitzrayim somewhere between 70-90 years. In that time, the Hebrews have multiplied exponentially (Shemot/Exo. 1:7). After the death of Pharaoh, who allowed the Hebrews to live in Goshen in peace, his son became the new ruler of Mitzrayim. The new Pharaoh became afraid that if Mitzrayim went to war against another country, that the Hebrews might unite with the invading country, to fight against Mitzrayim (1:8-10). The Hebrews were a mighty people, who continued to multiply causing the succeeding Pharaoh to fear the Hebrews in Mitzrayim. Notice the Scriptures say: *'unite also unto our enemies, and fight against us'* (1:10). Pharaoh did not say the Hebrews are the enemy, his statement is: If they do fight against us in combination with the enemy, we will be slaughtered. Pharaoh then came up with a plan on how to control the Hebrews, and to slowdown the Hebrews multiplying, and to weaken them as a people. Pharaoh's plan was to have his army roundup the Hebrews and to put them in bondage, under very harsh conditions (1:11-14). Also Pharaoh, in order to slowdown the rate of Hebrew births, Pharaoh ordered the midwives to kill the Hebrew male children at birth (1:16). However, TMH Elohim had blocked that order, and the midwives did not kill the male children because they feared The Most High Elohim (1:17). This is an interesting point to observe: the Egyptians have their own gods, and yet, they fear Elohim.

Now we come to several points of Scripture that are seldom, if ever discussed in the **_Ekklesia_** (Church). There was a man of the house of Levi, who took to wife a daughter of Levi. The woman became pregnant and delivered a male child. There was a decree in place that all Hebrew male infants should be put to death. The mother was able to hide the child for 3 months in Mitzrayim. At the end of 3 months, the wife felt she could not hide the infant any longer. Here is where the story becomes very interesting: The *nashim* (wife) put the child into a waterproof basket, and she put the basket into the river (2:1-3). This is the story of Mosheh; however, here you will see what is in the story you were not taught, and that has been grossly misused to enslave the minds of most people. Pharaoh's daughter found the basket with the infant in it (2:5). Pharaoh's daughter, after having called her maid to take care of the infant, Pharaoh's daughter decided she wanted to keep the child, and he became her son (2:9). This Egyptian woman brought the child into the house of Pharaoh to live. Here is the point: there is no way Pharaoh's daughter could convince anyone the child was hers, if the Hebrews and the Egyptians do not have the same physical characteristics. Pharaoh's daughter named the child Mosheh (2:10). We have established that the Hebrews have lived free in Mitzrayim for nearly a century; now Mosheh has been born and will be the vessel to deliver the Hebrews out of slavery. Line upon line, and precept upon precept. Now get this: The Hebrews were never in bondage in the lifetime of Yosef in Mitzrayim. It was when Pharaoh's son became the king, that fear of the Hebrews led to the bondage that was yet to come. Fear is always a catalyst that causes the oppression of one group by another group. The birth of Mosheh, the acts of Mosheh, and the purpose for Mosheh was not by accident. You see, as a *Prophet,* Mosheh was appointed to his position before he was ever conceived in his mother's womb: *I AM THAT I AM* sent Mosheh to lead the Hebrews out of Mitzrayim (3:14). As we have already observed in Bereshis, the rust and heavy metals have to be burned off of the Hebrews. HASHEM put the Hebrews through the fire to prepare them for battles to come, and most importantly, to prove the Hebrews worthiness to serve and worship HIM only. Mosheh was 80 years old when he began to deal with Pharaoh about freeing the Hebrews (7:7).

There were a number of acts that would have to be performed, miracles per se, before the Hebrews would be set free. Listen-up: One of those acts involved coloration of the skin. Here we will pull many verses together, along with science, and a repeat of some of the history we have previously discussed. The first act involved turning Mosheh's rod into a *serpent* (snake; 4:1-4). The next act was, *I AM THAT I AM*, Ordering or Commanding Mosheh to put his hand under his shirt, on his chest. Mosheh did as TMH Elohim instructed him to do. Before the people, Hebrews and Egyptians, Mosheh's hand went from **brown** to **white** (Leprous), back to brown (4:6-7). Now watch this: line and precept, pulling the Scriptures together.

Bamidbar/Num. 12:1-10 (AKJV):

'*And Miriam and Aharon spoke against Mosheh because of the* **Ethiopian** *woman whom he had married: for he had married an Ethiopian woman. 2 And they said, Has the HASHEM indeed spoken only by Mosheh? has HE not spoken also by us? And the HASHEM heard it. 3 (Now the man Mosheh was very meek,* **above all the men which were upon the face of the earth**.) *4 And the HASHEM spake suddenly unto Mosheh, and unto Aharon, and unto Miriam, Come out you three unto the tabernacle of the congregation. And they three came out. 5 And the HASHEM came down in the pillar of the cloud, and stood in the door of the tabernacle, and called Aharon and Miriam: and they both came forth. 6 And HE said, Hear now MY words: If there be a* **prophet** *among you, the HASHEM will make Myself known unto him in a vision, and will speak unto him in a dream. 7 MY servant Mosheh is not so, who is faithful in all MY house. 8 With him will I speak mouth to mouth, even apparently, and not in dark speeches; and the similitude of the HASHEM shall he behold: wherefore then were you not afraid to speak against MY servant Mosheh? 9 And the anger of the HASHEM was kindled against them; and HE departed. 10 And the cloud departed from off the tabernacle; and, behold, Miriam became* **leprous, white as snow**: *and Aharon looked upon Miriam, and, behold, she was* **leprous**.'

The following is not a statement of racism, but rather is Biblical evidence that: ALL OF THE PEOPLE LIVING AT THAT TIME WERE OF MELANIZED SKIN. White skin during that time period is representative of <u>death and disease</u>. Miriam in being afflicted with *Leprosy,* turning white, had the appearance of "***one dead***". Her appearance would be frightening to someone not familiar with seeing a Leprosy victim. In those days, white skin equated to disease and death. People of white skin, I feel your temperature rising, and the hate flowing like a river upon me for telling you the truth. I did not write the Scriptures, all I can do is to present what the Scriptures say. My duty is to tell you the truth, not to spare your feelings. The above Scriptures also give us a warning, a warning for us not to speak against the True Servant of TMH Elohim. WARNING, WARNING, WARNING! Do not speak against a True *P*rophet of Elohim, your fate could be destruction. Now don't get this twisted, these verses are not speaking on the <u>charlatans</u> standing in most pulpits today. Those crooks are agents of Hasatan, and are not the representatives of Elohim. Charlatans deceive the people with the doctrines of devils. One must be able to discern the *P*rophet from the false prophet. Now let us add more Biblical credence to the characters of the Bible being those of melanin skin.

Melachim Bais/2 Kings 5: 25-27 (AKJV):

'*But he went in, and stood before his master. And Elisha said unto him, Where came you, Gehazi? And he said, Your servant went no where. 26 And he said unto him, Went not mine heart with you, when the man turned again from his chariot to meet you? Is it a time to receive money, and to receive garments, and olive-yards, and vineyards, and sheep, and oxen, and menservants, and maidservants? 27 **The leprosy therefore of Naaman shall cleave unto you**, and unto your **seed** (children/ posterity) for ever. And he went out from his presence a **leper as white as snow**.*'

Gehazi did evil by doing what the *P*rophet refused to do: To take money and gifts for performing a miracle for Elohim. Gehazi thought he was acting without the knowledge of Elisha. Here is the thing: Elisha was filled with the Ruach Hakodesh, Who informed him of everything Gehazi did. Now get this, don't miss what these verses actually tell us: Elisha put a <u>generational curse</u> upon Gehazi turning not only Gehazi white with Leprosy, but every generation of his family-line to come after him.

Line upon line and precept upon precept. We have already seen in the KJ bible that brown skin in ancient days was the normal color of skin. Now let us look outside of the KJ bible to a book that has been labeled as *pseudepigraphical.*

Enoch 105:2:

> "*... the flesh of which was as white as snow*, and red as a rose; the hair of whose head was white like wool, and long; and whose eyes were beautiful. When he opened them, he *illuminated all the house, like the sun*; the whole house abounded with light."

This verse is in reference to Noah, the *albino*. Listen-up: To believe the stories of Mosheh, and Miriam to be true in the KJ bible, and then to discredit what is written in The Book of Enoch is an inconsistency to say the least. In order to bring a better perspective of this, Mosheh was told to put his hand into his bosom, and when he took his hand out of his bosom, his hand was white (Shemot/Exo. 4:6); Miriam was turned white (Bamidbar /Num. 12:10); and Gehazi was turned white (Melachim Bet/2 Kgs 5:27). Noah's eyes illuminated, being bright in color; bright-eyed or as defined "*bright dutch blue*" (Merriam Webster). The white skin, and blue or illuminated eyes are two great factors predicting what is to come to humanity after the flood.

As this book is Scriptural, Historical fact, and Science, let us look at some Scientific Data that lends credence to the above Scriptures:

How Europeans Evolved White Skin:

> "*Ancient genomic sequences* have started revealing the origin and the demographic impact of Neolithic farmers spreading into Europe1–3. ... By sequencing a ~*7,000-year-old Mesolithic* skeleton discovered at the La Braña-Arintero site in León (Spain), we retrieved the first complete pre-agricultural European human genome. Analysis of this genome in the context of other ancient samples suggests the existence of a common ancient genomic signature across Western and Central Eurasia from the Upper Paleolithic to the Mesolithic. The La Braña individual carries ancestral alleles in several skin pigmentation genes, suggesting that the *light skin of modern Europeans* was not yet ubiquitous in *Mesolithic times*.

*Next-generation sequencing (NGS) technologies are revolutionizing the field of ancient DNA (aDNA), and have allowed the sequencing of complete ancient genomes5,6, such as that of Ötzi, a __Neolithic human body found in the Alps__1.*

*Of the ten variants, the Mesolithic genome carried the ancestral and non-selected allele as a homozygote in three regions: C12orf29 (a gene with unknown function), SLC45A2 (rs16891982) and SLC24A5 (rs1426654) (Table 1). The latter two variants are the two strongest known loci affecting light skin pigmentation in Europeans20–22 and their ancestral alleles and associated haplotypes are either absent or segregate at very low frequencies in extant Europeans (3% and 0% for SLC45A2 andSLC24A5 respectively)"*

ncbi.nlm.nih.gov/pmc/articlespmc4269527

The first important factor in the above information is this: THE INFORMATION WAS WRITTEN BY WHITE SCIENTISTS AND HISTORIANS EMPLOYED BY THE U.S. GOVERNMENT. Listen, listen, do not allow the above fancy language to block your overstanding of what happened over many eons. The above information comes from the U.S. Government, and goes to something that is prevalent throughout this country and the world: AMERICA AND THE WORLD HAVE BEEN DECEIVED BY THE ELITE CLASS BY LIMITING THE EDUCATION AND THE BRAINWASHING OF THE PEOPLE WITH A SYSTEM OF MISEDUCATION. Simply put, what the above data tells us is, a 7,000 year old body was found in the ice in the Alps, an area that is ice covered almost always. The body was well preserved. Upon testing this ancient body by *deoxyribonucleic acid* (DNA), science has proven that the first inhabitants of Europe were of melanin skin. Over many years of living in the colder climates, the people that left Africa loss the genes they needed in the hot climate of Africa to produce a sufficient amount of melanin. The end result is what we see today: people, not affected by Leprosy, of none melanin skin. Allow me to give you a theory based out of my own mind: If the U.S.

closed its borders to all incoming and outgoing persons, it may take many millennia, but the end result would be one: Every person living here would eventually be of melanin skin, ranging from light brown skin, to very dark skin, depending on the region of the country they live.

Now we will return to the Shemot/Exodus:

Eventually, the Hebrews would be set free from Mitzrayim. One thing that most people don't overstand about the miracles performed by Mosheh is this: Almost every act Mosheh did, the Egyptians were able to duplicate: frogs (8:2); flies (8:31); cattle died (9:6); boils (9:9); hail (9:18); crops destroyed (9:31-32); locusts (10:4). Watch this: There was one of the plagues the magicians could not duplicate, the plague of the lice (8:16). Here is the thing that evades the minds of most readers of these verses: The gods of the Egyptians have power, and grant gifts to their people. The Egyptians made a great confession to Pharaoh that the gods of Mitzrayim could not match the Elohim of the Hebrews (8:19). The Egyptians have their gods, the fallen malachs. The last plague Elohim brought on Mitzrayim is what caused Pharaoh to let the Hebrews go, the death of the first born of the Egyptians, of their children, of the animals, every first born of all species (11:5). Listen-up: Chapter 12 of the Shemot is filled with information that pertained strictly to the Hebrew *Goyim* (Nations). Before the Hebrews were set free from Mitzrayim, Elohim decreed that the same month of the Hebrews release, will be the beginning of the Hebrew calendar (12:2). Elohim instructed Mosheh and Aharon on what this *New Year* would involve: a celebration called the *Passover*. The *Passover* occurred when Elohim sent HIS Ruach Hakodesh to strike-down the first born of **every** home that was not marked with the blood of the *Sacrificial Lamb* (12:5). Shemot, Chapter 12, tells us many fascinating points of Scripture: Hebrews are strictly forbidden to eat meat that is not fully cooked (12:9); the *Passover* is a perpetual celebration (12:14); the Passover celebration is a *Sacred Convocation* (gathering of the Hebrews; 12:16), which involves the *Feast of Unleavened Bread* (12:17), and the sacrifice of a *Lamb* (12:21), representing the time the *Ruach Hakodesh* passed over all of the houses marked with blood in Mitzrayim. The Passover celebration is marked with some significant information: First, this celebration is an annual event that is to take place every year on the same date on the Hebrew calendar, not the *Gregorian* calendar. The Passover takes place in the month *Abib* (13:4), which marks the *Hebrew New Year*. Here is another must overstand: The New Year is the time that the trees, and all vegetation that goes dormant in the fall, begin to spout-out new growth; it is the time the crops are ready for harvesting. For the new year to begin in the dead of winter is a misnomer that has been perpetuated upon the world by the fallen malachs.

After the Hebrews left Mitzrayim, the stiffnecked, stubborn, and disobedient Hebrews did foolishly, causing TMH Elohim to become angry with them. The Hebrews complained about the land which the HASHEM had given to them (Bamidbar/Num. 32:7-9). For the complaints, TMH made them to wander in the wilderness forty (40) years (Bamidbar/Num. 32:13). The point in all of this information about the Hebrews time in Mitzrayim, the scientific, and historical data above is this: Mosheh died at the age of one hundred twenty (120) years old (Devarim/Deu. 34:7). Looking at the age of Yosef and Mosheh, and when they each died, and that the Hebrews were freed under Mosheh, makes it impossible that the Hebrew enslavement in Mitzrayim to be the Hebrew enslavement prophesied in Devarim, Chapter 28. The Scriptures are scattered and have to be pulled together in order to get the full picture.

Mosheh was a man of power, who innately knew he was Hebrew, though raised as an Egyptian. This is important to overstand: Many of the Hebrews living today have awakened to the truth of who they are, it is that same innate ruach, that has awakened them to that truth. As an adult, Mosheh witnessed an Egyptian beating a Hebrew man. Mosheh slew the Egyptian and buried him in the sand (Shemot/Exo. 2:12). Here is another point of interest: the next day, two Hebrews, who had witnessed Mosheh slay the Egyptian, engaged Mosheh in conversation about the incident (2:13-14). The two Hebrews thought Mosheh was Egyptian; this is the second confirmation the Hebrews and Egyptians look the same. Listen-up, stop the ignorance of believing Egyptians during that time had non-melanin skin. Mosheh was in fear that what he did, killing the Egyptian, had reached the ear of

Pharaoh, and in fear, Mosheh fled to Midian (2:15). Here, we come to the third confirmation of the Hebrews and Egyptians having the same physical features. In Midian, the daughters of *Reuel* were watering their flock, when shepherds came and chased the daughters away from the well, preventing them from obtaining water for their heard (2:16-17). Mosheh witnessed what the shepherds did, and came in defense of the daughters, and Mosheh chased the shepherds away. The daughters were able to water their flock, and returned home much sooner than usual. The daughters dad asked them: How are you able to come home so soon today? The daughters replied: An Egyptian saved them from the shepherds, and helped them water the flock (2:19). This is the third time Mosheh has been identified as an Egyptian.

The lesson of the outer appearance of Mosheh is simply this: The Hebrews and the Egyptians in Scriptural History, were so close in resemblance, they were indistinguishable from one another; and even more striking is, they spoke the same language: ancient Hebrew. This brings us to another line upon line, and precept upon precept point of Scripture. Mosheh has received his Commission from The Most High Elohim; and has returned to Mitzrayim to confront Pharaoh. Elohim has instructed Mosheh on what to say, and what to do to persuade Pharaoh to let the Hebrews go. Elohim told Mosheh to put his hand into his bosom, which Mosheh did. When Mosheh removed his hand from his bosom, his hand was *"leprous as snow"*. After revealing his white hand, Mosheh was instructed to put his hand into his bosom again, and when he pulled his hand out the second time it was *"turned again as his other flesh."* (4:6-7). This is a strong statement or declaration to the skin hue of the bible characters of Old; they were people of brown, to dark brown skin hue. The enemy has rewritten history to hide this information, scattering parts here and there to make it difficult to follow historical lines. All of those bible characters were of melanin skin. Do not continue to be blinded by the *iconography* used to identify those bible characters as not having brown skin, they were all of melanized skin. Only lepers had "white" skin in those days.

The HASHEM Abba has Supreme power above all other life: the physical world, and the spiritual realm as well. Mosheh and Aharon have been instructed by TMH in what to do to convince Pharaoh to let the Hebrews go. Now let me preface what I am about to share in these verses: all of the acts done by Mosheh and Aharon are to show the Egyptians, and the Hebrews, that Elohim is the Supreme Elohim; not that there are no other gods. Additionally, TMH brought the plagues in increasing intensity to show that after the plagues reach a certain level, the Egyptians would not be able to match HIS power, instilling fear in the Egyptians. These points must be overstood for anyone seeking the truth of Scripture. The beginning or early acts performed by Aharon, the *P*rophet, were done to make Pharaoh resist and refuse to let the Hebrews go because Pharaoh knew his magicians could match those acts (Shemot/Exo. 7:3). When Aharon threw down his rod before Pharaoh, Pharaoh called his magicians, who were able to duplicate the act of turning rods into snakes (7:10-12). This tells us that as TMH has the power to perform a miracle, so can the gods of the Egyptians. Aharon's rod (snake) ate up the snakes of the magicians to demonstrate that TMH is the Superior power. Elohim knew the magicians would match this amazing act, and that Pharaoh's heart would be stiffened in not letting the Hebrews go (Shemot/Exo. 7:13). What TMH requires of the Hebrews is one simple act: TO SERVE THE MOST HIGH ELOHIM ONLY (7:16). After the snakes produced by the magicians had been eaten by Aharon's snake, and Pharaoh's heart was again hardened, the next act was turning the water into blood. This act was also matched by the magicians; therefore, Pharaoh's determination to keep the Hebrews enslaved grew even stronger (7:22). The third act done by Aharon was the plague of the frogs; and again, the magicians were able to duplicate this act, intensifying Pharaoh's resolve to keep the Hebrews captive. However, this time Pharaoh tells Mosheh and Aharon, to ask Elohim to remove the frogs, and Pharaoh will let the Hebrews go (8:7-8). Here is the fact of Scripture that is repeated throughout the Scriptures: The Hebrews have <u>one</u> main duty on this ***eretz*** (earth), to serve The Most High <u>only</u> (8:10). After the frogs were removed, Pharaoh's heart was again hardened to keep the Hebrews captive (8:15). That brings us to the fourth miracle, the act of the lice. This time the magicians could not duplicate the act, and said to Pharaoh: '*This is* *the finger of Elohim:'* (8:18-19). This is interesting because it tells us that, the Egyptians realize there is a Supreme Elohim, above all other gods. Now we come to the fifth miracle, the production of the flies. This too is very interesting because flies are such filthy creatures that can contaminate everything: the animals; the food; the water; and cause disease in the people. Therefore, TMH made sure not to afflict the Hebrews by keeping the flies out of the land where HIS people are living, the land of Goshen (8:22). After a lengthy conversation of Mosheh speaking to TMH, and to Pharaoh, Pharaoh agreed to let the Hebrews go once the flies were removed; but yet again, Pharaoh did not uphold his end of the deal (8:31-32). The Most High then tells us or rather declares to us the reason HE created the Hebrew people: the Hebrews were created to serve Elohim only (9:1). That brings us to the sixth miracle: the destruction of the animals. With this plague TMH made a divide between the animals of the Egyptians and the animals of the Hebrews; all of the animals of the Egyptians died, but none of the animals belonging to the Hebrews died (9:4-6). But even so, Pharaoh refused to let the Hebrews go. The seventh plague brings boils upon the people of Mitzrayim (9:9). The boils came and Pharaoh still refused to let the Hebrews go. Here is the entire scenario: TMH brought Pharaoh into power in Mitzrayim for the purpose of demonstrating HIS power to all of the people: Hebrew and Gentile:

Shemot/Exo. 9:16 (AKJV):

'*for this cause have **I raised you up**, for to show in you MY power: and that MY name may be declared throughout **all** the earth.*'

In the wording of verses 9:16-21, TMH has sent a message or is communicating with Pharaoh, letting Pharaoh know how and why Pharaoh is the leader of Mitzrayim; and TMH giving Pharaoh a warning that the hail will come on tomorrow. The hail and the fire came; this eighth plague was of such devastation that Pharaoh made a stunning admission:

Shemot/Exo. 9:27 (AKJV):

*'I have sinned this time; the HASHEM is righteous, and **I and my people are wicked**.'*

Pharaoh agreed to let the Hebrews go, but again reneged on the deal. The hardening of Pharaoh's heart, and the plagues that have been put upon Mitzrayim, are all done for one reason: to prove that HASHEM is the only power we should fear (10:2). Pharaoh's heart, even after the hail, continued to be hardened bringing on the ninth and tenth plagues: the locust (10:14), and the thick darkness (10:22). That brings us to the last plague that will lead to the Hebrews release from Mitzrayim. This plague will cause the firstborn of every Egyptian household to die (11:5). The Hebrews were freed, and the day they came out of Mitzrayim is referred to as, *The Passover*.

It is recorded throughout the Scriptures many times the word "***gods***", and yet, people are taught there is only one god? There is only One Supreme Elohim, but the Scriptures makes it perfectly clear, there is more than one god.

Melachim Bet/2 Kings 17:24; 17:31; 18:34; 19:13; Isa. 36:19 (AKJV):

*'And the king of Assyria brought men from **Babylon**, and from Cuthah, and from Ava, and from **Hamath**, and from **Sepharvaim**, and placed them in the cities of **Samaria** (Yisra'el) instead of the children of Yisra'el: and they possessed Samaria (Yisra'el), and dwelt in the cities thereof. 17:31: And the Avites made Nibhaz and Tartak, and the **Sepharvites** burnt their children in fire to **Adrammelech** and **Anammelech**, the gods of **Sepharvaim**. 18:34: Where are the gods of Hamath, and of Arpad? where are the gods of **Sepharvaim**, Hena, and Ivah? have they delivered Samaria (Yisra'el) out of MY hand? 19:13: Where is the king of Hamath, and the king of Arpad, and the king of the city of **Sepharvaim**, of Hena, and Ivah? Isaiah 36:19: Where are the gods of Hamath and Arphad? where are*

*the gods of **Sepharvaim?** and have they delivered Samaria*
(Yisra'el) *out of MY hand?'*

Line and precept: The children of Yisra'el because of their
disobedience to TMH Elohim, were put out of the land of Yisra'el,
and replaced by the children of Hasatan. These verses make it expressly
clear, the Hebrews of **Samaria** (Yisra'el) were replaced by *Sephardic*
people. Those people did not serve the Elohim of the Hebrews, they
served *Adrammelech* and *Anammelech,* their gods. Stop believing in
*monotheism*, it is a fallacy; *henotheism* is the reality of biblical history.
Henotheism is the system of multiple gods, but those gods are not
equal in power to the head God, the Elohim of the Hebrews, the God
of gods (Devarim/Deu. 10:17). For the Hebrews, that God is Elohim,
WHO created the Hebrews specifically to serve HIM only (Dev. 6:13-
14). Hebrews, it is not appropriate to use the epithet God in reference
to Elohim. The use of the word here is for clarity of the message only.
Hebrews begin to erase the use of said word from use in talking to or
in reference to Elohim. Let us pull these line and precept Scriptures
together a little closer. Not only did the *Sepharvites* take the place of the
Hebrews, their cousins also possessed the land of Yisra'el. Look at this:

Bereshis/Gen. 10:1-5 (AKJV):

*'Now these are the generations of the sons of Noah, Shem, Ham,*
*and **Yepheth:** and unto them were sons born after the flood.*
*2 The sons of **Yepheth; Gomer,** and Magog, and Madai, and*
***Yavan,** and Tubal, and Meshech, and Tiras. 3 And the sons of*
***Gomer; Ashkenaz,** and Riphath, and Togarmah. 4 And the*
*sons of **Yavan;** Elishah, and Tarshish, Kittim, and Dodanim.*
*5 By these were the **isles of the Gentiles** divided in their lands;*
*every one after his tongue, after their families, in their nations.'*

*Hamath* (Ancient Syria), the land of the giants is where The Most
High sent the *banim* (children) of Yisra'el, against the enemies of TMH
to '*prove Yisra'el by them*' (Yudges 3:1), of being worthy as HIS Chosen
people. Here is the deal: the people of that land were the offspring of

the fallen malachs, who worshiped *Baal*. The Sephardim had their own gods, and Ashkenaz were of the Gentile family-line of Yepheth. In the case of Yisra'el in their homeland, they failed to '*follow the Commandments of Elohim*' (Dev./Deu. 28:1). Their failure led to the **Ashkenaz** and **Sephardim** being the possessors of the land because Elohim was angry with HIS Chosen people, and allowed the enemy to replace the Hebrew Yisra'elites. You still don't get it: The *Ashkenazim* and the *Sephardim* took the place of the Hebrews. Those groups do not serve the Elohim of the Hebrews; the Ashkenazim and Sephardim have their own gods and or religion.

Not only are there other gods, there are specific gods of different groups of people, who are the products/descendants of the *Annunaki*, the fallen malachs.

Melachim Bet/2 Kings 23:13 (AKJV):

'*And the high places that were before Yerushalayim, which were on the right hand of the mount of corruption, which Shelomoh the king of Yisra'el had built for* **Ashtoreth** *the abomination of the* Zidonians, *and for* **Chemosh** *the abomination of the* Moabites, *and for* **Milcom** *the abomination of the children of* Ammon, *did the king defile.*'

Not only are there specific gods for specific people, those gods have names. Listen-up: Those other gods are no match for the Elohim of the Hebrews. Those gods, the fallen angels are written of in multiple books of Scripture. Briefly, here are some of those gods from the book of Enoch:

Enoch, Chapter 68:1-2:

"*After this penalty they shall be astonished and irritated; for it shall be exhibited to the inhabitants of the earth. 2 Behold the* names of those angels. *These are their names. The first of them is Samyaza; the second, Arstikapha; the third, Armen; the fourth, Kakabael; the fifth, Turel; the sixth, Rumyel; the* *seventh, Danyal; the eighth, Kael; the ninth, Barakel; the tenth, Azazel; the eleventh, Armers; the twelfth, Bataryal; the thirteenth, Basasael; the fourteenth, Ananel; the fifteenth, Turyal; the sixteenth, Simapiseel; the seventeenth, Yetarel; the eighteenth, Tumael; the nineteenth, Tarel; the twentieth, Rumel; the twenty-first, **Azazyel**."*

Azazyel is the *Chief Watcher*, and is responsible for teaching all manner of knowledge to humanity that humanity was not supposed to have at their early inception into the world. The truth of Scripture is found in reading and researching other books, not only the KJ bible. Azazyel taught the people the following acts, and more.

Enoch Chapter 8:1:

*"Moreover **Azazyel** <u>taught</u> men to make <u>swords, knives, shields, breastplates</u>, the fabrication of mirrors, and the workmanship of bracelets and ornaments, the use of paint, the <u>beautifying of the eyebrows</u>, the use of stones of every <u>valuable and select kind</u>, and all sorts of dyes, so that the world became altered."*

The information in this verse is poignant on multiple levels: Azazyel taught the art of war; the use of beautifying materials, and the value of <u>stones</u> (gold, and silver, etc.). The common element in this verse is that, what Azazyel taught to the people, was taught to specific people, who would come to rule the world in wealth, in power, in superiority, and in the world standard of beauty. I repeat, the only way to come to better overstanding of biblical history, one must incorporate information from multiple sources into their reading. The *Book of Ecclesiasticus* offers us the following on the personality of one, whose desire is to obtain wealth:

Ecclesiasticus (Septuagint) 13:21-26: 14:1-10:

*'A <u>rich man</u> beginning to fall is held up of his friends: but the <u>poor man</u> being down is thrust also away by his friends. 22 When a rich man is fallen, he has many helpers: he speaks things <u>not to be spoken</u>, and yet men forgive him: the poor man*

*slipped, and yet they rebuked him too; he spake wisely, and could have no place. 23 When a rich man speaks, every man holds his tongue, and, look, what he says, they extol (glorify) it to the clouds: but if the poor man speaks, they say, What fellow is this? and if he stumble, they will help to overthrow him. 24 Riches are good unto him that has no sin, and poverty is evil in the mouth of the ungodly. 25 The heart of a man changes his countenance, whether it be for good or evil. 26 A cheerful countenance is a token of a heart that is in prosperity: and the finding out of parables is a wearisome labor of the mind. 14:1: Blessed is the man that has not slipped with his mouth, and is not pricked with the multitude of sins. 2 Blessed is he whose conscience has not condemned him, and who is not fallen from his hope in the Hashem. 3 Riches are not comely for a **niggard**: and what should an envious man do with money? 4 He that gathers by defrauding his own soul gathers for others that shall spend his goods riotously. 5 He that is evil to himself, to whom will he be good? he shall not take pleasure in his goods. 6 There is none worse than he that envies himself; and this is a recompense of his wickedness. 7 And if he does good, he does it unwillingly; and at the last he will declare his wickedness. 8 The envious man has a wicked eye; he turns away his face, and despises men. 9 A covetous man's eye is not satisfied with his portion; and the iniquity of the wicked dries up his soul. 10 A wicked eye envies his bread, and he is a **niggard** at his table.'*

This is some very powerful information, it goes to the **countenance** and **greed** of an evil person. Some people will do unspeakable unrighteousness to obtain wealth. Their countenance is reprehensible to the point of savagery, for financial gain, and for power. The more power and wealth they gain, the more power and wealth they scheme to achieve. Those of evil countenance will speak slanderously of another who has not wronged anyone. Those who speak the truth will be castigated by the one filled with filthy concupiscence, and work diligently to steal that which those of good countenance have obtained. But in all of the above Scripture is this: It is those who seek the wealth and the power, those who treat others badly: the thief, the murderer, those with an evil countenance, who is the "***niggard***". Let me pull this together for you: The character traits of the most vile of persons is a *niggard.* You see, those who have stolen, killed, robbed, defrauded, and otherwise abused others, has in time taken a term meant to describe their own character of evil countenance, flipped the script, making the term niggard apply to people of good countenance. This is only a snap shot of what those of evil countenance have done to others.

In reading from the *Book of Ecclesiasticus* about the word "*niggard*", and to whom it applies is surely a revelation. Moreover, the *Septuagint* has a vast amount of information from the different books in the *Canon*; such as: *Baruch, the Epistle of Yeremy, Bel And The Dragon, and the Maccabees* about those of wicked intent. None of those books are included in the King James Bible. The Septuagint reveals who the true evil people of the *eretz* (earth) are. The greed, power, and desire for supremacy in Shamayim came to eretz by the fallen malachs. These books tell of the Hebrews being bought for slaves, who bought them, the stories of *Cleopatra*, and more. The Septuagint tells of the Hebrews in *Spain, India, Greece, and all of the West*. Briefly, in researching data, many other topics the researcher was not searching for will present itself. In example: While researching for information on the *African Diaspora*, and the close proximity of the *Iberian Peninsula* to Africa, and then doing an *etymological* search of *Iberia*, another connection to lands the Hebrews lived was discovered: *Ibrahim, Hebrew, Iberia, Eber, Ibrim, and Ibriyyim*, are all synonyms of *Abraham*. **Iberia**, in particular, is very important to overstand because that name was given to the Northeast most region of Europe, across from South Africa, called the *Iberian Peninsula. (Note: The directional information here is correct, as the maps have been drawn upside down)*. That means the Iberian Peninsula is named after the Hebrews, because the Hebrews lived there at some time in *Geographical History*. There is an excellent video on this topic that traces the history of the Spaniards, the Hebrews, and the Iberian Peninsula that can be found on *YouTube* under the title: *Hidden Hebrews- King David (Revelation) – part 2.*

In returning to what is written in Enoch 8:1, the knowledge of precious stones and metals is of Shamayim. The secrets of Shamayim were never intended for humanity, at least at that time in humanity. Those fallen malachs brought information to earth, implanted that information into their defiled offspring for the same purpose they attempted to overthrow Elohim: power and riches. The use of precious metals in Shamayim is well established in the Scriptures (Hisgalus/ Rev. 21:18-21). The fact that there is gold, and other precious materials in outer space, has been authenticated by modern science. This is what credible sources tell us:

> "It's long been known that earthly metals like _gold_ and _silver_ were forged in supernova explosions"

> Andrew Fazekas, For National Geographic News; Sep 9, 2012

_National Geographic_ is a world renown Institution of incredible integrity. Clearly we can see from the Scriptures and Science, there are divisions of people, and why some people believe they are superior to others. Those of a superiority complex desire to control others, and believe they are naturally entitled to wealth. Those hybrid people are the offspring of the fallen malachs. As to Azazyel teaching on the use of paints, bracelets, and eyebrow beautification, the Scriptures point to such adornments being associated with whoredom or other deceptive, and or cunning behavior. Line and precept. _The Book of Septuagint_ contains many writings not included in your KJ bible. From the _Septuagint_, we will exam how women adorning themselves can be used to overthrown men.

Yehuwiyth, Chapter 10:3-4 (Septuagint):

> 'She took off the **_sackcloth_** (shawl) she had on, laid aside the garments of her widowhood, washed her body with water, and anointed herself with **_rich ointment_**. She **_braided_** her hair, put on a **_bow,_** and dressed in the **_festive attire_** she had worn while her husband, Manasseh, was living. 4 She chose sandals for her feet, and put on her **_anklets, bracelets, rings,_**

*earrings, and all her other **embellishments**. Thus she made herself very **beautiful,** to entice the eyes of **all the men** who should see her.'*

These verses are perfect in the use of decorative adornments women can use to overthrow men. This knowledge was taught to women by *Azazyel*. The use of silver, and gold, and other precious materials was for Shamayim only at the time the malachs were confined to the eretz. The point of the story is this: Yehuwiyth's husband, *Manasseh* was killed by *Holofernes*, Chief Captain of the Assyrian Army, of the family-line of Esau and Moab (Yehuwiyth 6:8-10). The Assyrians were at war with Yisra'el, overthrowing, defeating Yisra'el in battle. After grieving the death of her husband, Yehuwiyth developed a plan on how to avenge Manasseh's death (8:32-34). Her plan involved the above verses, Yehuwiyth was adorned to the tens. After getting beatified, Yehuwiyth went on her way to meet Holofernes to carry out her plan. When she reached the camp of the Assyrians, the men met her at the gate, and asked her: *Of what people are you?* She replied: **I am Hebrew** (10:10-13). The Assyrians were so struck by her beauty, they said: "*Who would despise this people, that have among them such women? surely it is not good that one man of them be left, who being let go might deceive the **whole earth** (10:19)".* This verse alone is a whole other topic, allow it to sink into your mind what the message is in the words. Continuing on with Yehuwiyth's plan: She knew that she would eventually be presented to Holofernes, which she was (12:10-12). The Chief Captain was so taken with her, he drank wine to stupor (12:20). Holofernes, now in a drunken stupor was completely vulnerable and unaware of anything going on around him. Yehuwiyth's plan to avenge Manasseh can now be carried out: "*And she **smote twice upon his neck** with all her might, and **she took away his head** from him, 9 and tumbled his body down from the bed, and pulled down the canopy from the pillars: and anon (soon) after she went forth, and **gave Holofernes his head to her maid**; 10 and she put it in her bag of meat: so they twain went together according to their customs unto prayer: and when they passed the camp, they compassed the valley, and went up the mountain of Bethulia, and came to the gates thereof (13:8-10)".* As you can see from reading this story, women using beatifying ointments, and precious embellishments can and do cause some men to become non-thinking, and vulnerable to the beauty of a smart woman with a plan. Azazyel brought the secrets of Shamayim to eretz before the time for such knowledge to be given to humanity.

In returning to our reading of Shemot, many have been taught that the Hebrews were in bondage/enslavement in Mitzrayim for four hundred (400) years. Now let us examine the words as written in the KJ bible and the Orthodox Jewish Bible:

Shemot/Exo.12:40 (AKJV; OJB):

> 'Now the **sojourning** of the children of Yisra'el, who dwelt in Egypt, was four hundred and thirty years (AKJV). … Now the **moshav** (time period of residence) of the Bnei (Children) Yisra'el dwelling in Mitzrayim was four hundred and thirty shanah (years; OJB)'.

The first thing about the quote from the AKJV of Scripture is this: THERE IS NO "*J*" IN HEBREW; THEREFORE, THE WORDING OF THE VERSE IS FROM ITS ONSET IN ERROR. The OJB uses the word "**moshav**", and in parentheses provides the definition of "**moshav**". In researching the word **sojourning**, looking at the synonyms thereof is this: *Temporary residing as another's **guest**; stay, tarry, visit, field trip, homestay, sleepover, layover, stop, stopover, live, dwell, **reside**,* and more (Merriam-Webster). The OJB clearly uses wording for the Hebrews time in Mitzrayim that describes the event more accurately. Listen-up: The Hebrews time in Mitzrayim was initially as the guest of the first Pharaoh (Ber./Gen. 47:4-11). The Hebrews time in Mitzrayim was not all in enslavement, and the Scriptures do not support such teaching. The Hebrews enslavement written of in Devarim/Deu. 28, was *prophetic*, and today the Hebrews are in that enslavement because of disobedience to Elohim.

After the Hebrews left Mitzrayim, they were singing a new song to The Most High Elohim, the Song of Mosheh. Some of the words are:

Shemot/Exo. 15:11 (AKJV):

*'Who is like unto YOU, O HASHEM, among the **gods**? Who is like YOU, glorious in sacredness, fearful in praises, doing wonders?'*

We have to see pass the words written on the pages to find what is underneath the writing to get the full message(s) hidden in the text. Stop listening to those, who don't overstand that God and gods are not the same: G-d is Elohim; gods are the Annunaki, Hasatan, and their posterity. However, Hebrews should not use the word G-d in reference to Elohim. We will come to a great deal of information on why that word should not used in regard to Elohim in a lengthy line and precept segment to come. The Scriptures repeatedly use the word "**gods**," meaning either *polytheism or henotheism*; either way, it is not the *monotheism* you have been taught. Did you get the full overstanding of more than one god? Look at this verse:

Shemot/Exo. 18:15 (AKJV):

*'Now I know that the HASHEM is **greater** than all **gods**: for in the thing wherein they dealt proudly HE was **above** them.'*

Clearly this verse tells us there is One Supreme Elohim, and the other gods are not equal to TMH Elohim. Clearly the verse says: Elohim is **above** all other gods. *Polytheism* has more than one god, who are of equal significance; whereas, *henotheism* is more than one god, while upholding one god as the head of the gods. Elohim tells us HE is *'Elohim of gods'* Devarim/Deu. (10:17). Many believe they are *monotheists,* but in fact may be *henotheists.*

Let us now go back in the Scriptures to Shemot 15:15, because there is information written there which is crucial about the enemies of Elohim:

114

Shemot/Exo. 15:15 (AKJV):

'Then the **_dukes_** of **_Edom_** shall be amazed; the mighty men of
**_Moab_**, trembling shall take hold upon them; all the inhabitants
of **_Canaan_** shall melt away.'

This verse goes all the way back to Cain. In tracing the family-line
of Cain, one can see, the seed of Hasatan, and the fallen malachs. It is
that part of inhumanity, who has tormented the Hebrews for millennia.
Listen-up! One must have overstanding of what is written in Bereshis/
Genesis, Chapters 4 and 5. In chapter four (4) is the bloodline of Cain.
That bloodline includes some well known names such as, Enoch and
Lamech (v. 4:17-19). There is a problem in that bloodline because Cain
is the polluted bloodline, Cain is the child of Hasatan. Here is where
the clarity of those verses has to be overstood. In the family tree of
Aw-dawn, beginning in Bereshis 4:25 is this: "_Adam knew his wife ..._
_called his name Seth._" Then in chapter 5:3 is this: "_... and begat a son in_
_his **own** likeness, after his image; and called his name Seth._" From Aw-
dawn to Seth, and several generations later would come Enoch (not
the same Enoch of the family-line of Cain), to Methuselah. Here is the
overstanding: NO WHERE IN THE SCRIPTURES OF BERESHIS,
CHAPTER FIVE (5) WILL YOU FIND ANY GENEALOGY OF
CAIN BEING THE CHILD OF AW-DAWN. Did you catch it? From
Cain and his descendants are the evil family-line of Edom, who is Esau
(Bereshis/Gen. 36:1; 36:8). I have not made this clear to you: There
are two (2) kinds of people: those of the evil, wicked countenance of
Hasatan; and those of good countenance of Elohim. Now let us add
line and precept. The dukes of Edom are:

Ber./Gen. 36:19-21 (AKJV):

"_These are the sons of **Esau, who is Edom**, and these are their_
**_dukes_**. _20 These are the sons of **Seir** the Horite, who inhabited_
_the land; Lotan, and Shobal, and Zibeon, and Anah, 21 and_
_Dishon, and Ezer, and Dishan:_"

The most important name in this verse is **_Seir_**. The reason for that is this:

Malachi 1:3 (AKJV):

"And **_I hated Esau_**, and laid his **_mountains_** and his **_heritage waste_** for the **_dragons of the wilderness_**"

The mountains referenced in this verse is Seir. Now let us look at who lived in Mt. Seir.

Devarim/Deu. 2:20-23 (AKJV):

'That also was accounted a land of **_giants: giants_** dwelt therein in **_old time_**; and the **_Ammonites_** call them **_Zamzummims_**; 21 a people great, and many, and tall, as the **_Anakims_**; but the HASHEM destroyed them before them; and they succeeded them, and dwelt in their stead: 22 as HE did to the children of **_Esau, which dwelt in Seir_**, when HE destroyed the **_Horims_** from before them; and they succeeded them, and dwelt in their stead even unto this day: 23 and the **_Avims_** which dwelt in Hazerim, even unto Azzah, the **_Caphtorims_**, which came forth out of Caphtor, destroyed them, and dwelt in their stead.'

You can see from the above verses that there were many giant family-lines, produced from Esau. Those Beings were created by the *Annunaki* (fallen angels), and not by Elohim. The Nephilim were created through DNA manipulation when the Annunaki mated with the women Abba created (Ber./Gen. 6:4).

This is very interesting because Mt. Sinai is synonymous with Mt. Seir, which is the same mountain where Mosheh received the Ten Commandments (She./Exo. 20:2-17). Now look at this: Mt. Seir is where the fallen angels landed on earth as recorded in The Canon of Enoch; which states:

Enoch 6:6:

*'And they were in all two hundred (fallen angels); who descended in the days of Yared on the **summit of Mount Hermon**, and they called it Mount Hermon, because they had sworn and bound themselves by mutual **imprecations** (curses) upon it.'*

The Elite Class has labeled the *Book of Enoch* as *pseudepigraphical.* The children of the Annunaki lived in the highest mountains in the region, the *Caucasus Mountains.* Let's continue to follow the family-line of Cain.

Bereshis/Gen. 10:6-10:15 (AKJV):

*"And the sons of **Ham**; Cush, and Mizraim, and Phut, and **Canaan**. ...15 And **Canaan** begat **Sidon** his firstborn, and Heth,"*

In pulling all of this information together, the picture should be more clear. The seed of the Annunaki has a family-line that came to humanity by way of Chavvah, who bore contaminated Cain. Many of that family-line were giants; such as, **Sidon**. Stop allowing those of the mis-education system to plant into your brain that creatures like Sidon, are only *mythological.* The other giants that roamed the eretz came from Abraham's brother *Lot.* Let us briefly look at what happened to Lot that brought that part of the family into contaminated creatures as well.

Line upon line and precept upon precept: Both Yepheth and Ham are the natural enemies to Shem, the Hebrews, because those two parts of the family are polluted. Moab is from the family-line of *Lot.* That part of the family teamed up with, and interbreed with the children of Chemosh, one of the fallen malachs. Chemosh is the god of Moab:

Yudges 11:24 (AKJV):

*'Will not you possess that which **Chemosh your god** gives you to possess? So whomsoever the HASHEM our Elohim shall drive out from before us, them will we possess'.*

Bamidbar/Num. 21:29 (AKJV):

*'Woe to you, **Moab**! You are undone, **O people of Chemosh**: he has given **his sons** that escaped, and **his daughters**, into captivity unto Sihon king of the **Amorites**'.*

Chemosh is the god of Moab. In pulling the Scriptures together, past events are better overstood. It was Moab, who plotted against the Hebrews to destroy them. The Scriptures are scattered, and full overstanding of the Scriptures is confounded in how they are a piece here, and a piece there. Watch this: line and precept:

Bamidbar/Num. 22:7-12 (AKJV):

*'And the elders of Moab and the elders of Midian departed with the rewards of **divination** in their hand; and they came unto **Balaam**, and spoke unto him the words of **Balak**. 8 And he said unto them, Lodge here this night, and I will bring you word again, as the HASHEM shall speak unto me: and the princes of **Moab** abode with **Balaam**. 9 And Elohim came unto Balaam, and said, What men are these with you? 10 And Balaam said unto Elohim, Balak the son of Zippor, **king of Moab**, has sent unto me, saying, 11 Behold, there is a people come out of Mitzrayim, which covers the face of the earth: come now, **curse me them**; peradventure I shall be able to overcome them, and drive them out. 12 And Elohim said unto Balaam, You shall not go with them; you shall not curse the people: for they are blessed.'*

*I AM THAT I AM* had a conversation with Balaam warning him to keep his hands off of the Hebrews. Balaam possessed powers that can be viewed as witchery and magic, and he had the ability to see things yet to come. Balaam had a gift that used according to good is no less than a *Seer*; however, if used for evil is to curse. As a diviner, Balaam could be sought out by those seeking the cause of good or of evil. Divination is defined as:

*"The art or practice that seeks to foresee or foretell future events or discover hidden knowledge usually by the interpretation of* **omens** *or by the aid of supernatural powers* (Merriam-Webster)".

An *Omen* is a future event and can be good or evil. These next line upon line writings tell us why Balak and Moab wanted Balaam to curse the Children of Yisra'el.

Bamidbar/Num. 22:1-3 (AKJV):

'And the children of Yisra'el set forward, and pitched in the **plains of Moab** on this side Yarden by Yericho. 2 And **Balak the son of Zippor** saw all that Yisra'el had done to the **Amorites**. 3 And Moab was very afraid of the people, because they were many: and Moab was distressed because of the children of Yisra'el.'

One of the greatest emotions a person can have is *fear*. Balak knowing what was done to the **Amorites** by Yisra'el, and now the Yisra'elites being in the flat lands of Moab, Balak is stressed out because he realizes, his army cannot stand against the Hebrews.

Moab is in fear of Yisra'el, and they have great cause for concern. For this point, let us examine the writing from both the KJ bible, and the OJB:

Bamidbar/Num. 24:17 (AKJV; OJB):

'I shall see him, but not now: I shall behold him, but not nigh: there shall come a **Star** out of Ya'aqov, and a **Sceptre** shall rise out of Yisra'el, and shall smite the corners of **Moab**, and destroy all the children of Sheth.' ... 'I see him, but not now; I behold him, but not karov (near); there shall come a **Kokhav (Star, i.e. Moshiach**, see Targums) out of Ya'akov, and a **Shevet (Sceptre)** shall rise out of Yisroel, and shall strike through the temples (i.e., sides of the head) of Moav, and destroy all the Bnei Shet.'

The Amorites knew Elohim was with Yisra'el. In Numbers 22:12, Elohim told Balaam not to attempt to curse the children of Yisra'el, as Balak wanted Balaam to do. Now we know why: Out of Yisra'el will come *Ha Mashiach* from Ya'aqov. The Promise to Abraham, Yitzhaq, and Ya'aqov will be fulfilled by this bloodline. The polluted seed of the Annunaki will be destroyed by the pure people, the Hebrews.

In the story of *Lot* (Ber./Gen., Chapter 19), is the story of the two Malachs sent from Elohim. The Malachs came to see what was going on in the city of **_Zoar._** In order to bring this story into full perspective, we have to look at Bereshis, Chapter 14. Line and precept: In verses 14:1-2, it tells us who the rulers of the lands are. In verses 5-6, it tells us the names of the nations of people living there: *Zuzims, Emims, Ham,* and more. These are cursed groups of people, descendants of the fallen malachs. Now don't get this twisted, not everyone of Ham is cursed, like everyone else, Hamites must choose on their earthly travel, who they serve. There was all manner of wickedness, lewd behaviors of all sorts going on in Zoar, and the surrounding areas, as it was in the pre-flood era. We will look at those behaviors when we come to the *Book of Law* (Leviticus). As the Story of Lot is written: Lots daughters did evil by way of incest (19:32-36), and the following verse is the result of the rape of Lot.

Bereshis/Gen. 19:37 (AKJV):

*'And the firstborn bare a son, and called his name **_Moab_**: the same is the father of the **_Moabites_** unto this day.'*

In pulling all of these parts of Scripture together, now one can better see why: *'Woe to you, **_Moab_**! You are undone, **_O people of Chemosh_** ... And the elders of **_Moab_** and the elders of Midian departed with the **_rewards of divination_**'* are vital parts of the full story. These people are all part of the bloodline of the Annunaki. Now watch this:

Bereshis/Gen. 36:8 (AKJV):

*"Thus dwelt Esau in **_mount Seir_**: Esau is Edom."*

Here is the point: All of the descendants of the fallen malachs at some point have occupied the area of *Mt. Seir*, which is the area surrounding the *Caucasus Mountains*. According to many books, Mt. Seir is where the Annunaki first landed on the eretz. Line and precept, look at these verses; they tell us without a doubt, who have occupied Mt. Seir.

Devarim/Deu. (AKJV) 2:20-21 (AKJV):

'*That also was accounted a land of **giants: giants** dwelt therein in **old time**; and the **Ammonites** call them **Zamzummims**; 21 a people great, and many, and tall, as the **Anakims**; but the HASHEM destroyed them before them; and they succeeded them, and dwelt in their stead: 22 as HE did to the children of **Esau, which dwelt in Seir**, when HE destroyed the **Horims** from before them; and they succeeded them, and dwelt in their stead even unto this day.*'

The above verses take us all the way back to:

Bereshis 32:3 (AKJV):

'*And Ya'aqov sent messengers before him to Esau his brother unto the land of **Seir**, the country of Edom.*'

Altogether, these verses tell us the enemy of the Hebrews are the Edomites, and Hamites, and where they originally lived on the eretz before spreading out to many regions of the eretz. Now we will look at some historical information about the location of Mt. Seir.

"*What Do **Mt. Horeb**, The Mountain of God, **Mt. Paran** and **Mt. Seir** Have to Do with **Mt. Sinai**? The short answer to our title question is that the Mountain of God, Mt. Horeb, Mt. Sinai and Mt. Paran are **all names for Mt. Sinai**, and Mt. Seir is important for determining the location of Mt. Sinai. The long answer, which is the subject of this article, is that each of these names provides important clues for determining where Mt.*

121

*Sinai is located. The location of Mt. Sinai is one of the major mysteries in Biblical research. Yohanan Aharoni has stated, "To-day the problem of identifying the route of the Exodus and <u>Mount Sinai itself</u> is one of extraordinary difficulty, far more than any other problem of Palestinian Biblical topography" (1962: 118)."*

biblearchaeology.org/research/exodus-egypt4012

Accordingly, what this information from researchers tells us is: The most knowledgeable geologists have determined that Mt. Sinai's exact location cannot be determined. This is simply my speculation, but the location of Mt. Sinai today cannot be authenticated because it was part of the Garden of Eden, which Elohim sealed off from humanity. And, furthermore, because Mt. Herman/Sinai is where the Annunaki first landed on the eretz. And, moreover, Mt. Sinai is where Mosheh met with Elohim, and the mountain is sacred, not to be trodden upon by man.

*Topographical* maps show the location of Mount Hor, and Yerushalayim (*en.wikipedia.org/wiki/File:Map Land pf Israel.jps*). Another great source of this information is found at *Georgraphy Skillbuilders:Interpreting Maps, Trade in the Roman Empire, A.D. 200.* The maps also gives us the center of the land of Yisra'el, which is approximately Yerushalayim, which is the land given to the Levites.

What those maps show us is how close the *Caucasus Mountains* are to the land of Yisra'el. The big difference in the climate of Yerushalayim and Mt. Seir results from the land elevation of Seir, which is 7,497, the height of Mount Hermon. Esau lived in those cold, snow/ice covered mountains, which that cold climate would eventually cause physical changes in their external features. Those, who have studied how climate effects our bodies have concluded the following:

*"40,000 – 10,000 BC Late Stone Age; Rise of **<u>brown-skinned</u>** Homo Sapiens, spreading to **<u>all major regions</u>** of the world and adapting to variations in **<u>climate and environment</u>**; Development of bow and arrow; evidence of rock paintings;*

*Hunter gathering lifestyle; Arrival of the **Grimaldian Negroid in Europe**.*"

African Diaspora II International Migration

The fallen ones landed at Mt. Seir. Esau eventually lived in that region in caves with environmental changes causing changes in the outer appearance of Edomite people. This is line and precept information to keep in mind as we continue to research the line and precept moments of Scripture. There is another aspect to be discussed about the region called Seir. That mountain is where the Annunaki first descended from Shamayim to *HaAretz* (The Earth), it was not by accident that Elohim called for Mosheh to meet HIM on Sinai. Mosheh had to go through a purging or cleansing process before he could come near to The Most High Elohim on that mountain. Mosheh and the mountain were purged of the foul pollution of the Annunaki, and made sacred by Elohim. The reason Sinai was chosen was to block Sinai from being the route of travel the fallen malachs would try to get back into Shamayim. Watch this:

Bereshis 28:12; 17 (AKJV):

*'And he dreamed, and behold a **ladder** set up on the earth, and the top of it reached to **heaven**: and behold the malachs of Elohim ascending and descending on it. ... 17 And he was afraid, and said, How dreadful is this place! This is none other but the house of Elohim, and this is the **gate** of heaven.'*

Ya'aqov, who would be the Progenitor of the Twelve Shevets of Yisra'el, was allowed to see the Mountain of Elohim, where Mosheh went to receive the Ten Commandments of Elohim. Ya'aqov dedicated the mountain to Elohim (Ber./Gen. 28:18-19). But get this: Prior the Ya'aqov dedicating the mountain to TMH Elohim, Elohim told Ya'aqov, the land where the mountain is located will be the land given in the Promise with Abraham and Yitzhaq (13-14). Here is the main point: The exact location of the mountain is in dispute unto this day as noted by *biblearchaeology*. In my assessment of the reason the mountain is in dispute is one: Yisra'el is scattered, and until the Hebrews come back together as one family, there will be no homeland for the children of Ya'aqov. When Elohim decides it is time, when the Hebrews reunite in <u>obedience</u> to Elohim, then and only then will that land be restored to the Hebrews. No one else will be allowed to live in the house of Elohim (13).

Now we will return to Shemot. *I AM THAT I AM* said to HIS people.

Shemot/Exo. 20:1-7 (AKJV):

> '1 You shall have **<u>no other god before ME</u>**. 2 You shall not make unto yourself **<u>any graven image</u>**, or any **<u>likeness of any thing</u>** that is in **<u>heaven</u>** above, or that is in the **<u>earth</u>** beneath, or that is in the **<u>water</u>** under the earth: You shall not bow down yourself to them, nor serve them: for I the HASHEM your Elohim am a qanna (envious) Elohim, visiting the iniquity of the fathers upon the third and fourth generation of them that hate ME; And showing mercy unto thousands of them that love ME, and keep MY commandments. 3 You shall not take the name of the HASHEM your Elohim in vain; for the HASHEM will not hold him guiltless that takes HIS name in vain.'

Here is the point: Why would Elohim give us the First Three Commandments to worship <u>no</u> other god **before** HIM, or not to worship any idol, and for us not to give recognition to any other god? This alone gives credence to the existence of another deity. The Hebrews must not give credit to another god for the work of HIS hands. *Chemosh* is another god, as is *Milcom, Baal,* and *Hasatan.* If there is no other god, that would make Elohim psychotic. Elohim forbid! I have to make this absolutely clear and would be totally remiss if I don't say this: TAKE THAT CROSS OFF OF YOUR NECK, OUT OF YOUR CHURCH, AND THAT FISH SYMBOL OFF OF YOUR CAR, IT IS IDOLATRY. (Also see Shemot/Exo. 23:32-33; the gods are real).

I tell you of a truth, you have been misled to believe lies all of your life. The shocking stories of the Scriptures are of themselves fascinating. Let us continue to tear-down the belief there is only one god theory.

Shemot/Exo. 22:20 (AKJV):

'He that sacrifices unto **any god, except** unto the HASHEM only, he shall be utterly **destroyed**.'

This is one of the statutes given to the children of Abraham, Yitzhaq, and Yisra'el; it would be completely stupid for the Omniscient HASHEM to give such an order for a fictitious deity. All I'm pointing out to you is this: Be sure that no matter what is going on in life, remain steadfast in The Most High Elohim only. Abba did not tell us not to worship any other god but HIM for no reason, HE gave us the Commandment because of the Annunaki, and what they have done since their fall from Shamayim. You are still not convinced of this truth, here we go, line and precept.

Shemot/Exo. 22:28 (AKJV):

'You shall **not revile** (verbally abuse) the gods, nor curse the ruler of thy people.'

Is this shocking or what? This is telling us to leave those other gods alone. How much more convincing do you need? Listen-up: not only should Hebrews not be involved with those other gods, Hebrews must leave the people alone who worship those other gods. Those gods have their own people. No one, except the Hebrews are created to serve Elohim, no one but the Hebrews. The Hebrews are a completely separate entity from other people (Dev. 14:2; 7:6; Psl. 4:3; Amos. 3:2; Yer. 1:5; and more). This is not about bias and hate, it is Scripture. In Isaiah 49:5, the verse is directly speaking to the Hebrews telling them, they are from the womb created to bring Yisra'el together in worship of Elohim. There is more than one god, but only One *Omnipotent, Omniscient, Omnipresent* Elohim.

Out of the mouth of unlearned men and women comes the words

of complete abstention from any alcoholic beverages. These unlearned people create ***ekklesia*** (church) ***orthodoxy*** (rules) stating that members of their ekklesia must be free from alcohol. As shocking as what I am about to say is, that kind of thinking and teaching is *antithetical.* Now let us give credence from the Scriptures to nullify such nonsense:

Shemot/Exo. 22:29 (AKJV):

'You shall not delay to offer the first of your ripe fruits, and of your ***liquors****: the firstborn of your sons shall you give unto ME.'*

This verse is telling us to dedicate the first of everything the HASHEM provides for us, back to HIM; even of the ***liquor****. Would it shock you to know that we are instructed to have a wine offering to the HASHEM once each year?

Shemot/Exo. 29:40; Bamidbar/Num. 18:12 (AKJV):

*'And with the one lamb a tenth deal of flour mingled with the fourth part of an hin of beaten oil; and the fourth part of an hin of ****wine*** for a drink offering ... All the best of the oil, and all the ****best of the wine****, and of the wheat, the first fruits of them which they shall offer unto the HASHEM, them have I given to you.'*

Shocking, isn't it? Most people have no idea the Hebrews are to solute The Most High Elohim with a celebration of food and wine each year (She./Exo. 30:10). No more needs to be said on this point; however, let us build upon this shocking revelation because teaching abstention from alcohol is not Scriptural. There can be no denial that we have been Commanded to drink the wine. Not only are we to drink the wine, the festival of wine is supposed to be the best wine we have. Look at this next verse:

Devarim/Deu. 16:13 (AKJV):

*'You shall observe the <u>feast of tabernacles</u> seven days, after that
you have gathered in your corn and your **wine**.'*

This verse tells us the Hebrews are to gather yearly for a week-long
celebration of The Most High Elohim, eating and drinking. I'm not
trying to tell anyone, who does not drink to start drinking. My duty is
to tell you the shocking <u>truth</u> of Scripture. My duty does not include
taking the bitterness of Scripture, adding sugar to the mix, making it
sweet to be pleasing to you; I have to be pleasing to TMH <u>only</u>. Stop
listening to ignorant men and women standing in the pulpit teaching
antithetical lies; using the Scriptures to control you, and to keep you in
a state of stupidity. Remember, the Scriptures are scattered, and must
be viewed in a line upon line, and precept upon precept manner to
ascertain the truth of what is hidden in plain sight in the Scriptures.
There are many Scriptures that cannot, and do not stand alone. Selah.

*I AM THAT I AM* gave Mosheh Laws that pertain to supporting
the priesthood.

Shemot/Exo. 30:16 (AKJV):

*'And you shall take the atonement **money** of the children of
Yisra'el, and shall appoint it for the <u>service of the tabernacle of
the congregation</u>; that it may be a memorial unto the children
of Yisra'el before the HASHEM, to make an <u>atonement for
your **souls**</u>.'*

This verse alone dispels one of the most misused ideologies of modern
religion. The collecting of money from the people was always about
supporting the priests, working in the tabernacle. Those priests were
preparing the sacrifices, the meals, and conducting all of the festivals.
The money was never intended to make the priests rich. Indeed, the
animals, fruits, vegetables brought into the tabernacle were to be used
in ceremonies of cleansing for the *nefesh* (soul). Let us pull the parts
of Scripture together pertaining to giving, and very importantly, the

cleansing of one's *nefesh* (soul). Hopefully in bringing the parts together a better overstanding of why the doctrines of today are antithetical to what *I AM THAT I AM* requires in giving to the **ekklesia** (church), and purifying the nefesh.

The priests not only collected the tithe to support themselves in the *Tabernacle of the Congregation* (Bamidbar/Num. 18:26), they also distributed food and other supplies to the widows; the fatherless, the strangers in the land, and those who lacked basic subsistence (Devarim/ Deu. 26:12). The use of tithes today is an abominable act against TMH, and against humanity. The tithe was never meant to make your pastor, and the heads of the church rich. Elohim forbid! The fact of Scripture is, Malakhi/Mal. 3:8: "*Will a man rob Elohim*"? has nothing to do with money, the tithe has always been foodstuffs (Nechemyah/Neh. 13:5). The tithe is a welfare system set-up by TMH to assure everyone in the village were taken care of; not a means to gather riches for the **Kohen** (Priests). In reading Malachi, Chapter 2, you will see why the question of: "*Will a man rob Elohim*"? was asked to begin with, and why TMH said to the Kohen, HE will "*spread dung upon your faces*". Because some of the priests had corrupted themselves with greed, HASHEM raised the question in Malachi 3:8. There are also others the tithe was meant to support: The singers, and the **porters** (custodians), who cleaned the tabernacle (Nechemyah/Neh. 13:5). The Bible is scattered in its presentation, and takes a great deal of study to grasp the line upon line, and precept upon precept basis of Scripture.

The Hebrew people are highly intelligent people for one main reason, they are given good knowledge by *I AM THAT I AM*. The sad part of the Hebrews being intelligent is this: they oftentimes fail to use wisdom along with that intelligence. The Hebrews are a stubborn, hardheaded people, who fall in behind other people, following after their religious practices. This has been true throughout Biblical History, and in many instances leading the Hebrews into bondage and servitude. You see, it is not as much the pleasurable, physical acts or sins the Hebrews should not participate in; it is the worshiping of another god, and the the Hebrews taking up the religious practices of the heathens that has caused the Hebrews to transgress from Elohim. Listen-up! The gods of the heathens gives rewards to their people, and manifold pleasures, many of those pleasures for the heathens, the Hebrews are to abstain therefrom. The Hebrews are Commanded not to bother the heathen, nor seek their riches (Dev./Deu. 23:6). It is seeing the riches those people get from their gods, and observing how they live so lavishly, that makes following them a temptation for many. Do you get it? The gods of the heathens gives rewards to their people, and manifold pleasures, many of those pleasures for the heathens, the Hebrews are to abstain therefrom. There were many acts of pleasure in Shamayim that the fallen ones brought to HaAretz (The Earth), the fallen ones shared that knowledge with the humans. That knowledge went against what Elohim planned for humanity at that time. As time went on and the people multiplied, laws were given to the Hebrews to prevent them from committing some of the acts of the heathens. That is why the Hebrews have six hundred thirteen (613) rules under the *Law*. In Enoch, Chapters 8:1; 9:5; 10:12-13, the offspring of the Annunaki were taught by Azazyel the secrets of Shamayim, humanity was not equipped for such knowledge at that time. That knowledge became evil in the hands of humanity because that knowledge leads to ways of dominating over other people. Now let us look at the knowledge and wisdom Elohim gave to the Hebrews, and the reasons for the knowledge received from Elohim. This is what *I AM THAT I AM* gave to Mosheh:

Shemot/Exo. 31:1-5 (AKJV):

'And the HASHEM spoke unto Mosheh, saying, 2 See, I have called by name <u>**Bezaleel**</u> the son of Uri, the son of Hur, of the tribe of <u>**Yehuwdah**</u>: 3 and I have <u>filled him with the Ruach of Elohim</u>, in <u>wisdom</u>, and in <u>understanding</u>, and in <u>knowledge</u>, and in <u>all</u> manner of workmanship, 4 to devise cunning works, to work in <u>gold</u>, and in <u>silver</u>, and in <u>brass</u>, 5 and in cutting of <u>stones</u>, to set them, and in <u>carving of timber</u>, to work in <u>all</u> manner of workmanship.'

No one else had the talents and skills Elohim gave to the Hebrews. This is tremendously important because it explains what happened to the Hebrews everywhere they were in the world. In order to inform this comment, we have to visit/revisit some crucial information. After the Hebrews were freed from Mitzrayim, and finally reached the Promised Land (Bamidbar/Num. 34:13-15), there would be many more captivities to come, due to the Hebrews <u>disobedience</u> to Elohim (Bamidbar 21:29; Devarim 28:41; 2 Kings 24,25). In the final exile, and splitting-up of the Hebrews, it was the Babylonians, who over threw the Hebrews. When the Hebrews fled, some escaped on ships, built by the *Shevet* (Tribe) of *Zebulun* (Bereshis/Gen. 49:13; Melachim Alef/1Kgs. 9:26). Many of the Hebrews escaped on foot into Mainland Africa; reaching all points of the continent, with the larger contingents reaching East Africa and North Africa. The Hebrews that fled on ships, possessing knowledge of the sea, (1 Kings 9:26) navigated to *Turtle Island* (The Americas). Here is the main perspective into the importance of why the Hebrews were sought out: Indeed it had to do with the curses of Devarim 28; moreover, it was because the Hebrews were skilled, knowledgeable craftsmen, who could do all labor skills. Not only did the Hebrews have the skills to build, they were given the knowledge of the *apothecary* (natural medicine; Shemot/Exo. 30:25-35; 37:29).

When the Europeans came to East Africa and North Africa seeking the Hebrews, they knew who they were looking for and why; however, they could not locate the Hebrews without the help of the Hamites. The Arabs also played a part in capturing Hebrews. In fact, one of the earlier groups to enslave the Hebrews were the Arabs: *The Arab Slave Trade* occurred prior to *The Trans Atlantic Slave Trade*. An excellent historical perspective of this can be found online: *Islam, Archaeology and Slavery in Africa by J. Alexander, Vol. 33, No. 1, pages 44-60*, informs this topic. Upon the Europeans locating the Hebrews, capturing them, loading them onto ships: THIS HAS TO BE ABSOLUTELY OVERSTOOD, THE ABOVE INFORMATION TELLS US WITHOUT A DOUBT, NOT ALL HEBREWS CAME TO *TURTLE ISLAND* (THE AMERICAS) ON SHIPS OF ENSLAVEMENT, THEY CAME TO TURTLE ISLAND ON THE SHIPS BUILT BY SHELOMOH BY THE SHEVET OF ZEBULUN (1 Kings 9:26). The enslaved Hebrews built houses for the enslavers in America; the enslaved built the WHITE

HOUSE IN WAHSINGTON, D.C. Not only did the enslaved Hebrews build the White House, they DESIGNED, ENGINEERED, AND CRAFTED, every intricate detail of its décor. This is very important information to overstand, first because: THIS IS INFORMATION THAT HAS BEEN KEPT SECRET OR AT MINIMUM LEFT OUT OF THE EDUCATION SYSTEM, ESPECIALLY ON THE PUBLIC SCHOOL LEVEL. THERE ARE HOWEVER, SOME HISTORICALLY "BLACK" INSTITUTIONS THAT TEACH THIS HISTORY. The first public acknowledgment of the Hebrew slaves building the *White House* came on July 25, 2016, when the first Hebrew First Lady, *Mitchell Obama*, gave a speech before the Democratic National Convention (DNC), in Philadelphia stated very eloquently: '*That she is living in the house built by slaves.*' The history of the White House and its construction can be easily verified online. Simply type into the search engine: *Mitchell Obama, Slaves built the White House.*

The Hebrews used mathematical calculations for structural integrity of the building. How did they know how to do such artistry? The knowledge is Elohim provided. It is part of who the Hebrews are by the Ruach Hakodesh. Elohim gave the knowledge as follows:

Shemot/Exo. 35:35-36 (AKJV):

> '*And HE has put in his heart that he may teach, both he, and Aholiab, the son of Ahisamach, of the tribe of Dan. 7 Them hath HE <u>filled with **wisdom**</u> of heart, to work <u>all</u> manner of work, of the **engraver**, and of the <u>cunning workman</u>, and of the **embroiderer**, in blue, and in purple, in scarlet, and in fine linen, and of the weaver, <u>even of them that do any work,</u> and of those that devise <u>cunning work.</u>*'

The skills the Hebrews possessed of the Ruach of Elohim were phenomenal. After the Europeans had exhausted the available Hebrews in *Turtle Island* (America), by working them to dealt, maiming, and murder, they needed replacements. In order to resupply the needed free labor force, the Europeans then went to Africa to find the Hebrews there, thus began *The Trans Atlantic Slave Trade.*

The Hebrews were a wealthy people, with many wise, intellectuals among them. There were many of the men involved in making the needed items for worship in the Tabernacle of the Congregation. The people brought so much material, it was requested that the people not bring anymore material to finish making the needed vessels for the sanctuary (She. 36:1-7). The Hebrews were master builders, there was nothing they could not make. Overstand this without any doubt: While the Hebrews as a whole, had great skills and knowledge, those gifts were given to the Shevet of Yehuwdah (She. 38:22).

The most mineral rich continent on earth is Africa. *I AM THAT I AM* gave the Hebrews an abundance of precious stones, and gold, and silver, and fine linens (She. 38:21-24; 39:10-14). After approximately 250 years are so of the *Trans Atlantic Slave Trade,* and more Europeans invading and colonizing more of Africa, the Europeans recognized that, not only could they use the Hebrews as slaves in America, they could also use Hebrews, and Hamites as slaves in their own land. Over the course of time the Europeans realized the richness of Africa beyond that of a cost free, forced labor source. The attention of the Europeans then turned to becoming wealthy by raping the African Continent of it precious resources. By the might of the Europeans they began to use slave labor to mine the gold and silver, and diamonds, extracting tonnage of precious minerals, and loading it on ships for transport to Europe. You can find detailed information pertaining to the raping of minerals from Africa online. A good source is: *Britannica.com/place/ South-Africa/Black-Coloured-and-Indian-political-responses.* With that said, there is a saying which fits this scenario perfectly:

> *Assertion: There is a truism that I must express boldly, declaring fact finding speech, and writings of White Historians and Theologians; and that is, when these White brothers and sisters speak and write from the data they have studied, any information they render an opinion that does not uphold supremacy of the White Race, that information should be viewed as accurate,*

*based upon the historical information they have researched. True Historians and Theologians uphold the findings of the historical evidence, without inserting their own personal bias. True Historians and Theologians, regardless of their personal upbringing, tell the truth, whether positive or negative. Their findings are neither: racial; discriminatory; sexist; chauvinistic; ethnic; subjugating, or of supremacy.*

Anthony J. Vance, October 1, 2016

The Hebrews are a strong intelligent people, created by Elohim for the express purpose of serving and worshiping HIM only. Now let us return to the reason for the *Levitical Priesthood*; to whom it is established; and what the *Law* is intended to do. To keep the Children of Yisra'el in order Elohim took a portion of the family, setting them aside from the main body of the family to do the work required to cleanse a Hebrew, who sinned (worshiped another god). The work of the *Levitical Kohen* (Priests) also involved sacrifices for the **atonement** of the *nefesh* (soul) that sinned. Overstand this: Sin and transgression are not terms of equal value though oftentimes the words are used interchangeably: sin is of the flesh, transgression is of the ruach (spirit). Let's pull this all together to inform us on why the Priesthood was brought into existence, and to whom **atonement** is to cover. Now watch this:

Devarim/Deu. 24:16 (AKJV):

*'The fathers shall not be put to death for the children, neither shall the children be put to death for the fathers: every man shall be put to death for his own sin.'*

This is one of those verses that is contradictory to the writings of the NT, in the sacrifice of a human, for another human(s). No person can be sacrificed for another person. Let's keep going, these line and precept moments will dispel many false teachings and doctrines of devils.

Ezekiel 18:20 (AKJV):

'The **nefesh** (soul) that **sins** (worships another god), <u>it shall die</u>.
The son shall not bear the iniquity of the father, neither shall
the father bear the iniquity of the son: the <u>righteousness of the
righteous shall be upon him, and the wickedness of the wicked
shall be upon him</u>.'

What is in this verse is a reinforcement that: NO PERSON CAN
BE SACRIFICED FOR ANOTHER PERSON(S). The nefesh, who
goes over to the side of the fallen malachs, at death of the flesh, will
also die the death of the **nefesh** for their **sin**. In other words, for their
transgression.

She./Exo. 32:30 (AKJV):

'And it came to pass on the morrow, that Mosheh said unto the
people, <u>You have sinned a great sin</u>: and now I will go up unto
the HASHEM; peradventure I shall make an **atonement** for
your sin.'

Mosheh had been called to the top of Sinai by The Most High
Elohim to receive the First Ten Commandments. While Mosheh was
in the mountain, the people went into idolatry. Elohim was going to
destroy the very people HE created to serve and worship HIM only
(32:8-10). In addition to destroying the Hebrews, Elohim was going to
make a new people with Mosheh as the *Progenitor* of this new people
(32:10). Listen-up: Mosheh engaged *I AM THAT I AM* in conversation.
Hear me well in this: You too can talk to Elohim directly, but you
must recognize HIM, and HIM alone as Sovereign. Mosheh spoke to
HASHEM on behalf of the people, speaking like a defense attorney at
trial (32:11-13). Now get this: Elohim listened to the voice of righteous
Mosheh, and changed HIS mind about destroying the Children of
Yisra'el (32:14). What led to Elohim coming close to destroying HIS
people is found in Shemot/Exo., Chapter 30. In close observation of
Chapter 30, it tells us what sin is: **Sin** is **idolatry**, the worshiping

another god: whether of wood, stone, gold and silver, or a demigod such as, Chemosh. One has to discern the difference between a sin such as: having the pleasure of a prostitute, and not paying for the service; and the sin of idolatry and worshiping another god.

VaYikra/Lev. 1:1-2 (AKJV):

*'And the HASHEM called unto Mosheh, and spoke unto him out of the tabernacle of the congregation, saying, 2 <u>Speak unto the children of Yisra'el</u>, and say unto them, If any man of you bring an offering unto the HASHEM, you shall bring your offering of the cattle, even of the herd, and of the flock.'*

Line and precept, here we go. These verses are speaking to the requirements necessary for a sinner to be cleansed of their sin. *I AM THAT I AM* is instructing Mosheh on what HE requires the idolater to do to be clean, after the person has ventured into worshiping another god, whether it is one of the Annunaki or an idol. Here is the point: redemption has to come by way of animal sacrifice to the HASHEM. This has to be emphatically announced: THERE IS NO HUMAN SACRIFICE FOR SIN OF ANY KIND, TO ELOHIM THAT INVOLVES THE SACRIFICE OF A HUMAN. Let's keep going, line and precept.

Bamidbar/Num. 8:19 (AKJV):

*'And I have given the Levites as a gift to Aharon and to his sons from among the <u>children of Yisra'el</u>, to do the <u>service of the children of Yisra'el</u> in the tabernacle of the congregation, and to make an **<u>atonement</u>** for the <u>children of Yisra'el</u>: that there be no plague among the <u>children of Yisra'el</u>, when the <u>children of Yisra'el</u> come near unto the sanctuary.'*

This verse drives the point home as to whom the **<u>redemption</u>** or **<u>atonement</u>** applies thereto. Repeatedly, it tells us redemption, by animal sacrifice, conducted by the Levites, applies only to the Hebrews. The

Hebrews are the only people Elohim specifically created and called, get this: HIS Chosen People. No other person or people has this first place status with TMH Elohim. Now don't get this twisted! We will come to the redemption of Gentiles as we continue this study.

1 Chronicles 6:49 (AKJV):

*'But Aharon and his sons offered upon the altar of the <u>burnt offering</u>, and on the altar of incense, and were appointed for all the work of the place most sacred, and to make an **<u>atonement for Yisra'el</u>**, according to all that Mosheh the servant of Elohim had commanded.'*

This verse reinforces who the **atonement** process is for, *The Children of Yisra'el*. The burnt offering is always of the choices animals of the herds. *I AM THAT I AM* spoke to Mosheh instructing him on what HE requires for the *sinner* (demigod worshiper, idolater) to be restored to HIM. Let us add reinforcement to this scenario.

2 Chronicles 29:24 (AKJV):

*'and the <u>priests killed them</u>, and they made **<u>reconciliation with their blood upon</u>** the altar, to make an **<u>atonement</u>** for all Yisra'el: for the king commanded that the burnt offering and the <u>sin offering should be made for all Yisra'el</u>.'*

All of the animals for sacrifice were supposed to be brought to the *Kohen* (Priests), who would kill the animal, and use its blood on the altar, to make ***reconciliation*** for the demigod worshiper and or idolater. To be reconciled means to be: forgiven, to repent, to be in remission. Over and again the Scriptures tell us: the process of **atonement** is for the Hebrew, who for whatever reason, ventured into the practices of the enemy: All people that are not Hebrew. Listen-up: All people not of the blood-line of Abraham, Yitzhaq, and *Ya'aqov* (Yisra'el) is the enemy of the Hebrews. That is fact of Scripture, but do not get the wrong takeaway from that. Elohim made provision for non-Hebrews to be acceptable to HIM. This too will be a line and precept moment as we uncover more of what is contained in the Scriptures. One other point of the above verse is this: The sprinkling of the blood of animals should register a very important act performed by TMH Elohim: The act of the *Passover.*

Nehemiah 10:33 (AKJV):

'*for the shewbread* (twelve (12) loaves of bread, one representing each shevet), *and for the continual meat offering, and for the continual burnt offering, of the <u>Shabbaths</u>, of the <u>new moons</u>, for the <u>set feasts</u>, and for the sacred things, and for the <u>**sin**</u> <u>offerings</u> to make an <u>**atonement**</u> <u>for Yisra'el</u>, and for all the work of the house of our Elohim.*'

The word **_atonement_** appears in the Scriptures seventy (70) times, sixty nine (69) times in the Old Testament, and in each case pertains to repenting to Elohim for *idolatry*, which is worshiping another god. The word **_sacrifice_** appears in the Scriptures three hundred ten (310) times, of which two hundred seventy (270) times in the Old Testament. The commonality involved with both words atonement and sacrifice is this: Of the Old Testament, these words are almost always used in reference to Yisra'el. This is very important because, while Yisra'el is the Sir name of all Twelve *Shevets* (Tribes), there is a distinction between Yisra'el and Yehuwdah. We will look at this more in reviewing 2 Samuel 21:1-5. But for now, let us continue to breakdown what a sacrifice is, to whom it applies, and WHO it is in honor thereof.

Zechariah 14:21 (AKJV):

'*Yea, every pot in **Yerushalayim** and in **Yehuwdah** shall be sacredness unto the HASHEM of hosts: and all they that **sacrifice** shall come and take of them, and seethe* (cook, boil, soak) *therein: and in that day there shall be <u>no more the</u> <u>**Canaanite**</u> in the **house** <u>of the HASHEM of hosts.</u>*'

There is something very interesting in the use of the words: **_atonement_** and **_sacrifice_**, as we have seen in all of the above Scriptures. But in the verse directly above, there are some aspects to point out: 1. There is another division in the verse; **_Yerushalayim_** is also separate from **_Yehuwdah_**, though both are Hebrew; 2. The Canaanite shall not be allowed into the "**_house_**" of Elohim. Did you catch it? Yerushalayim is the land of the *Levitical Priesthood*, separate from both Yisra'el and Yehuwdah. Yisra'el is three (3) separate divisions: The Levites, the Yisra'elites, and the Yehuwdites. Canaan will be banned from the house of the HASHEM. Canaan goes back to the time of Ham, and Ham being cursed because Ham was the vehicle by which the fallen malachs returned after the flood. That is a line and precept moment.

In the *Old Testament* the words sacrifice and atonement are used in direct connection to Elohim; whereas, in the *New Testament* the meaning changes from Yisra'el making atonement for violating the *Ten Commandments*, to offering sacrifice for *Gentiles*. The verse below shows the error of *New Testament Doctrine*, and is one of the many reasons the New Testament is not *plenary* (all authoritarian). Listen-up Hebrews: Do not throw-out the NT in its entirety, but rather use a discerning eye, and allow the Ruach Hakodesh to inform that which is written to be the truth of Scripture, or if the Scripture had been embellished.

1 Corinthians 10:20 (AKJV):

'But I say, *that the things which the* **Gentiles sacrifice, they sacrifice** *to devils, and not to Elohim: and I would* **not** *that you should have fellowship with devils.*'

This verse is case in point. The Old Testament does not include **Gentiles** offering sacrifice to the Elohim of the Hebrews. The Gentiles have invented their own religions, and serve the gods of their predecessors, those from whom they are descended, the fallen *malachs* (angels: Annunaki). No one is to make sacrifice for **atonement** except the Levitical Priests. Hebrews participating in such acts are involved with demonism. This verse cannot be more clear: Any Gentile offering sacrifice, the so-called Sun-day morning *"Lord's Supper"*, is of the devil, because Gentiles cannot offer sacrifice, and because their Sun-day *"Lord's Supper"*, is representative of human sacrifice. Elohim forbid! Hebrews come out of the ways of the Gentiles, and return to the praise, worship, and honor of Elohim only. Now watch what occurred in these next verses, they are packed with varying topics we have already touched on, and will discuss more line and precept.

2 Samuel 21:1-5 (AKJV):

> *'Then there was a famine in the days of Daviyd three years, year after year; and Daviyd inquired of the HASHEM. And the HASHEM answered, It is for __Saul, and for his bloody house, because he slew the __Gibeonites__. 2 And the king called the Gibeonites, and said unto them; (now the Gibeonites were __not__ of the children of Yisra'el, but of the remnant of the Amorites; and the children of Yisra'el had sworn unto them: and Saul sought to slay them in his zeal to the children of Yisra'el and Yehuwdah.) 3 Wherefore Daviyd said unto the Gibeonites, What shall I do for you? and wherewith shall I make the __atonement__, that you may bless the inheritance of the HASHEM? 4 And the Gibeonites said unto him, We will have no silver nor gold of Saul, nor of his house; neither for us shall you __kill__ any man in Yisra'el. And he said, What you shall say, that will I do for you. 5 And they answered the king, The man that consumed us, and that devised against us that we should be destroyed from remaining in any of the coasts of Yisra'el,'*

There was dispute after dispute between the family-line of the giants, the children of the Annunaki, and the Hebrews. The **Gibeonites** are descendants of the **Amorites** (v.2), a branch of the giants. This is a long story that covers several chapters. In brief, a Hebrew by the name of **Sheba,** from the Shevet of **Benoni** renounced his allegiance to Yisra'el (20:1). In fact, there was so much division going on at that time that Yisra'el was at odds with the *Shevet* (Tribe) of **Yehuwdah** (19:41-42). The bottom-line of the story comes to this: Sheba was under the influence of the Annunaki, **_Belial_** (Hasatan; 2 Sam. 20:1). What has to be overstood is: Yisra'el went into demigod worship many times, of which, the end result was Devarim/Deu., Chapter 28. Another point that has to be pointed out in the above verses is: There is a distinction between Yisra'el and Yehuwdah. Daviyd was attempting to make restitution to the Gibeonites for the murders of some of their men by Saul (20:1). The HASHEM told Daviyd the famine came into the land because of the murders. What Saul did was not ordained of The Most High Elohim. The Scriptures tell the Hebrews in Devarim/Deu. 7:3-4, not to involve themselves, Hebrews, with other people. Daviyd is offering to make **restitution, not atonement** for the deaths of the Gibeonites. The reason for such an assessment is one: No where have we read of human sacrifice for any act of repentance to Elohim. Moreover, sacrifice is restricted to certain animals for specific acts of transgression and or sin.

Now get this, Saul's offer was refused by the Gibeonites (2 Sam. 21:4). We are coming to the point of Saul's actions. Saul became contaminated for <u>disobedience</u> to Elohim (1 Sam. 15:22-28). Saul was a fighting force, ordering the killings of many of the contaminated family-line of the Annunaki. Saul had animals taken in victory over the contaminated **Amalekites** sacrificed to Elohim, which the animals were supposed to destroyed, directly <u>disobeying</u> that which *I AM THAT I AM* instructed Saul to do (1 Sam. 15:3; 15:15; 15:19). Here is the point: Saul went over to the Hasatan side, resulting in Saul being punished by Elohim (1 Sam 13:10-13).

All of these points from 2 Samuel 21:1-5 are many; and yet, there remains another point to be made: The Shevet of **Benoni**, the Shevet of Saul has other untoward behaviors which resulted in Benoni also becoming polluted. We will examine the contamination of Benoni in full detail as we continue these line and precept lessons of the Scriptures.

All of the hardships of Hebrew suffrage is self-inflicted; whether of a physical nature of being enslaved, or the theft of precious metals the Hebrews owned, or the loss of the Hebrew homeland. If the Hebrews had not <u>disobeyed</u> what Elohim instructed the Hebrews to do in ancient days unto this day, the Hebrews would be on top today, and not:

Devarim/Deu. 28:37 (AKJV):

*'And you shall become an astonishment, a proverb, and a byword, among **all** nations where the HASHEM shall lead you.'*

Hebrews, come out of her, and return to *I AM THAT I AM*, WHO created you from Shem (Ber./Gen. 10:21, 25; 11:18-20, 22, 24, 26), as a whole other people for the express purpose of serving and worshiping HIM only. Selah!

# THE LAWS TO GOVERN THE PEOPLE

The Book of VaYikra/Leviticus is the Book of Law. The *Laws* are written to provide specific instructions on certain topics to direct, and to guide the Hebrews on how to live their daily lives to the benefit of the Hebrews as a whole. Some of the *Laws* are of the Hebrew man *Mosheh,* and are referred to as *Mosaic Law.* However, the most important *Laws* come from *I AM THAT I AM.* Breaking the Law can result in a multitude of unfortunate outcomes. But even so, the punishments to come from breaking the *Law* may not be as substantial as compared to breaking a *Commandment,* and most importantly: *THE TEN COMMANDMENTS.*

A *Commandment* means: It is imperative, and that there is no other option: Do not veer to the left or to the right, stay the course. The *Law* has to do with the customs of a people, and what is the prescribed behavior for the community as a whole. The words Law and Commandment are used interchangeably; however, they are not interchangeable because, the two words do not bear the same importance.

*The Book of VaYikra/Leviticus* tells us more about the ***Torah*** (Law), also referred to as the *Pentateuch.* The Torah is the First Five Books of Scripture: Bereshis/Genesis; Shemot/Exodus; VaYikra/Leviticus; Bamidbar/Numbers; and Devarim/Deuteronomy. The Torah (*Pentateuch*) is what the Hebrew Yisra'elites are to use to conduct their daily lives therefrom. Many Hebrews only know about the *Ten Commandments*; the truth is, there are 613 rules in the Torah, written to the Hebrew Yisra'elites only. The fact of the *Old Testament* is: From Bereshis/Gen. to Malachi, the entire book is the book of the Hebrews. The focus in these lessons is to bring out the most important aspects of the Torah. Let me say this: I speak wisdom: To sustain all of the rules under Torah was near impossible in ancient days; in modern times, it is a completely impossible task to accomplish: Imagine everyone having to offer up sacrifice for **<u>sin</u>** (idolatry and or demigod worship); there would have to be millions of animals slaughtered each day to cover our sins: men and women would be stoned to death in the streets daily for the sins we commit; and many Hebrews would not be able to keep employment because the Hebrews are not permitted to work on the *Shabbath Day*. Now to the point at hand: The Ten Commandments are what the Hebrews must maintain throughout all generations; the Shabbath Day is a Commandment, not a Law. Here is Wisdom: though today we have occupations that require us to work on the Seventh Day, that does not equate to not being able to honor the Seventh Day. If you must work on the Shabbath Day, set some time aside in the Shabbath Day, reserved for you and the Abba only. Work your occupation, which is the means by which you earn wages to take care of your family. However, if you are cutting the grass; washing your car on the Shabbath Day, I speak boldly: You are wrong. Having a wounded animal on the Shabbath Day, for goodness sake, please take care of the wounded animal. You get the point. Some things we have to take care of even on the Shabbath Day; know the difference between a chore, and doing that is necessary. *I AM THAT I AM* Commanded us to keep the Seventh Day sacred.

Though this section of our reading mostly deals with the Book of VaYikra, let us examine some specific verses from Shemot first, as Shemot gives the absolutely best information regarding a Commandment of Elohim.

Shemot/Exo. 20: 1-11 (AKJV):

> 'And **<u>Elohim spoke</u>** all these words, saying, 2 I AM the HASHEM your Elohim, which have brought you out of the land of **<u>Mitzrayim</u>** (Egypt), out of the house of **<u>bondage</u>** (Egypt). 3 **<u>You shall have no other gods before me</u>**. 4 You shall **<u>not make unto you any graven image, or any likeness</u>** of any thing that is in **<u>Shamayim</u>** (heaven) **<u>above</u>**, or that is in the **<u>earth beneath,</u>** or that is in the **<u>water under the earth</u>**. 5 You shall **<u>not bow down thyself</u>** to them, nor serve them: for I the HASHEM your Elohim am a envious Elohim,

*visiting the iniquity of the fathers upon the **children unto the third and fourth generation** of them that **hate ME**; 6 And showing mercy unto thousands of them that **love ME**, and keep MY Commandments. 7 You shall not take the **name of the HASHEM your Elohim in vain**; for the HASHEM will not hold him guiltless that takes HIS name in vain. 8 Remember the **Shabbath day**, to keep it sacred. 9 Six days shall you labor, and do all your work: 10 But the **Seventh Day is the Shabbath of the HASHEM your Elohim** : in it you shall not do any work, you, nor your son, nor your daughter, your manservant, nor your maidservant, nor your cattle, nor your stranger that is within your gates: 11 For in six days the HASHEM made heaven and earth, the sea, and all that in them is, and rested the Seventh Day: wherefore the HASHEM blessed the Shabbath Day, and hallowed it.'*

HASHEM has told us explicitly to <u>obey</u> HIS Commands, and that HIS Commands are to the Hebrews. How do we know this is only to the Hebrews? Because it says: Have no other gods, and it is to those who love HIM. Those other people serve their gods, and not the Elohim of the Hebrews. HE tells us exclusively to keep the Shabbath Day. No where in the Scriptures will you find Elohim, Ha Mashiach, or Mosheh say, to make Sunday a day of worship or that Sunday is of sacredness. Sunday is the first day of the week. The reason the world worships their gods on Sunday has to do with *Constantine,* and the *Roman Catholic Church.* When Constantine was the Emperor, he ordered the change that was given to him, that was ordained by *Pope Julius the First,* and is to this day sanctioned by the *Roman Catholic Church.* This change came about in the time Rome was dominating Europe. The time period this occurred is called the *Hellenizing Period.* It was during this time period the *Roman Empire,* under *Constantine,* forced Christianity upon the people. This new religion was based mostly in Roman Superiority. From Rome, the Vatican, the entire world would eventually suffer from the effects of the Christian doctrine forced upon many. Even though in time, many would come to Christianity willingly, they had no idea they were operating under mind manipulation. There is something else

145

in these verses, slapping us right in the face: There is a plurality in these Commandments that is not acknowledged by most people, and that is the word **gods**. Hear me well in this: Molech, Baal, Lucifer, Hasatan, and many more are gods, they are demigods, who have power but not the power of The Most High Elohim.

*I AM THAT I AM* continued to speak to HIS servant Mosheh, continuing to give Mosheh Commands for the Hebrew people.

Shemot/Exo. 20: 12-17 (AKJV):

> '12 Honor_**your father and your mother**: that your days may be long upon the land which the HASHEM your Elohim give you. 13 You shall **not kill**. 14 You shall not **commit adultery**. 15 You shall **not steal**. 16 You shall **not bear false witness** against your neighbor. 17 You shall not covet your neighbor's **house**, You shall not covet your neighbor's wife, nor his manservant, nor his maidservant, nor his ox, nor his ass, nor any thing that is your neighbor's.'

Let me ask you a question: Where in the Scriptures is it written that Ha Mashiach changed any of the Ten Commandments? No where is the answer. The Fourth Commandment establishes the Shabbath Day as the Seventh Day (Shemot/Exo. 20:8-10). The Shabbath Day is an everlasting memorial of the Day of Rest. This is explained in:

Shemot/Exo. 31:14 (AKJV):

> 'You shall **keep the Shabbath** therefore; for it is sacred unto you: every one that **defiles it shall surely be put to death**: for whosoever does any work therein, that soul shall be **cut off from among his people**.'

*I AM THAT I AM* has made it perfectly overstood: This Day is sacred unto HIM, and those, who willingly violate the Shabbath are to be put away from the family. Let me be absolutely clear in stating the following: I am not advocating for anyone to be put to death; I am simply presenting you with the written Scriptures. To practice first day of the week rest is in direct violation of the Scriptures. Something else I have to also say is: In overstanding the Scriptures, is to understand why Christianity and Hebrew Spirituality are in opposition to one another: Christianity is religion that serves pagan ritualism; whereas, Hebrew Spirituality is serving the True Creator of the Hebrews, The Most High Elohim. The Scriptures must be pulled together for better overstanding. Here, the Commandments in VaYikra, the Book of the Law have been pulled into Shemot, in order to show how some Hebrew regulations are of Elohim directly, and some are of Mosheh. Let us now delve into some of the Laws that came from Mosheh. Keep in mind that the Ten Commandments are direct orders from Elohim, and that the *Mosaic Laws* are about community. Furthermore, laws are created for control of community behaviors. Laws come about when something in society becomes a problem, and those behaviors are having an adverse effect on the people.

VaYikra/Lev. Chapters 1-7, concern the dietary Laws for offerings; what the purpose of dietary regulation is, and to whom the offerings apply to in carrying out the sacrifice: the priests. The laws pertaining to offerings cover meats (v. 2:7-13), and vegetables (v. 2:14). For most people reading VaYikra is dry, boring reading; however, there are some parts of VaYikra that are conceptual rules that should be strictly adhered thereto. Overstand this: The Scriptures use a redundancy to make some points stand out as important. When it comes to meats, make no mistake about how it is to be cooked for consumption.

VaYikra/Lev. 3:17; 7:26 (AKJV):

> '*It shall be a **perpetual statute** for your generations throughout all your dwellings, that you **eat neither fat nor blood**. ... Moreover you shall **eat no manner of blood**, whether it be of fowl or of beast, in any of your dwellings.*'

These verses makes it apparently clear, no Hebrew is to eat any meat that is not completely cooked. Eating meat rare, medium rare, or that is still pink on the inside is against the *Law*: it is unclean. Eating the fat is really bad for one's health, it can and does lead to damage in the body's circulatory system. Fat causes <u>heart disease, high cholesterol, leading to cardiovascular collapse</u>, and many other health issues. For all who believe there are no contradictions in the bible, and that the bible is *plenary* (all authoritative), it is not. The New Testament in many instances is anti-Torah. Let us examine some New Testament verses that are absolutely in opposition to the above verses:

St. Mattithyahu 26:26-28 (AKJV):

> 'And as they were eating, **_J-sus_** took bread, and blessed it, and broke it, and gave it to the disciples, and said, Take, eat; this is **_my body_**. 27 And he took the cup, and gave thanks, and gave it to them, saying, Drink you all of it; 28 for this is **_my blood_** of the **_new testament_**, which is shed for many for the remission of sins.'

These verses are not of Elohim, they are of Hasatan. The Hebrews are strictly forbidden to eat raw meat, and certainly are not allowed to drink blood. The representation in these verses is that of cannibalism, though it is supposed to be a spiritual encounter, it is not. It is Hasatanic. Hebrews following the New Testament are not following Torah. Is there any credence to the NT? Indeed there are parts of the NT that line-up with the Torah. However, let us look at what Ha Mashiach had to say about the Law. Mattithyahu 2:15, 17, 23; 4:14; 8:17; 12:17; 13:14, and many more verses speak on fulfilling the Law, as the Prophets Yeremiah, and Esaias laid out for the Hebrews. The Laws of Torah has never been overturned by the Abba, Ha Mashiach, or the Ruach Hakodesh. Mashiach Himself said in Mattithyahu 5:18 (AKJV):

> 'For verily I say unto you, Till heaven and earth pass, one jot or one tittle shall in **_no wise pass from the law_**, till **_all_** be fulfilled.'

Overstand this, there is no letter "J" in the Hebrew language; therefore, the above verse cannot be the exact words of Ha Mashiach,

Who spoke Hebrew. But even more important to know is this, and you can check multiple sources such as, *Thesaurus,* for the words "jot" and "tittle". Be no longer deceived by cleverly written passages of Scripture, the language being changed by those of evil intent. What the verse is actually saying is: *'Not one damning word of the Torah, not even the smallest piece, shall be removed from the Law until all of the Prophesy is Fulfilled'.* This is another reason all of the parts of Scripture, scattered in many places of the bible have to be pulled together for better overstanding of Scripture. The transcribing of the Hebrew Scrolls to *Greek,* to *Arabic,* to *Latin,* and on to *English,* the Scrolls lost much of their meaning in translation. In fact, when all of those languages began to have some words used commonly between them, is when English actually began to form as a language about 1,000 A.D.. The combination language that formed of <u>Italian, French, Arabic, Spanish, and Greek</u> is referred to as the *"Lingua Franca"*.

When you look at the historical information available to us, and combine that information with word definition, and most importantly Scripture, the blinders will drop from your eyes. This is what the *Historian John Wycliffe* wrote about the English language:

# HISTORY OF THE ENGLISH LANGUAGE BIBLE

*"The Pre-Reformation History of the Bible From 1,400 BC to 1,400 AD*

*The story of how we got the English language Bible is, for the most part, the story of the Protestant Reformation which began in the <u>late 14<sup>th</sup> Century AD with John Wycliffe</u>. Indeed, <u>if we go back more than just one thousand years, there is no language recognizable as "English" that even existed anywhere</u>. The story of the Bible is much older than that, however"*.

greattimeline.com

There is one other crucial piece of information to consider about words written in English with regard to Scripture. In order to transcribe a manuscript accurately, it has to be a *transliteration*. In other words: words found in the manuscript being transcribed, that do not have an exact match in the receiving language, that word should be added to the *Lexicon* of the receiving language, otherwise the full meaning is lost in translation. In example, the first *First King James Bible*. That bible, the first 1611 publication contains no *"J"* words because the letter *"J"* had not been invented at the time of publication. The name *"James"* was spelled *"Iames"*, as the letter *"J"* was created from the letter *"I"*. What more proof can one have than seeing the book, with the king's name spelled "Iames"? You can find this book for sale at various book sellers.

Any book you are reading about history or Scripture prior to 1611 using the letter *"J"* to spell any words, and most importantly, the names of cities, countries, or people is a fabrication to distort the truth of who the Hebrews are, and where they originally lived. Watch this!

*"The form of 'J' was unknown in any alphabet until the 14<sup>th</sup> century. Either symbol (J,I) used initially generally had the consonantal sound of Y as in year. Gradually, the two symbols (J,I) were differentiated, the J usually acquiring consonantal force and thus becoming regarded as a consonant, and the I becoming a vowel. It was not until 1630 that the differentiation became general in England."*

The Encyclopedia Americana

Everything in history since the advent of written language has been documented somewhere, by someone. The above history on the letter "*J*" comes from a source of great credibility. There should be no words, absolutely zilch, written in the Old Testament spelled with a "*J*". The names in the Scriptures were changed to hide the truth of the characters of Scriptures, the Hebrews.

Now to a topic that is antithetical to the Scriptures. Many *ekklesia* (churches) have covenants that state: '*Abstain from all alcohol*'. That is not what *I AM THAT I AM* instructed for the Hebrews. Anyone with an overstanding of the Torah will know that kind of institutional commitment is not Scriptural. Let us now pull the Scriptures together for clarity.

VaYikra/Lev. 10:9 (AKJV):

'*Do not drink wine nor strong drink, you, nor your sons with you, when you go into the Tabernacle of the Congregation, because you will die: it shall be a <u>statute for ever throughout your generations</u>:*'

These are the instructions Elohim gave to Aharon, the *Progenitor* of the *Levitical Priesthood* (VaY./Lev. 10:8). As Elohim had spoken to Aw-dawn, Abraham, Yitzhaq, Ya'aqov, and Mosheh, HE also spoke directly to Aharon. The instructions were to assure the *Kohen* (Priests) had clarity of mind in performing the duties of the tabernacle. The order of operations for the tabernacle require no deviation from the direction

Elohim prescribed. For this segment of our study, we will group several verses together, followed by expounding upon what the verses tell us collectively. Now watch this line and precept.

> Shemot/Exo. 22:29 - 29:40 ; Yudges 9:13; 2 Kings 18:32; Bamidbar/Num. 18:12 (AKJV):

> *'You shall not delay to offer the first of your ripe fruits, and of your **liquors**: the firstborn of your sons shall you give unto ME. ... 29:40: And with the one lamb a tenth deal of flour mingled with the fourth part of an hin of beaten oil; and the fourth part of an hin of **wine** for a <u>drink offering</u> ...Yudges 9:13: And the vine said unto them, Should I leave my **wine**, which cheers <u>Elohim and man</u>, and go to be promoted over the trees? ... 2 Kings 18:32: until I come and take you away to a land like your own land, a land of corn and **wine**, a land of bread and **vineyards**, a land of oil olive and of honey, that ye may live, and not die: and hearken not unto Hezekiah, when he persuade you, saying, The HASHEM will deliver us. ... Bamidbar/Num. 18:12: All the best of the oil, and all the **best of the wine**, and of the wheat, the first fruits of them which they shall offer unto the HASHEM, them have I given to you.'*

There is no need to beleaguer the point. These verses spell it out line by line. To teach complete abstention from alcohol is *antithetical*. To throw out drinking alcohol means, not keeping the *Law* Elohim gave us for the *Passover* (VaY./Lev. 23:5), and the *Festival of Wine* (VaY./Lev. 23:13). Did you catch what that means? It means that, when the Hebrews are brought back together from the scattering, these festivals will come into play, and if not, the Hebrews are once again in <u>disobedience</u>. We will now transition the topic to hygiene and sexually transmitted disease.

Have you ever read in the Scriptures anything pertaining to <u>venereal disease</u> or a <u>woman on her period</u>? As shocking to some as it might be, the Scriptures do speak to issues of life the *ekklesia* (church) will not discuss, for fear of indecency. I have to ask, if it is in the Scriptures, how can a topic be indecent or taboo? No doubt about it, the fifteenth chapter of VaYikra/Lev. is related to sex. The man having sex, and then developing a disease causing his semen to continually flow from his penis has likely been infected with gonorrhea or syphilis, and he is unclean (15:2-3). The infected person is to wash anything that he has come into contact with, and he is to bathe himself. If the infected person touches someone else, before he has washed all of the garments he has touched, and washed himself, whomsoever he has touched is dirty, and must wash their clothes, and bathe (15:10). If you don't believe this is talking about sexually transmitted disease, and sex in general, look at this:

VaYikra/Lev. 15:16-18 (AKJV):

*'And if any man's **semen of copulation** go out from him, then he shall wash all his flesh in water, and be unclean until the evening. 17 And every garment, and every skin, whereon is the semen of copulation, shall be washed with water, and be unclean until the evening. 18 The woman also with whom man shall have **sex with reaching orgasm**, they shall both bathe themselves in water, and be unclean until the evening.'*

What these verses are telling us is: take a bath after having sexual intercourse, it is about cleanliness. Speaking firmly in language we use today, these verses say: After having your pleasure, go and wash your personal parts, don't lay all night with vaginal fluid on the man, and his semen still inside the woman, at least the part that is leaking from her. That is disgusting if left for hours and hours, and does lead to odor and possible infection. The first fifteen verses of VaYikra, Chapter 15, is about venereal disease, and how to be cured from the disease. Verse 16 transitions into good hygiene after having sex. Not washing after exchanging body fluids with another person is filthiness.

Now look at what the Scriptures say about the woman on her period:

VaYikra/Lev. 15:19; 24 (AKJV):

*'Also you **<u>shall not approach</u>** unto a woman to uncover her nakedness, as long as she is put apart for her uncleanness. ...
24 And if any man have sex with her at all, and her menses be upon him, he shall be **<u>unclean seven days</u>**; and all the bed whereon he slept shall be unclean.'*

Having sex when a woman is on her period is one of the most filthy acts men and women commit. This is a line upon line, and precept upon precept moment. The laws of men and women dealing with semen, and blood are all found in VaYikra/Lev., Chapter 18. Many men and women commit this abomination monthly because of our great sexual prowess and desire. The truth in Scripture says: DO NOT HAVE SEX WITH A WOMAN HAVING HER MENSES. VaYikra 18 tells us about bestiality, homosexuality, incest, and moreover, hear this well: Having sex with anyone under the influence of a demigod; such as, Molech. You could possibly been invaded by and evil spirit (VaY./ Lev.18:21). The conclusion of all of the acts listed in Chapter 18 is this: *'For all these abominations have the men of the land done, which were before you, and the land is defiled; (18:27)'* To have sex with a woman on her period, is no different than homosexuality, bestiality, or offering sacrifice to another god; it is all <u>abomination</u>. Are you shocked to know the common practice of having sex with a wife/woman on her period is an abomination? The thing is, in the *ekklesia* (church) today, the pastors fail the people in teaching because they don't teach according to the Laws of Scripture that matter. This Law is about your cleanliness before the Elohim. Discontinue allowing the half-truths, and untruths of the ekklesia to lead you in the wrong direction. Believe it or not, if your pastor is not teaching you from the Torah, he is an agent of Hasatan. Grace will not and cannot replace the *Law*. Many will perish because of a lack of following the Law. These laws are about your fitness of <u>redemption</u>; the Law of sexual cleanliness is vital to your <u>obedience</u> to Elohim. I would be in complete error not to say this also: There is nothing new under the sun. All of the acts covered in VaYikra, Chapter

28 have been going on since the time of the fallen malachs. How say you? The mention of Molech for one (18:21), and even more telling is verse 24, Elohim said: The other nations, which HE separated the Hebrews therefrom, all committed all of the acts listed in the chapter.

Next we will look at information about the Hebrews in slavery, and the *Law*. The Hebrew ancestors knew the *Law*, but they broke the *Law*. That <u>disobedience</u> to *I AM THAT I AM* would cause difficult times for the Hebrews for many years to come. The Law tells the Hebrews what to do, and what not to do.

> VaYikra/Lev. 26:1-2 (AKJV):
>
> *'You shall make you **no idols nor** <u>graven image</u>, neither rear you up a <u>standing image</u>, neither shall you set up <u>any image of **stone**</u> <u>in your **land**</u>, to bow down unto it: for I AM the HASHEM your Elohim. 2 You shall <u>keep MY Shabbaths</u>, and **reverence** MY sanctuary: I AM the HASHEM.'*

<u>No means no; nor means no; rear-up means to build; stand-up means to erect.</u> The very house of worship most people attend are an abomination to The Most High Elohim. That wooden or metal cross symbol is either an **idol** or **graven image.** In some lands the enemy has erected massive statues of religious figures. Some countries in South America, and Africa, have wasted many resources building some of the largest statues in the world in their land. Most people have no idea they are in violation of the **Shabbath Day** by not keeping the Shabbath Day, a day of rest, which Day is the **Seventh Day**, not sun god day. Now don't get this twisted: In modern times, many have to work on the Shabbath Day because the **enemy** has set-up the system that way in <u>disobedience</u> to Elohim. However, that does not mean, one cannot set some time aside in the Shabbath Day to spend time with the Abba.

Now watch this! *I AM THAT I AM* has told us what will happen when the Hebrews go into <u>disobedience</u>. What must I do to be pleasing to Elohim?

VaYikra/Lev. 26:15-17 (AKJV):

*'and if you shall* <u>*despise MY statutes*</u>*, or if your soul* <u>*abhor*</u>
*MY rulings, so that you will not do* <u>*all*</u> *MY Commandments,*
*but that you break MY covenant: 16 I also will do this unto*
*you; I will even appoint over you* <u>*terror*</u> (police brutality, hate
groups)*,* <u>*consumption*</u> (unhealthy food or the lack of food),
<u>*and the burning ague*</u> (disease such as malaria; Corona virus),
*that shall consume the eyes, and cause sorrow of heart. and you*
*shall sow your seed in vain,* <u>*for your enemies*</u> *shall eat it. 17 And*
*I will set MY face against you, and you shall be* <u>*slain before your*</u>
<u>***enemies***</u> (knee on the neck; shot in the back)*: they that* <u>*hate*</u>
<u>*you shall* **reign** *over you*</u> (inequitable laws; imprisonment)*;*
*and you shall flee when none is in pursuit of you.'*

This Prophetic Promise from Elohim to HIS people is in full effect
unto this day. The Hebrews are dissident to the only ONE WHO can
protect them from the enemy. We have seen in this reading repeatedly
who the enemy is: the offspring of the fallen malachs. The hunger
and wasting away of some people in the world is this curse. The
<u>enemy</u> trodding many underfoot: the *amalgamation* of the Hebrews
everywhere in the world the Hebrews fled in the *Babylonian Exile*, the
enemy came in pursuit of the the Hebrews: befriending the Hebrews,
learning from the Hebrews how to live in the land. After learning what
they needed to know about the land, the enemy would then put their
plan into action on how to overthrow the Hebrews, and take Hebrew
lands by whatsoever means necessary. After taking over the land, the
enemy would begin the next step in the process: the *acculturation* of the
Hebrews. In this phrase of the overthrow, the cultural practices of the
Hebrews would be slowly replaced with the culture of the enemy, until
the Hebrew culture would be lost, and all of the practices of the enemy
become the norm to the Hebrews. The last phase of the overthrow
is *assimilation*. This part of the overthrow is at minimum a two-fold
scheme of trickery. Assimilation is the inclusive, and simultaneously,
exclusive portion of the enemy controlling the Hebrews everywhere in
the world the Hebrews live. Listen-up and hear me well: This part of

the plan is even more heinous than *amalgamation* and *acculturation*. *Assimilation* is where the Hebrew outwardly is given the facade of being equal to the enemy, but inwardly, is ostracized into an inferior lifestyle. What I mean by this is: the Hebrew has the appearance of being on equal footing of the enemy in society; however, when it comes down to a dispute between the Hebrew and the enemy, if the issue has to go before the courts, the biased inequity system is preset to rule against the Hebrew. Moreover, in the assimilation part of the scheme is this: The financial system of the enemy is based upon the Hebrew. Hear me well in this: the Hebrew is the basis of the *stock market* in many lands: the Hebrew is either the free labor system by enslavement, or imprisonment, or are paid the lowest wages compared to the pay of the enemy. The Hebrews were scattered to all lands for one main cause: <u>Disobedience</u> to TMH Elohim.

All of the above *tenants*: amalgamation, acculturation, and assimilation all lead to another tenant known as *intersectionalism*. What this means is, when it comes to where the Hebrews live is controlled by pricing homes in certain areas above the affordability of the low wage earners. The invisible line of intersectionalism then goes into, where tax money is collected and its use. In example: tax money collected and then dispersed for public education is disproportionately used to fund schools in affluent areas where the enemy lives, and only a small portion of that money is used to fund schools in areas where the Hebrews live. That too then leads to disparity in education: creating the intersection where the Hebrew and the enemy are kept at a distance in quality education. The two corners keeping the Hebrew on one side of the street, and the enemy on the other side of the street. This in-turn leads to greater poverty in Hebrew neighborhoods, and increased criminal activity by desperate people. Poor education leads to less opportunity for the Hebrew to gain wealth. Do you overstand what all of this comes down to? The Hebrews left the Laws Elohim gave to them, and in <u>disobedience</u>, all of the Prophetic Promises in VaYikra/Lev. 26:15-17 are in full effect. Watch this! Line upon line, and precept upon precept, here we go.

VaYikra/Lev. 26:3-4; 36-39 (AKJV):

*'If you <u>walk in MY statutes</u>, and keep MY <u>Commandments</u>, and do them; 4 then I will give you rain in due season, and the land shall yield her increase, and the trees of the field shall yield their fruit. … 36 And upon them that are <u>left alive of you</u>* (not thrown into the sea, or hung, or starved to death) *I will send a faintness into their hearts in the <u>lands</u> of their **enemies*** (the lands of the kidnappers); *and the sound of a shaken leaf shall chase them; and they shall flee, as fleeing from a **<u>sword</u>*** (gun); *and they shall fall when none pursue. 37 And they shall <u>fall one upon another</u>* (killing their own people), *as it were before a sword, when none pursue: and you shall have **<u>no power</u>*** (two sets of rules under the laws) *to stand before your **enemies**. 38 And you shall <u>perish among the **heathen**</u>* (the oppressors), *and the land of <u>your **enemies**</u>* (captors) *<u>shall eat you up</u>. 39 And they that are left of you shall pine away in their iniquity in your **enemies' lands**; and also in the <u>iniquities of their fathers</u> shall they pine away with them.'*

The Hebrews failed to keep the Commandments of Elohim, and as a result, they were punished by Elohim. The Hebrews of every land are in peril: trodden under foot; discriminated against; in fear of persecution; murdered; in fear of their children leaving home, and never returning at the hands of the enemy; in want of food, starving to death in many lands. The acts and <u>disobedience</u> of the ancestors to HASHEM, centuries past, have continued to plague the Hebrews unto this day. The one reason why is this: The <u>disobedience</u> of the forefathers is still in play today. The only way forward for the Hebrews is to come out of the religious practices of the **enemy**, and to return to Elohim in <u>obedience</u> to the *Laws* HE gave the Hebrews to live by. Do you overstand? The enemy, the children of the fallen *malachs* (angels) are in control of this planet, and have persuaded the world to follow their gods, the *Annunaki*. There is one other point of focus in these verses: "***enemies' lands***". This plurality means: Wheresoever the Hebrews have been exiled: North and South America, Africa, Asia, or Europe, multiple lands, the heathens will rule over the Hebrews, until the Hebrews return to the ONE, Who created them to serve and worship HIM only. Line and precept. Next let us examine what the *Historians* have to say about religion.

> 1444 – Present *"While the **African continent is being raped**, the Pan-African synthesis starts on the slave ships and evolves into an even greater synthesis in the Americas. An African-based legacy creates a **Neo-African culture** manifested in **religion, language – sermons, oratory** and other forms of oral literature, music, dance, quiltmaking, cuisine."*

> AFRICAN DIASPORA IV Period of Enslavement, Colonialism and Resistance, See Painter – Chapter 2; Caldwell

> *"The forces here were swiftly followed by reinforcements so that, within 7 years, the **Muslim conquerors**, who came to be known as **The Moors**, were in control of most of the peninsula – a situation that was to remain more or less intact for the next 400 years – but, in some parts, for the next 700.*

> *Initially, **Islamic Spain – known as Al-Andalus** – formed a part of the North African province controlled by Damascus, the capital of the Islamic world. In effect this meant that the caliphs, or leaders, in Spain were little more than puppets."*

spanish-fiestas.com/history/moors

What is reflected in this historical data is this: The enemy of the Hebrews are the children of Ishmael, and their cousins, who became the Spaniards. Both groups enslaved the Hebrews, forcing their gods, and their religions onto the Hebrews. The Moors came from Ham, and were the first inhabitants of the whole of Europe. The picture should be more clear in this: The Moors played a huge role in the enslavement of the Hebrews. This will be brought out in great detail in our study of Devarim/Due. Now let us incorporate what the *Historian* and *Theologian* James Cone wrote about the enslaved Hebrews.

> *"The record shows clearly that black slaves believed that just as God had delivered Moses and the Israelites from Egyptian bondage, God also will deliver black people from American slavery. And they expressed that theological truth in song.*
>
> *Oh Mary, don't you weep, don't you moan,*
> *Oh Mary, don't you weep, don't you moan,*
> *Pharaoh's army got drowned,*
> *Oh Mary, don't you weep.*
>
> *That truth did not come from white preachers; it came from a liberating encounter with the One who is the Author of black faith and existence. As theologians, we must ask: What is the source and meaning of freedom expressed in this spiritual?*
>
> *Oh Freedom! Oh Freedom!*
> *Oh Freedom, I love thee!*
> *And before I'll be a slave,*
> *I'll be buried in my grave*
> *And go home to my Lord and be free.*
>
> *Here freedom is obviously a structure of, and a movement in, historical existence. It is black slaves accepting the risk and burden of self-affirmation, of liberation in history. That is the meaning of the phrase, "And before I'll be a slave, I'll be buried in my grave." But without negating history, the last line of this spiritual places freedom beyond the historical context, "And go home to my Lord and be free." In this context, freedom is eschatological. It is the anticipation of freedom, a vision of a new heaven and a new earth. Black slaves recognized that human freedom is transcendent-that is, a constituent of the future-which made it impossible to identify humanity exclusively with meager attainment in history."*

Cone, James H., GOD of the OPPRESSED, Orbis Books, Mary Knoll, NY 1054500308, ISBN: 978-1-57075-158-5, 1997, pages 10-11

Note: Eschatological, the cycle of life: life, death, heaven, hell.

What this tells us is: Though the enslaved were in bondage, many of them realized the god of the enemy is not the Elohim of the Hebrews. However, there were multifactoral elements occuring at the same time. Not only were the Hebrews in enslavement, they were being stripped of their Hebrew Heritage; they were not allowed to speak the Hebrew language or to teach their history to their children. In fact, the enemy would use the most heinous of tactics to prevent the transfer of data from the older generation to the younger generation. This too will be discussed in great detail in our study of Devarim/Deu..

During the time of Hebrew enslavement and beyond, the Hebrew was viewed as nothing more than an animal; to be specific, the Hebrew was *chattel* (human livestock). However, not all of the envaders of lands where Hebrews lived; such as, the Americas, South Africa, and more, were all of evil influence. In America, the envaders of good countenance, and those of evil countenance would have to reach an agreement on their enslaved chattel. The following is the compromise reached by the Government of the United States of America with regard to their enslaved population of Hebrews.

*"Article I, Section. 2 [Slaves count as 3/5 persons]*

*Representatives and direct Taxes shall be apportioned among the several States which may be included within this Union, according to their respective Numbers, which shall be determined by adding to the whole Number of free Persons, including those bound to Service for a Term of Years, and excluding Indians not taxed, **three fifths of all other Persons [i.e., slaves]**."*

*"Before the Civil War ended, Congress passed, and sent to the states for ratification, the **Thirteenth Amendment which abolished "slavery" and "involuntary servitude"** and authorized Congress to enact "appropriate legislation" implementing the abolition."* Adopted: December 18, 1865.

wiseconservatism.com/2011/01/06/35th-clause-in-the-constitution-what-is-it-and-why-was-it-put-in/

The *Thirteenth Amendment* of itself is a document filled with deception. While it reads that the Hebrews are now free, they were not. Hold this in memory because this is also a precursor to The Book of Devarim/Deu. The captors of the Hebrews used the bible as one tactic to reinforce their dominant position over the enslaved. The very book the captors used to keep their superior position, they violated what the *Law* informed on slavery. What the captors did to the Hebrews went against the very bible they used to keep the Hebrews in enslavement, and their own people in the mindset of superiority. The *Torah*, the third book of the Torah speaks on the year of *Yowbel* (Yubile). Mind you, what the captors did was outright theft of the people and property; but even so, the year of *Yowbel* is the time when every possession sold or bond servant was to be liberated.

VaYikra/Lev. 25:10 (AKJV):

*'And you shall __hallow the **fiftieth** year__, and proclaim liberty throughout all the land unto __all__ the inhabitants thereof: it shall be a Yubile unto you; and you shall __return every man unto his possession__, and you shall __return every man unto his family.__'*

This section of the Bible alone tells us, the Hebrew enslavers were wrong on many levels: Their gods are not the Elohim of the Hebrews because if so, they would have released the Hebrews at the time of *Yowbel*. The captors also committed theft, violating the Commandments of Yowbel; many of the captors had sexual intercourse (raped) betrothed

Hebrew women and men; they coveted (stole) another man's property. You get the idea, they violated every one of the Ten Commandments. Then the captors violated the Commandment to free the people (Lev. 25:39-40): their land, possessions, and so forth in the year of Yowbel. Yowbel is one of the most Sacred Days to honor Elohim (Lev. 25:12). The entire Chapter of Leviticus 25 is about <u>equity</u> for all.

Leviticus 25:42-44 (AKJV):

'*For they are MY servants, which I brought forth out of the land of Egypt: they* ***shall not be sold as bondmen***. *43* ***You shall not rule over him with rigor****; but shall fear your Elohim. 44 Both your bondmen, and your bond-maids, which you shall have,* ***shall be of the heathen*** *that are round about you; of them shall you buy bondmen and bond-maids.*'

What the enslavers did was to turn the Scriptures upside down: making the Hebrews the heathen and the heathen the Hebrews. They stole everything from the Hebrews: land, possessions, riches, and people. And yet, this all falls on the Hebrews for their recurring <u>disobedience</u> to Elohim by taking up the ways of the heathens, worshiping the gods of the enemy.

Furthermore, in overstanding the Scriptures is to understand why Edom and the Hebrews are enemies unto this day. The Hebrew people need to stop trying to welcome in our enemies (Ezra 9:12). Finally from the Book of VaYikra/Lev. is something that has to be pointed out about the Covenants of Elohim, many have not recognized that there have been many Covenants. This is what *I AM THAT I AM* said to Mosheh:

VaYikra/Lev. 26:42 (AKJV):

'*Then will I remember MY Covenant with* ***Ya'aqov****, and also MY Covenant with* ***Yitzhaq****, and also MY Covenant with* ***Abraham*** *will I remember; and I will remember the land.*'

The Covenants Elohim made with the three of them were all

separate entities, and yet intertwined coming down the family-line in the establishment of a *New People* called the Hebrews. Others in this family-line of the Covenant include <u>Mosheh, Yosef, and Ha Mashiach</u>. To Elohim is all of the honor and glory. Selah.

# COMBINING THE CANONS THAT DISCUSS REPRODUCTION

I have chosen this section of the Scriptures to discuss sexuality because most people don't read *The Book of Bamidbar/Num.* for various reasons. This segment will present in all line upon line and precept upon precept format. *Sexuality*: bestiality; prostitution; homosexuality; rape; incest: All of these topics are in the Scriptures, but even so these topics are not discussed in the *ekklesia* (church). Without a clear overstanding of the sexual content in Scripture, one will never come to the knowledge of *eretz* (earth), and of *Shamayim* (Heaven); of the fallen *malachs* (angels; Annunaki); of the division of people; and of who the gods are. Most importantly, WHO the Elohim of the Hebrews is. In this section of our reading, I have chosen to pull all of the Scriptures together related to sex exploitation. Open your eyes, your mind, and *ruach* (spirit) to what we are about to explore. Without having all of your senses intact in reading this, some will be offended, though this is contextually in line with the Scriptures. Do not allow *Cognitive Dissonance* to continue to block you from comprehending in truth. Do not allow anyone to continue to tell you that books outside of the AKJV of the Bible are illegitimate books of Scripture, and that all other books are *pseudepigraphon* (false).

The Scriptures often speak on the topic of sex; more than most people realize. The reasons the Scriptures speak on sex so often are several; two thoughts that came into my *ruach* (spirit) are these: The *malachs* (angels) were given much knowledge in *Shamayim* (Heaven), and retained that knowledge (sexuality), after their failed attempt to overthrow Shamayim; and two, perhaps after the malachs witnessed the animals having sex is how they learned what sex is. It is not clear in the Scriptures how the malachs knew what sex is, but clearly from Bereshis

6:4, they had a knowledge of sex. It is most likely that *Azazyel*, who taught the secrets of Shamayim to the people, was the one who taught people about sex. This entire section is from multiple books, line and precept. Let us begin by examining some correlating information from other books prior to examining the contents of the Bamidbar. *The Book of Enoch* tells us the following:

Enoch 10: 10-12:

'*10 Restore the earth, which the **angels have corrupted**; and announce life to it, that I may revive it. 11 All the sons of men shall not perish in consequence of **every secret, by which the Watchers** have destroyed, and which they have **taught, their offspring**. 12 All the earth has been corrupted by the effects of the **teaching** of **Azazyel.** To him therefore ascribe the **whole crime**.*'

From the beginning of beginnings the fallen ones were very sexual Beings, of great sexual prowess. Most people reading the Scriptures are clueless about the sexual content in the Scriptures. Folks, there was sex in Shamayim, and there will be sex in Shamayim when Elohim brings His Chosen People back to Shamayim. When the *Watchers/Fallen Malachs (Angels)/Annunaki* rebelled against the *Mamlachah* (Kingdom) of Elohim, and Abba had them thrown out of the Mamlachah, HE did not remove their knowledge. Now watch this: Clearly the Watchers "***corrupted***" the life on *eretz* (earth) that was created by The Most High Elohim. The Watchers "***taught***" who? "***Their offspring***". Do you comprehend what this means? There are children to this day on the eretz possessed of the spirit of the *Watchers*. Those, who rule this eretz are the offspring of the Watchers, and their offspring control your churches, banks, and governments. The Watchers are able to control the world by building armies to fight against the children of Elohim. The Watchers use tactics; such as, wealth, supremacy, and power to make their minions steadfastly loyal to them, those workers of iniquity not realizing they are pawns on the chess board. Who received the blame for teaching the secrets of Shamayim to the people? The leader of the Watchers, *Azazyel.*

If you recall, in Bereshis/Genesis 6:4, the malachs were having sex with the daughters of men. Moreover, and you will definitely not hear this from your pastor: Most preachers don't tell the truth of Scripture, some know the truth, but most of them do not. Many preachers are in need to be taught themselves (Yehudi/Heb. 5:12). The truth is, the flood came about because the malachs were having sex with everything they desired: the birds, animals, sea creatures, the women, and the men. With that said, let us look at two issues dealing with the sexually active woman. Let us pull the Scriptures together, this is a line and precept moment from VaYikra/Lev., and Bamidbar/Num..

VaYikra/Leviticus 19:29 (AKJV):

*'Do not **prostitute** your daughter, to cause her to be a **whore**; because the land will fall to whoredom, and **the land become full of wickedness**.'*

Bamidbar/Num., Chapter 5:20-22 (AKJV):

*'... and if you be defiled, and <u>some man have had **sex** with you, beside your husband</u>: 21 Then the priest shall charge the woman with an **oath of cursing**, and the priest shall say unto the woman, The HASHEM will make your thigh to rot, and your belly to swell; 22 And this water that causes the curse shall go into your bowels, to make your belly to swell, and your thigh to rot; And the woman shall say, Selah, Selah.'*

A father, who sells his daughter into **prostitution** has no respect for women. What sticks out to me in this verse about forcing one's own daughter into sexual slavery is this: There is no punishment listed in the Scriptures for the father committing such a despicable act. I am absolutely baffled by this verse because there is no punishment listed for the dad; only that the country will fall apart because the prostitution will lead to more immorality. In Bamidbar/Num., Chapter 5, is the discussion of how to deal with the **spirit** (5:14) of envy in the husband, who suspects his wife has committed adultery. The woman is to be brought before the priest for an oath of *fidelity*; after giving the oath, the woman has to drink bitter water (5:19). There are two outcomes in the woman drinking the bitter water: If she has not committed adultery, all is well, and there are no consequences. However, if she is guilty of adultery, the curse will come upon her (5:17-22). The gist of the story as a take away is this: Many of the sexual stories of the Scriptures involve punishment of some kind for the women, and the men are not punished, except in the case of rape. The way the Scriptures are written there can be no doubt of the dominance of men, and how it is tolerated to the highest levels of society. *Misogyny* is built into the system, it appears, from Shamayim itself. The point being, sex is something that needs to be discussed openly and honestly; sex has always been and always will be in life. The most important teaching that can ever be done on the topic of sex is this: Sex is the only vehicle, outside of the *Hashilush Hakadosh* (Abba, Son, Ruach) that effectively and efficiently transfer spirits. Having sex with those of evil countenance, can transfer evil spirits from one person to another. Everything that looks good, ain't good for you. Sex can defile you, as the women were defiled in Bereshis 6:4. The world became polluted by the sexual knowledge of the fallen malachs. Selah.

*The Book of Bamidbar/Num.* does not contain much information in the way of sexuality; however, many other books are filled with sexual content. Some books speak to sex openly and frankly, while some books cloak sex with clever language. Line and precept, let us look at many sexual acts of Scripture, from multiple sources.

Yudges 19:16 is the opening story-line of this segment because it introduces us to whom the story is about: The *Shevet* (Tribe) of Benoni. Watch this, line and precept. There was an old man, who lived in Gibeah with the Shevet of Benoni. There were travelers the old man had interaction with, and in conversation, the old man learned the travelers had no place to sleep for the night. The old man provided the travelers with lodging for the night (19:18-21). Now watch what happened as the old man and the travelers were in the house exchanging pleasantries.

Yudges 19:22 (AKJV):

*'Now as they were making their hearts merry, behold, the **men** of the city, certain **sons** of **Belial** (Hasatan), **beset** (encroached) the house round about, and beat at the door, and spoke to the master of the house, the old man, saying, Bring forth the **man** that came into your house, that we may **know him**.'*

The **men**, the carnally minded sons of "**Belial**" have surrounded the house, beating on the house demanding the old man to send the male traveler out to them. This verse is one of the many verses throughout Scripture, that does not present the story in language that is commonly used as we speak today. The cloaked word in the verse is "**know**". The word "**know**" is an *euphemism* for sex. I realize at this point someone is saying, blasphemy. Hang on, watch this:

Yudges 19:25 (AKJV):

*'But the **men** would not listen to him: so the man took his **concubine** (the woman), and brought her forth unto them; and they **knew her**, and **abused her** all the night until the morning: and when the day began to spring, they let her go.'*

To *know*, present tense; *knew*, past tense. The men wanted the man sent out to them; but the old man sent the woman out to them. The **men** wanted to have sex with the **man**; the men had sex with the woman, taking turns raping her all night long. The word "**know**" is defined as: *"Archaic: to have sexual intercourse with"* (Merriam-Webster). Those men gang raped the female over and again. The sons of Belial did a terrible thing in raping the concubine; who is the concubine, and who are the sons of Belial?

Yudges 20:4 (AKJV):

*'And the Levite, the **husband** of the woman that was slain, answered and said, I came into Gibeah that belongs to **Benoni**, I and my concubine, to lodge.'*

Many don't overstand what a concubine is: The concubine is one of many *nashim* (wives) of one man, but is not the first or number one nashim. Clearly Yudges 20:5 tells us the concubine was raped: "**forced**". The men of Gibeah were ruffians, who were involved in many forms of lewdness. When the old man cut his concubine in twelve pieces, he sent one piece to each of the Twelve *Shevets* (Tribes). The Yisra'elites asked the men of Benoni: '*What wickedness is this that is done among you?*' (Yudges 20:12). Who are the men of Gibeah? Watch this line and precept.

Yudges 20:13 (AKJV):

> '*Now therefore deliver us the **men**, the children of **Belial**, which are in Gibeah, that we may put them to death, and put away evil from Yisra'el. But the children of **Benoni** would not listen to the voice of their brothers the children of **Yisra'el**.*'

The men of Gibeah are Benonites, who are under the influence of **Belial** (Hasatan). They are acting under the influence of their previous captors in *Mitzrayim* (Egypt; Yudges 19:30). When the other shevets received word of what Gibeah had done they went to the *Ekklesia* (Temple, Sanctuary) of Elohim, asking HASHEM: What should they do? Elohim told the Yisra'elites to prepare for war against the Benonites, and that Yehuwdah should be the first to fight against Benoni (20:18). The Benonites were a capable fighting force, and they defeated Yehuwdah, killing twenty two (22) thousand Yehuwdites (20:21). The Yisra'elites then went back to Elohim, and were instructed to go to war the second time against Benoni (20:23-24). Once more Benoni defeated Yisra'el killing eighteen (18) thousand Yisra'elites (20:25). After Yisra'el was defeated the second time by Benoni, Elohim stepped-in to help Yisra'el defeat Benoni (20:35-48). The slaughter of twenty five (25) thousand Benonite men decimated the shevet, and the men of Yisra'el made a vow not to give their daughters to the remaining Benonite men (21:1). The end result to thousands of Benonite men being slaughtered, and the Yisra'elite men refusing to allow marriage of their daughters to Benoni, are the following verses:

172

Yudges 21:3 (AKJV):

*'and said, O HASHEM Elohim of Yisra'el, why is this come to pass in Yisra'el, that there should be to day **one Shevet (Tribe) lacking in Yisra'el?'***

Yudges 21:6-7 (AKJV):

*'And the children of Yisra'el repented them for **Benoni** their brother, and said, There is **one Shevet cut off from Yisra'el** this day. 7 How shall we do for **wives for them** that remain, seeing we have sworn by the HASHEM that we will **not give them of our daughters to wives?'***

Because of the evil Benoni committed in the rape of the concubine, and the demand that the old man send out the male traveler for them to "**know**", essentially Benoni is now outcast from the rest of the family. However, they have not been completely disowned by Yisra'el. Line and precept: What happened next to Benoni comes in Yudges 21:8-10: All of Yisra'el, including Benoni was to go before the HASHEM for the census. No one from Benoni came to the meeting place in Mizpeh. As a result of Benoni's disobedience, the leadership made a decision in the following verse:

Yudges 21:11 (AKJV):

*'And this is the thing that you shall do, You shall utterly destroy **every male**, and **every woman** that has had **sex by man**.'*

Did you catch the full meaning of the verse? What the men of Benoni were involved with was *bisexuality*. Some of the Benonite men had pleasure in women, and men, and in particular boys. Listen-up: This is not the first time men of Yisra'el have committed such acts. In Bamidbar/Num. 31:15-18, is a story of similar appearance, and verse 17 reads: *'Now therefore **kill every male** among the **little ones**, and **kill every woman** that has **had sex with man** by **lying with him**'*. Come out of *Cognitive Dissonance*, allow your brain to connect to what your eyes have read. Stop allowing cleverly written phrases to obstruct the meaning in the verse(s). Here is the main issue in both of these scenarios: The Yisra'elites have come under the influence of evil spirits. All of the behaviors: other god worship; rape; bisexuality, were all activities learned in *Mitzrayim* (Egypt; 19:30). After the slaughter of the women and males, who had had sex with the men of Benoni, there were four hundred (400) young virgins found there (21:12) that the innocent men left of Benoni took as wives; however, there were more men of Benoni left that needed a *nashim* (wife) (21:14). After all of those events, all of Yisra'el came together at Rimmon, including the innocent men of Benoni. The men of Benoni said: How then will we get wives for ourselves (21:16). Listen-up! The men of Yisra'el have repeatedly done evil, resulting in women, and male children being killed (Bad./Num. 31:35). Because of Benoni not coming to the census meeting at Mizpeh, a decree was made against Benoni, part of which was to **curse** any man of Yisra'el, who gives his daughter to Benoni (21:15-18). Therefore a plan was developed on how to obtain wives for the remaining men of Benoni. The plan involved the men of Benoni to go to Shiloh, and when the women come out to dance, that Benoni, who was hiding in the vineyards, would come out of the vineyards and capture the women (21:21) for nashim for the remaining Benonite men.

Line upon line and precept upon precept. Here we go. Let us now look at a relationship that has been controversial among religious people for a long time. Some have concluded that to say: There are those, who distort the story, and are speaking blasphemy; while others say: There is more to the story than most people are willing to accept, for one reason only: They refuse to believe that such stories are written about in the *Sacred Writings*. There is a saying that applies to the text, and it is: '*There is nothing new under the sun*' (Ecclesiastes 1:9). Let us venture into the verses dealing with Yonathan and Daviyd.

1 Samuel 20:17 (AKJV):

'And <u>Yonathan caused Daviyd</u> to swear again, because **<u>he loved him</u>**: for **<u>he loved him</u>** as he loved his own soul.'

This verse is something that <u>every</u> Hebrew man, woman, and child should possess: love for one another in togetherness. If the Hebrews today, realized who they are, they would stop disrespecting one another, and stop fighting and killing each other. Watch this!

1 Samuel 18:1 (AKJV):

*'And it came to pass, when he had made an end of speaking unto Saul, that the **soul** of Yonathan was **knit** with the **soul** of Daviyd, and Yonathan loved him as **his own soul**.'*

These two Hebrew men were so <u>in love</u> with one another, their souls were "**knit**" together, no different than a husband and wife, who truly love one another. This verse is another example of word play found throughout the Scriptures; words intended to hide what is truly the topic of discussion. The truth of the meaning of the verse is hidden in the word "**knit**". In looking at multiple sources for the meaning of *knit*, it is: Intermingle, united, become one, closer, bond, and more. Above those meanings is this: The word *knit*, of the Hebrew prime root word **qashar** is to be "*in love*" (7194; *Strong's Exhaustive Concordance of the Bible*). The love of Yonathan and Daviyd is so strong it is repeated again in verse 18:3. The story of these two Hebrew men contains: <u>valiance, strength, bravery</u>, and above anything else, the story contains the <u>love of Elohim for Yonathan and Daviyd</u>. This story is long, covering many chapters that causes the story to be difficult to follow and boring. Saul was introduced to Daviyd in verses 16:20-21, and again in verse 17:58. The point being, Yonathan and Daviyd had a long standing relationship before Daviyd was ever known to Saul. There are long stories in the Scriptures that require much attention to what is scattered, and interwoven into the story. Going backward in the verses, chapter 16 tells us more about Daviyd. Verse 16:12 tells us that Daviyd was of a great countenance, and very attractive. This is again written in verse 17:42. Hear me well in this: In verse 18:4, Yonathan strips of all of his clothing, and gave them all to Daviyd. Yonathan was naked before Daviyd. The thing is: What is the point of that part of the story?

The love of Yonathan and Daviyd is reiterated in verses 20:17-18. The Scriptures use redundancy to iterate very specific, important information. Yonathan tells Daviyd that he will be greatly missed at the *Feast* of the *New Moon* on tomorrow. Yonathan knew that Saul was not pleased with Daviyd (20:13), and they two developed a plan on how to signal if it was safe for Daviyd to attend the festival or not. At the festival, Daviyd's seat was empty. Saul began to ask himself, What is in the spirit of Daviyd? Saul said: "*he is not clean; surely he is not clean (20:26)*". Saul began to question Yonathan about Daviyd not being at supper for the last two days (20:27). Yonathan gives his father an explanation for the absence of Daviyd (20:28-29); however, Saul was not pleased, and his words in this next verse reveals what was in Saul's heart.

1 Samuel 20:30 (AKJV):

'*Then Saul's anger was kindled against Yonathan, and he said unto him, <u>You son of the perverse rebellious woman,</u> do not I know that you have chosen the son of Yesse to your <u>**own confusion**</u>, and unto the confusion of thy mother's <u>**nakedness**</u>?*'

Saul is angry with his son Yonathan, over his relationship with Daviyd. Saul unleashed openly what he had already known from his ruach. The ruach sent from Elohim informed Saul of the relationship between Yonathan and Daviyd (19:9). However, it was not a problem until the envy of Saul came into play for the victory Daviyd had in killing the Philistines (18:27), and the women singing more praises to Daviyd than they attributed to Saul (18:7-8). After Saul's failed attempt to kill Daviyd (20:33), Yonathan knew Daviyd could not remain in the land. The two of them met in a secluded place and remained together until they knew the time was at hand for Daviyd to leave the country.

1 Sam 20:41 (AKJV):

'*... and fell on his face to the ground, and bowed himself three times: and <u>they **kissed** one another</u>, and <u>**wept** one with another</u>, until Daviyd exceeded.*'

The two Hebrew men kissed, and wept together until the time that Daviyd should leave to travel safely. In parting ways, the men made an agreement:

1 Samuel 20:42 (AKJV):

*'And Yonathan said to Daviyd, Go in peace, for as much as we have <u>sworn both of us</u> in the name of the HASHEM, saying, The HASHEM be between me and you, and <u>between my seed and your seed forever</u>. And he arose and departed: and Yonathan went into the city'*

These Hebrew men were Elohim fearing men. They each pledged a blessing upon the children from both of them that would eventually be born to both of them. Daviyd departed and traveled to the city of Nob., where he met Abimelech, the priest of Nob (21:1). Upon arrival, Daviyd asked Abimelech for bread/food. The only food the priest had was sacred bread. The interesting thing about Daviyd receiving the food, he had to be without sexual pleasure for at least three (3) days. In the time Daviyd left Naioth in Ramah (1 Sam. 19:20), many things have come to pass, Saul and Yonathan have been killed (2 Samuel 1:4). Watch what Daviyd said in response to Yonathan's death.

2 Samuel 1:26 (AKJV):

*'I am distressed for you, my brother Yonathan: very pleasant have you been unto me: <u>your **love** to me was wonderful</u>, **passing** the love of **women**.'*

Parts of the story of Yonathan, Saul, and Daviyd are love stories, as well as murder, and spirit possession (1 Sam. 19:9). There are other books containing information about the same stories that are not included in the AKJV of Scripture, but even so, the KJ sometimes references other Books. In the case of Daviyd there is more information written in *The Book of Yashar* (2 Sam. 1:18). There is so much sex and nudity, and all manner of acts recorded in the Scriptures that most people have no clue is written in the Scriptures, or they have no clue of the interpretation thereof. In 1 Samuel 19:24, it talks about Saul stripping off his clothes, prophesying before Samuel: *"And he **stripped off his clothes** also, and **prophesied** before **Samuel** in like manner, and lay down **naked** all that day and all that night."* What is the reasoning behind Saul Prophesying in the nude? Some would never equate this verse to anything sexual, and in fact it likely was not sexual. Folks, let me give you another example of being a man of Elohim, capable of Prophesy, while being in the nude:

Isaiah 20:2 (AKJV):

*'At the same time spoke the HASHEM by Isaiah the son of Amoz, saying, Go and <u>loose the sackcloth from off your **loins**</u>, and put off your shoe from your foot. And he did so, <u>walking **naked** and barefoot</u>.'*

*I AM THAT I AM* Commanded Isaiah to undress, and to remove his shoes from his feet. The man was in his birthday suit in honor of HASHEM. Isaiah walked around three (3) years naked, prophesying in honor of Elohim. Aw-dawn and Chavvah were naked in the Garden of Eden (Ber./Gen. 3:7). Listen-up: Being nude is our nature, it is not obscene in honor of the Abba. Sex in and of itself is not the problem, it is violence associated with sex, or wickedness associated with sex, that makes sex dirty, foul, polluted, and unclean. In the story of Tamar and Amnon, 2 Samuel 13:8-28, Amnon raped Tamar his sister. It was not the sex that was wicked because of the incest, it was the act of rape. Yes, the incest is against the *Law* but does not have the same weight as rape. Watch this!

Yashar 34:52; 60 (AKJV):

*'And Judah answered his father, saying, Was it for naught my brothers Simeon and Levi killed all the inhabitants of Shechem? Surely it was because Shechem had <u>**humbled our sister**</u>, and transgressed the Command of our Elohim to Noah and his children, for <u>Shechem took our sister **away by force**</u>,*

> *and committed **adultery with her**. ... 60 Stand forth each
> man, girt with his weapons of war, his **bow and his sword,**
> and we will go and fight against these uncircumcised men; the
> HASHEM is our Elohim, HE will save us.'*

*The Book of Yashar* is one of those books not in the AKJV of
Scripture, but even so, the KJ recognizes the story (2 Sam. 1:18) as
accurate, and not as *pseudepigraphical* (false). As a result of the rape of
Tamar, the Shevets of Simeon and Levy killed the people of Shechem,
and the <u>Chief Shevet of Yehuwdah</u> gave full approval of the slaughter.
This goes back to Shechem, who also committed rape against Dinah
(Ber./Gen. 34:2-26). Shechem is of the evil offspring of the Annunaki,
a Hivite. The Hivites are of the family-line of cursed Canaan (Ber./
Gen. 10:15-17). Did you catch it? It is not the sex or nudity, it is evil
wickedness that defiles. The love shared between two consenting adults
is not dirty or foul. Your opinion, or what you have been led to believe
is irrelevant against the Scriptures. The story of Yonathan and Daviyd
is a love story, that was in agreement of mutual consent of the two (2)
men, and prayer sent to Elohim for the two (2), and their posterity to
come (1 Sam 20:41-42).

Now let us look at the story of Chavvah and Aw-dawn again. Both
of them participated in the events of the *Garden of Eden*. Look at the
verse again.

Bereshis/Gen. 3:6 (AKJV):

> *'And when the **woman** saw that the tree was good for food, and
> that it was **pleasant** to the eyes, and a tree to be **desired** to
> make one wise, she took of the **fruit thereof**, and did eat, and
> <u>gave also unto her **husband**</u> with her; and **he did eat**.'*

Do you see it? Many people, who study the Scriptures and have
overstanding know this verse is about sex. Therefore, anyone whose
overstanding is open realize, that with Chavvah having sex with the
Being in the Garden, that so did Aw-dawn. Argue if you will but
you argue with the Scriptures because you do not comprehend the

Scriptures. Continuing forward, let us look at another verse of Scripture, alluded to in the KJ bible, but is cloaked in cleverly written form to hide what it is saying from unlearned persons (Ber./Gen. 9:22). Moving forward with more writings from books you may not have heard of before, and yet, those books parallel the KJ bible, but with a better description of the story.

THE CABALA/TALMUD; Midrash Rabbah 1:292-293:

*Cabala/Talmud*:

*"Because you have abused me (**sodomized**/buggered me) in the darkness of the night, your children shall be born **black and ugly**... because you have twisted your head to cause me embarrassment, they shall have kinky hair and red eyes... because your lips mocked at my exposure, theirs shall swell... and because you **neglected my nakedness**, they shall go naked with their **shamefully elongated male members** exposed to all to see..."*

Midrash Rabbah - Genesis XXXVI:7

Some will read this and say, it is blasphemy, rather than question why this story is not clearly overstood in reading other books about the curse of Ham? Ham raped Noah, and as a result, Noah cursed Canaan, his grandson. This is recorded in the KJ bible but is not thoroughly discussed (Ber./Gen. (9:22). What cannot be stated conclusively is this: Who actually committed the rape: Ham or Canaan? The truth is, it does not matter because both Ham and Canaan were possessed of evil spirits. Prior to the flood Ham was possessed by the Annunaki, and the family-line of Ham became the giants, and other heathen family-lines. Canaan is of that family-line. This book too, *The Midrash Rabbah*, was labeled as *pseudepigraphical*. This too is backed-up in *The Book of Enoch*.

Enoch 7:11:

*'And the women **conceiving brought forth giants**,'*

If you don't believe what is written in Enoch about the giants, you cannot possibly believe the KJ bible either, Bereshis/Genesis 6:4. The information is a match. You cannot have it both ways. Now look at this!

Enoch 15:8:

> 'Now the **giants**, _who have been born of **spirit and of flesh**_, shall be called **upon earth evil spirits**, and on **earth shall be their habitation. Evil spirits shall proceed from their flesh**, because they were created from above; from the **sacred Watchers** was their **beginning** and primary foundation. Evil spirits shall they be **upon earth**, and the **spirits of the wicked shall they be called**. The habitation of the spirits of heaven shall be in heaven; but upon earth shall be the habitation of **terrestrial spirits**, who are **born on earth**.'

The Watchers/Annunaki/fallen malachs (angels) rebelled against The Most High Elohim. When the fallen ones saw the beautiful women Elohim created, the fallen malachs raped them, producing contaminated offspring (Ber./Gen. 6:4). How can one say the malachs raped the women? Once again for the KJ bible only readers, this is what it says in the KJ bible:

Bereshis/Gen. 6:2 (AKJV):

> '... they were beautiful, and they **took** them wives of all which they **chose**'.

In no biblical text anywhere will you find that it was consensual sex between the **terrestrial** women Elohim created, and the fallen malachs. This is what it says in the Orthodox Jewish Bible.

Bereshis/Gen. 6:2:

> 'they were **tovot** (good); and they **took** them nashim of all which they **chose**.'

Every source we have examined presents the exact information, the women were raped. Now look at this from *The Book of Yashar*.

Yashar 4:18:

*'And their magistrates and rulers went to the **daughters of men** and **took** their wives by **force** from their husbands according to their **choice**, and the sons of men in those days took from the cattle of the earth, the beasts of the field and the fowls of the air, and taught the mixture of* <u>*animals of **one species** with the*</u> <u>***other***</u>*, in order therewith to provoke the HASHEM;'*

All of the above books are in agreement. The Annunaki took, chose, forced themselves upon the beautiful women Elohim created from the *eretz* (earth; terrestrial). What more can be said on this one topic. Rape is a condition that causes or allows the evil spirits to permeate another person. There is another point in Yashar that has to also be addressed: the mixing of species. This goes back to the great flood, all of the animals were destroyed along with the people. The question has to be asked: Why would Elohim destroy the innocent animals along with the contaminated people? Because the animals too were contaminated by the sexual exploitation of the Annunaki.

In The Book of VaYikra, the *Laws*, are the rules pertaining to sexual indiscretion. Anyone who does not comprehend the extensive amount of sexual discussion in the Scriptures, do one simple thing: Read VaYikra/Lev., Chapter 18. In particular verses 18:22-24. Verse 18:30 tells us all of the indecency involved with sex came before the Hebrews were a people, and that all of those acts came from the knowledge of the Annunaki. Hopefully, this segment of our reading has brought enlightenment on the topic of sex: whether of immorality, or of the love in your life. Selah!

# COVERING MOST OF DEVARIM/DEUTERONOMY

Some of the most shocking verses of Scripture are found in *The Book of Devarim*. In breaking-down the sensational information of Devarim, we will visit reference sources; such as, *The Book of Enoch, The Book of Yehoshua; The Book of Hisgalus/Revelation*, and more. The book of Devarim is a detailed history, a synopses of the Hebrews from their inception as a people, going back to the time of the first to be called *Hebrew:* The Patriarchs- *Abraham, Yitzhaq, and Ya'aqov.* While the entire Old Testament is about the Hebrews, *The Book of Devarim* is of the most important books Hebrews need to overstand. Hopefully, anyone, Hebrew or Gentile, reading this compilation of Scripture, Science, and History, will gain a clear overstanding of who, *The Chosen People* of Elohim are unto this day. Let us begin with Devarim/Deuteronomy, Chapter 1.

Mosheh is talking to the Hebrews, giving them instructions, after the Hebrews had defeated their enemies: King Og, and the Amorites (Devarim/Deu. 1:4). First, one has to overstand who Og and the Amorites are: They are the offspring of the fallen *malachs* (angels), the Annunaki. Those people were living in the land that the Annunaki first landed on *HaAretz* (The earth). It was this land that the malachs were using to go back and forth between *Eretz* (Earth) and *Shamayim* (Heaven; Bereshis/Gen. 28:12). Let me make this clear: This land is to be occupied by the Chosen People only, because it is the gateway to Shamayim. Watch this!

Shemot/Exo. (OJB) 33:2:

*"And I will send a **Malach** (Angel) before thee; and I will **drive out** the Canaanite, the **Emori** (Amorite), the **Chitti** (Hittite), the **Perizzi** (Perizzite), the **Chivi** (Hivite), and the **Yevusi**;"*

These *shevets* are of Ham, of which some of them are the cursed of humanity, are actually the children of the **Annunaki** (fallen angels). Some of the shevets from this family were polluted, contaminated Beings, who serve their gods, and not the Elohim of the Hebrews. Here is the point: *The Promised Land* is the land of *Canaan*; is the land of the fallen malachs; is the land of Mt. Horeb, Mt. Hermon, Mt. Seir, Mt. Sinai. All of these names are synonymous: This land was Promised to the Hebrews, who were created to occupy the land around the Mountain of Elohim. Did you catch it? The Hebrews were created for the sole purpose of keeping the enemy, the children of the fallen malachs out of the land of Yisra'el, and to serve Elohim only. However, there are conditions the Hebrews have to meet. Watch what happens as we add to this study. Let us look at the borders of the Promised Land.

Devarim/Deu. 1:7-8 (AKJV):

*'Turn you, and take your travel, and go to the <u>mount of the Amorites</u>, and unto all the places near thereunto, in the **plain**, in the **hills**, and in the **vale**, and in the **North**, and by the **sea side**, to the <u>land of the **Canaanites**</u>, and unto **Lebanon**, unto the great river, the river **Euphrates**. 8 Behold, I have set the land before you: go in and possess the land which the HASHEM swore unto your <u>fathers, Abraham, Yitzhaq, and Ya'aqov</u>, to give unto them and to their children after them.'*

The first thing to overstand in the verses is this: Where is the <u>mount of the Amorites</u>? Scholars have determined that the exact location of Mt. Sinai/Hermon/Seir, and so on, is undetermined. What is known in following the Scriptures unrelentingly is this: The mountain of the Amorites is *Heshbon,* which is the same region as Mt. Sinai (Yehoshua

9:10; Nehemiah. 9:22; Yeremiah. 48:45; Yudges. 11:19). Logic then tells us that area is the landing place of the Annunaki when they came to earth from Shamayim, and where their offspring lived after mating with the women Elohim created. Elohim wanted them out of that land for HIS people to inhabit the land to secure the mountain or gateway. And yet, there is still another problem that has to be taken care of before the Hebrews can secure the land.

Devarim/Deu. 1: 42 (AKJV):

*'And the HASHEM said unto me, Say unto them, Go not up, neither fight; for I AM not among you; less you be **defeated before your enemies**.'*

The Hebrews themselves had been <u>disobedient</u> to Elohim. The Hebrews were led to the area of *Heshbon* by Elohim in the appearance of fire by night, and a cloud by day (1:33). After reaching the area, the Hebrew men were instructed to scout out the area for the best route to mount an offensive for war against the Amorites. The scouts went to the land, and when they saw the giant Amorites, they were in fear, and reported back to Mosheh a discouraging report; they showed cowardice (1:28-31). The Hebrews had no confidence they could defeat the giants though Elohim had been with them, and HE told them not to fear the Amorites or <u>any</u> man (1:17). The Hebrews had been placed in *Mitzrayim* (Egypt) by Elohim to prepare them for this very purpose: to destroy the offspring of the fallen *malachs* (angels) living at Heshbon. Because the Hebrew men showed such cowardice, Elohim denied them entry into the land (1:34). *I AM THAT I AM* tells the Hebrews that, if they choose to go to war with the Amorites that HE, Elohim, will not be with them for their cowardice (1:40-42), and that they will be defeated (1:43). *I AM* also informed the Hebrew men that they will die in the wilderness for their <u>disobedience</u>, but their children will inherit the land (1:39-40). Did you catch it? Chapter 1 of Devarim tells us why the Hebrews were sent to Mitzrayim in the first place: to toughen and strengthen them into a people ready to stand against the enemies of Elohim. And, moreover, for the Hebrews to fear <u>no one</u> because Elohim is with them, as long as they are in <u>obedience</u> to HIM.

In Chapter 2 of Devarim/Deu., is some very important information about the Hebrews, Lot, and Esau. After the Hebrews had lived on the coast of the Red Sea for many years, giving time for those <u>disobedient</u> Hebrews to die out (2:16), Elohim told the Children of Yisra'el: It is time for them to go into the mount of the Amorites to kill them (2:24), and for them to fulfill their purpose: To occupy the land surrounding the Mountain of Elohim (2:1-2). Listen-up! All of the names of the mountains in the region have been confounding for most people. Let us look at why the Scholars have said, It is not possible to determine which mountain is actually Sinai. Elohim gave *Seir* to Esau (2:4). Elohim tells the Hebrews not to engage with Esau in any fashion except to buy food and water (2:5-6). As the Hebrews continue their travel toward *Heshbon,* they will come to the land of the Moabites. Elohim again tells the Hebrews not to bother the Moabites, the progeny of Lot (2:9). Interestingly enough, it was Esau who killed the giants of the land, the Emims, Anakims, Horims, and so forth (2:10-12). Two points: Esau is a warring people capable of great destruction; and, Esau is a mountain man or people (2:12). The Hebrews are also told by *I AM THAT I AM* not to bother Ammon (2:19). Hebrews, here is one reason you are hated:

Devarim/Deu. 2:25 (AKJV):

> 'This day will I begin to put the **_dread_** of you and the **_fear_** of you upon the nations that are under the <u>whole heaven</u>, who shall **_tremble_**, and be in **_anguish_** because of you.'

Everywhere in the world the Hebrews live, they are hated by the people of that land. Not for the color of their skin, but rather, because the Hebrews are the Chosen People of the One and Only, true Elohim. All of those other people are the products of the Annunaki. The fact is, those other people know, the Hebrews are the only direct descendants of Elohim. On top of that, those people know who the Hebrews are, another reason many have suppressed, oppressed, and with tremendous effort have tried to wipe-out the memory of the Hebrew people, and or tried to take the place of the Hebrews, claiming Hebrew heritage as their own. Elohim forbid. Every country in the world that has original artifacts of Hebrews, those artifacts show the truth of Hebrew heritage. In some countries, many of those artifacts have been concealed in facilities, locked-up in secret chambers to prevent the general public from knowing the truth. In secret places; such as: *The Smithsonian; Vatican City; The British Museum; The Russian Museum; Archaeological Museums, and in Artifacts of Ancient Mitzrayim (Egypt)*. Those in possession of those original paintings of the saints bow, and pray before those paintings, and or artifacts. I have to say this: All such items are sacrilege because we are to have no representations of any such items; whether of Shamayim above; in the eretz below; or of the water under the eretz (Shemot/Exo. 20:4; Devarim/Deu. 5:8).

Many people doubt that giants ever existed on earth; to those skeptics I say: You are not a believer of Scripture because clearly the Scriptures speak on the existence of giant people in those days. Next we will examine information about the Children of Yisra'el preparing for battle against King Og, of the family-line of the giants. The cities the giants lived in were gated cities with very high walls (Devarim/Deu. 3:1-5). The Children of Yisra'el are commanded to destroy all of the people of *Edrei*; and to keep the cattle, and possessions of the slain for themselves (3:6-9). Here is where this fascinating information hidden in plain sight in the Scriptures begins to intensify: King Og and his people live in *Bashan*, the land of the highest point in all the land of Yisra'el, and surrounding areas: *Mount Hermon*. Mount Hermon is the home of the giants (3:9-11). This is very substantial to comprehend because, Mt. Hermon is thought to be the first place the *Annunaki* landed on the **eretz** (earth). This is what Enoch tells us about Mount Hermon:

Enoch 6:6:

*"And they were in all two hundred (fallen angels); who descended in the days of Yared on the **summit of Mount Hermon**, and*

> *they called it Mount Hermon, because they had sworn and*
> *bound themselves by mutual **imprecations** (curses) upon it."*

Some have labeled *The Book of Enoch* as *pseudepigraphical*, as they did *The Book of Sirach* of the *Apocrypha*. Some ancient writings have been labeled as false to continue deceiving the world about who the Hebrews are. The Annunaki descended from Shamayim, first appearing on the eretz on Mt. Hermon. Hermon being the gateway for their travel, and thus the reason Elohim closed the gateway, and then appointed a special people to live in the land surrounding Mt. Hermon.

Many people have no idea that the Hebrew Yisra'elites did not all live in Yisra'el. The **Shevet** (Tribes) of Reuben, Gad, and half the Shevet of Manasseh lived in the mountain land East of Yisra'el (Yehoshua 12:6). The land of the giants was given to them after they helped the other Shevets defeat the giants (3:12-16). Did you catch what was repeated in this paragraph? The word **giant** is a redundancy, all of the land West of Mt. Hermon, and East of Mt. Hermon were inhabited by the giants.

Yehoshua 11:17 (AKJV):

> *'Even from the mount Halak, that goes up to **Seir**, even unto*
> ***Baalgad** in the valley of **Lebanon under mount Hermon**:*
> *and all their kings he took, and smote them, and slew them.'*

The most important word in the entire verse is "***under***". We will add onto the use of under as we build to the height of this lesson. Before going farther into the word under, we must look at the Sidonians because in *Mythology,* the giant *Sidon* is a mystical fairy-tale creature of giant statue. Not so folks, Sidon was a giant of the family-line of Canaan, the cursed of The Most High Elohim. The Sidonians too, were defeated, and their land given to Yisra'el (Yehoshua 13:4-6). There is another important word in the above verse, and that word is *Baalgad*. This word is important because Baalgad is the city of the god of the giants: the Canaanites. In fact, Baal is the word the *Anakims* (Annunaki) use for their leader, their god, one of the fallen **malachs** (angels). *I AM THAT I AM* is the name of the Elohim of the Hebrew Yisra'elites (Shemot/

Exo. 3:14). Think about it: Why would Elohim tell us in the Ten Commandments not to have any other god before HIM? It is because there are other gods.

Let us continue to build upon these shocking, and rather revealing Scriptures. In order for the Hebrews to occupy the land of the giants, they had to cross the *Yarden River*. In order to do that the Yarden River had to be stopped, so the Hebrews could cross on dry ground. In order to dry-up the Yarden River, the Priests had to carry the *Ark of The Covenant* with them. When the Priests stepped into the water, the water dried-up as in the parting of the *Red Sea* (Yeh. 3:13-17). Before the Hebrews came to the Yarden River, they had to kill the remainder of the giants in Bashan, Og and his people (2:10). The land of Og is where the two and a half shevets would live: Reuben, Gad, and half the Shevet of Manasseh. The war between the Hebrews, and the giants have a recurring theme in who the Hebrews continue to battle: THE CANAANITE, **AMORITE**, HITTITE, PERIZZITE, YEBUSITE, and so on (Yeh. 11:3). Do you overstand this? The enemies of Elohim, and of the Hebrews, are all the other people on the eretz. The giants and other regular size people are not the creation of Elohim, they are the products of the Annunaki. Listen-up: All of you *monotheist,* read and overstand:

Devarim/Deu. 3:24 (AKJV):

> *'O HASHEM Elohim, YOU have begun to show your servant Your greatness, and Your mighty hand: for what **elohim** is there in **Shamayim** or in **Eretz**, that can do according to Your works, and according to Your might?'*

This verse is a conversation between Elohim and Mosheh. Clearly, in speaking to Elohim, Mosheh has acknowledged other **elohim** in Shamayim, and other **gods** on eretz. You did not catch it. The other elohim of Shamayim are the Ruach Hakodesh, Ha Mashiach, and the other heavenly Beings; such as, Michael the Archangel, Gabriel, and Raphael. The gods of eretz are Hasatan, Baal, Molech, and the other fallen malachs. Here is the point: There is only One Supreme Elohim. All of those other elohim/gods, have power but not equal power to Elohim, WHO created everything that is, of Shamayim and of the Eretz. However, everything became mutant with the *War in Shamayim*, what had been all good was now polluted. The contamination had to be cleaned out of Shamayim, therefore was the eretz turned into the prison for the fallen malachs. Folks, this is hell! The mountain the malachs were transcending to and from had to be secured, the Hebrews were created to be the guardians of Elohim's Mountain.

After the Hebrews slew Og at the battle of Edrei, they traveled on toward Heshbon, the land of the Amorites, which land is Yarden. The interesting part is, the land that Og lived would become the land of Reuben, Gad and half the Shevet of Manasseh (Dev./Deu. 3:1-15). When all of the battles ended in victory for the Hebrews by the Mighty Hand of *I AM THAT I AM*, Elohim spoke to Mosheh at the base of *Horeb* Mosheh was instructed to gather the Hebrews together for a very important meeting (4:10-11). This meeting is very significant for two main reasons: All of the Hebrews will hear the instruction of Elohim; they will hear HIS voice, but not see HIS presence (4:12). This monumental because there should be no doubt in the people that: They serve the True and Living Elohim. *I AM* gave the Hebrews Ten Commandments (4:13). This meeting took place on the other side of Yarden in *Mount Horeb* (4:15), where the two and a half Shevets will live. This brings us to the instructions Elohim gave specifically to the people HE created to serve and worship HIM only.

Devarim/Deu. 4:16-19 (AKJV):

> 'Lest you corrupt yourselves, and make you a **graven image**, the similitude of **any figure**, the likeness of **male or female**, 17 the likeness of **any beast** that is on the earth, the likeness of **any winged fowl** that flies in the air, 18 the likeness of any thing that **creeps** on the ground, the likeness of **any fish** that is in the **waters** beneath the earth: 19 and lest you lift up your eyes unto heaven, and when you see the **sun, and the moon, and the stars**, even all the host of heaven, should be driven to

**_worship them, and serve them_**, *which the HASHEM your
Elohim has divided unto all nations under the whole heaven.'*

These verses are crucial to comprehend. Listen-up! This goes so
deep into the psyche of people in every land on this planet, though it is
written to the Hebrews. <u>There is to be no statue, no image, no carving,
of any kind that we are to have in our possession</u>: No bird, no fish,
no man, no woman, no planet, that represents **deity**. Do you get it?
Those paintings of Ha Mashiach, whether painted black, brown, white,
purple or green, are blasphemy. That cross you wear around your neck
is blasphemy. Moreover, the Hebrews must not follow the ways of other
people, who worship their gods, and not the Elohim of the Hebrews.
Say what you will but the Scriptures speak for themselves. The religion
you practice in houses made by man, with crosses, and paintings of
*Cesare Borgia*, are houses of blasphemy. Even the NT tells us, those
houses are not the House of Elohim (Acts 7:48). Elohim forbid. I have
to say this also because I know someone will think to themselves: But
the New Testament? The New Testament is a *Greco/Roman Book*, that
in all aspects does not pass the smell test. Case in point: The *Law* is
done away with in grace and mercy. That is an untruth from the pit of
fire. Ha Mashiach Himself said:

Matthew 5:18 (AKJV):

'*For verily I say unto you, Till heaven and earth pass, **one jot**
or one **tittle** shall in **no wise** pass from the **Law**, until **all** be
fulfilled.'*

This is what the verse is actually saying: *Not one damning word of
the Torah, not even the smallest piece, shall be removed from the Law until
all of the Prophesy is fulfilled.* Do not, I repeat, do not allow yourself to
continue to be brainwashed by those standing in the puppet-pit telling
you grace and mercy will save you. What saves you is recognizing and
accepting the only Elohim of the Hebrews. There is no other **Redeemer**,
no other **Savior** (Isa. 49:26; Hosea 13:4).

*I AM THAT I AM* gave us this Law Himself. A Law that was

reinforced by Ha Mashiach. Let us continue to pull these line and precept points together. The Hebrews are a difficult people due to their own stubborn ways, and disobedience. Mosheh knowing who he is dealing with said to the people:

Devarim/Deu. 4:26-27 (AKJV):

> 'I call heaven and earth to <u>witness against you</u> this day, that you shall soon <u>utterly perish from off the land</u> where unto you go over **Yarden** to possess it; you shall not prolong your days upon it, but shall utterly be destroyed. 27 And the <u>HASHEM shall **scatter** you</u> among the nations, and you shall be left **<u>few in number among the heathen</u>**, where the HASHEM shall lead you.'

Mosheh knew that because the Hebrews had pushed back on leaving Mitzrayim; their complaints about not having food in the desert; their failure to remain obedient, that at some point, the Hebrews would go into other god worship. What Mosheh is telling the Hebrews is this: Today, I am warning you that if you transgress the *Law* Elohim has given to you, the eretz and Shamayim bear witness of what I am relaying to you. Essentially, Mosheh has told the Hebrews, when you transgress these rules, you will be cursed and punished by Elohim. Don't get this twisted. Cursed here does not mean everlasting punishment. The Hebrews always have the opportunity for forgiveness in serving and worshiping Elohim only (4:29-31). This warning from Mosheh will come to fruition as we continue line and precept.

The Scriptures make it perfectly clear that the only people that belong to Elohim are the Hebrews (Dev./Deu. 4:35). The Hebrews living at that time heard the voice of Elohim, and HE showed them miracle after miracle (4:33-34). All of this is reinforced in verses 5:3-4. Then we come to the most important *Laws* of Laws: *The Ten Commandments*: 1- *You will not have any other god before ME*. This is important because it does not say, there is no other god, it says: Those gods are not your Elohim. 2- Reinforces not to have any *<u>images</u>* or *<u>likenesses</u> of anything representing deity*. 3- Do not use the *name of Elohim in a negative way*, or equate HIS name to *anything evil*. 4- Be sure to keep the *Seventh*

*Day* of the week sacred by reframing from work. The *Shabbath Day*, the Day of Rest, is in remembrance of Elohim ending all that HE planned for creation at that time. Let me make this clear: Until Elohim decides to bring the New Shamayim and HaAretz (Isa. 65:17; His./Rev. 21:1), HE will not create anything further. 5- *Never disrespect your mother and father*, and if you transgress this *Law*, your days may be shortened on the eretz. 6- *Do not kill* your brother are sister, a fellow Hebrew. 7- *Do not lay down with an espoused person*. 8- *Do not steal*. 9- *Do not tell lies* against your family or friends. 10- *Do not defraud anyone* in order to obtain that which belongs to them.

This next verse tells us something that most people completely miss in reading all Scripture. There has been much disputation about keeping the *Law*. There are 613 rules for the Hebrews in the Torah. The first thing is this: How are the Hebrews to follow 613 rules, when the Hebrews don't even keep the Ten Commandments? And moreover: THE HEBREWS ARE STILL IN CAPTIVITY, IN WANT OF EVERYTHING; STILL BEING SHACKLED, AND PUT IN CHAINS; MURDERED IN THE STREETS; OWN NOTHING; AND DO NOT KNOW WHICH LAND IS TRULY THE LAND ELOHIM PROMISED TO ABRAHAM, YITZHAQ, AND YA'AQOV. Let us look at what is actually written in the Scriptures on this topic.

Devarim/Deu. 5:22 (AKJV):

> 'These words the HASHEM spoke unto **all your assembly** in the mount out of the middle of the fire, of the cloud, and of the thick darkness, with a **great voice**: ...'

I have ended the verse there because we have to look at the succeeding verses for this line and precept moment of overstanding of what is in this verse. The Hebrews had been summoned to meet with Elohim at *Horeb*, The Mountain of Elohim (Dev./Deu. 5:2). All of the people heard HIS voice, not only Mosheh, all of the Hebrews heard HIS voice.

Devarim/Deu. 5:23-24 (AKJV):

*'And it came to pass, <u>when you heard the voice</u> out of the middle of the darkness, (for the mountain did burn with fire,) that you came near unto me, even **all** <u>the heads of your Shevets (Tribes)</u>, and your **elders**; 24 and you said, Behold, the HASHEM OUR Elohim has shown us HIS glory and his greatness, and <u>we have heard HIS voice</u> out of the midst of the fire: we have seen this day that Elohim <u>does talk with man, and he lives</u>.'*

Though the Hebrews heard the voice of Elohim, they did not see Elohim. The point here is: You, Hebrew man, Hebrew woman, can and should talk to Elohim in your divine gift of being one of HIS Chosen people. To the remainder of verse 5:22. Watch this!

*'... **and HE added no more**. And HE wrote them in <u>two tables of stone</u>, and delivered them unto me.'*

Did you catch it? HE (Elohim), gave the Ten Commandments, and **nothing more**. You can agree or disagree, but the assessment or takeaway in this is: While those other rules are there to direct the lifestyle of the Hebrews; those rules are not, are not of equal merit to the *Laws* Elohim specifically wrote in stone. Do you get it? Those rules are set in stone signifying permanence. Now don't be saying I am giving anyone permission to break the rules, I am presenting to you what is in the Scriptures, not the lies you have been subordinated to all of your life.

*I AM THAT I AM* said to the Hebrews:

Devarim/Deu. 6:14 (AKJV):

*'You shall not go after other **gods**, of the **gods** of the people which are <u>round about you</u>;'*

This goes to the people the Hebrews had to defeat to come into the land surrounding Horeb. It is speaking about the Emims, the Anakims, the Moabites, and so on (2:10-12). This is also talking about Esau (2:40, and the Moabites (2:9), and every person, who is not Hebrew. What

THE PLIGHT AND TRAVELS OF THE HEBREWS

gods are these? **_Ashtoreth, Chemosh, Milcom_** (Melachim Bet/2 Kings 23:13); **_Baal_** (Bamidbar/Num. (22:41); **_Lucifer_** (Isaiah 14:12); **_Hasatan_** (Yob 1:7-8) and others. Do you get it? These are the fallen malachs; they are the demigods. These gods have power but not the power of Elohim. I have to state this also, those gods provide gifts to their people, as Elohim gives gifts to the Hebrews. Monetary rewards Hebrews, are not always of Elohim, Hasatan can and does reward people to accomplish his goals on HaAretz (The Earth).

Devarim/Deu. 6:21 (AKJV):

*'Then you shall say unto your **son**, We were Pharaoh's bondmen in Mitzrayim (Egypt); and the HASHEM brought us out of Mitzrayim with a mighty hand.'*

All of the miracles done in Mitzrayim, were done to show the power of Elohim is superior to the power of the other gods. Think on this: All of the miracles performed by Mosheh and Aharon, were also done by the priests of Mitzrayim; however, when their priests could not match the reproduction of the lice, admitting: The Elohim of the Hebrews, is the God of gods (She./Exo. 8:19). Pharaoh himself then admitted the Elohim of the Hebrews was the most powerful force in existence (She./Exo. (9:27)). The interesting thing about the Hebrews that is so disturbing is this: After the Hebrews were freed from Mitzrayim, they still had this mind-set of, preferring to be back in Mitzrayim to serve in bondage, because the food and water was in low supply as they traveled toward the Promised Land (Shemot/Exo. 14:11-12; 16:3). All of the acts done in Mitzrayim, Elohim did to show HIS power, HE used Pharaoh for this purpose (She./Exo. 9:12; 16). Unto this day, the Hebrews remain *recalcitrant* (stubborn) and disobedient to Elohim. It is for this reason that the Hebrews remain in bondage.

We will now look at a large volume of information that involves mixing of Hebrews with non-Hebrew heritage, and the special status of the Hebrews to Elohim.

Ezra 9:9-12 (AKJV):

*'For we were bondmen; yet our <u>Elohim has **not** forsaken us in</u> <u>our bondage</u>, but has extended mercy unto us in the sight of the kings of Persia, to give us a reviving, to set up the <u>house of our</u> <u>Elohim</u>, and to repair the desolation thereof, and to give us a wall in Yehuwdah and in Yerushalayim. 10 And now, O our Elohim, what shall we say after this? for we have <u>forsaken Your</u> <u>Commandments</u>, 11 which YOU have Commanded by Your servants the Prophets, saying, The land, unto which you go to possess it, is an **unclean** <u>land</u> with the **filthiness** <u>of the people of</u> <u>the lands</u>, with their **abominations**, which have filled it from one end to another with their **uncleanness**. 12 Now therefore give **not** <u>your daughters unto their sons</u>, **neither** <u>take their</u> <u>daughters unto your sons, nor seek their</u> **peace** <u>or their</u> **wealth** <u>for ever</u>: that you may be strong, and eat the good of the land, and leave it for an inheritance to your children for ever.'*

These verses are the follow-up to what had occurred at Yerushalayim. The Priests, and Levites, and others, have been intermingling with contaminated people: The Ammonites, Moabites, Egyptians, Hittites, and more (Ezra 9:1-2). *I AM THAT I AM* has Commanded the Hebrews at Mount Horeb, not to have anything to do with the people of other lands (Dev./Deu. 2:9-12; 40). Those other people are polluted by the blood-line of the Annunaki. Here they are described as: **filthy, unclean, abominable** creatures. They are unclean because they were contaminated through *Deoxyribonucleic Acid* (DNA) mixing by the fallen malachs by way of sexual reproduction. It is because of that cross contamination that the Hebrews are to keep separate from other people. Moreover, the Hebrews are told **not** to seek **peace** with the enemy, and **not** to seek their **wealth**. Do you get it? The Hebrews are to be a pure blood-line from Ya'aqov, who became Yisra'el after his encounter with the Malach of Elohim (Ber./Gen. 32:24-25). Many believe that Abraham is the father of the Hebrews, which is true. However, Abraham's part in the Hebrews becoming a people, came from Abraham being <u>obedient</u> to Elohim in his willingness to sacrifice his son Yitzhaq (Ber./Gen., Chp.

22). Here is a point which is a must overstand: Elohim would never have allowed Yitzhaq to be sacrificed to HIM. No where in the Old Testament will you find human sacrifice to Elohim, only animals. The role of Abraham in the Promise ended with that selfless act of obedience. Ya'aqov had a totally different Covenant than Yitzhaq, and Abraham, and yet, the Promise still had another part to come in Yosef (Ber./Gen. 41:50-52). The context of the verses is this: The Hebrews are supposed to be a self-reliant family, supporting one another in all ways, and are not to intermingle the blood by sexual reproduction with them, Esau, Hittite, no other people. Now let us back-up the above information.

1 Kings 11:2 (AKJV):

'... _You shall **not** enter into marriage with them_; neither shall they with you, for certainly they will sway your heart after their **deities**.'

*I AM THAT I AM* Commanded the Hebrews **not** to marry those other people. Who are those other people? The Moabites, the **Ammonites**, the Hittites, and so forth. But most importantly of all, the Edomites (1 Kings 11:1). There is a common theme in everything we have read in these lessons: All of the other people are the offspring of the Annunaki. Let's go: line and precept.

Nehemiah 13:3, 23, 25, 27 (AKJV):

'And it came to pass, when they had heard the Law, that they separated from Yisra'el all the **alien mixture**... Also in those days, I saw the _Hebrews who had **married** Ashdodite, Ammonite, and Moabite women_... And I quarreled with them, and I **cursed** them, and I **struck** some of them, and I **plucked** out their hair, and I **admonished** them by Elohim, _You shall_ **not** _give your daughters to their sons nor take their daughters either for your sons or for yourselves_... Shall we then hearken to you to do all this great **evil** to betray our Elohim to _marry_ **foreign** women?'

Do you see it now? The theme continues, leave those contaminated people alone. Do not mix with them. Nehemiah was very wrought with the Hebrews so much so, he cursed at them; used his fists on some of them; pulled the hair from their heads and beards; and rebuked them in the name of Elohim. It is wicked for a Hebrew to marry an Edomite, or other of those contaminated people. Is this racism? Indeed it is; however, this is not the racism that we see today. This racism has to do with serving Elohim or serving the Annunaki gods. It is Commanded by The HASHEM Elohim of the Hebrews, WHO brought the Hebrews out from those contaminated people by a Ruach transformation. Once the blood-line of those purified people was purged, it became sin for the Hebrews to go back into that contaminated flock. I cannot express this strongly enough: Only the Hebrews are of Elohim, all other people are "***alien mixture***". Let's keep going.

Shemot/Exo. 19:5 (AKJV):

*'Now therefore, if you will obey MY voice indeed, and keep MY Covenant, then you shall be a **peculiar treasure** unto ME above all people: for all the earth is Mine.'*

The key words of this verse are "***peculiar***" and "***above***". To be ***peculiar*** is defined as: *Characteristic of only one person, group, or thing*; ***above***: *superior to; in or to a higher place than* (Merriam-Webster). Did you catch the gist of this? The Hebrews, though taken from the other contaminated people, have been purified by Elohim to serve and worship HIM only. Now listen-up! The main takeaway in this is: Yes, the Hebrew in the eye of Elohim is above all other people, when those other people recognized what had occurred in Hebrew transformation, they began to plan and plot how they would take the place of the Hebrews. This topic will be exposed more and more as we continue the study of Devarim/Deuteronomy.

Psalm 33:12 (AKJV):

*'Blessed is the nation whose Elohim is the HASHEM; and the
people whom HE has __chosen for HIS Own inheritance__.'*

This verse is phenomenal. The hidden information in the verse is
this: Though the Hebrews are the select people of Elohim, all other
people are not lost. Here is the key: Those other people have to renounce
their gods, and serve Elohim only. This renouncing of other gods goes
back to what happened to Abraham when he discovered what his father
*Terah* was involved in. The story of Abraham in the KJ bible is not
complete. Stay with me on this. We will come to the missing part of the
story in *The Book of Yashar*. Do you get it? To renounce the other gods
takes the person into a spiritual transformation, that will wash-out the
pollution of the Annunaki. Unfortunately, the spirit of the Annunaki
is very powerful; therefore, it is difficult for this to be accomplished.
This is even difficult for many Hebrews, which is why the Hebrews
were enslaved repeatedly in Scriptural History. Now let us look at the
beginning of the Hebrew family: The transformation.

Psalm 135:4 (AKJV):

*'For the HASHEM has __chosen Ya'aqov unto Himself__, and
__Yisra'el__ for HIS __peculiar treasure__.'*

Ya'aqov was the set-apart appointee of Elohim to give the Twelve
Shevets a commonality for the whole of the Shevets. In wrestling with
the Malach (Ber./Gen. 32:24-28), this set-apart man, this peculiar
treasure, would be the catalyst for the Twelve Shevets of Yisra'el. In that
transformation, the Hebrews have a Sir-name, Yisra'el.

This next verse relates to Yehoshua reviewing the history of the
Hebrews, that is, the family-line even prior to the great flood. This is
what Yehoshua said to the Hebrews.

Yehoshua 24:22 (AKJV):

*'And Yehoshua said unto the people (Hebrews), You are witnesses
against yourselves that you have **chosen you the HASHEM**, to
serve HIM. And they said, We are witnesses.'*

This is a pledge the Hebrews swore to Yehoshua. The ancestors prior
to the flood were worshiping the Annunaki, as were the children of
the Annunaki (Yeh. 24:2). When Elohim decided to make a new race
of people, that race would have to be tried and tested. Elohim chose
Abraham as the beginning of this new race (24:2). Elohim sent those
new people into Mitzrayim to purge the filth off of them, in other
words: The Hebrews would have to go through the fire to burn the filth
of other god worship off of them. Elohim used the plagues of Mitzrayim
to show HIS new race, the Hebrews, that those other gods are not as
powerful as HE is (24:4). However, Esau was not counted as Hebrew,
and was sent to live in the Caucasus Mountains, Mount Seir (24:4).
Who else lived at Seir? *'That also was accounted a land of **giants: giants**
dwelt therein in **old time**; and the **Ammonites** call them **Zamzummims**;
21 a people great, and many, and tall, as the **Anakims**;'* (Devarim/
Deu. (2:20-21). Listen-up: We have seen repeatedly who the children
of the Annunaki are: The Perizzites, the Canaanites, the Hittites, the
**Amorites**, and so on (24:11-12). Yehoshua tells the Hebrews again
about their forefathers serving the gods of those other people (24:14-15).
Yehoshua gives the Hebrews warning: If you serve other gods, Elohim
will cause you to suffer (24:19-20). Verse 22 says: The Hebrews made
a pledge to serve Elohim only. The problem with the Hebrews is their
willful <u>disobedience</u> to Elohim, and they have repeatedly gone into
enslavement as a result.

As in any society there has to be leadership. The message in the
below verse has two basic tenants. Let us look at this verse for what it
contains.

1 Chronicles 28:4 (AKJV):

*'Howbeit the HASHEM Elohim **of Yisra'el** chose me before all the house of my father to be king over Yisra'el for ever: for HE has **chosen Yehuwdah** to be the **ruler**; and of the house of Yehuwdah, the house of my father; and among the sons of my father HE liked me to make me king over **all** Yisra'el.'*

First of all, this verse tells us that **all** of Yisra'el is supposed to be united as one. Though Yisra'el has twelve divisions, how does Yehuwdah being the head of the family relate to the topic of the Hebrews worshiping only Elohim? It goes to what will happen that will result in Yisra'el splitting into the *Northern and Southern Kingdoms*. The rulers of the Twelve *Shevets* (Tribes) is the Shevet of Yehuwdah. Yehuwdah must recognize who they are, and take the reigns of leadership. We will look at this more as we build line and precept.

Devarim 7:4-7 (AKJV):

*'**For they will turn away your son** from following ME, that they may serve **other gods**: so will the **anger of the HASHEM be kindled against you**, and destroy you suddenly. 5 But this is how you shall deal with them; you shall **destroy their altars**, and break down their **images**, and cut down their **groves**, and burn their **graven** images with fire. 6 For you are an **sacred people** unto the HASHEM your Elohim: the HASHEM your Elohim has chosen you to be a **special people** unto Himself, **above all** people that are upon the face of the earth. 7 The HASHEM did not set HIS love upon you, nor choose you, because you were more in number than any people; for you were the **fewest** of all people.'*

The first sentence in the above verse speaks volumes with regard to marrying out of the Hebrew family. For a Hebrew man to marry a Gentile, the woman can influence him into her way of worship, Shelomoh is a prime example (1 Kings 11:3). Not only did Shelomoh break the *Law*, guess who he married? The forbidden offspring of the fallen malachs (1 Kings 11:1). Here is the thing: The Hebrew man marrying a Gentile is breaking the Law of Elohim, the result of that is, the Hebrew man may have put his own life in peril as a result. The other important aspect of these verses is, Elohim choose this group of people to become the Hebrews because, they were the smallest group of all the people on the eretz. There were possibly millions if not billions of hybrid people before Abraham was separated from them to become the Hebrews.

There are many hidden treasures of information in the seventh chapter of The Book of Devarim/Deuteronomy. Elohim said to the Hebrews that in obedience to HIM, the Hebrews are blessed more than any other people of the eretz (7:14). All of the other people of the eretz will hate the Hebrews because of their number one status to the True Elohim, and the Hebrews will not have sickness among them (7:15). The other people that inhabit the land the Hebrews are to take over are the Hittites, The Amorites, Canaanites, and so forth (7:1); those people are the descendants of the fallen malachs. Many of them are mightier, and stronger than the Hebrews. Elohim tells the Hebrews not to be afraid of them because HE is with them (7:19-21). By the mighty hand of Elohim, those people have no chance of defeating the Hebrews. When Elohim lifts HIS mighty hand against the enemy, they will be slaughtered with a great slaughter, so much so, that Elohim tells the Hebrews not to kill them all at once, otherwise the wild animals will then overtake the Hebrews (7:22). Here is what is hidden in the verse: Many of the giants in the land require a large volume of food, and that required a large volume of animals to feed them, animals of all types: birds, fish, elephants, both carnivorous and non-carnivorous animals. In killing all of the wicked people at once, the carnivorous animals would then multiply exponentially leading to many Hebrews possibly being consumed by lions, and other meat eating wild beasts. In defeating the wicked of the land, who desire silver and gold, *I AM THAT I AM* tells the Hebrews not to collect any of their precious metals because, the desire of riches leads to evil (7:25). I hear your question: Why does the desire for silver and gold lead to wickedness? *"It's long been known that earthly metals like gold and silver were forged in supernova explosions*

(Andrew Fazekas, For National Geographic News; Sep 9, 2012); *the use of stones of every valuable and select kind* (Enoch 8:1); *She chose sandals for her feet, and put on her **anklets, bracelets, rings, earrings**, and all her other **embellishments**. Thus she made herself very **beautiful**, to entice the eyes of **all the men** who should see her.* (Yehuwiyth 10:4); *And the Gibeonites said unto him, We will have no silver nor gold of Saul,* (2 Samuel 21: 4)". The topic of riches goes all the way back to the Annunaki in their fall from Shamayim. Multiple proofs of the greed for riches from science and Scripture tell us why, the desire for such metals can and does lead to wickedness. Those elements are originally of Shamayim reserved for the *Mamlachah* (Kingdom) of Elohim. Let's give this more credence:

> Shemot/Exo. 24:10 (AKJV):

> *'and they saw the Elohim of Yisra'el: and there was under HIS feet as it were a **paved** work of a **sapphire stone**, and as it were the **body of Shamayim** in HIS clearness'.*

Pardon the pun: Elohim is the Gold Standard of Shamayim and HaAretz. This goes to when the Hebrews were gathered at Mt. Sinai to receive the Commandments of Elohim. Their description of Elohim is that of splendid excellence, the best of the best.

> Song of Shelomoh 3:10 (AKJV):

> *'He made the pillars thereof of **silver**, the bottom thereof of **gold**, the covering of it of purple, the midst thereof being **paved** with love, for the daughters of Yerushalayim'.*

This is from the love letter wherein Shelomoh is describing his love of Ha Mashiach. Every precious thing there is, is for the *Hashilush Hakadosh* (Sacred Trinity). In Chapter 1 of Shelomoh there is listed most every precious ointment, oil, gem, mineral, and metal of value used in the description, and love of Shelomoh to Ha Mashiach. Did you get it? The evil Annunaki desired the best of the best for themselves, thus the planned coup of Shamayim. In taking over Shamayim, they would have the power, the wealth, and the superiority. When they were thrown out of Shamayim, that same mind-set remained in them, which they passed on to their offspring.

The Hebrews were sent into Mitzrayim to prove them, try them, and to test their worthiness to become Elohim's Chosen people. The Hebrews purpose in Mitzrayim was to also save them from the drought to come upon the eretz (Ber./Gen. 45:7-8). In returning the Devarim, we will next look at Hebrew travel. After the Hebrews were freed from Mitzrayim, they did foolishly by rebelling against Elohim (Dev./Deu. (9:7). The Hebrews began to complain about having little food available to eat (8:3). Devarim 8:2 repeats why the Hebrews were sent to Mitzrayim.

Devarim/Deu. 8:2 (AKJV):

*'And you shall remember all the way which the HASHEM your Elohim led you these forty years in the wilderness, to **humble you**, and to **prove you**, to know what was in **your heart**, whether you would **keep HIS Commandments**, or no.'*

The rust and heavy metals needed to be burned off of the Hebrews. The Hebrews having been taken from contaminated flesh, the children of the Annunaki. There is the possibility of the Hebrews regressing to serve other gods is embedded in them because the Hebrews came from the heathens. Elohim showed the Hebrews time and again, that HE is the ultimate power, but even so, the innate presence of contamination in the Hebrew, though *infinitesimal* (miniscruel, very small), it is still in them, though the Hebrew has been purged repeatedly. Listen-up: Lilith became infected: *'In the **Talmud**, Lilith becomes not only a spirit of darkness, but also a figure of uncontrolled sexuality. The Babylonian Talmud (Shabbat151a) says: 'It is forbidden for a man to sleep alone in a house, lest Lilith get hold of him.' Lilith is said to fertilize herself with male sperm to give birth to other demons'.* Lilith is also referenced in the AKJV of Scripture in Isaiah 34:14. In the *Orthodox Jewish Bible* it refers to Lilith in the following: '*The tziyyim (martens) shall also encounter iyyim (wild cats), and a sa'ir (wild goat) calls to its companion, and* **lilit** *(night creature) dwells there and finds for itself a mano'ach (place of rest)*: (Yeshayah/Isa. 34:14)'. Aw-dawn I (Bereshis/Gen. 1:26-27), and Aw-dawn II (Bereshis/Gen. 2:7) became infected. Chavvah became infected (Bereshis/Gen. 3:3-7). Ham and Canaan his son, became infected (Bereshis/Gen. 9:18-25). Shelomoh became infected (1 Kings 11:1; 2 Kings 23:13) in marrying contaminated *nashim* (wives), the offspring of the Annunaki; and then building a temple for his nashim to worship their god, **Chemosh.** Saul became infected for his <u>disobedience</u> (1 Samuel 15:22-23). You get the picture. The duty of the Hebrew is to not allow that innate part of them to cause them to break the Commandments, in particular, the *Ten Commandments*, and apart from the Ten Commandments, for the Hebrew not to mix with those other people. The Hebrew blood-line has been purified, and that blood-line, the only pure blood-line is Yehuwdah, The Shevet from which *Ha Mashiach* was to come (Matthew 1:1-17). In reading the *genealogy*, do not get confused as some of the names sound familiar, but they are not the same character you may be familiar with; in example, **Manasses** is not **Manasseh.** The point in all of this is: Singularly it is *Yehuwdah*, who carries that specific and direct link to Elohim (Ber./Gen. 49:8-12; 1 Kings 12:21). All of the Shevets of Yisra'el have specific roles to play. With that being said, all of Yisra'el must be <u>obedient</u> to the *Laws* of Elohim, and not follow after the ways of the offspring of the fallen malachs. The good news is, even the people the Hebrews came from, can decontaminate in renouncing their gods, and following the Laws Elohim gave to the Hebrews. However, the Annunaki themselves cannot be purged, the offspring though, of the fallen malachs can be purged, as were the Hebrews, which took many generations. The children of the fallen malachs, after renouncing their gods, after the third generation are allowed among the Hebrews (Devarim/Deu., 23:2-8). We will discuss this in detail more as we build line upon line, and precept upon precept.

*I AM THAT I AM* said to the Hebrews in the remainder of chapter 8, that HE will take care of them, providing them with food (8:10), herds, flocks, silver, gold, and houses (8:12-13). Now watch this, this is a conditional promise.

Devarim/Deu. 8:19-20 (AKJV):

'And it shall be, if you do at all __forget__ the HASHEM your Elohim, and walk after __other gods__, and serve them, and worship them, I testify against you this day that you shall __surely perish__. 20 As the nations which the HASHEM destroyed before your face, so shall you __perish__; because you would not be __obedient__ unto the voice of the HASHEM your Elohim.'

These verses are self-explanatory. In <u>obedience</u> you are blessed with the best of the best, in <u>disobedience</u> you will perish. This warning is given because the Hebrews are about to face something tremendously difficult to do, and an impossibility if the Hebrews go into disobedience. Here we go, line and precept.

Devarim/Deu. 9:2 (AKJV):

'a people __great and tall__, the children of the __Anakims__, whom you know, and of whom you have heard say, Who can stand before the children of __Anak__'!

The land the Hebrews are to possess is the land of the giants, who are the offspring of the Annunaki, the fallen angels. We have previously discussed the events of Mt. Hermon, as being the place the Annunaki first landed on the eretz. Now, Elohim is about to bring the Hebrews into this land to secure the land, blocking the Annunaki offspring from trying to use the land to find a way for them to get into Shamayim. The gateway the fallen malachs were ascending and descending from Shamayim to eretz was closed off by Elohim (Ber./Gen. 28:12). Those people were massive in size and could easily defeat the Hebrews. However, Elohim was with the Hebrews. Watch this!

Devarim/Deu. 9:4-5 (AKJV):

'*Speak not you in your heart, after that the HASHEM your Elohim has cast them out from before you, saying, For __my righteousness__ the HASHEM has brought me in to possess this land: but for the __wickedness of these nations__ the HASHEM do drive them out from before you. 5 __Not for your righteousness, or for the uprightness__ of your heart, do you go to possess their land: __but for the wickedness of these nations__ the HASHEM your Elohim do drive them out from before you, and that HE may perform the word which the HASHEM swore unto your fathers, __Abraham, Yitzhaq, and Ya'aqov.__'*

Elohim had selected the Hebrews for HIS Own people, and is ready for the Hebrews to come into the land HE Promised to the progenitors. The Hebrews too have oftentimes been disobedient, and therefore, Elohim is letting them know: Not by your righteousness am I giving you this land; rather, it is because those other people are wicked, and they conspired to do evil in this place. There is something more very significant in verse 5: Abram, whose name was changed to Abraham (Ber./Gen. 5:17) was the first to be called Hebrew (Ber./Gen. 17:5). How did Abraham gain the favor of The Most High Elohim when everyone else was corrupt, worshiping other gods? This is another line and precept moment.

Book of Yashar 9: 11-13:

'*And __Abram__ the son of __Terah__ was waxing great in those days in the house of Noah, and no man knew it, and the HASHEM was with him. 12 And the HASHEM gave Abram an understanding heart, and he knew all the works of that generation were vain, and that __all their gods__ were vain and were of no avail. 13 And Abram saw the sun shining upon the earth, and Abram said unto himself Surely now this sun that shines upon the earth is Elohim, and HIM will I serve. 18 And in the morning when it was light and the sun shone upon the earth as usual, Abram saw all the things that the HASHEM Elohim had made upon earth.*'

Abram had observed that all of the gods the people were serving were lifeless, made of wood, and stone. Elohim opened up the ruach of Abram, connecting to the Ruach Hakodesh, allowing Abram to see the truth. Now observe what Abram witnessed. This too is not recorded in the KJ bible, and leaves the story as recorded in the KJ bible weak in its presentation on how and why Abram became the Progenitor of the Hebrews, a new race of people.

Book of Yashar 9:19, 23-24, 28-31:

'19 And Abram said unto himself Surely these are _not gods that made the earth and all mankind_, but these are the servants of Elohim, and Abram remained in the house of Noah and there knew the HASHEM and HIS ways' and he _served the HASHEM all the days of his life_, and all that generation _forgot_ the HASHEM, and served _other gods of **wood** and **stone**_, and _rebelled_ all their days. 23 And all the families assembled consisting of about six hundred thousand men, and they went to seek an extensive piece of _ground to build the city and the **tower**_, and they sought in the whole earth and they found none like one valley at the east of the _land of **Shinar**_, about two days' walk, and they traveled there and they dwelt there. 24 And they began to make bricks and burn fires to build the _city and the **tower**_ that they had imagined 28 And behold these **_ascended and others descended_** the whole day; and if a brick should fall from their hands and get broken, they would all weep over it, and if a man fell and died, none of them would look at him. 29 And the HASHEM knew their thoughts, and it came to pass when they were building they cast the arrows toward the heavens, and all the arrows fell upon them _filled with **blood**_, and when they saw them they said to each other, _Surely we have slain all those that are in heaven_. 30 For this was from the HASHEM in order to _cause them to **err**_, and in order; to destroy them from off the face of the ground. 31 And they built the **_tower_** and the city, and they did this thing daily until many days and **_years_** were elapsed.'

Abram had observed that gods of inanimate materials could not possibly be the Elohim, Who created the heavens and the earth, and the people, who came under the influence of the Annunaki. The people had forgotten the True Elohim, and created their own gods. One day the children of wickedness decided they wanted to build a city, and a tower. They sought to build the tower in order to reach Shamayim. This tower is the story of the *Tower of Babel* (Ber./Gen. 11:1-9). Did you catch it? It was the giants who were building the tower. In the midst of this Abram remained steadfast and loyal to The Most High Elohim. The people began to build the tower, and as the tower reached higher and higher over the years, the people began to shoot arrows into heaven to kill the heavenly Beings. When the arrows came back to eretz, the people shooting the arrows thought they had killed the angels in Shamayim because the arrows were blood stained. What the people did not know was, Elohim had stained the arrows to make them believe they were successful in killing the Beings of heaven. Elohim had placed a snare for their destruction. Additionally, these verses reveal to us the possibility of Beings in Shamayim, who have blood in their veins. Did you catch it? There is possibly human life somewhere beyond our own knowledge of existence.

Yashar 11: 22-25:

*'And **Terah bowed down to his gods**, and he then went away from them, and Abram, his son, went away with him. 23 And when Abram had gone from them he went to his mother and sat before her, and he said to his mother, Behold, __my father has shown me those who made heaven and earth, and all the sons of men.__ 24 Now, therefore, quickly and fetch a kid from the flock, and make of it __savory meat__, that I may bring it to my __father's gods__ as an __offering for them to eat__; perhaps I may thereby become acceptable to them. 25 And his mother did so, and she fetched a kid, and made savory meat thereof, and brought it to Abram, and Abram took the savory meat from his mother and brought it before his father's gods, and he drew nigh to them that they might eat; and __Terah his father, did not know of it.__'*

Terah, Abrams father was leading Abram in the wrong direction, Terah was an idolater, and a worshiper of the Annunaki. Abram not knowing any better prepared to make offering to the gods of his father. Abram had an idea on what to do to be pleasing to those false gods. Watch this!

Yashar 11:26-32:

'26 And Abram saw on the day when he was <u>sitting amongst them, that they had no **voice**, no **hearing**, no **motion**, and not one of them could **stretch forth his hand**</u> to eat. 27 And Abram **mocked them**, and said, Surely the savory meat that I prepared has not pleased them, or perhaps it was too little for them, and for that reason they would not eat; therefore tomorrow I will prepare fresh savory meat, better and more plentiful than this, in order that I may see the result. 28 And it was on the next day that Abram directed his mother concerning the savory meat, and his mother rose and fetched three fine kids from the flock, and she made of them some excellent savory meat, such as her son was fond of, and she gave it to her son Abram; and Terah his father did not know of it. 29 And Abram took the savory meat from his mother, and brought it before his father's gods into the chamber; and he came nigh unto them that they might eat, and he placed it before them, and Abram sat before them all day, thinking perhaps they might eat. 30 <u>And Abram viewed them, and behold they had neither voice nor hearing, nor did one of them stretch forth his hand to the meat to eat.</u> 31 And in the evening of that day in that house <u>Abram was clothed with the spirit of Elohim.</u> 32 And he called out and said, **<u>Woe unto my father and this wicked generation</u>**, whose hearts are all inclined to vanity, who serve these idols of wood and stone which can neither eat, smell, hear nor speak, who have mouths without speech, eyes without sight, ears without hearing, hands without feeling, and legs which cannot move; like them are those that made them and that trust in them.'

Terah, Abram's father, and the other people made themselves

statues, and other replicas of their gods, the Annunaki. The interesting and most fascinating part of this is: Elohim knew what the people were doing before Abram's rebellion, but Elohim had done nothing to stop the children of the fallen malachs from worshiping their gods. Why was that so, you ask? The fallen malachs were already in punishment: THE PUNISHMENT OF THE FALLEN MALACHS IS THEIR OUSTER FROM SHAMAYIM, AND BEING IMPRISONED ON THE ERETZ; THEY WERE CAST-DOWN FROM SHAMAYIM (His./Rev. 12:7-12: Yude 6; Isa. 14:12-15). THE ERETZ IS THE CONFINEMENT PLACE, THE PRISON FOR THE REBELLIOUS ANGELS, WHO LEFT THEIR FIRST ESTATE (Yude 6). THEIR BANISHMENT FROM SHAMAYIM IS THEIR REWARD UNTIL THE DAY OF SENTENCING (Yehudi/Heb. 10:27; Yude 6, 15). DID YOU CATCH IT? EVERY ONE ON HAARETZ IS POLLUTED FROM THE TIME OF LILITH, AW-DAWN, AND CHAVVAH.

Yashar 11:33-40:

'33 And when Abram saw all these things his anger was kindled against his father, and he hastened and took a **hatchet** in his hand, and came unto the **chamber of the gods**, and he **broke all his father's gods**. 34 And when he had done breaking the images, he placed the **hatchet in the hand of the great god** which was there before them, and he went out; and Terah his father came home, for he had heard at the door the sound of the striking of the hatchet; so Terah came into the house to know what this was about. 35 And Terah, having heard the noise of the hatchet in the room of images, ran to the room to the images, and he met Abram going out. 36 And Terah entered the room and found all the idols fallen down and broken, and the hatchet in the hand of the **largest**, which was not broken, and the savory meat which Abram his son had made was still before them. 37 And when Terah saw this his anger was greatly kindled, and he hastened and went from the room to Abram. 38 And he found Abram his son still sitting in the house; and he said to him, What is this work thou hast done to my gods? 39

*And Abram answered Terah his father and he said, <u>Not so my</u>
<u>lord</u>, for I brought savory meat before them, and when I came
nigh to them with the meat that they might eat, they <u>all at once</u>
<u>stretched forth their hands to eat</u> **before the great one** <u>had put</u>
<u>forth his hand to eat</u>. 40 And the large one saw their works that
they did before him, and his anger was violently kindled against
them, and he went and took the hatchet that was in the house
and came to them and broke them all, and behold the <u>hatchet</u>
<u>is yet in his hand as you see</u>.'*

Abram came up with another plan in dealing with those false
gods for their failure to speak, to eat, to move. Abram used their very
inabilities to speak or to move to destroy them. Abram was wise enough
to even come up with what to tell Terah about what occurred in the
room of images. Terah absorbed the story hook, line, and sinker.

Yashar 17:17-19:

*'At that time the HASHEM **appeared** to him and HE said
to him, **<u>I will make MY Covenant</u>** between ME and you,
and I will greatly multiply your seed, and this is the **<u>Covenant</u>**
which I make between ME and you, that every male child be
circumcised, you and your seed after you. 18 At eight days old
shall it be circumcised, and this Covenant shall be in your flesh
for an everlasting Covenant. 19 And now therefore your <u>name</u>
<u>shall no more be called Abram but</u> **Abraham**, and your wife
shall <u>no more be called Sarai but</u> **Sarah**.'*

The story of Abraham is crucial in overstanding the beginning of the
beginning of humanity. All of the people were products of manipulation
by the Annunaki, and then their offspring: the Amorites, the Emims,
the Zamzummims, and so on. What occurred in the Garden of Eden,
the first fall of humanity, the second fall of humanity, was related to
the Annunaki first, who by some form of *deoxyribonucleic acid* (DNA)
cross contamination, were able to breed with humans; and then those
forbidden creatures mated with the women (Ber./Gen. 6:4), who were
made from the brown soil of the eretz. Listen-up: this statement is

accurate because the women the sons of Elohim mated with were the descendants of Aw-dawn, who was taken from the ground (Ber./Gen. 2:7). What Abram did exposed the weakness in believing an inanimate figure could possibly be a true deity. When Elohim saw that Abram broke the images, and renounced those defiled figures as deities, The HASHEM Elohim spoke to Abram, and entered into a *Covenant* with him. Hear this well! All of the people prior to Abraham were contaminated, excluding Noah. All of those Progenitors contamination was passed down from Aw-dawn, who committed sexual acts in the Garden of Eden with the creatures in the garden (Talmud, Yebamoth, 63a). Before Noah there was Enoch, who was righteous before The HASHEM our Elohim, and because Enoch was righteous to Elohim, he was taken up to Shamayim without dying the death of the flesh (Ber./Gen. 5:24). Here is the main point in all of this: What Abram did caused Elohim to reconsider humanity, to provide another opportunity to reconcile man to Himself. To do that Elohim entered into the Covenant with righteous Abram, to begin a new race of people: The Hebrews. Therefore, his name was changed to Abraham, meaning: father of many (*dictionary.com*). However, I have determined the name Abraham to be more accurately defined as: A New Beginning.

We left off Devarim discussing the name change of Abram to Abraham, now let us return to Devarim, and the Hebrews in their travel to the Promised Land.

Devarim/Deu. 9:18 (AKJV):

*'And I fell down before the HASHEM, <u>as at the **first**</u>, forty days and forty nights: <u>I did neither eat bread, nor drink water</u>, because of all your sins which you sinned, in doing **<u>wickedly</u>** in the sight of the HASHEM, to provoke HIM to anger.'*

What occurred leading to this verse is the Hebrews doing that which the heathens had done; the Hebrews made an <u>idol</u> to worship as their god (Dev./Deu. 9:16). They broke the First Three Commandments though they had seen miracle after miracle, and been freed from the oppression of other groups by Elohim. That innate portion of the Hebrews that remained in them when the Hebrews were severed from the wicked children of the fallen ones, is always fighting against the portion of them that desires to serve and worship Elohim. Did you catch it? Their is a war going on inside of the Hebrews to always do that which is pleasing to Elohim, and yet, there is that part which desires to be naughty. Listen-up: For the Hebrews to do right they have to know what sin is versus what transgression is. Don't allow the spin on words to make you believe sin and transgression to be identical partners for they are not. Sin is more aptly like scheming to defraud someone or soliciting a prostitute, and then stiffing him or her for the payment (Ber./Gen. 34:12; She./Exo. 22:17). It is not the sex that becomes the sin, it is the theft of sex by not paying the agreed price (Ber./Gen. 5:19). Transgression, however, is breaking *The Ten Commandments*. We must clearly overstand the difference in the Laws of sin and The Ten Commandments (She./Exo. 34:7; Bam./Lev. 16:16, 16:21; Yehoshua 24:19). The Scriptures clearly tell us in Bereshis 5:22: after Elohim gave The Ten Commandments: *"and HE added no more"*. What that tells us is: there is no law, no ordinance, no statute, equal to the Commands Elohim gave the Hebrews, written in stone. That indicates there is no variability in these rules whatsoever, do not veer left, do not veer right. Keep your course straight down the middle of the road.

There is something else hidden in plain sight in verse 9:18. Watch this! Some will not believe this though it is written in the Scriptures: Mosheh, neither ate food or drunk water for forty days and forty nights. Does that sound familiar? Ha Mashiach did not eat or drink for forty days and forty nights (Mat. 4:2); Mosheh delivered the Hebrews out of Mitzrayim: The Deliverer (Acts 7:35); Ha Mashiach delivered the word of Elohim to the Hebrews: The Deliverer (Rom. 11:26); Mosheh performed miracles (Dev./Deu. 11:3); Ha Mashiach performed miracles (Acts 2:22); Mosheh was placed in a straw basket (She./Exo. 2:3); Ha Mashiach was laid in a straw manger (Lk. 2:7). The similarities are not by chance. Mosheh was buried in a secret place by Elohim, and no one knew the place of his burial (Dev./Deu. 34:6); Ha Mashiach has no place of burial (Eph. 4:8-10). Look at this: Melchizedek was '*1 For this*

*Melchizedek, king of Salem, <u>priest of The Most High Elohim</u> ... 2 King of righteousness 3 Without father, without mother, <u>**without descent,** having neither **beginning** of days, nor **end** of life;</u> but made like unto the <u>**Son of Elohim**</u>. Abides a priest continually* (Heb. 7:1-3)'. What this tells us is this: Ha Mashiach has been on eretz more than once: He came in the person of Melchizedek, Mosheh, and Ha Mashiach. Listen, listen: No normal human can live forty days without eating food, and especially, not drinking water. Ha Mashiach can come to eretz whensoever He chooses. As for Mosheh, Elohim said: *'And the HASHEM said unto Mosheh, See I have made you an **elohim to Pharaoh**: and Aharon your brother shall be **your prophet**'* (Ber./Gen. 7:1) Elohim Himself declared Mosheh to be an elohim. The purpose of Mosheh was to pave the way for the next time Ha Mashiach would come to HaAretz.

Many religions teach consciously or unconsciously a belief system of *monotheism*. Throughout our reading we have seen the words <u>gods,</u> and <u>God</u> used to describe deity. Now let us look at the importance of discerning the intent behind some word usage.

Devarim/Deu. 10:17 (AKJV):

'*For the HASHEM your Elohim is Elohim of gods, and HASHEM of lords, a great Elohim, a mighty, and a terrible, which regards not persons, nor take reward.*'

Were you able to find the errant word usage in this verse? First let us examine what *I AM THAT I AM* said to the Hebrews, paraphrasing; I the HASHEM your Elohim, *I AM* the Highest Elohim of all gods, and all lords, no matter who or what you recognize as a god. Now to this, use of language per the English Lexicon. This is the breakdown of the parts of the English language:

**PLEONASM**: *the use of more words than those necessary to denote mere sense (as in <u>the</u> man <u>he</u> said):* <u>redundancy</u>.

*DATIVE: of, relating to, or being the grammatical case that marks typically the indirect object of a verb, the object of some prepositions, or a possessor:*

*Origin and Etymology of DATIVE:*

*Medieval Latin datives subject to appointment, from Latin, assigned (of a guardian), from datus, past participle of dare to give; dative*

*Definition of DATIVE for English Language Learners:*

*Grammar: the form of a noun or pronoun when it is the indirect object of a verb.*

Merriam-Webster.com

These parts of speech in the English language are very important to overstand because the words change the meaning or hide the meaning within the texts. Above, what the *pleonasm* and dative tell us in relationship to Scripture, that things are not as they always appear in the bible. The redundancy in a *pleonasm* is like unto: *The **lady**, **she** said*; rather than: The **lady said**. The *dative* is where in Scripture word usage significantly changes the story. A *dative* represents something already in existence, a person, place or thing. In other words, the word or the thing or both already in existence, has been given a new name or identity or both. In example: Elohim to God; Ya'aqov to Yisra'el; Old Testament to bible. You get the point. Now look at the etymology of the following words.

God:

*"Old English god "supreme being, deity; the **Christian God**; image of **a god**; godlike person," from **Proto-Germani**  ***guthan** (source also of Old Saxon, Old Frisian, Dutch god, Old High **German got**, German Gott, Old Norse guð, **Gothic** guþ), from PIE *ghut- "that which is invoked" (source also of*

*Old Church Slavonic zovo "to call," Sanskrit huta- "invoked," an **epithet of Indra**), from root \*gheu(e)- "to call, invoke."*

etymonline.com

Lord:

*"**Mid-13c.**, laverd, loverd, **from Old English** = hlaford "**master of a household**, ruler, feudal lord, superior; husband," also "God," translating Latin dominus, Greek **kyrios** in the **New Testament**, **Hebrew Elohim** in the Old (though Old English drihten was more frequent). Old English hlaford is a contraction of earlier hlafweard, literally "**one who guards the loaves**," from hlaf "bread, loaf" (see loaf (n.)) + weard "keeper, guardian" (from PIE root \*wer- (3) "perceive, watch out for")."*

etymonline.com

Holy:

*"**Old English halig** "holy, consecrated, sacred; godly; ecclesiastical," from **Proto-Germanic \*hailaga**- (source also of Old Norse heilagr, Danish hellig, Old Frisian helich "holy," Old Saxon helag, Middle Dutch helich, Old High German heilag, German heilig, Gothic hailags "holy"), from PIE \*kailo- "whole, uninjured" (see health). Adopted at conversion for Latin sanctus."*

etymonline.com

Savior:

*"1300, "one who delivers or rescues from peril," also a title of J-sus Christ, from Old French sauveour, from Late Latin salvatorem (nominative salvator) "a saver, preserver" (source also of Spanish salvador, Italian salvatore), from salvatus, past participle of salvare "to save" (see save (v.)). In Christian sense, **a translation of Greek** soter "savior." Replaced Old English*

*hælend, literally "healing," noun use of present participle of hælan"*

etymonline.com

Savior as a noun:

1. As a noun: one that saves from danger or destruction
2. One who brings salvation; *specifically, capitalized* : J-sus

1. First Known Use: 14ᵗʰ century
   Merriam-Webster.com

All of the information above on specific word usage is invaluable to the truth of Scripture. The words God, god, lord, and so on, are errant in their use as being representative of the HASHEM Elohim of the Hebrews, and the *Hashilush Hakadosh* (Sacred Trinity) in totality. A <u>lord</u> is a man, a servant of low status in society. The word god is representative of the gods of the heathens. Here is what the parts of speech teach us about verse Devarim 10:17. Elohim is telling the Hebrews that, the gods of the other people, and the lords of the other people have no power as compared to HIS power. Moreover, the verse tells us that any heathen, who renounces the gods of the Anakims, the Anak, are acceptable to HIM (Dev./Deu. 9:2). Did you catch the parallel? It equates to the same type of conversion Abraham experienced as written in the Book of Yashar, Chapter 11.

Now we have to look at information *I AM THAT I AM* said to the Hebrews with regard to obtaining a blessing, and how being blessed can be changed into a curse for disobedience.

Devarim/Deu. 11:26-28 (AKJV):

'Behold, I set before you this day a <u>blessing and a curse</u>; 27 a **<u>blessing</u>**, if you **<u>obey</u>** the Commandments of the HASHEM your Elohim, which I Command you this day: 28 and a **<u>curse</u>**, if you will **<u>not</u>** obey the Commandments of the HASHEM your

*Elohim, but turn aside out of the way which I Command you
this day, to go after other gods, which you have not known.'*

The fundamental essential element in Scripture is "*other gods*". This
cannot be stated enough or over stated. It comes down to this simple
premise: Have no other god(s) period, whether of the Annunaki, or of
wood, or of stone, or gold, or silver, or anything representative of deity.
Blessings come in loyalty and obedience to Elohim only. Let's go, line
and precept.

Devarim/Deu. 12:2 (AKJV):

*'You shall utterly destroy all the places, wherein the nations
which you shall possess served their gods, upon the high
mountains, and upon the hills, and under every green tree.'*

Elohim told the Hebrews to destroy everything the heathens
possessed to purge the land of the wickedness that had gone on in those
lands. Where are those lands? The lands surrounding the Mountain
of Elohim: the land of the Amorites, Girgashites, Canaanites (Dev./
Deu. 7:1); which is also the land of Esau, who destroyed the Horims at
Mount Seir (Dev./Deu. 2:20-23). Elohim has told the Hebrews that in
obedience is blessing, and in disobedience is cursing. Watch this!

VaYikra/Lev. 26:14-17 (AKJV):

*'But if you will **not** listen to ME, and will **not** do all these
Commandments; 15 and if you shall despise MY statutes, or
if your soul abhor MY authority, so that you will not do all
MY Commandments, but that you break MY Covenant: 16 I
also will do this unto you; I will even appoint over you terror,
consumption, and the burning fever, that shall consume the
eyes, and cause sorrow of heart: and you shall sow your seed in
vain, for your **enemies** shall eat it. 17 And I will set MY face
against you, and you shall be **slain** before your enemies: they
that **hate** you shall **reign** over you; and you shall flee when
none pursues you.'*

Here Elohim has told the Hebrews: Do as I have Commanded you to do. Keep the Covenants I have made with Abraham, Yitzhaq, Ya'aqov, Mosheh, and all of the Prophets. Elohim also tells the Hebrews what will happen to them if they go into <u>disobedience</u>. This is a line and precept moment that will intensify as we continue our study of Devarim. Now to a topic that many dispute about in the Hebrew community on a daily basis, restricted meats.

Devarim/Deu. 12:15 (AKJV):

*'Notwithstanding you may kill and eat flesh in all your gates, **whatsoever** your soul lusts after, according to the blessing of the HASHEM your Elohim which HE has given you: <u>the **unclean** and the clean may eat thereof</u>, as of the **roebuck**, and as of the **hart**.'*

This verse is controversial because we know that the dietary Laws forbid certain animals from being consumed as food (VaYikra/Lev., Chapter 11). This verse reads like, the **unclean** person, and the **clean** person may eat the **roebuck** (young deer) and the **hart** (old deer). Is the verse referring to the person or the meat? Let us pull this together.

Devarim/Deu. 12:20-21 (AKJV):

*'When the HASHEM your Elohim shall **enlarge** <u>your border</u>, as HE has promised you, and you shall say, <u>I will eat **flesh**</u>, because your soul longs to eat flesh; you may eat flesh, **whatsoever** <u>your soul lusts after</u>. 21 If the place which the HASHEM your Elohim has chosen to put HIS name there <u>be **too far** from you</u>, then you shall kill of your herd and of your flock, which the HASHEM has given you, as I have Commanded you, and you shall eat in your gates **whatsoever** <u>thy soul lusts after</u>.'*

This verse tells us that whatsoever animal Elohim has put in the land where you are, kill and eat. This is referring to: The Hebrew, who is a far distance from the Promised Land, and that person has no clean animal to kill and eat, that whatsoever animal HE sends to you, you may eat that animal. Do you get it? When the Hebrew was in travel long distance from where the Hebrews keep the sanctioned animals for food, that then, and only then, could they kill and eat an unclean animal. It is not permitted for the Hebrew to have unclean animals in the Promised Land. Let us follow the flow from The Book of Yashar:

Yashar, Chapter 9:8:

'And *Terah had twelve gods* of large size, made of wood and stone, after the *twelve months of the year*, and he served each one monthly, and every month Terah would bring his **meat offering** and drink offering to his gods; thus did Terah all the days.'

# Meat, animal flesh, has been from the beginning a source of contamination. This goes to what the Annunaki did before and after the events that took place in the Garden of Eden. The fallen malachs contaminated almost all of the animals with sexual DNA contamination. That contamination led to the great flood.

Book of Yashar 83:26-29:

'At that time the children of Yisra'el continued their travel from the wilderness of Sinai, and they took a travel of three days, and the cloud rested upon the wilderness of Paran; there the anger of the HASHEM was kindled against Yisra'el, for they had provoked the HASHEM in asking HIM for **meat**, that they might eat. 27 And the HASHEM listened to their voice, and gave them **meat** which they ate for one month. 28 But after *this the anger of the HASHEM was kindled against them, <u>and</u> <u>HE smote them with a great slaughter</u>, and they were buried there in that place. 29 And the children of Yisra'el called that place Kebroth Hattaavah, because there they buried the people that <u>lusted flesh</u>.'*

The Hebrews were away from their camp, where they had animals acceptable for food. They were three days on foot away from the camp, and had no clean meat to eat. They asked Elohim to provide them meat to eat, Elohim gave them what animals were available around them to eat; however, HE was not pleased with them for the request to eat the unclean animals. Elohim's anger was such that, HE caused them to eat the same unclean animals for a full month as punishment. Because those Hebrews requested the unclean meat, ate the unclean meat, Elohim then took vengeance on them, and killed all of those, who ate the meat. Now let us look at several verses related to meat/flesh. In order to follow clean versus unclean animals we have to go back to the Fifth Day of Creation.

Let us now visit Scripture going back to the beginning of the Creations Stories. On day five of the creation, Elohim created all of the animals, fowl, and sea creatures (Ber./Gen 1:20-21). Listen-up: All of those creatures are clean. How can that be so? In verse 1:22 is the answer: *'And Elohim blessed them ... Be fruitful, and multiply ...'.* The reaffirmation of the non-human life being clean comes in verse 1:31: *'And Elohim saw everything that HE had made, and, behold, it was very good.'* There was nothing contaminated at that time. Hold on, this will become clear as we continue to pull the verses together. Elohim sent every creature HE made to Aw-dawn to be named (2:19). After Aw-dawn completed naming all of the creatures, Elohim also made a companion for Aw-dawn (2:22-23). Now we come to where the problem with the animals comes into play. Hasatan is in the Garden of Eden (3:1); this corrupt creature is going to cause many changes to come to the animal world (3:14), the plants (3:18), and humanity (3:19). Watch this! Because of the sexual acts committed by Chavvah, Hasatan, and Aw-dawn, came the contamination of all that Elohim had *blessed* and called *good*. Bereshis/Gen. 6:12 reads: '*And Elohim looked upon the earth, and, behold, <u>it was corrupt; for **all flesh** had been **corrupted**</u> his way upon the earth*'. There was not one form of life left unaffected by what the three of them did in the garden. Aw-dawn and Chavvah were never supposed to be in contact with Hasatan, the tree in the middle of the garden. Everything Elohim had created on the eretz, even the eretz itself, was now contaminated by the mixing of a spiritual creature(s) with flesh and blood creatures, Aw-dawn and Chavvah. The acts done by the three of them, led to Bereshis 6:4, the production of the giants. Elohim in HIS anger decided then to destroy the life HE had made in the great flood (6:17). However, Elohim decided to preserve a small amount of creatures of all kinds to begin life again (7:2-3); even the creeping things (7:14). In this restart, after the flood, Elohim tells all life to reproduce to fill the earth again (8:17). Now watch this! After the flood and all of the life is reproducing, Elohim tells them: '***<u>Every moving thing that lives</u>** shall be **meat** for you; <u>even as the green herb</u> have I given you all things* (9:3). Did you catch it? Everything is once more clean. How do we know that? Elohim made a *Covenant* with all of the life (9:15-17), not to destroy all life with a great flood again. But even though the contamination of the creatures is cleaned-up, the wickedness is not gone. Now look at this: As we have previously discussed, the wickedness would return to humanity, contaminating the life again. The return came by way of Ham, who raped Noah (9:22). Some will not believe what the Scriptures actually tell us in this story, and will deny that Ham raped Noah. One of the reasons we know for sure that the rape occurred is this: '*And Noah awoke from his wine, and **knew** what his younger son **had done** unto him* (9:24)'. Say what you will, but the Scripture has laid-out for us in the decency of wording what happened to Noah. Folks, one cannot awaken from a drunken stupor, and know someone saw them naked when their eyes are closed, and moreover, they are semi-comatose. This rape ushered in the return of curses (9:25). Here is the part of the story on contaminated animals, and people that pulls it all together: '*But in the fourth generation <u>they shall come here **again**</u>: for the <u>iniquity of the **Amorites**</u> is **not** yet full* (15:16)'. This goes back to Bereshis 10:16, and 14:13, the contaminated offspring of Ham, to Canaan, to the Amorites.

Did you overstand what happened with certain animals being good for food, and other animals deemed contaminated? The above verses explain why the Hebrews were put to death while traveling away from their camp. They requested meat to eat while they were in the wilderness, away from their homeland. The animals outside of the camp should not have been requested for food, leading those Hebrews to a death sentence. All of the above events are of the Annunaki. All of those contaminated people, the Zamzummims, the Emims, the **Amorites**, the Hittites, and all of those people are wicked, of whom, their offspring are the enemies of the Hebrews. Who are those people? The descendants of Ham and Yepheth, who became infected by the fallen malachs. Now let us look at a how some of those wicked people have worshiped their gods.

Devarim/Deu. 12:31 (AKJV):

'You **shall not** do so unto the HASHEM your Elohim: for every abomination to the HASHEM, which HE hates, have they done unto their gods; for even their **sons** and their **daughters** they have **burnt** in the fire to their gods.'

This is very important for the Hebrew to grasp. There is no human sacrifice for remission of sin Commanded by Elohim in the Torah, or the entirety of the Old Testament. Human sacrifice is not, I repeat, human sacrifice is not of Elohim. Human sacrifice is of Hasatan. Listen-up clearly: The very thought of human sacrifice is against the Commandments of Elohim written in stone (She./Exo. 20:13). Let this be clearly overstood: The Commandment not to kill is about a Hebrew killing a Hebrew, not the enemy. There is no Commandment in the Old Testament that is even suggestive of human sacrifice for sin. Those, of evil countenance came up with human sacrifice to honor their gods, Elohim never suggested human sacrifice as a way to remit sin to HIM. In fact, when Elohim told Abraham to offer up Yitzhaq, it was only a test, never was the act to come to an actuality (Ber./Gen. 22:1-12). No man or woman can be sacrificed to atone for another persons sins. All human sacrifice is of wickedness (Yeremiah 7:30-31; Psalm 106:37-38; 2 Chronicles 28:1-3; 2 Kings 21:6; Leviticus 18:21, and more). You have missed a connection point in Scripture. Allow me to pull it together for you: Elohim told Abraham to sacrifice Yitzhaq for one purpose only, Abraham needed to be tested for his commitment and worthiness to become a new race of people, the Hebrews. Remember, Abraham destroyed the idols his father Terah worshiped. Elohim was making sure that Abraham had not *apostatized* (stopped believing in Elohim only) or blasphemed into other god worship. Do you get it? No man can die for the redemption of another man's sins. Elohim forbid. Let us look at Scripture counter to human sacrifice in redemption to Elohim.

> Devarim/Deu. 24:16 (AKJV):
>
> *'The father shall **not** be put to death for the son, **neither** the son be put to death for the father: every man shall be put to death for his **own** sin.'*

> Psalm 49:7 (AKJV):
>
> *'**No man can by any means redeem** his brother or give to Elohim a ransom for him.'*

> Ezekiel 18:20 (AKJV):
>
> *'The person who sins will die. The son will **not** bear the punishment for the father's iniquity, **nor** will the father bear the punishment for the son's iniquity; the righteousness of the righteous will be upon himself, and the wickedness of the wicked will be upon himself.'*

What many have been taught about redemption has nothing to do with the Elohim of the Hebrews. Human sacrifice is antithetical in all forms of presentation. The OT cannot be overturned by modern day writings. The enemy to the Hebrews has poisoned many people's minds with what they have written in newer books from A.D., and forward. Most of what is written in those books is anti-Torah. The teachings of those newer writings is a tool of the Annunaki, meant to deceive the people into what they desire in sacrifice to them. We will build on human sacrifice, line and precept, but for now let us add to the information about eating meat.

In returning to our discussion of eating meats, there is another element of eating meat that the Hebrews have to absolutely adhere thereto. I personally know Hebrews, who eat meat that is not fully cooked: pink to red on the inside. Folks, keeping the Ten Commandments is of complete necessity, but there are other Laws that the Hebrews must also keep. Not only are there certain animals that are to be offered for sin, and of festivals in honor of Elohim, there is a rule governing how well-done the meat is to be cooked. All meats offered in sacrifice, or that which is termed an *oblation,* is not to be wasted but eaten by the Hebrews. This is what the Scriptures say about eating the sacrifice:

Devarim/Deu. 12:23 (AKJV):

*'Only be sure that you **eat not the blood**: for the blood is the life; and you **may not eat the life** with the flesh.'*

This *Law,* not to eat any bloody meat, is fully covered in the Book of VaYikra/Lev. 17:1-14. The specificity in the Law to abstain from eating blood comes from the ritualistic practices of the heathens, the offspring of the fallen malachs, who offered human sacrifice to their gods (Dev./Deu. 12:30-31). The Laws given to the Hebrews all have a commonality: The Hebrews are not to follow any acts that came from the **Amorites**, the Canaanites, and any of those groups the Hebrews were to destroy. Here, I have highlighted *Amorite* again, because, if you have not noticed, the Amorite has been the greatest opponent in all of our reading to the Hebrews. You see, the sons of *Belial,* of the Annunaki, gave wicked, evil worship practices to their offspring (Dev./Deu. 13:13). Those offspring are the same people Elohim told the Hebrews to destroy their cities, and to kill the heathens, including the animals (Dev./Deu. 13:15). There is a very interesting point in that Scripture: For the Hebrews to kill the cattle along with the people. The heathens, in their religious practices, also did animal sacrifice to their gods; thereby, those animals were deemed as unclean for the Hebrews to keep. The Hebrews must never allow anything into the camp that is polluted, after they have cleaned-out, removed all contamination from the Promised Land.

The Hebrews are a set-apart people, peculiar to Elohim only, a people above all other people of the eretz (Dev./Deu. 14:2). There are specific animals the Hebrews are to keep herds thereof: Oxen, sheep, deer, goats, *pygarg* (antelope), and the *chamois* (a type of goat; 14:4-5). Another Law pertaining to clean and unclean meats is this: The clean animal that dies of its own, is not to be eaten by the Hebrew, but is okay to give to a stranger that is in the camp, or it may be sold to an *alien* (extraterrestrial; 14:21). The alien is an offspring of the fallen malachs. The point being, those of non-Hebrew blood can eat whatsoever they please: the carcass of a dead animal, fat, and blood (VaY./Lev. 3:17), all of which is deemed as contaminated, and thereby forbidden for the Hebrew to eat. The Hebrew eating such flesh is polluted, requiring a purification period to be restored as clean. I have to also say this: Hebrews today are not all together in their homeland due to <u>disobedience</u>, which makes following the *Dietary Laws* impossible to keep. The reason this is impossible for the Hebrews today is this: The Hebrews have not all been brought back together in their own homeland, as one family, who raise their own animals, and grow their own crops. Do you overstand this? The Hebrews are still in bondage, being ruled by the heathens in every land they live, and are dependent on their enemies, in want of all things (Dev. 28:48). The Hebrews today saying they are awake, and that they are in complete compliance to Torah are not in truth. That Hebrew or those Hebrews do not, I repeat, do not overstand we are not in the time of our reconciliation to Elohim. Most of the Hebrews living today don't even know they are Hebrews, and moreover, the dominant portion of the Hebrews today are practicing religion, not spirituality. Once the Hebrews return to worshiping Elohim only, coming out of the ways of the heathens, then and only then will Elohim bring the Hebrews together as a whole, collecting them from every land where they have been scattered (Dev. 30:3). However, Hebrews can keep the *Law* of not eating the fat, and the blood. Furthermore, Hebrews can avoid eating the flesh of forbidden animals.

Now to a topic that many people, Hebrew and non-Hebrew alike either do not realize exist, or they have no comprehension of what the Scriptures reveal to us. Look at this verse:

Devarim/Deu. 21:22-23 (AKJV):

*'And if a man have committed a <u>sin worthy of death</u>, and he be to be <u>put to death</u>, and you **<u>hang</u>** him on a **<u>tree</u>**: his body shall not remain all night upon the **<u>tree</u>**, but you shall in any wise <u>bury him that day</u>; (for he that is **<u>hanged</u>** is **<u>accursed</u>** of Elohim;) that your land be not defiled, which the HASHEM your Elohim gives you for an inheritance.'*

There is a multitude of valuable information in these verses: Anyone committing a crime worthy of death is to be hung on a tree, not pierced through with a sharp weapon, not shot with a pellet, not stoned to death. Watch this!

Bereshis/Gen. 40:19; 40:22 (AKJV):

*'yet within three days shall Pharaoh lift up your head from off of you, and shall **<u>hang you on a tree</u>**; and the birds shall eat your flesh from off of you. ... 40:22: but he **<u>hanged</u>** the chief baker: as Yosef had interpreted to them.'*

This is the story of Yosef in the prison of the Pharaoh of Mitzrayim, after the queen falsely accused Yosef of attempted rape (39:11-16). Two of the kings men, the chief baker, and the chief butler were also imprisoned at that time (40:2-3). The end result of the story was death for the chief baker, who was condemned for his crime, and <u>hanged on a **tree**</u>.

Bamidbar/Num. 25:4 (AKJV):

*'And the HASHEM said unto Mosheh, Take all the heads of the people, and **hang** them up before the HASHEM against the sun, that the fierce anger of the HASHEM may be turned away from Yisra'el.'*

This verse goes to the topic of serving other gods. The men of Yisra'el committed transgression by marrying the women of the Moabites, the offspring of the fallen angels (25:1-2). Moreover, the women were able to convince their Hebrew husbands to worship the gods of the Moabites, angering the Elohim of the Hebrews (25:3). Because of that, all of the Hebrews, who participated in the crime were cursed by Elohim, WHO ordered Mosheh to **hang** them all (25:4). For the Hebrew to marry out of the Hebrew race is prohibited by Elohim, and the worship of any other god is to be cursed, whether a god of wood, stone, metal, or of the Annunaki gods.

Yehoshua 10:26 (AKJV):

*'And afterward Yehoshua smote them, and slew them, and **hanged** them on five trees: and they were **hanging** upon the trees** until the **evening**.'*

What led to this verse was a war of the Hebrews against the **Amorites**, and their five kings (10:6). Once more we see the offspring of the fallen malachs, in this case the Amorite family. Yehoshua and the Hebrews defeated the Amorites but all of the kings escaped, and hid in the mountains, in a cave (10:18). When Yehoshua was informed of where the kings had escaped, they pursued them, finding them in the cave (10:22). Here is an interesting observation about the five kings: Those were the kings of Hebron, Yarmuth, Lachish, Eglon, and Yerushalayim (10:5). Did you catch it? Hebron, a suburb of Yerushalayim, and Yerushalayim are all under the control of the **Amorites**. All of the afore mentioned cities are the region roundabout the *Promised Land*. The lands were occupied by the Amorites, Canaanites, Hittites, Perizzites, Yebusites, and Hivites all around Mount Hermon (11:3). This is not news, the entire *Torah* places great emphasis on who those people are, the enemies of the Hebrews. To the point at hand: To be hung on a tree is to be the cursed of Elohim.

2 Samuel 4:12 (AKJV):

*'And Daviyd commanded his young men, and they slew them, and cut off their hands and their feet, and **hanged** them up over the pool in Hebron. But they took the head of Ish-bosheth, and buried it in the sepulcher of Abner in Hebron.'*

In this story, Daviyd was informed by the young man, who killed Saul, that Saul was dead (1:10; 4:10). The young man thought he was informing Daviyd of good news because of the evil acts Saul had committed by becoming involved with familiar spirits, bringing up the spirit of Samuel from the dead (1 Sam 28:7; 15). However, Daviyd rebuked the young man, and had him executed, and his body <u>hung on the tree</u>. Hanging being the ultimate of cursing to the body.

Ezra 6:11 (AKJV):

*'Also I have made a decree, that whosoever shall alter this word, let **timber** <u>be pulled down from his house</u>, and being set up, let him be **hanged** thereon; and let his house be made a dunghill for this.'*

In this story, Darius the king, made a decree to rebuild the House of Elohim that had been robbed and torn down by Nebuchadnezzar (6:1-5). Darius ordered all of the builders of the temple to be paid at his expense (v.8). Darius then issues the warning above that, if anyone violate his orders in rebuilding the temple, be **hanged** <u>from timber</u> taken from <u>his own **house**</u> (6:11). The violator to be viewed as nothing more than dung. Hanging is the greatest insult that can be given to a person, especially the Hebrew. Those who are hung are seen as the lowest of the lowest in society. Let's keep going, line upon line.

Esther 2:23 (AKJV):

*'And when inquisition was made of the matter, it was found out; therefore they were both **hanged on a tree**: and it was written in the Book of the Chronicles before the king.'*

The underlying stories behind this verse are the love of the King Ahasuerus for Esther (2:16-17); and hatred toward anyone of Hebrew heritage (3:13). The Babylonians had overthrown Yerushalayim, and taken many of the Hebrews captive (2:6). Where these events occurred is very interesting, the land was all under the control of King Ahasuerus, and his conquest covered land from India to Ethiopia (1:1). In captivity in India, Esther was told by her uncle, Mordechai, not to reveal her identity of being a Hebrew to their captors (2:10). Here is the thing in this: the Indians and the Hebrews have the same language and characteristics; otherwise, how could Esther keep her identity a secret? What lead to the above verse is that, Haman felt disrespected by Mordechai because Mordechai refused to honor him (5:9). Haman told his wife Zeresh of the incident, and Zeresh then called for a gallows to be built to hang Mordechai thereon (5:14). Esther found out of the plan to hang her uncle, Mordechai, and by that time Esther had become the queen (7:3). The king loved the beautiful queen and would do whatsoever she requested of him. When the king heard the words of his wife (7:3-6), he then ordered the wicked Haman to be **hanged** on the gallows made from **trees** (7:9).

Acts 5:30; 10:39 (AKJV):

*'The Elohim of our fathers raised up Messiah, Whom you slew and **hanged on a tree**. ... 10:39: And we are witnesses of all things which He did both in the land of the Hebrews, and in Yerushalayim; Whom they slew and **hanged on a tree**.'*

In all our reading in the Old Testament, pulling many pieces of Scripture together, we have seen that sacrifice in honor of Elohim is always an animal, and that all human sacrifice is wicked, evil practice done by the children of the Annunaki. We have also seen that **hanging** is the most dishonorable death in all of humanity. Here, I must put in some more information from word *etymology*. After the insertion of word research, and many more Scriptures, will will resume where we left off in The Book of Devarim. In the above verse, the person, hung on that tree has been falsely represented as Ha Mashiach, when in actuality it is representative of **_Zeus_**. When you look at word etymology for the person, whose name I removed from the verse is this: **_Greek_** *form of* **_Joshua_**, *used variously in* **_translations_** *of the Bible. From late* **_Latin_** **_Iesus_** *(properly pronounced as three syllables), from* **_Greek_** **_Iesous_**: *Zeus:* *supreme god of the ancient* **_Greeks_** *and master of the others, 1706, from* **_Greek_**, ... *Old* **_Persian_** *daiva-* "*demon, evil god*" (etymonline.com). Do you see the picture? The Scriptures have been infused, in many aspects, with a false narrative to deceive the people into worshiping a demon. Ha Mashiach was hung on a tree, but that was an act of the wicked, evil children of the fallen malachs. LISTEN-UP: HA MASHIACH IS THE HEBREW MESSENGER, WHO CAME TO DELIVERY THE **LAW** OF ELOHIM; HA MASHIACH WAS NOT SENT TO BE A HUMAN SACRIFICE TO SAVE EVERYONE, WHO BELIEVES ON HIS NAME; HA MASHIACH TOLD US TO KEEP THE **LAW**; HA MASHIACH'S NAME WAS TRANSLATED OVER AND AGAIN. No where in the entirety of the Old Testament will you find any human sacrifice from Elohim. Elohim told us to worship HIM, and HIM only. Watch this:

Isaiah. 43:10-11 (AKJV):

'You are MY witnesses, says the HASHEM, and MY servant whom I have **chosen**: that you may know and believe ME, and understand that I AM HE: **before** ME there was no Elohim formed, **neither** shall there be after ME. 11 I, even I, AM the HASHEM; and beside ME there is **no Savior**.'

*I AM THAT I AM* has told us explicitly there was **no** Elohim before HIM or after HIM. The other gods are the Annunaki, Whom Elohim made, and by their evil coup of Shamayim became the enemy. Once the evil Annunaki saw the beautiful people Elohim made, they invaded humanity by sexual DNA manipulation, causing the fall in the Garden of Eden, and again after that in their offspring, produced from the fallen malachs mating with the children of Elohim in Bereshis 6:4, resulting in some of the offspring being giants, corrupted flesh. Line upon line and precept upon precept. Moving forward.

Isaiah. 45:21-25 (AKJV):

*'Tell you, and bring them near; yea, let them take counsel together: who has declared this from ancient time? Who has told it from that time? have not I the HASHEM? And there is __no Elohim else__ beside ME; an alone Elohim and a __Savior__; there is __none__ beside ME. 22 Look unto ME, and be you __saved__, all the ends of the earth: for I AM Elohim, and there is __none__ else. 23 I have sworn by Myself, the word is gone out of MY mouth in righteousness, and shall not return, That unto ME __every knee shall bow__, every tongue shall swear. 24 Surely, shall one say, in the HASHEM have I righteousness and strength: even to HIM shall men come; and all that are incensed against HIM shall be ashamed. 25 In the HASHEM shall __all__ the seed of Yisra'el be validated, and shall glory.'*

These verses are contradicted by the writings of the NT. Here, again Elohim has declared to us that, HE and HE alone is the **Savior.** Let me say this: The Savior and the Messiah are not synonyms. The Savior is the life giver; whereas, the Messiah is the Messenger sent from Elohim, to reinforce the rules of Law given to another Messenger, by the name of Mosheh. The words __no__ and __none__ are beyond variability, there is not wiggle room up, down, left, or right. Moving forward.

Isaiah. 49:26 (AKJV):

*'And I will feed them that oppress you with their own flesh; and they shall be drunken with their own blood, as with sweet wine:*

*and all flesh shall know that I the HASHEM AM your **Savior**
and your **Redeemer**, the **Mighty One** of Ya'aqov.'*

Here, Elohim once more tells us, HE is the **Savior**. Now the
word **Redeemer** has been inserted into the reading. The synonyms for
Redeemer include, but is not limited thereto are: *deliverer, rescuer, saver,
savior, defender, guardian, protector, and keeper* (Merriam-Webster).
What this tells us is: Elohim is saying to the Hebrews, in <u>obedience</u> to
ME, no one can harm you, or take your place as MY Chosen People,
as I gave you the Promise in Ya'aqov. Let's keep going.

Hosea 13:4 (AKJV):

'Yet I AM the HASHEM your Elohim from the land of
*Mitzrayim, and you shall know **no god but ME**: for there is **no
Savior** beside ME.'*

Isaiah told us repeatedly that the One Savior we have is Elohim,
now in the line and precept methodology, Hosea has reinforced that
fact as recorded in the Scriptures. Listen-up: The Messiah of the NT is
not the Ha Mashiach of the OT. Those, who translated the Scriptures
embellished the Scriptures with teachings that are ascribed to the
children of the fallen malachs. Hebrews following the ways of NT
doctrine are following pagan practices, Elohim is the Redeemer of the
Hebrews.

No where in the Old Testament will you find the worshiping of the
Ruach Hakodesh, or of Ha Mashiach. Elohim has told us over and over
that, HE alone is our Supreme Creator. However, the Ruach Hakodesh
was sent to teach us, to guide us, and to grant the gifts of the Ruach.
Ha Mashiach came to deliver the *Law* of Elohim, the same Law Elohim
gave to Mosheh. Human sacrifice is strictly forbidden in the OT, and
much of what is written in the NT amounts to deceptive garbage, ready
for the dung hill. Elohim did not break HIS Own Law by having Ha
Mashiach sacrificed for the Hebrews, or the world, and especially not
for the heathens, who have been a plague to HIS Chosen People from
the beginning. Elohim is the Elohim of gods, and the <u>only Elohim</u> of

the <u>Hebrews only</u>. All non-Hebrew people have to renounce their gods, and commit to following the Laws Elohim gave to the Hebrews in order to be acceptable to Elohim. The belief that the human sacrifice written of in the NT is but foolery, perpetrated upon the world to deceive the whole world into believing a lie (His./Rev. 12:9).

I would be totally remiss to leave this topic without addressing something found in the *New Testament*: *Eli, Eli, Lama Sabachthani?* This is very interesting because it is one of the only verses found in the NT written in Hebrew. Think on that! Why would the transcribers leave those Hebrew words in the NT, an actual *transliteration*, and not a *translation*, of those Hebrews words in their book, and then render the interpretation of those words? The interpreted being as follows: *'My Elohim, My Elohim, why have YOU forsaken Me* (Mat. 27:46)? 1 Samuel 2:12: *'Now the sons of Eli were sons of Belial; they knew not the HASHEM'*. The first thing we have to overstand is, who is Eli? The answer to the question is found in 1 Samuel 3:13-14 (AKJV):

> *'For I have told him that I will <u>punish his house **forever** for</u> <u>the iniquity</u> which he knew of; because his sons made themselves **vile**, and he restrained them not. 14 And therefore I have sworn unto the house of **Eli**, that the iniquity of Eli's house <u>shall **not** be purged with</u> **sacrifice** nor offering **forever***.'

For the evil the sons of Eli did, that part of the family-line of the Hebrews were forever cursed. Eli knew that his sons had violated the process of sacrifice (1 Sam:13-16). The sons of Eli were also rapists (2:22). Elohim had shown Samuel in a vision or dream what the sons of Eli had done (3:1-6). Here is another interesting truth of Samuel, at the time of the vision, Samuel had not met Elohim (3:7). The vile things that Eli's sons did caused the curse of the house of Eli (3:13-14). Additionally, the sons of Eli, Hophni and Phinehas, have the Ark of the Covenant (4:4). That act caused Elohim to slay both Hophni and Phinehas (4:11). Line and precept; here we go. Abiathar had become the priest, and he too did a terrible thing by offering **sacrifice** not commissioned by Elohim (1 Kings 1:19-25). Shelomoh is now the king and has the following words for Abiathar:

1 Kings 2:27 (AKJV):

'*So Shelomoh thrust out Abiathar from being priest unto the HASHEM; that he might fulfill the word of the HASHEM, which HE spoke concerning the house of **Eli** in Shiloh.*'

Under the *mamlachah* (kingdom) of Shelomoh came the fulfillment of the curse of Eli. There are many sources of information that tell us the messiah written of in the NT is not the Ha Mashiach. Eli is cursed, so the question has to be: The person in the NT tortured and hung on a tree (Acts 10:39), was that the Mashiach or the agent of Hasatan? Here is more information vaguely found in the NT (Acts 2:27). Watch this!

THE CABALA/TALMUD:

"Jesus is in hell, being boiled in hot excrement" Gittin 57a

"She (Mary) who was the descendant of princes and governors played harlot with carpenters" Sanhedrin 106a

"All gentile children are animals" Yebamoth 98a

"Adam had sexual intercourse with all the animals in the Garden of Eden" Yebamoth 63a

"Even the best of the gentiles should be killed" Soferim 15, Rule 10

"Satan had sexual intercourse with Eve in the Garden and Cain was their issue; therefore, all of humanity is basically demonic/evil EXCEPT the Hebrews whom became purified when Moses went to the Mountain (Mount Sinai)."

These verses fill-in much of what is missing from the AKJV of

Scripture; and moreover, reveals to us why the messiah of the NT shouted out: "*Eli, Eli Lama Sabachthani?*" The messiah of the NT was abandoned by his god, who is not the Elohim of the Hebrews. Listen-up: the Savior, the Messiah, the Redeemer of the Hebrews is the same Elohim, WHO transformed Abraham into a new race of people. The Elohim of the Hebrews is the same Elohim, WHO transformed Ya'aqov into Yisra'el. The transformation was spiritual, not physical. Now look at this information from different books.

Five Deaths of the Cabala/Talmud:

'*Jesus Stoned: Then "__hanged__" or crucified, Sanhedrin 43a-43b; 67a (Jewish Encyclopedia)*
*Jesus' Apostles: All killed, Sanhedrin 43a and their names decoded by the Jewish Encyclopedia.)*
*Jesus Crucified: As a "blasphemer." (Sanhedrin 46a; Jewish Encyclopedia)*
*Jesus Burned: Sanhedrin 52a: Manner of burning; Yebamoth 6b: Verified by Jewish Encyclopedia under "Balaam." He is "lowered into __dung__ up to his armpits then a hard cloth was placed within a soft one, wound round his neck and the two loose ends pulled in opposite directions forcing him to open his mouth. A Wick was then lit, and thrown into his mouth so that it descended into his body and burnt his bowels...his mouth was forced open with pinchers against his wish..." And: "The death penalty of 'burning' was executed by pouring molten lead through the condemned man's mouth into his body, burning his internal organs."*
*Jesus Strangled: "He was lowered into __dung__ up to his armpit, then a hard cloth was placed within a soft one, wound round his neck, and the two ends pulled in opposite directions until he was dead." (Sanhedrin 52a; Repeated Sanhedrin 106b, verified by Jewish Encyclopedia)*
*Jesus in Hell: Where His punishment is "boiling hot semen," Gittin 57a identified as Jesus in footnote to same, and in Jewish Encyclopedia under "Balaam."*

*Christians in Hell: In the above passage punished by "boiling hot excrement" which is the punishment for all who mock "at the words of the sages." (Talmud)*
*Jesus: "Committed bestiality," "corrupted the people," is "turned into hell." (Sanhedrin 105a)*
*Jesus "Limped on one foot" and "was blind in one eye," "he practiced enchantment by means of his membrum (penis)," "he committed bestiality with his ass," he was a fool who "did not even know his beast's mind. (Sanhedrin 105a-105b)*
*Jesus: Attempts to seduce woman, is excommunicated by a Rabbi and then worships a brick, was a seducer of Israel, and practiced magic. (Sanhedrin 107b, Jewish encyclopedia)*
*Jesus' Resurrection cursed: "Woe unto him who makes himself alive by the name of **God**." (Sanhedrin 106a)'*

All of these sources cannot be labeled as *pseudepigraphon*, leaving only the AKJV of Scripture as valid. We have looked at information from *The Book of Enoch, The Orthodox Jewish Bible, The Cabala Talmud, The Book of Yashar, The King James Bible, The Jewish Encyclopedia,* and more. Information that when pulled together presents a more complete picture. Moreover, we have looked at word displacement from various sources explaining the origin of words, and how many words of Scripture have been changed, hiding the true meaning in certain verses of Scripture. This is not by accident; but rather, is intentional deceit, by the descendants of the Annunaki, to blind the world to the truth, the whole world should believe a lie (2 Thes. 2:11). It is all the work of the sons of Elohim, who defiled themselves in the attempted coup of Shamayim, the war in Shamayim (His./Rev. 12:7-12). The AKJV of Scripture itself leaves some clues to the relevance of other sources as being legitimate *Canons* of Scripture: Yehoshua 10:13; 2 Samuel 1:18: Bereshis/Gen. 4:17-18, 5:18-19, 5:21-24: Yehudi 11:5: Yude 1:14.

Because the Scriptures have been manipulated, it presents us with topics that we may never know the answer to, and or perhaps, we are not to overstand. However, there is something else that has to be presented on the life of Ha Mashiach, and that of the New Testament messiah.

First thing is this: Who is this messiah in the NT? This next verse from *The Book of Maccabees* reads as follows.

1 Maccabees 3:48:

*'And laid open the book of the **Law**, wherein the **heathen** had sought to paint the **likeness of their images**.'*

Listen-up: The Hebrews have been displaced from their land repeatedly, brutalized, demoralized, castigated, and more for <u>disobedience</u> to Elohim. What this verse tells us is: Now the heathen, the enemy to the Hebrew has now plotted on how to steal the identity of the Hebrews. The Hebrew people are Shemetic people, who live in Yisra'el. The Hebrews require no skin protection from the sun, their skin is made to endure the heat of a desert environment. To see the figures inserted into the Scriptures, look at the *KJ Family Bible*. The pictures in that bible show all of the Hebrew patriarchs to be Caucasian. It does not even make logical sense for that region, the figures show what the heathens have done in producing their own bible. Let me say this because if I don't say this, someone will try to present me as a racist for telling the truth of Scripture: Not all people of non-melanin skin are the children of Hasatan. These truths are not about skin color, but rather, are proof positive of what the Scriptures said was to come. The Hebrews are of brown skin hue. The Scriptures themselves bare-out this fact because humanity was taken from the brown eretz (Ber./Gen. 2:7).

The very fact in putting these images in a book, and calling them the Hebrews is *iconography* at its best. These pictures are in direct violation of the Scriptures because we are to have no images of deity, period (She./Exo. 20:4; Dev./Deu. 4:16-18, 23, 4:25, 5:8). This is the very methodology used to promote superiority of the children of the fallen malachs. Anyone with a modicum of intelligence about history, will recognize that such renderings: painted-over, repainted, recreated, from the days of Biblical History simply cannot be accurate. *The Book of Maccabees* got it exactly right. The use if *iconography* is one of the most powerful ways to influence a belief, to support and promote a lie. Line and precept here we go.

Isaiah 54:7-10 (AKJV):

'For a **small moment** have I **forsaken you**; but with great mercies will I gather you. 8 In a little **wrath** I hid MY face from you for a **moment**; but with everlasting kindness will I have mercy on you, saith the HASHEM your **Redeemer**. 9 For this is as the waters of Noah unto ME: for as I have sworn that the waters of Noah should no more go over the earth; so have I sworn that I would **not** be wroth with you, nor rebuke you.'

These verses are a predetermined reality check for what will happen to the messiah written of in the NT. This determination tells us something is amiss that is yet to come. Let us look at some parallel verses from the AKJ Bible and the *Septuagint*:

Isaiah 43:10-11:

'You are MY witnesses, says the HASHEM, and **MY servant** whom I have **Chosen**: that you may know and believe ME, and understand that I AM HE: before ME there was **no** Elohim formed, **neither** shall there be **after** ME. 11 I, even I, AM the HASHEM; and beside ME there is **no savior** (AKJV).......

'Be you MY witnesses, and I too AM a **WITNESS**, says the HASHEM Elohim, and **MY servant** whom I have **Chosen**; that you may know, and believe, and **understand** that I AM HE: before ME there was **no** other Elohim, and after ME there shall be **none**. 11 **I AM Elohim**; and beside ME there is **no Savior** (Sept.).'

The first difference in these parallel verses is that Elohim Himself says: HE bears witness that HE will send HIS servant, to deliver the word of truth to the people. Elohim makes a specific point that has to be considered in overstanding the historical value of Scripture from the

240

first word written: Elohim staunchly said twice: There is **no** Elohim but HIM, and that there is **no** Savior but HIM. Now let us look at some verses from the New Testament for a comparative read to Isaiah 43:10-11.

> Luke 5:20, 22:69-71; Mattithyahu 14:33, 28:9-10; Y'hochanan 8:58 (AKJV):
>
> *'And when he saw their faith, he said unto him, Man, <u>your</u>* *<u>sins are **forgiven you**</u>. ..... 22:69-71: Hereafter shall the Son* *of man sit on the right hand of the **power of Elohim**. 70* *Then said they all, Are you then the Son of God? And he said* *unto them, You say that I am. 71 And they said, What need* *we any further witness? for we ourselves have heard of his own* *mouth. ..... Mattithyahu 14:33: Then they that were in the* *ship came and **worshiped him**, saying, Of a truth you are the* *Son of God. ..... 28:9-10: And as they went to tell his disciples,* *behold, "Jesus" met them, saying, **All hail**. And they came and* *held him by the feet, and **worshiped him**. 10 Then said "Jesus"* *unto them, Be not afraid: go tell my brethren that they go into* *Galilee, and there shall they see me. .....* Y'hochanan 8:58: *"Jesus" said unto them, Verily, verily, I say unto you,* **Before Abraham was, I am**.*

Oftentimes the reading of OT Scriptures does not match that of NT doctrines. The first thing that must be pointed out on the forgiveness of sin comes in the form of a question: Who has the authority to forgive sin? Watch this!

> Psalms 32:5, 51:4; Daniel 9:9; Isaiah 43:25; 1 Kings 8:39 (AKJV):
>
> *'I acknowledged <u>my sin to YOU</u>, and I did not cover <u>my iniquity</u>;* *I said, I will <u>confess</u> my transgressions to the HASHEM, and* *you <u>forgave</u> the iniquity of my sin. Selah, ... 51:4 Against YOU,* *YOU **only**, have I **sinned** and done what is **evil** in Your sight,* *so that YOU may be affirmed in Your words and blameless*

> *in Your punishment. ...* Daniel 9:9: *To the HASHEM our Elohim belong <u>mercy and **forgiveness**</u>, for we have rebelled against HIM ...* Isaiah 43:25: *I, I AM HE who blots out your <u>transgressions</u> for MY Own sake, and I will **<u>not remember</u>** your <u>sins</u>. ...* 1 Kings 8:39: *Then hear in heaven Your dwelling place and **<u>forgive</u>** and act and render to each whose heart YOU know, according to all his ways (for YOU, **<u>YOU only</u>**, know the hearts of all the children of mankind)'*

All of these verses tell the Hebrews to pray for remission of transgression and sin to The Most High Elohim. Believe what you have been taught about forgiveness, or believe the Scriptures, that is up to you. Overstand this: New Testament Scriptures sometimes conflict with the Old Testament. Let me say this: Whatever you are reading in the NT that is not supported by the OT must need scrutiny; the NT is not written by the Hebrews, it is a *Greco-Roman* book. The next question on forgiveness and the power to forgive also comes in the form of a question: Does the Son have the power of the Abba?

Isaiah 40:18, 25, 46:5 (AKJV):

> *'To whom then will you **<u>liken</u>** Elohim? Or what likeness will you **<u>compare</u>** unto HIM? ... 25 To whom then will you **<u>liken ME</u>**, or shall I be **<u>equal</u>**? Says the **<u>Sacred One</u>**. ... 46:5 Elohim says, To whom will you **<u>liken ME</u>**, and make **<u>ME equal</u>**, and **<u>compare ME</u>** that we may be **<u>alike</u>**?'*

These verses inform the Hebrews that there is no other entity period that has the power of Elohim. I hear your thoughts: But the *Hashilush Hakadosh* (Trinity)? Let this permeate throughout your thinking: The word *Trinity* is not found anywhere in the Scriptures, OT or NT. According to the *Stanford Encyclopedia of Philosophy*, the term *Trinity* is a modern day invention, derived from religious doctrine, with the intent to make equal Elohim, Mashiach, and the Sacred Ruach. The above verses are the recorded words of Elohim to the Hebrews; thereby, as being the words of Elohim, how then can any entity be equal to HIS Supremacy? Let not *cognitive dissonance* continue invade what you read.

When you examine the verses of Luke 5:20, 22:69-71; Mattithyahu 14:33, 28:9-10; and Y'hochanan 8:58, Elohim did not sacrifice the messiah of the NT. Listen-up: There is no Scripture of sacrifice to Elohim that involves a human Being. Human sacrifice is of the fallen malachs. The people, hearing the words "Jesus" spoke, making himself equal to Elohim, tortured and killed him for blasphemy. "Jesus" did not rebuke the people for bowing down, worshiping him, when per the Scriptures, we only bow in honor of Elohim. "Jesus" also implied himself to be the patriarch of the Hebrews, and that his power is equal to Elohim. I have presented you with multiple Scriptures showing that Elohim is of Himself Sovereign, and to be the Redeemer of the Hebrews, and of anyone, willing to renounce their religions, and then following the rules laid-out by Elohim for the Hebrews. It is up to you to receive or expel this information, Selah.

We will now return to Devarim/Deuteronomy. We will resume with the false prophet. Any prophet telling a Hebrew to practice any-kind of religion or to worship any entity except Elohim, is a false prophet. A true *P*rophet, is one who serves Elohim only, and who does not sway the Scriptures in any direction. Let us look at what the Scriptures say about the false prophet.

Devarim/Due. 13:6-7 (AKJV):

> *'If your brother, the son of your mother, or your son, or your daughter, or the wife of your bosom, or your friend, which is as your own soul, entice you secretly, saying, **Let us go and serve other gods**, which you have not known, you, nor your fathers; 7 namely, of **the gods** of the people which are **round about you**, near unto you, or far off from you, from the one end of the earth even unto the other end of the earth;'*

These verses spell-out what we have been seeing from multiple books in our reading: The Elohim of the Hebrews is not the god of other people. That is the message in the Talmud, the Jewish Encyclopedia, and every source studied for this book. Look! This is true even from the AKJV of Scripture. When you read the above verses, there are two points that should stick-out: One: *gods*, meaning more than one, dispelling *monotheism*; and two, *gods of **other people***, meaning those other people are serving the fallen malachs. No one else is this written to except the Hebrews.

Devarim/Deu. 13:13 (AKJV):

*'Certain men, <u>the children of **Belial**</u>, are gone out from among you, and have withdrawn the inhabitants of their city, saying, **<u>Let us go and serve other gods</u>**, which you have not known;'*

This goes to the pollution that creeps into the Hebrew camps, something that has plagued the Hebrews since the time of Abraham. What happens is: The offspring of the fallen malachs are very cleverly deceitful, and cunning; they are masters of disguise, and excellent persuaders in falsehood. These wicked spirits invade a Hebrew, who is either not well versed in the truth of Elohim, or is tempted with material gain, or sexual pleasure, whatever their weakness is. The enemy uses that weakness to convince the Hebrew to follow after their god. The Hebrew must at all times be mindful of who, he or she mingles with, and to keep their circle of association small. Watch this!

Devarim/Deu. 14:2 (AKJV):

*'For you are an sacred people unto the HASHEM your Elohim, and the HASHEM has **<u>chosen</u>** you to be a **<u>peculiar people unto Himself</u>**, above **<u>all</u>** the nations that are upon the earth.'*

Do you overstand the straight-up fact, not an implication, of what this verse is saying to the Hebrews? The Hebrew only is of Elohim, and no one else. The Hebrew is a peculiar treasure to Elohim, created for the express purpose to follow Elohim only. The word *peculiar* means: *Special quality or identity; distinguished; class; unique; eccentric*, and much more

(Merriam-Webster). *Peculiar of the Hebrew word: **cegullah** (seg-ool-law): feminine. Pass participle, of an unused root meaning: to shut-up; wealth (as closely shut-up):-jewel, peculiar (**treasure**), proper good, **special** (5459: Strong's Exhaustive Concordance of the Bible).* The Scriptures, word definition, and word etymology tells us that the Hebrew is the envy of the world because the Hebrew is the select of Elohim; a people brought forth from the heathens, purified by the Ruach Hakodesh. A people separated from the heathen class, who are the contaminated offspring of the fallen malachs. From the time of Aw-dawn, unto the time of Abraham, every human was polluted by the fallen malachs. Not only were the people polluted, so were all of the creatures of the eretz. Listen-up: It was the contamination of humans, animals, fish, and fowl by the Annunaki that caused Elohim to clean the eretz in the great flood (Bereshis/Gen. 7:16-24). Hebrews, do you grasp the complete concept of all these scripted writings? You, Hebrew man, Hebrew woman, are hated and envied by the world because you, and you alone are the children of The Most High Elohim, Abba asked little in return for your creation and separation from the heathen: Obedience! This will be a line and precept moment as we continue to follow the Scriptures.

Now to something every Hebrew should also overstand: Brotherly, and sisterly love, and support of one Hebrew for another.

Devarim/Deu. 15:1-2 (AKJV):

> *'At the end of every seven years you shall make a **release**. 2 And this is the manner of the release: Every creditor that lends ought unto his neighbor shall release it; he shall **not** exact it of his **neighbor**, or of his **brother**; because it is called the HASHEM'S release.'*

Simply what these verses are telling us is, to help one another out in supply of food and basic subsistence. If the Hebrew you have helped is still in debt to you at the end of a seven year period, that debt is to be expunged to give that person a fresh start. That kind of support will keep the family together and strong, leaving no one destitute. Elohim being very aware that not everyone will have the same capabilities to sustain themselves gave this Law because there will always be poor among the Hebrews (Dev./Deu.15:7, 11). The Hebrew in debt to another Hebrew, this is important to overstand: Hebrews don't borrow from heathens, the Hebrew serving domestically to another Hebrew for their debt, no matter how much they owe, or the years they have served, are freed from the debt, and server-ship in the seventh year (v.12). However, if the Hebrew man or woman chooses to remain with the Hebrew they are in debt thereto, that Hebrew is to remain in service to the lender for the rest of their life (v. 17). This is the Law of the Release for Hebrew servitude.

Line and precept: the Hebrews are not only to help one another, the Hebrews are to come together in the first month of the year to celebrate and commemorate their freedom from Mitzrayim.

Devarim/Deu. 16:1, 13-14 (AKJV):

*'Observe the month of __Abib__, and keep the Passover unto the HASHEM your Elohim: for in the month of __Abib__ the HASHEM your Elohim brought you forth out of Mitzrayim by night. ... 13 You shall observe the feast of tabernacles seven days, after that you have gathered in your corn and your wine: 14 and you shall delight in your feast, you, and your son, and your daughter, and your manservant, and your maidservant, and the Levite, the __stranger__, and the fatherless, and the widow, that are within your gates.'*

The value in these verses is tremendously important. First, overstand this: The month *Abib* is the first month of the year to the Hebrews. Secondly, the month Abib is representative of the Hebrews freedom from Mitzrayim, and the event which led to their freedom, *The Passover*. The celebration of Passover then leads to all of the feasts the Hebrews are to celebrate annually. Furthermore, these verses tell us, who can participate in the celebrations. Listen-up: This is a must overstand, when the __stranger__ is in your camp, he or she is welcome to celebrate with you in the feasts. Make no mistake about who this stranger is: the stranger is a Hebrew from another camp, not a heathen. Heathens should not even be allowed into the camps, and if they are, they should not be allowed to remain there. Three times in the year all of the Hebrew males are to come together to present themselves to Elohim for the celebrations of *Unleavened Bread, The Feast of Weeks, and The Feast of Tabernacles* (v.16). And very importantly, when the men all come to celebrate the feasts, each man is to bring an offering to the functions. Each man is to bring what he can provide, no matter how small his contribution may be. And his contribution must not be viewed as insufficient by the other Hebrew males, for there is to be no respect of persons, they are family (v.19). When is the start of these celebrations? *Abib* begins in the growing and harvesting period. When it is time to harvest the crops, is the time the month Abib begins (vs. 16:9, 13).

We have discussed diligently the antithetical doctrine of *monotheism*. Now let us examine this as line and precept further to debunk such teaching as monotheism.

Devarim/Deu. 17:2-4 (AKJV):

'2 If there be found among you, within any of your gates which the HASHEM your Elohim gives you, man or woman, that has wrought wickedness in the sight of the HASHEM your Elohim, in **transgressing** HIS **Covenant**, 3 and has gone and **served other gods, and worshiped them,** either the **sun, or moon, or any of the host of Shamayim** (heaven), which I have not commanded; 4 and it be told you, and you have heard of it, and inquired diligently, and, behold, it be true, and the thing certain, that such abomination is wrought in Yisra'el.'

All throughout the Old Testament, we have seen the words, Serve or served other gods. Now the Hebrews have been freed from Mitzrayim, and are in camps, and are now to celebrate sacred days. The Hebrews are told again: Not to serve or worship any deity except the Elohim of the Hebrews. Other gods can be idols made of wood, metal, stone, and so forth; while serving another god can be any god of the heathens: Molech, Hasatan, or any of the Annunaki gods. It does not matter which of these a Hebrew gives reverence thereto, it is transgressing the Covenant of Elohim. Once more, I must say this: Elohim is not schizophrenic to Command the Hebrews not to worship or serve another god if there are no other gods. Listen-up: Even those, who give praise to the <u>stars, and the moon, and the sun</u> may possibly be in transgression. Transgression is such wickedness that Elohim has mandated that: Any Hebrew found guilty of transgression be put to death (17:5). Folks, come out of *cognitive dissonance, monotheism* is a fallacy. In actuality, many, who practice religion, are in the belief system of *henotheism:* The belief in multiple deities, but with one central god as the head of gods. The Hebrews over many centuries repeatedly went into idol worship or recognized the gods of other people. Sometimes serving the gods of the Moabites, the Ammonites, and so on (23:3). In each case, it resulted in the Hebrews suffering great affliction, and or death.

There are certain people who will be ordained of Elohim to provide guidance to the Hebrews as directed by Elohim. Here we will discuss the roles of the priest, the Levites, and the *P*rophet versus the *p*rophet.

Devarim/Deu. 18:1, 15, 20 (AKJV):

*'The priests, the Levites, and all the **Shevet** (tribe) of Levi, <u>shall have no part nor inheritance with Yisra'el</u>: they shall eat the offerings of the HASHEM made by fire, and HIS inheritance. ...15 The HASHEM your Elohim will raise up unto you a **Prophet** from the middle of you, of your brethren, like unto ME; unto him you shall listen; ... 20 But the **prophet**, which shall presume to speak a word in MY name, which I have not commanded him to speak, or that shall speak in the **name of other gods**, even that prophet shall die.'*

The priests and the Levites are a separate group, not a separate people, from the main body of Yisra'el. They are set-apart from those, who are set-apart. You did not catch it. The priests and the Levites have special duties to perform that requires many hours per day, six days per week. Their duties and responsibilities are such that, working normal farming and husbandry would be a monumental task for the priesthood to accomplish with their duties over the Tabernacle of the Congregation. The Levites are not counted among the other shevets (Bam./Num. 1:47; 1:50). The Levites were taken from the sons of Aharon (Bam./Num. 3:9), this is backed-up in verse 3:12: *'And I, behold, I have taken the Levites from among the children of Yisra'el instead of all the firstborn that open the matrix among the children of Yisra'el: therefore the Levites shall be mine;'* I AM THAT I AM said, the sons of Levi would become the priesthood. That priesthood would have land provided to them from all of the shevets for the sole purpose of managing the Tabernacle of the Congregation, the place that the sacrifices, and all of the ceremonies would be performed. The Levites were given land out of the Twelve Shevets land to be their own cities (1 Chr. 6:64-81). There is something more in the above verses that has to be pointed out: There are *P*rophets, and there are *p*rophets. The difference in these *epithets* (titles) is this: The Prophet is sent of Elohim; whereas the prophet is a self-proclaimed man, who is filled with lies and deception, one, who is serving his god(s), and is not sent by Elohim. Below is a concept of what a Prophet is:

# THE PROPHET

The word prophet evokes images in our thoughts and minds of Scriptural characters of Old. Howbeit, what is a prophet? In the Old Testament, the word prophet recognizes those men and women (prophetess') who foretold the things of Elohim to come. Prophets are endued with wisdom, knowledge, and overstanding, concerning the things of Elohim. They inspired others for the ministry of Elohim, to increase the number of Elohim's people, and to broaden the importance of Elohim's plan. Many of them could touch and heal, or touch and cause disease to come upon an individual; or they might simply speak into existence a plague or disease process; such as, the curse Elisha placed upon Gehazi in 2 Kings, Chapter 5. They were filled with authority from Elohim to orchestrate oracles and writings for the Sacred Scriptures. They were men and women of Elohim, set on course by Elohim, to do HIS tasks and lay the foundation for all generations. This is not the textbook definition of a prophet; it is the inspired meaning of the word prophet from someone, who has also been endued with great foresight, and inspiration from Elohim.

Are there still prophets today? Some say, No. However, I boldly proclaim, Yes! Are they the same as in the days of Old? Yes. The difference being, the prophets of Old had great responsibility in contributing to the writings and acts recorded in the Sacred Scriptures. They laid the foundation for everyone coming after them to embrace Elohim through the inspired word they received from the Ruach hakodesh. Prophets of today have a different calling from Elohim. The word is already written, and is not to be changed because it would be akin to changing Elohim. There are two *immutable* (unchangeable) things that exist, Elohim and that Elohim does not lie. So, in today's world, what is a prophet? In today's world, a prophet is someone endued with special gifts from

Elohim, acting under the influence of the Ruach hakodesh. They possess special insight into the things of Elohim. They have foresight and vision in and about the Word of Elohim. They are directors of vision for directing and leading the people in the right direction in their earthly travel. They see visions telling them what things that are written in the Scriptures, and the correct interpretation thereof, and what things are still to come to fulfillment, as written in the Scriptures. They are men and women, who prophesy over others, and lead the church in growth, both in size of building and in souls coming to Elohim.

Even more significantly, a prophet today, is a man or woman, who knows the Word of Elohim, and then, rightly dividing the Word of Elohim for soul saving in, *I AM THAT I AM*. Moreover, they bring out the true meaning of the Scriptures and present the word to us bringing it to the forefront of our minds in modern times. The prophet or prophetess expounds and expands upon the Word of Elohim, fully explaining the Word, in a manner that is clearly overstandable to the audience. Additionally, they are filled with vision for all aspects of life: church growth, outreach programs, care of the old, children, widows, and the poor. They stand strongly and boldly before the Throne of Elohim, spreading the good news about our Hashem, Ha Mashiach. They rebuke false teachings and those, who are in business (preaching) for the money and not for the saving of souls unto life. Simply put, they are under the influence of the Ruach hakodesh, to the honor and glory of Elohim, for the administration of and up-building of HIS Kingdom.

Are these modern-day prophets perfect? Absolutely not! However, they strive and fight each day for the up-building of Elohim's Kingdom. Do they sin? Absolutely, Yes! They are no different than the most prolific Scripture writer of the Sacred Scriptures, the Apostle *Shaul* (Paul). Shaul said about himself, *"I die daily"*. Meaning each day, I have to go before my Abba in prayer asking forgiveness for my sins. My brothers and sisters of Elohim, there are none of us, who sins not. Those with the gift of prophesy must use that gift to help others in order to increase Elohim's flock. Halleluia. Selah.

Now we will return to and continue with pulling the Scriptures together from Devarim/Deuteronomy. This next verse gives us a theme that has been repeatedly discussed throughout the Scriptures; the children of the fallen malachs.

Devarim/Deu. 23:3 (AKJV):

> 'An **_Ammonite_** or **_Moabite_** _shall **not** enter into the congregation of the Elohim_; _even to their tenth generation shall they not enter into the **congregation** of the Elohim **for ever**.'_

The children of the Ammonites, the Moabites, the Canaanites, the Hittites, and so on, are the contaminated offspring of the Annunaki. The Scriptures make it perfectly clear, they are not of Elohim, and they are not permitted into the camps of the Hebrews. Hebrews must stay away from intermingling with them in marriage, producing children, and most importantly, entering into the worship ceremonies in honor of the HASHEM. Shelomoh is a perfect example of how such intermingling and marriages can lead one away from The Most High Elohim (1 Kings 11:3-8). Shelomoh was influenced into building houses of worship for the gods of his *nashim* (wives): *Ashtoreth, Chemosh, and Milcom* (2 Kings 23:13). The above verse makes it implicitly clear: Those hybrid people are "**for ever**" excluded from the "**congregation**" of Elohim. Do you get it? Those people are the enemies of Elohim, and thereby, the enemies of the Hebrews.

In verse 23:3, the Ammonites, and Moabites are forever to be kept out of the Tabernacle of the Congregation. There are also Laws Elohim gave concerning the Edomites and the Egyptians. Watch this!

Devarim 23:7-8 (AKJV):

> 'You shall **not abhor an Edomite**; _for he is your brother: you shall **not abhor an Egyptian**; because you were strangers in his land. 8 The children that are begotten of them **shall enter into the congregation** of the HASHEM in their third generation.'_

Many have said or believe Edom, who is Esau, is a particular race of people. I contend that Edom is not a particular people; but rather is a spirit of opposition to Elohim. The spirit that dwells in Edom is the same pollution that infected the Moabites, and the Ammonites. However, the Egyptians, and the Edomites are given a reprieve for the behaviors they inflicted upon the Hebrews, and their adversity to Elohim. Allow me to pull this together for you: *Mitzrayim* (Egypt) enslaved the Hebrews, the chosen of Elohim. Watch this! Shemot/Exo. 7:3-4: '*And I will <u>harden Pharaoh's heart</u>, and multiply MY signs and MY wonders in the land of Mitzrayim. 4 But Pharaoh shall **not** listen to you, <u>that I may lay MY hand upon **Mitzrayim**</u>, and bring forth MY armies, and MY <u>people the children of Yisra'el</u>, out of the land of Mitzrayim by great authority*'. It was by Elohim that Pharaoh enslaved the Hebrews. Did you catch it? The Hebrews too needed to be purged of the contamination of the fallen malachs. Remember in the story of Terah and Abraham, the family-line the Hebrews would eventually emerge therefrom, Terah was a polluted idolater (Yashar 11:22-25). We have previously examined a large amount of genealogy, but for this segment of the study, repeating some information is necessary for clarity to bring the line and precepts of these verses together: Ber./Gen. 36:9: '*And these are the **generations of Esau** the father of the **Edomites in Mount Seir**.*' Folks, Ya'aqov and Esau are brothers! Esau however, did some awful things, such as selling his birthright (Ber./Gen. 25:31-33). Moreover, Esau was cross contaminated with the Annunaki. The following are some of the hybrid people, who lived in the land surrounding *Mt. Hermon*, also known as *Mt. Seir*: Devarim/Deu. 2:20-23 (AKJV): '*That also was accounted a land of **giants: giants** dwelt therein in **old time**; and the **Ammonites** call them **Zamzummims**; 21 a people great, and many, and tall, as the **Anakims**; but the HASHEM destroyed them before them; and they succeeded them, and dwelt in their stead: 22 as HE did to the children of **Esau, which dwelt in Seir**,*' Did you see it? All of these polluted people lived in the land that was to become the *Promised Land*, the land that the fallen malachs inhabited when they were thrown out of Shamayim to the *eretz* (earth) in their failed coup of Shamayim. Here is the tie-in: There were many family-lines of the giants; look at this: 1 Kings 11:1: '*But Shelomoh loved many strange women, … **Moabites, Ammonites, Edomites, Zidonians, and Hittites**;*' Bereshis/Gen. 19: 37-38: '*And the* *firstborn bare a son, and called his name **Moab**: the same is the father of the **Moabites** unto this day. 38 And the younger, she also bare a son, and called his name Ben-ammi: the same is the father of the children of **Ammon** unto this day.'* These verses are the story of *Lot* and his two daughters. The daughters gave their father alcohol to drink to the point of being in a drunken stupor, and they each had incest with their dad on separate nights. They both became pregnant by their dad. Though these events occurred prior to any sexual Laws, it was not something that should be done; thereby, from that reproductive process came contaminated races of people.

In pulling all of these Scriptures together, the specific points are this: The Ammonites and the Moabites are of the direct descendants of the fallen malachs; and the fallen malachs are their gods. Those groups of people are the adversaries of Elohim, and thereby, are not permitted to enter the Temple of Elohim **forever**. The Annunaki, the Anakims, the Anak, the Ammonites, are all fallen angels. Their family-line has been continued unto this day by the descendants of Moab and Ammon, who are the fruit of incest. The Edomite, who is Esau, has reprieve because he carries Hebrew blood. However, because Edomites are of Hebrew blood, mixed their blood with the seed of the offspring of the fallen malachs, it takes three generations for an Edomite, once the Edomite renounces their gods, to be acceptable to enter into the Congregation of the HASHEM. The Egyptians also gain reprieve to enter the congregation of Elohim after the third generation, because Elohim used the Egyptians to purge the Hebrews from the pollution of Terah, the idolater. What is a must overstand in all of this is: There are some people that can never enter the *Mamlachah* (Kingdom) of Elohim. Those people are the Annunaki, who left their first estate (Ber./Gen. 6:1-4; Yude 1:6), and have been on eretz since that time reaping havoc on humanity. They are capable of transferring from body to body, and when the host body is in dying, they transfer to another body of the family-line: An Ammonite or Moabite. Who are those people? Those, who hold all of the power, all of the wealth, and supremacy over all of the eretz.

Many of the *Laws* in Scripture are written in the Book of VaYikra/

Lev., however, there are also many Laws laid-out in the Book of Devarim/Deu.. Let us now examine several of those Laws.

Devarim/Deu. 23:17-18 (AKJV):

'There shall be **no whore** of the daughters of Yisra'el, **nor a Sodomite** of the sons of Yisra'el. 18 You shall not bring the hire of a whore, or the **price of a dog**, into the **house** of the HASHEM your Elohim for any **vow**: for even both these are **abomination** unto the HASHEM your Elohim.'

In these verses the first thing we have to overstand is the word **vow**. The word vow has many synonyms, to name a few: *promise, swear, pledge, covenant, contract, affirm,* and much more (Merriam-Webster). Therefore, the message in the verses is this: There are whores (VaY./ Lev. 21:7; 21:9; Dev./Deu. 22:21; Isa. 57:3), and sodomites (1 Kings 14:24; Yudges 19:22), in Yisra'el, and that anyone, who is a **whore** or a **sodomite** must not be used to make promises thereby to the HASHEM. Elohim does not honor such vows because the whore and the sodomite are unclean for use as a pledge, offered in the House of Elohim. Why this was written is not fully spelled-out in the verses. But even so, when one looks at the synonyms of **abomination** it means: *abhor, detestable, loathing, execrate, hate, disgusting,* and more (Merriam-Webster). To use an *analogy*, this can be viewed as a person, who would never eat meat that is not fully cooked being presented with a medium rare steak to eat. That person would immediately become disgusted with such a presentation, and require the meat to be fully cooked for consumption. The bottom-line to this is: pledges and promises to Elohim, have to be purged as even the priests had to purge themselves before entering the *Tabernacle of the Congregation*; in particular, the *Sacred of Sacreds* (She./ Exo. 26:33-37)). There is another part of the above verses that is very relative, and requires more input from multiple sources, and that is: the word **dog**: Shemot/Exo. 11:7: *'But against any of the children of Yisra'el shall not a **dog** move his tongue, against man or beast: that you may know how that the HASHEM do put a **difference between** the Egyptians and*

_Yisra'el'_. Yudges 7:5: '_So he brought down the people unto the water: and the HASHEM said unto Gideon, Every one that **laps** of the water with his tongue, as a **dog laps**, him shall you set by himself; likewise every one that bows down upon his knees to drink'_. What lead to this verse was the disobedience of the Hebrews; they had sought-out others gods (Yudges 5:8). The Hebrews were worshiping _Baal_ and _Ashtoreth_ (Yudges 2:13)), and paying homage to the **gods of the Amorites** (Yudges 6:10). Once again the backsliding Hebrews had been placed in bondage for worshiping another god. Elohim in talking to the Hebrew man, _Gideon_ (6:13-14), was about to bring HIS people out of bondage. First the enemy needed to be defeated, and the plan was to have every Hebrew man who laps water with his tongue as does a **dog** (7:5), would be the army Elohim would use to defeat the Midianites (7:7). Keep this in mind, the dog lapping with its tongue as we read the history of the dog, but now we have to look at what a dog is.

> "_In the King James Version of the Bible, the word dog appears 41 times and only in limited ways does it refer to the animal, **the dog**. Strangely enough it referred mostly (30x's) to male prostitutes (Thedogplace.org)_".

> "_In other **religions the dog** and several other animals are revered as **sub-gods**. The dog's history begins about 13,000BC with the great granddad of all dogs, **the wolf**. In ancient Egypt, the jackal-dog **Anubis** was the **god** of the dead, protector of the **afterlife**. But nowhere can I find any reference suggesting any name for the creative deity was a dog. ... Most breeds are **designed by man** but the domestic dog was no accident of nature_ (Ancient.eu/Anubis)".

> "_Anubis: **jackal-headed god of Egyptian religion**, identified by the later Greeks with their **Hermes**, from Greek Anoubis, from Egyptian Anpu, Anepu_ (etymonline,com)".

There is a lot of information to unpack in all of these sources. First, have you ever heard the word **dog** is word play for the word **god**? The word dog goes back to Ancient Mitzrayim, and is representative of the god of the afterlife, **Anubis**. This god, Anubis, dates from the: *"First Dynasty of Egypt (c. 3150-2890 BCE)"*, and images of Anubis are found on royal tombs from as early as the: *"Predynastic Period in Egypt (c. 6000-3150 BCE)"*. Use of the word god in English writings came about in thirteenth century AD, and is: *"Old English god "supreme being, deity; the **Christian God**; image of **a god**; **godlike person**,"* (etymonline.com). The first exact date of the English language use of god is not known specifically but is believed to be circa thirteenth century AD. The word god has even more disturbing meaning: *"The **anthropomorphic god Indra** ... the **Vedic** religion ... figure in **Hinduism** ... deity of **Buddhism** ... The formidable thunderbolt-wielding Indra strikes an imposing figure but as **king of the gods** ..."* (ancient.eu/Indra). All of this information has to have some validity in history, and in combination with Scripture, makes a strong stand against the use of god in reference to the Hebrew Elohim.

Note: *anthropomorphic*: the equivalent of giving human characteristics to a god.

Elohim's plan to select the men to fight the Midianites was to distinguish men, who would doggedly fight to the death, as a dog would do against invaders. The men who lapped the water were selected by Elohim for war (Yudges 7:5). The Hebrews who bowed-down to drink water were not selected for the war because they were not brutal or fierce enough for the battle (Yudges 7:5). The inferred reference to the dog being a male prostitute from historical sources and the Scriptures, is that of being a sell-out; someone who would retreat in battle. In the Hebrew language, the word dog is **keleb**: *"to yelp, or else to attack; a dog; hence (by euphemism) a **male prostitute**"* (Strong's Exhaustive Concordance of the Bible). The inference in the Scriptures to the male prostitute has to be considered as less than honorable, and or to yell out in fear. Then there is this: wolves have been genetically altered by *deoxyribonucleic acid* (DNA) manipulation into a new creature called a dog. Even unto this day, a man cannot befriend a wolf, the wolf is a vicious carnivore that has no fear of people, and will rip a human apart, and feast upon the carcass. The next point about the dog is this: According to the dates above,

13,000BC, the vicious wolf was in existence, and this ferocious, vicious fighter was determined to be a figure of honor, worthy of becoming one of the gods of Mitzrayim; in this case the god *Anubis*. Watch this! Is this only by chance or is this word association relevant and revealing? *The Annunaki, the Anakims, the Anak, the Ammonites, and Anubis.* This information is crucial because it tells us that, from the fall of the *malachs* (angels), it has been this same progeny, who has plagued the Hebrews from Hebrew inception as a race. Mitzrayim is where Elohim sent the Hebrews to begin the process of purging them from the wicked, evil influences the fallen malachs had inflicted upon the *eretz* (earth). In more modern times, the word dog, has been spelled backward to hide what it truly represents, the dog-headed god of Mitzrayim by the name of *Anubis*. This information is vitally important to the Hebrew: the use of **god** in reference to Elohim must be removed from your vocabulary. One of the most striking elements in the above information is that: god can be <u>a man, an image, or any deity</u>. The use of god is in relationship to **religion**, not Hebrew Spirituality. Listen-up: It was the Greeks who first mimicked the Hebrews by transcribing the Hebrew Scrolls into the Greek language. However, the Greeks had their own gods also. One of the main Greek gods was *Hermes*. Now with the knowledge of Anubis from the Egyptians, came the Greeks own god-dog, Hermes. Folks, this stuff is not make believe! What is written in the Scriptures is real, but scripted in such a way the meanings embedded in the Scriptures, elude most people reading the Scriptures. Now we will examine information on the Hebrews being set-apart from other people, and yet the Edomites and the Egyptians can be part of this special people.

*I AM THAT I AM*, separated Abram from all other people living at that time, and Elohim changed Abram's name to Abraham (Ber./Gen. 5:17).

Devarim/Deu. 26:18-19 (AKJV):

'and the HASHEM has avouched (affirm) you this day to be HIS **peculiar people**, as HE has promised you, and that you should keep all HIS Commandments; 19 and to make you *__high above all nations__ which HE has made, in praise, and in name, and in honor; and that you may be an __sacred people__ unto the HASHEM your Elohim, as HE has spoken.'*

Make no mistake about what this is saying, Abraham, the Progenitor of the Hebrews, is to become a new race of people, a people different from all other people, although taken from the other people. This people, the Hebrews, will not appear in the natural totally different physically, and yet they are different. Some have the misguided belief that Hamites and Hebrews are the same people. That is simply not the case. Listen, though all people are able to procreate, all people are not replicas of one another. In example, the Hamites skull is not the same as the Hebrews; Hamites, true Hamite females do not grow long hair, and Hamite men, do not have full beards, and moreover, the muscularity is not the same (Africans and Negroes Are Not the Same People; Youtube). Hebrews and Asians are easily distinguished from one another in several ways: hair texture, facial features, and skin color in particular. Of course obviously the Hebrew is different from the Caucasian. The only reason Hebrews have been called African is one: the color of the skin. To the point at hand, the Hebrew is a peculiar people. We looked at this previously in She./Exo. 19:5, but the definition of peculiar is necessary to reiterate: "*__peculiar__*" and "*__above__*". To be *__peculiar__* is defined as: *Characteristic of only one person, group, or thing*; *__above__*: *superior to; in or to a higher place than* (Merriam-Webster). This definition alone clearly distinguishes that when Elohim separated Abraham from the other people, that characteristically, they would have somewhat of a different look from everyone else. In addition, Elohim has said, this new people will be regarded above all other people, and in obedience to HIM are a sacred people. That is no greater or higher position on eretz than being a Hebrew. Overstand this: the position of the Hebrews is a conditional position. This next segment will be intensely line upon line and precept upon precept, and will contain History, Science, and Scripture, that will detail the plight and travel of the Hebrews.

Chapter 27 of Devarim begins to tell us the destructive plight and travel of the Hebrews. For this segment of our study, we will first visit VaYikra/Lev., Chapter 26 extensively. The books of VaYikra 26, and Devarim 28, will uncover the true identity of the Hebrews. Also included in this section will be a great amount of history, as recorded by the *British Imperial Government, the U.S. Imperial Government, and the Roman Catholic Church*. Before opening Devarim 28, we will begin in VaYikra/Lev., Chapter 26. The reason for that is, VaYikra, Chapter 26 brings out the conditions for the Hebrews to be successful, and or fall to desperation.

VaYikra/Lev. 26:1-13 (AKJV):

*'You shall make you __no idols__ nor __graven image__, neither rear you up a __standing image__, neither shall you set up any __image of stone__ in your land, to bow down unto it: for I AM the HASHEM your Elohim. 2 You shall __keep__ MY Shabbaths, and reverence MY Sanctuary: I AM the HASHEM. 3 If you walk in MY __statutes, and keep MY Commandments__, and do them; 4 then I will give you rain in due season, and the land shall yield her increase, and the trees of the field shall yield their fruit. 5 And your threshing shall reach unto the vintage, and the vintage shall reach unto the sowing time: and you __shall eat your bread to the full__, and dwell in your land safely. 6 And I will give peace in the land, and you shall lie down, __and none shall make you afraid__: and I will rid evil beasts out of the land, neither shall the sword go through your land. 7 And __you shall chase your enemies__, and they shall fall before you by the sword. 8 And five of you shall chase an hundred, and an hundred of you shall put ten thousand to flight: and your enemies shall fall before you by the sword. 9 For I will have respect unto you, and make you fruitful, and multiply you, and establish MY covenant with you. 10 And you shall eat old store, and bring forth the old because of the new. 11 And I will set __MY Tabernacle among you__: and __MY soul shall not abhor you__. 12 And I will walk among you, and will be your Elohim, and you shall be __MY people__. 13 I AM the HASHEM your Elohim, which brought you forth out of the land of Mitzrayim, that you should not be their bondmen; and I have broken the bands of your yoke, __and made you go upright__.'*

These verses represent a victory march for the Hebrews. Elohim has promised the Hebrews that all of their needs are secure in <u>obedience</u> to HIM. *I AM THAT I AM* reiterates HIS Command, not a request, to have **no idols** of any kind that represent deity. All of those statues standing in houses of blasphemy today are wickedness. It cannot be emphasized enough, that cross on the *ekklesia* (church), around your neck; that fish symbol, are all evil. Some countries have erected giant statues of a false messiah in public parks, promoting blasphemy. In obedience to Elohim, the Hebrews will lack nothing: fruit and vegetables to the plenty; fresh water and wine to drink; and very importantly, the Hebrews will not have fear of anyone. This cannot be stated enough: *Hebrews must be obedient to Elohim*! Listen clearly to the messages in these verses: There is something else that has to be overstood, the enemy, everywhere in the world the Hebrews have been scattered, have an innate fear of the Hebrew. You see, the word is clear: "<u>*and **none** shall make you **afraid**: and I will rid evil beasts out of the land,*</u>". Do you get it? What this tells us is that, the fear of the Hebrew is prevalent among the enemy. The Hebrew in obedience to Elohim is protected and mighty before the HASHEM. The enemy is aware of that, and therefore, when it comes to violence against a Hebrew, it is forceful, it is sudden, it is deadly. This tells us why, the Hebrew is killed without mercy by authority figures. This tells us why upon sight, some will clutch their purse immediately, though the Hebrew had displayed no actions to warrant clutching their purse. Do you overstand? The Elohim in you, causes immediate fear in some people, the mere presence and sight of the Hebrew, in particular, the Hebrew male of large statue. That fear of the Hebrew is what drives the discrimination and hate the enemy directs upon the Hebrew. Now let us add to the line and perceptual Commandments of Elohim.

The promises of Elohim for good to the Hebrews also come with warning from *I AM THAT I AM*.

VaYikra/Lev. 26:14-26 (AKJV):

*'14 But if you will not listen unto ME, and will not do all these Commandments; 15 and if you shall despise MY statutes,*

*or if your soul abhor MY rulings, so that you will not do all MY Commandments, but that you break MY Covenant: 16 I also will do this unto you; I will even appoint over you terror, consumption, and the burning ague, that shall consume the eyes, and cause sorrow of heart: and you shall sow your seed in vain, for your enemies shall eat it. 17 And I will set MY face against you, and you shall be __slain before your enemies__: they that __hate you shall reign over you__; and you shall flee when none pursue you. 18 And if you will not yet for all this hearken unto ME, then I will punish you seven times more for your sins. 19 And I will break the pride of your power; __and I will make your heaven as iron, and your earth as brass__: 20 and your strength shall be spent in vain: for your land shall not yield her increase, neither shall the trees of the land yield their fruits. 21 __And if you walk__ **contrary** __unto ME__, and will not listen unto ME; I will bring seven times more __plagues__ upon you according to your sins. 22 I will also send __wild beasts__ among you, which __shall rob you of your children__, and destroy your cattle, and make you __few in number__; and your high ways shall be desolate. 23 And if you will not be __reformed__ by ME by these things, but will walk contrary unto ME; 24 then will I also walk contrary unto you, and will punish you yet seven times for your sins. 25 And I will bring a sword upon you, that shall avenge the quarrel of MY Covenant: and when you are gathered together within your cities, I will send the pestilence among you; and you shall be __delivered into the hand of the__ **enemy**. 26 And when I have broken the staff of your bread, ten women shall bake your bread in one oven, and they shall deliver you your bread again by weight: and you shall eat, and not be satisfied.'*

These warnings, if not heeded thereto, will be devastating to the Hebrews. The Hebrews will be murdered in the streets; their children will not be safe, the children will leave the house, and the parents will worry, will my child return home safely or be shot dead, laid-out on the ground? Now overstand this: The murderer will not regard the loss of life of the child, but will rather applaud their death. All of the goodness of Elohim toward the Hebrew will be turned to cursing in disobedience. It is only in <u>obedience</u> to the rules spoken by Elohim that the Hebrew will remain the number one people of the *eretz* (earth). When the disobedient Hebrews were chased out of their land, arriving in other lands, the enemy came searching them because the enemy knew, Elohim was not protecting HIS chosen people, who forsook HIM. The reason the enemy searched out the Hebrews is crucial to overstand: though the Hebrews had gone into disobedience, they had something of great value: Shemot/Exo. 31:2-5 (AKJV): '*... of the tribe of <u>**Yehuwdah**</u>: 3 and I have <u>filled him with the Ruach of Elohim</u>, in <u>wisdom</u>, and in <u>understanding</u>, and in <u>knowledge</u>, and in <u>all</u> manner of workmanship, 4 to devise cunning works, to work in <u>gold</u>, and in <u>silver</u>, and in <u>brass</u>, 5 and in cutting of <u>stones</u>, to set them, and in <u>carving of timber</u>, to work in <u>all</u> manner of workmanship.*' Do you see it? The enemy did not possess the knowledge and skills of the Hebrews. It is the gifts of skill and knowledge that made the Hebrew the best source of free labor to build cities and towns for the enemy. Moreover, recognize who these skills are given to: The Shevet of Yehuwdah, the head shevet of the Hebrew Yisra'elites, the Negroes.

VaYikra/Lev. 26:27-37 (AKJV):

'*27 And if you will not for all this listen unto ME, but walk contrary unto ME; 28 <u>then I will walk contrary unto you also in **fury**</u>; and I, even I, will **chastise** (punish) you seven times for your sins. 29 And you shall **<u>eat the flesh of your sons, and the flesh of your daughters</u>** shall you eat. 30 And I will destroy your high places, and cut down your images, and cast your carcasses upon the carcasses of your idols, and my soul shall **<u>abhor</u>** (hate) you. 31 And I will make **<u>your cities waste</u>**, and bring your sanctuaries unto desolation, and I will not smell the savor of your sweet odors. 32 And I will bring the land into desolation: and your enemies which dwell therein shall be astonished at it. 33 And I will scatter you among the heathen, and will draw out a sword after you: and your land shall be desolate, and your cities waste. 34 Then shall the land enjoy her **<u>Shabbaths</u>**, as long as it lies desolate, and you be in <u>your enemies' land</u>; even*

*then shall the land rest, and appreciate her Shabbaths. 35 As
long as it lies desolate it shall rest; because it did not rest in your
Shabbaths, when you dwelled upon it. 36 And upon them that
are left **alive** of you I will send a **faintness** into their **hearts** in
the lands of their enemies; and the sound of a shaken leaf shall
chase them; and they shall flee, as fleeing from a sword; and they
shall fall when none pursues. 37 And **they shall fall one upon
another**, as it were before a sword, when none pursues: and you
shall have **no power** to stand before your enemies.'*

The most devastating behavior a Hebrew can have is in being
disobedient to the Commandments of Elohim. The end result will be
punishment of grave proportion, resulting from the disobedience of the
Hebrews, ushering in the fury, great anger, of the Abba. The cities the
Hebrews build will be trampled down, and overrun by the enemy. All
Hebrew possessions not destroyed by the enemy will be confiscated by
the enemy. The Hebrews will not be allowed to celebrate high sacred
days in their captivity, and laws will be developed by their captors to
prevent the Hebrews from serving the Elohim of their ancestors. The
Hebrews will be so overwhelmed by the fierceness of their enemies, the
Hebrews hearts will change its beats, causing many to tremble in fear
at the mere sight of the enemy in their presence. In fact, upon sight, the
Hebrew will run away to prevent contact with the enemy; however, the
Hebrew will not escape. The chase will ensue and the enemy by way of
weaponry will catch-up to the Hebrew, taking the life of the Hebrew,
and no one will care. Rather, the enemy will uphold the death(s) under
their system of law. The Hebrew will tremble in fear, and will have no
power against the enemy.

VaYikra/Lev. 26:38-46 (AKJV):

*'And you shall perish among the **heathen**, and the land of your
enemies shall eat you up. 39 And they that are left of you shall
mourn away in their iniquity in your enemies' lands; and also
in the iniquities of their fathers shall they mourn away with
them. 40 If they shall confess their iniquity, and the iniquity of*

*their fathers, with their trespass which they trespassed against ME, and that also they have walked contrary unto ME; 41 and that I also have walked contrary unto them, and have brought them into the land of their enemies; if then their uncircumcised hearts be humbled, and they then **accept of the punishment of their iniquity: 42 then will I remember MY Covenant with Ya'aqov, and also MY Covenant with Yitzhaq, and also MY Covenant with Abraham will I remember; and I will remember the land**. 43 The land also shall be left of them, and shall appreciate her Shabbaths, while she lies desolate without them: and they shall accept of the punishment of their iniquity: because, even because they despised MY rulings, and because their soul abhorred MY Statutes. 44 And yet for all that, when they be in the land of their enemies, **I will not cast them away**, neither will I abhor them, to destroy them utterly, and to break MY Covenant with them: for I AM the HASHEM their Elohim. 45 But I will for their sake remember the covenant of their ancestors, whom I brought forth out of the land of Mitzrayim in the sight of the heathen, that I might be their Elohim: I AM the HASHEM. 46 These are the statutes and rulings and laws, which the HASHEM made between HIM and the children of Yisra'el in mount Sinai by the hand of Mosheh.'*

The Hebrews are a stubborn people, who have time after time, refused to remain committed to the Elohim, Who separated them from all other people to serve and worship HIM only. The Hebrews were called: *MY Chosen People* by The Most High Elohim, and a *Peculiar Treasure* unto Himself. It is only the Hebrew, who can say: Abba Elohim. In disobedience to Elohim, the hard-headed Hebrews time after time were turned over to the hands of the heathens for punishment. The descendants of the Hebrew Progenitors, by disobedience, caused Elohim to suspend, not do away with the Covenants HE made with Abraham, Yitzhaq, and Ya'aqov. The Hebrews were so *recalcitrant* (stubborn, difficult) that even the land they had would become like poison, not producing the fruits and vegetables any longer. But even so, all is not lost to the Hebrews; they have one simple Command to follow: Be obedient to Elohim in HIS Commandments, Rulings, and Statutes. Selah.

We will now take a look at who the Hebrews are from the Biblical perspective, followed by the history and scientific evidence of who the Hebrews are. These verses leave no doubt about the Hebrews plights and travel, and where the Hebrews are today.

Devarim/Deu. 28: 25 (AKJV):

'The HASHEM shall cause you to be **beaten** _before your_ _enemies_: you shall go out one way against them, and _flee seven_ _ways before them_: and shall be _removed into **all** the kingdoms_ _of the earth_.'

This verse goes to the _Arab Slave Trade_ of the Hebrews. Watch this!

Since the time of Yi**shma'el**, the cousins of the Hebrews, the other child of the family-line of Abraham, the Yishma'elites, have been opponents to Hamites and to Hebrews for millennia. It was Yishma'el who actually began slave trading: _The Arab Slave Trade_, which occurred prior to the _Trans Atlantic Slave Trade_. The Arab Slave Trade began around 1500 years before the Trans Atlantic Slave Trade. Here are two articles dealing with real history, not the omitted and or false history taught in schools. I have called it false because the details of what actually happened is passed over except in schools of higher learning.

> "_for the **Islamic** world," Clarke continues, "Slavs provided the_ _major source of slaves in the 250 or so years between the defeat at_ _the battle of Poitiers in AD 732 that forced the consolidation of_ _their dramatic conquests across **North Africa** and the **Iberian**_ _**peninsula**, cutting back the flow of war captives, and the_ _expansion of the import of **black Africans** across the Sahara_ _from around AD 1000._"

newafricanmagaz.com/16616

> *"In East Africa a **slave trade was well established before the Europeans arrived on the scene**. It was driven by the sultanates of the **Middle East**."*

bbc.co.uk/worldsevice/africa/features/storyof

The Hebrews had been taken captive many times for the same reason: <u>disobedience</u> to Elohim. In the *Babylonian Exile* of Yisra'el, the Hebrews fled in many different directions. Some of them escaped on foot into Africa; some on ships to different lands, including the *Iberian Peninsula*, present day Spain. In our reading about Shelomoh, we discussed the Iberian Peninsula. With this history of Iberia, the picture should be becoming more clear, in why Iberia is very important in Hebrew history. Two points here that will be reinforced as we continue in this segment of our reading are: ships, and Iberia.

The Hebrews down-trodden status is by their own making, for failure to keep the Commandments of Elohim. Look at this crucial information that reflects more of the disparaging characteristics of the Hebrews of the Scriptures.

Devarim/Deu. 28:29-30; 32-33 (AKJV):

> *'and you shall grope at noonday, as the blind grope in darkness, and <u>you shall not **prosper** in your ways</u>: and you shall be <u>only **oppressed** and spoiled evermore</u>, and no man shall save you. 30 You <u>shall betroth a **nashim** (wife), and another **man shall lie** (have sex) with her</u>: you shall **build** an house, and you shall not dwell therein: you shall plant a vineyard, and shalt not gather the grapes thereof. 32 <u>Your sons and your daughters shall be **given unto another people**</u>, and your eyes shall look, and fail with longing for them all the day long: and there <u>shall be **no might** in your hand</u>. 33 The fruit of your land, and all your labors, <u>shall a **nation** which you know not eat up</u>; and you shall be only <u>oppressed and **crushed** always</u>:'*

The Hebrews have no light in the suppression and oppression they are under. No different than a masked animal led to the cliff, with a hundred foot drop below, awaiting that dreadful step to doom, surely the rocks below will be its fate. Can you imagine another man coming into another man's house, ordering the husband out of the house so the brutal intruder can have sex with the man's *nashim* (wife), or the husband being forced to watch as the brute rapes the nashim? Imagine, building a house, and a brute forces you out, and takes your home as his own. You've planted a vineyard, and vegetable garden: the fruits and vegetables are harvested, now comes the brute and takes all of the fruit of your labor. You have children, and now the brute comes, and kidnaps your children, and you watching what is going on: the children screaming, and crying: Daddy help me. You being powerless, fall down on your knees in anguish because, you have no power to do anything to stop the kidnapper. If you know history, you should know from reading this, who the Hebrews of Scripture are. In history there has never been another race of people to suffer such horror as the Hebrews have endured over thousands of years of suffering for their own *disobedience*. The Hebrews have suffered under the rule of Nebuchadnezzar, the Ishmeelites, the Babylonians, the Egyptians, and in modern times, the Europeans. Hebrews, get your act together. Return to worshiping, and serving the Elohim, who created you to heal the world in spirituality. Continuing on, line and precept.

Devarim/Deu. 28:36; 41; 43-44;48; 68 (AKJV):

'*The HASHEM shall bring you, and your king which you shall set over you, unto a nation which neither you nor your fathers have known; <u>and there shall you serve other **gods**, wood and stone</u>. 41 <u>You shall beget sons and daughters</u>, but you shall not comfort them; <u>for they shall go into **captivity**</u>, 43 The **stranger** that is within you shall get <u>up above you **very high**</u>; and you shall come down **<u>very low</u>**. 44 He shall **<u>lend</u>** to you, and you **<u>shall not lend</u>** to him: he shall be the **<u>head</u>**, and you shall be the **<u>tail</u>**. 48 therefore shall you **<u>serve your enemies</u>** which the HASHEM shall **<u>send against you</u>**, in **<u>hunger</u>**, and in **<u>thirst</u>**, and in **<u>nakedness</u>**, and in want of **<u>all</u>** things: and he shall put a **<u>yoke of iron upon your neck</u>**, until he have destroyed*

> you. 68 And the HASHEM shall bring you into Mitzrayim
> (bondage) again with **ships**, by the way whereof I spake unto
> you, You shall see it no more again: and there you shall be **sold
> unto your enemies** for bondmen and bondwomen, and **no
> man shall buy you**.'

There is much information in these verses that must be unpacked. The Hebrews have been so disobedient to Elohim that HE is bringing down the harshest wrath upon them. The stranger came into the land of the Hebrews, and in time by the process of *amalgamation*, and then *acculturation*, the Hebrew was taken very low, and the stranger very high above the Hebrews in their own land. No one will **hire** (buy) the Hebrew, there is no need to do so, the Hebrew is captured and forced into servitude by the invading forces. The third part in overthrowing a people is missing in this scenario: *assimilation*. That part of invading the Hebrews was never in the plan because to assimilate the Hebrew into their society would remove the free labor needed to build a country for the invaders. Here we will insert a large volume of U.S. History, drawing the parallels between history and Scripture.

> "More than a century later, in **1916, President Woodrow
> Wilson** signed an executive order designating "The Star-
> Spangled Banner" as the national anthem, and in **1931, the
> US Congress confirmed the decision.** The tune has kicked
> off ceremonies of national importance and athletic events ever
> since. ... And where is that **band** who so **vauntingly** swore,
> That the havoc of war and the battle's confusion **A home and a
> Country should leave us no more**? Their **blood has wash'd
> out their foul footstep's pollution**. **No refuge** could save the
> **hireling and slave** From the **terror of flight or the gloom of
> the grave**, And the star-spangled banner in triumph doth wave
> O'er the land of the free and the home of the brave."

lyrics.com/track/508956

What is contained in the Scriptures above, and the words of the Star-Spangled Banner are perfectly aligned in the history of the Hebrews in

*Turtle Island* (America). The language in the anthem is nothing new, it has been going on in this country for centuries. It is exactly language, such as: "***hireling and slave*** *From the* ***terror of flight or the gloom of the grave***," that have not been taught in the schools across America that has kept the identity of the Hebrews hidden. In all of the captivities the Hebrews endured, the Hebrews fled the *Babylonians* on the **ships of Shelomoh**, arriving in *Turtle Island* and *Iberia* long before any other people came to Turtle Island. It is exactly this kind of information that has eluded the general population in America, hiding the truth of who the Hebrews are in this land. It is fundamentally harder to keep a people down "***very low***" when those people know, who they are. There have been some Hebrews, though on a very small scale, who have known the history of the Hebrews for many decades: one such person was, *Dr. Martin L. King Jr.*. This is what Dr. King told America on *August 28, 1963* in his "*I Have a Dream Speech*":

> "*100 years later* ***the Negro is still not free*** *... One hundred years later the Negro is still languished in the corners of American society and finds himself* ***in exile in his own land***."

(archives.gov/files/press:pg.1).

Listen-up: It does not matter what race you have been assigned from birth, what matters here is the truth. All of the words to the "*I Have a Dream Speech*" are available for anyone to see and read online. What has to be pointed-out about the speech, in addition to its powerful statement, in declaring the Hebrews were here before the Europeans arrived it that, these truths are archived, and authenticated by the *United States Government*. Do you get it? Those, who enslaved the Hebrews in this land, have always known the **Negro is the Hebrew**. I have to state straight-up: HEBREWS DROP ALL OF THE EPITHETS THAT HAVE BEEN PUT UPON YOU; EPITHETS SUCH AS: COLORED, BLACK, AFRICAN AMERICAN ARE ALL DESIGNED TO SUBORDINATE YOU INTO A STATUS OF NON-CITIZENRY. THE REASONING BEHIND REMOVING

THE DESIGNATION OF NEGRO FROM THE EPITHET OF THE HEBREW, IS BECAUSE THE EPITHET NEGRO IS SYNONYMOUS WITH THE EPITHET HEBREW. When the Hebrews fled Yisra'el, eventually because of their disobedience to Elohim, the curses of Devarim, Chapter 28 would follow the Hebrews wheresoever they traveled. Thereby the Hebrews who fled to *Iberia*, were eventually overrun by the Spaniards; and overrun by the British in *Turtle Island*. There is another element in Dr. Kings speech that has to be pointed out, and that is: that statement is in reference to the *Thirteenth Amendment to the United States Constitution*, the **abolition of slavery**, signed by the *Senate April 8, 1864*. This is how the Thirteenth Amendment reads:

> "*13th Amendment*
>
> *Section 1. Neither slavery nor involuntary servitude, except as a punishment for crime whereof the party shall have been duly convicted, shall exist within the United States, or any place subject to their jurisdiction.*
>
> *Section 2. Congress shall have power to enforce this article by appropriate legislation.*"

The U.S. Government has always known who the Hebrews are, as have some key historical figures like Dr. King. Listen-up: When a society is headed-up by a Government, who upholds rhetoric as contained in the Star-Spangled Banner, it is obviously apparent, it will work diligently to hide the identity of its free labor system. Of course there is this: Absolute control over the enslaved by any means necessary, such as, "**yoke of iron upon your neck**". To those people, who are down very low, though freed by the Thirteenth Amendment, you should know, as do those, who have enslaved the Hebrews, the captors know who you are. After the Thirteenth Amendment the Hebrews were free, and yet continued in enslavement. You, Hebrew man, Hebrew woman continue unto this day to be denied equity in society. Hebrew man, Hebrew woman, by now you should know who you are. Those who ruled over the enslaved made sure those freed by the Thirteenth Amendment made it of absolute necessity to keep that population from knowing their history. The captors made sure to keep the now freed Hebrews poor, lending to them, and never allowed to be the lender. The captors developed methodology to break apart the emancipated family units, automatically weakening the Hebrew population as a whole.

Only you can draw an interpretation of the language of the 13th Amendment for yourself. The wording of the *Thirteenth Amendment* is a revealing story in and of itself. In close observation of this document is something hidden in plain sight. You see, when you read, you must see pass the words printed on the page, reaching into the absolute meaning or message contained therein. This Amendment clearly is in today's times, even more-so than in the time it was written, is a means of incarceration to continue the free labor system of slavery in America. Do you get it? The prisons today are filled with enslaved Hebrews, who work making different products for the *oligarchs* (powerful), and the elite *plutocrats* (wealthy), who manage and own the prisons. The *Thirteenth Amendment* clearly says, if a person (Hebrew) commits any crime, the Hebrew can be put into slavery. Therefore, after the 13th Amendment was signed into law came other laws to continue the free labor system unabated: *Jim Crow*, and *Sundown Laws*, and so forth. A Hebrew could be imprisoned for simply being outside at night, or not getting off of the sidewalk to allow a non-Hebrew to pass.

There are pictures from the 1800's showing who the true Aboriginal peoples of this land are, and those pictures can be found at: *images.search.yahoo.com*, and can also be found in the book *Negro Hebrew Heritage And Enslavement, Free Yourself.* This is so important because the true history of the *Indigenous* of this land is recorded in pictures. That which is captured in antique photos; etched in stone; or captured in minted coins, cannot be changed by *iconography* (words that don't match the story or paintings that have been redrawn from the original, but changing the characteristics of the people; i.e., from melanin skin to that of white skin). What the superior minded do is, they redraw/make a duplicate artifact to reflect history as being that of European in origin. They then hide the original works in exclusive museums. Clearly, though the enslavement of the Hebrew in America began in 1619, and the photos available were taken in the 1800's, the physical features of the Indigenous Hebrews, nearly 200 years later remains unchanged. Unto this day, Hebrews, maintain their distinct characteristics: the Hebrews then, and Hebrews today have the same features; the Hebrews have not changed. Who the Europeans saw when they first arrived in this land were the Negro Hebrew Yisra'elites. Listen-up and hear this clearly: The Mongoloids, who came to *Turtle Island* (America), came here across the *Bering Straits from Asia by way of Russia* (History of the Bering Land Bridge Theory nps.gov/National Preserve Alaska). The Hebrews were already in this land after fleeing Yisra'el on ships in the *Babylonian Exile*. The Scripture reference to "*The **stranger** that is within you shall get <u>up above you</u> **very high**; and you shall come down **very low**.*" is in relationship to the Hebrews escaping the Babylonian Exile, fleeing on ships to other lands, ships built by Shelomoh (1 Kings 9:26-28). The Hebrews were in Turtle Island for centuries before the Europeans arrived in the land. The Hebrews will serve their enemies in the Hebrews own land. The Hebrews will live in deplorable conditions: starvation, the lack of clean drinking water, and be deprived of adequate clothing. For food, the Hebrews would have to eat the worst parts of the animals slaughtered for their enslavers to eat: the feet, lips, brains, and intestines. No man shall buy the Hebrews refers to the Hebrews being overrun, and forcefully placed into enslavement.

Let us now examine why Yisra'el split into the Northern and Southern Kingdoms.

# THE WAR BETWEEN YEHUWDAH AND YISRA'EL (EPHRAIM)

In studying the Scriptures, and researching other biblical documents, a picture began to form in my mind that would only continue to form and intensify; there is a troubling breakdown in the unity of the Twelve Shevets of Yisra'el. In the disunity of Yisra'el first of all is this, though the shevets are all one family, they are not all one **_Goyim_** (Nation). In close observation of the Scriptures, _Levi_ is a Goyim; _Yehuwdah_ is a Goyim; and _Ephraim_ (Yisra'el) is a _Goyim_, all three being one, and yet separate. From the onset of this lesson know this: the name _"Jacob"_, was never the name _Yitzhaq_ (Isaac) gave to his son _Ya'aqov_. _"Jacob"_ is the anglicized version of Ya'aqov to present the Scriptures as of being European in origin. Also know this, the Scriptures will show us how _Yisra'el_ and _Ephraim_ became _synonymous_. Ya'aqov's name was changed to _Yisra'el_ when he wrestled with the **_malach_** (angel). And, moreover, the names _Yisra'el_ and _Ephraim_ are completely _interchangeable_. Yehuwdah is the point on the star of _Daviyd_ (David), the Lead **_Shevet_** (Tribe) of all Yisra'el. In other words, Yehuwdah is the Promise made to _Abraham_, _Yitzhaq_ (Isaac), and _Ya'aqov_, to Daviyd, to _Shelomoh_ (Solomon), the Shevet of Promise to the world. From the bloodline of Yehuwdah would come Ha Mashiach: The Messenger or Anointed One or Leader of the Hebrews. A family can have only one leader, and the Shevet of Yehuwdah is designated by The Most High Elohim to head the Hebrew Yisra'elite family: all Twelve Shevets. You will see in this segment of our study how chaos and division came about in the family causing the family to split into separate Goyim. The following verses show us part of the problem that exist between Yehuwdah and _Ephraim_ (Yisra'el) unto this day.

Here is the conversation between Yosef and *Yisra'el* (Ya'aqov). Don't be confused about the names for "*Jacob*", and I repeat, "*Jacob*" was never his name. After Ya'aqov wrestled with the **malach** (angel), TMH Elohim gave Ya'aqov a new name: YISRA'EL.

Bereshis/Gen. 48:17-20 (OJB):

> "*And when Yosef saw that **aviv** (his father) laid his **yamin** (right hand) upon the **rosh** (head of) Ephrayim, it displeased him; and he took hold of **yad aviv** (hand of his father), to remove it from **rosh** (head of) Ephrayim unto **rosh** (head of) Menasheh. 18 And Yosef said unto **aviv** (his father), Not so, **Avi** (My Father); for this is the **bechor** (firstborn); put thy **yamin** (right hand) upon his **rosh** (head). 19 And **aviv** (his father) refused, and said, I know it, **beni** (my son), I know it; **he also shall become a people**, and he also shall be great; but truly **achiv hakaton** (younger brother) **shall be greater than he**, and his **zera** (seed) shall become a multitude of **Goyim** (Nations). 20 And he made a **brocha** (blessing) on them that day, saying, In thee shall **Yisra'el bless**, saying, Elohim make thee like Ephrayim and like Menasheh; and he **set Ephrayim before Menasheh**.*"

What is going on in these verses is that *Ya'aqov* (Yisra'el), Yosef's dad is nearing death, and is performing the duties of an elder leader before his death: to *brocha* (bless) the grandchildren. If you recall, Yosef is the completion of the Twelve Shevets of Yisra'el, in that his two sons, Ephraim and Manasseh, make the eleventh and twelfth shevets. (Yisra'el is the Hebrew *Sir-name* and refers to the family as a whole). Here is the situation: In this case, Ya'aqov has chosen to *brocha* (bless) the younger grandchild above the blessings of the older grandchild. Yosef is not pleased with that, and verbalizes his displeasure strongly to his father. The main issue in the verses is this:

Bereshis/Gen. 48:19 (OJB):

> "... **_achiv hakaton_** *(younger brother) shall be greater than he,*
> *and his **_zera_** (seed) shall become a multitude of Goyim."*

The Shevet of Ephraim shall become many Goyim that will lead to problems within the family. Here is what is not evident in the verses: As Ephraim gains strength, and increase in numbers (Divrei Hayamim/1 Chr. 7:20; children of Ephraim), that part of the family will rise up against Yehuwdah, the Shevet of Ha Mashiach. In looking at charts that breakdown who the Twelve Shevets are, Ephraim is Puerto Ricans. If those charts are correct, that information is of significant importance in the relationship of the Puerto Ricans and the Negro Hebrews unto this day.

Yerushalayim is a set-apart nation (city), the Nation of Levi'im. The *Kohen* (Priests) were always a separate Goyim from Yisra'el: now don't get this twisted, I did not say a separate people. In the division of the land: Gad, Reuben, and the half shevet of Manasseh are going to live East of the *Yarden* River. In time, this separation will become an issue for the whole of Yisra'el.

Now observe what is going on with Ephraim and Manasseh. Keep in mind as we go thru this, Ephraim and Manasseh are the children of Yosef, not the sons of Ya'aqov, and they are the fulfilling of the Twelve Shevets of Yisra'el. Yehoshua 14:3 clearly informs us that *"two tribes, Manasseh and Ephraim"* are not Ya'aqov's sons, they are his grandsons.

Yehoshua 16:9-10 (OJB):

> *"And the towns set-aside for the **Bnei** (Children of) Ephraim*
> *were **inside** the **Bnei** (Children of) Manasseh, all the towns*
> *with their villages. 10 And they drove not out the Canaanites*
> *that dwelt in Gezer: but the Canaanites **dwell among the***
> ***Ephraim** unto **yom hazeh** (this day), **and serve under***
> ***forced labor.**"*

The *Bnei* (Children of) Yosef, the two shevets comprised of Hebrew and Egyptian heritage, are now separated into their own Goyim. However, the Ephraimites have made a terrible mistake: they did not drive out the Canaanites; and are now in bondage to the Canaanites. Do you get the gist of this? The Shevet of Ephraim is in bondage to their cousins, who are Hamites (Ber./Gen. 10:6). This is fascinating information because Ephraim is in bondage to Canaan, though Ephraim is surrounded by the Tribe of Manasseh. Here is the genealogy of Ham:

Bereshis/Gen. 10:6; 15-19 (OJB):

> "And the sons of **Ham**; Cush, and Mizrayim, and Phut, and **Canaan**. ... 15 And Canaan fathered Tzidon his **bechor** (firstborn), and Chet, 16 And the Yevusi, and the Emori, and the Girgashi, 17 And the Chivvi, and the Arki, and the Sini, 18 And the Arvadi, and the Tzemari, and the Chamati; and afterward were the **mishpechot** (families of) the Canaanites spread abroad. 19 And the boundary of the Canaanites was from Tzidon, as thou comest to Gerar, unto Gaza; as thou goest, unto Sodom, and Gomorrah, and Admah, and Tzevoyim, even unto Lesha."

Do you recall the story of Yosef in Egypt, and how Yosef was given *Asenath* to wife, the Egyptian woman, who bore Ephraim and Manasseh (Bereshis/Gen. 41:45)? The point in this is, Ephraim and Manasseh are half Egyptian, which will explain some of the reasons *Ephraim* (Yisra'el) and *Yehuwdah* will eventually war against one another. The problem in the Ephraimites not destroying the Canaanites is this: the Canaanites are the offspring of *Ham*, whose son Canaan, was cursed by Noah. Listen-up Yehuwdah, and any Gentile willing to follow Yehuwdah: Ephraim and Manasseh are part Hamite; and though they are included in the Twelve Shevets, they are not of the *Promise:* the only Shevet of Promise is Yehuwdah. Yehuwdah is the only line of the family from Noah not infected with the evil spirits of the Annunaki; Hamites and Yephites are polluted. Use your *ruach* (spirit) Yehuwdah, to discern the truth of Scripture. Elohim blocked any attempts to infiltrate the Shevet of the Promise with the evil spirits of Ham. *Ham's* family-line were the giants, and of the curse of Canaan. *Yephites* are the other Gentiles who stand against Yehuwdah. Because of who those two sons of Noah are, it makes those portions of the Twelve Shevet family antagonists to Yehuwdah.

Yehuwdah and Ephraim are having difficulties; Ephraim committed a terrible act against the Levi'im that would further push Yehuwdah and Ephraim to the brink of war.

Divrey Hayamim Bais/2 Chr. 11:14 (OJB):

*"For the Levi'im abandoned their commonlands and their **achuzzah** (possession, estate) and came to Yehuwdah and Yerushalayim; for **Yarov'am** and his **banim** (sons) had cast them off from executing the office of **Kohen** (Priests) unto **Hashem**."*

Yarov'am is a leader in Yisra'el, who did some awful acts as a leader of the people. Yarov'am was evil, and kicked the *Kohen* (Priests) out of the office of the priesthood; and even more significantly, Yarov'am cut off the worshiping of The Most High Elohim. Yarov'am spent many years in Mitzrayim, where he most likely worshiped the gods of *Kemet*. So what this amounts to is: now the half Kemetian shevets of Ephraim and Manasseh have a leader potentially in place who is of Kemetic influence. This has to be overstood, because it helps to bring clarity into the split of the family: *Yehuwdah* from *Ephraim* (Yisra'el).

We are building line upon line, and precept upon precept. The acts of Yarov'am caused wars between the Northern and the Southern Kingdoms many times.

Divrey Hayamim Bais/2 Chr. 12:15 (OJB):

*"Now the acts of Rechav'am, **harishonim** (first) and **ha'acharonim** (last), are they not written in the **Divrei Shemayah HaNavi** (Book of Shelomoh The Prophet), and of **Iddo HaChozer** (The Seer) with genealogies? And there were **milchamot** (wars) between Rechav'am and Yarov'am **continually**."*

You can see from the above verse, the ***milchamot*** (wars) were ongoing battles between the two kingdoms; those *milchamot* went on for many years. Both Yehuwdah and Ephraim had a substantial fighting force:

Divrey Hayamim Bais/2 Chr. 13:1-3 (OJB):

> *"Now in the eighteenth year of **Melech** (King) Yarov'am began **Aviyah** to reign over Yehuwdah. 2 He reigned 3 **shanim** (years) in **Yerushalayim**. And the **shem immo** (name of his mother) was Michayah bat Uriel of Giveah. And there was **milchamah** (war) between **Aviyah and Yarov'am**. 3 And Aviyah led the **milchamah** (war) with an army of **gibborei** (valiant men) **milchamah** (of war), even 400 **elef ish bachur** (thousand men chosen). Yarov'am also drew up for **milchamah** (the war) against him with 800 **elef ish bachur** (thousand men chosen), **gibbor chayil** (valiant, mighty men)."*

Aviyah came into power in *Yehuwdah* after the reign of Rehoboam. That was after a period of eighteen years (18) of fighting between Yarov'am and Rehoboam. Here is something that is not well known today: Notice that, Aviyah reigned 3 years from the city of *Yerushalayim*. You see, Yerushalayim was a separate land from the Northern and Southern Kingdoms. Yerushalayim was the land of the Priests situated between Palestine, and the Northern and Southern Kingdoms of Yisra'el.

Yerushalayim was neither in *Ephraim* (Yisra'el), to the North, or *Yehuwdah*, to the South; it was located between the two kingdoms; Yerushalayim is on the dividing line of what we call Israel and Palestine today. The broken line indicates the separation of Yisra'el and Palestine. As you can see from the map, Yerushalayim is in both Israel and Palestine. Yerushalayim today is very controversial in that, Israel and Palestine both claim it as their land. The truth of the matter is: and this is bible country: the land belongs to the Hebrew Priests: period; a whole separate *Goyim* (Nation):

Bamidbar/Num. 8:14 (OJB):

*'Thus shall you set apart as separate the Levi'im from among the Bnei (Children of) Yisra'el; and the Levi'im shall be Mine.'*

The Hebrew **Kohanim** (Priests) were set-apart for the work of TMH Elohim. The following verses begin to explain what happened between the Northern and Southern Kingdoms.

Divrey Hayamim Bais/2 Chr. 13:4-6 (OJB):

*"And Aviyah stood up upon Mt Zemaraim, which is in the hill country of Ephraim, and said, Hear me, thou Yarov'am, and **kol** (all) Yisra'el. 5 Ought ye not to know that Hashem Elohim Yisra'el gave the **Mamlachah** (Kingdom) over Yisra'el to David **l'olam** (forever), even to him and to his **banim** (sons) by a **Brit Melach** (Covenant)? 6 Yet Yarov'am **ben** (son of) Nevat **eved** (servant of) Shelomoh **ben** (son of) David is risen up, and hath rebelled against **Adonav** (his Lord)."*

We have already seen what Yarov'am did by removing the *Kohanim* (Priests) from their land, and forbidding the worship of The Most High Elohim, bringing hostility between the shevets. We have also seen how Shelomoh committed acts as despicable as Yarov'am by allowing his *nashim* (wives) to worship the *Annunaki*. Aviyah is telling *Ephraim* (Yisra'el) that: You should know better than trying to rule over *kol* (all) Yisra'el for it is not of TMH Elohim; the *Bais* (House of) Daviyd is to remain forever under the leadership of the Shevet of Yehuwdah. Aviyah is reminding Yarov'am that as Shelomoh rebelled against TMH, so is he in his defiance of Elohim's Commandment.

Yarov'am is a man of dishonor; when Rehoboam was very young, Yarov'am sought to overthrow and usurp the kingdom out of the *yad* (hand) of Rehoboam.

Divrey Hayamim Bais/2 Chr. 13:7 (OJB):

*"7 And there are gathered unto him **anashim rekim** (vain men), the **Bnei Belial** (Children of Hasatan/Satan), and have strengthened themselves against **Rechav'am** (Rehoboam) **ben** (son of) Shelomoh, when Rechav'am was **na'ar** (young) and **rakh levav** (fainthearted), and could not withstand them."*

Like all demon evils (d-e-v-i-l-s) Yarov'am was evilly, deceitfully, and cunningly crafty. Yarov'am gathered a band of undesirables, the "**Bnei Belial**" (children of Hasatan), to fight against and overthrow the young Rehoboam. Here is the thing: when Elohim is with you, no one can defeat you.

Divrey Hayamim Bais/2 Chr. 13:8 (OJB):

*"And now ye think to withstand the **Mamlechet (Kingdom) HASHEM** in the **yad** (hand) **Bnei** (Children of) David; and ye be a great multitude, and there are with you **eglei zahav** (golden calves), which **Yarov'am** made you for **elohim** (g-ds)."*

In reading this verse with your eyes wide open, you will see something that you will miss in casual reading of the verse. The Promise to *Ya'aqov* was the last Promise given to the Hebrews, with the fulfilling of the Promise being given *"in the **yad** (hand) **Bnei** (Children) of David;"*

There is something else in Divrey Hayamim Bais/2 Chr.13:8 that has to be pointed out: *eglei zahav* (golden calves), which Yarov'am made you for elohim. Yarov'am took the Northern Kingdom into idolatry. While the Scriptures do not directly state what caused Yarov'am to commit such an *egregious* (shocking, appalling, harmful) act, one can surmise that his time in *Mitzrayim* had some impact on Yarov'am breaking the First Three Commandments.

In addition to breaking the First Three Commandments, Yarov'am thought that because he was older, and had a larger army than Rehoboam, that if war came, the North could easily defeat the South. Aviyah tried to warn Yarov'am against any attempt to usurp the entire kingdom by informing Yarov'am that Elohim had given the Southern Kingdom or Yehuwdah, which includes Benoni, to Daviyd forever (Melachim/1Kings 12:23). You see, when Elohim rend the kingdom from Shelomoh, or rather Rehoboam his son, it was not forever; the family was to eventually come back together under the Shevet of *Yehuwdah*. Additionally, the entire kingdom was never taken away from the Shevet of Yehuwdah, the shevet or family-line from which Ha Mashiach would eventually be born.

The separation of the family, Yehuwdah and Benoni from Yisra'el, is only in the fledgling stage at this point. Rehoboam, and the **_Yisra'elites_** (Ephraim) both continued to do evil, resulting in a war of words between the North and the South. These next verses provides us the result of the division in the family.

Divrey Hayamim Bais/2 Chr. 13:13-19 (OJB):

> *"But Yarov'am caused a **ma'arav** (congregation or gathering) to come about behind them so that they were before Yehuwdah, and the **ma'arav** (congregation or gathering) was behind them. 14 And when Yehuwdah turned, **hinei** (behold), the **milchamah** (army) was before and behind, and they cried unto **Hashem**, and the **Kohanim** (Priests) sounded the battle trumpets. 15 Then the **Ish** (Men) **Yehuwdah** gave a shout, and as the **Ish** (Men) **Yehuwdah** shouted, it came to pass, that **HaElohim** routed Yarov'am and **kol** (all) Yisra'el before Aviyah and Yehuwdah."*

Shout, shout, shout-out to The Most High Elohim. I assure you that no matter what force is coming against you, in calling on Elohim, your enemy is defeated. I can tell you without any doubt whatsoever, the victories I have had over the enemy have all come as a result of calling on The Most Supreme Being in all of Eternality: Elohim. Yarov'am planned an ambushment for the *milchamah* (army) of Rehoboam. When the enemy began to encroach upon Rehoboam, the *Kohanim* (Priests), and the *Ish* (Men) called upon TMH Elohim. You did not get it; they did what the Hebrews must always do to defeat the enemy; to call upon Elohim, never bowing down to any other entity.

Divrey Hayamim Bais/2 Chr. 14:10 (OJB):

"*Therefore, **hineni** (behold), I will bring **ra'ah** (evil) upon the **Bais** (House of) Yarov'am, and will cut off from Yarov'am **mashtin b'kir** (him that urinates against the wall, i.e., every male), **atzur** (bond) or **azuv** (free) in **Yisra'el**, and I will sweep out after the Bais Yarov'am as one sweeps out the **dung**, till it be all gone.*"

Did you catch the specificity of this verse? This is written to *Ephraim* (Yisra'el), and has no bearing on *Yehuwdah*; they are separate *Goyim*. The **ish** (men), **azuv** (free) or **atzur** (bond) are cursed for allowing those lewd, foul **kohanim** (priests) to bring idolatry into the kingdom. Here is a point that has to be overstood: Not only was Yisra'el the country, and Yisra'el the people split apart, there was always separate land for the Shevet of Levi'im.

Now we are coming to the great fight between the **Bais** (House) of **Daviyd** (Yehuwdah), and the *Yisra'elites* (Ephraim). Let us now examine what brought this battle to the forefront, and how it all got started.

Melachim Alef/1 Kings 12:19-20 (OJB):

"*So **Yisra'el has been in rebellion against the Bais** (House) David unto this day. 20 And it came to pass, when **kol** (all) Yisra'el heard that Yarov'am was come again, that they sent and called him unto the **Edah** (Congregation), and made him **melech** (king) over **kol** (all) Yisra'el; there was **none that followed the Bais David**, but the **Shevet Yehuwdah** only.*"

Houston, we have a problem: the Kingdom has now split apart: the Northern Kingdom, headed by Yarov'am, and the Southern Kingdom headed by Rehoboam, the **ben** (son) of Shelomoh. Because Shelomoh did evil by allowing his **nashim** (wives) to follow the practices of their people: the worship of the *Annunaki*. Elohim told Shelomoh the *mamlachah* (kingdom) would be rend or taken away from his son, Rehoboam (v. 11:11). When Shelomoh learned that the people preferred Yarov'am to become *melech* (king) of *kol* (all) Yisra'el, Shelomoh became angry that Yarov'am was the choice of the other shevets to become the melech, and sought to kill Yarov'am (v. 11:40). Yarov'am finding out the plot to kill him, fled into Mitzrayim. After the death of Shelomoh, Rehoboam became the melech, and Yarov'am returned from Mitzrayim. Upon Yarov'am's return an overwhelming part of the people demanded that Yarov'am be the melech of Yisra'el, and not Rehoboam. That caused the *mamlachah* (kingdom) to become the Northern and Southern Kingdoms. Because of what Shelomoh did, the mamlachah would become separate countries. As Shelomoh messed-up so would Yarov'am: Yarov'am did evil in the following acts.

Melachim Alef/1 Kings 13:33 (OJB):

*"After this thing Yarov'am returned not from his **derech har'ah** (evil way), but installed again of the **lowest of the people as kohanim** (priests) of the high places; whosoever desired, he filled hands of [i.e., ordained] him, and he became one of the **kohanim** (priests) of the [idolatrous] high places."*

Yarov'am was supposed to be a man of honor, and that is why he was chosen to lead the Northern Kingdom by the people; however, Yarov'am turned to idolatry, and to demigod worship; which is the worse crime any Hebrew or Yisra'elite can do. Remember why the *mamlachah* (kingdom) was split in the first place? Shelomoh allowed his **nashim** (wives) to worship the gods of their people. What Yarov'am and Shelomoh did was something that Yisra'el would do over their entire history: to turn away from serving Elohim only; each time leading them into punishment and or enslavement. Yarov'am selected the worst of the people to put into the office of the **kohanim** (priests).

We know from previous reading that the **Bais** (House) Daviyd has been at odds with the Ephraimites; we also know there are actually three divisions of the family. Examine the following verse closely, it is filled with information on the three segments of this family.

Melachim Alef/1 Kings 12:21 (OJB):

*"And when Rechav'am was come to **Yerushalayim**, he assembled all the <u>Bais Yehuwdah</u>, with the <u>Shevet Benoni</u>, an hundred and fourscore thousand **bachur oseh milchamah** (chosen men of war), to fight against the Bais Yisra'el, to regain the kingdom for Rechav'am **Ben** (Son of) Shelomoh."*

Did you catch what is hidden in plain sight in the above verse? You see, the *"Bais Yehuwdah"*, and the *"Bais Yisra'el"*, are clearly shown in the verse to be separate *Goyim*. Yerushalayim is on the dividing line between the Northern Kingdom, the Southern Kingdom, and Palestine. Rechav'am came to Yerushalayim, neutral ground, to meet with Yehuwdah and Benoni, to strategize how they would *"fight against the Bais Yisra'el,"* Clearly this verse tells us, Yerushalayim, is a separate parcel of land from both the Northern and Southern Kingdoms. The Hebrew Yisra'elites are comprised of Yehuwdah, Ephraim, and Levi'im, *kol* (all) of which are separate Goyim, with separate roles to administer in <u>spirituality</u>, and yet, they are all one family.

There you have it folks, information most Hebrews, and world has not known: Yisra'el has always been at war, sometimes with common enemies, sometimes within the family. Hear the Word of the *Hashem*, people of the Hashem: it is Yehuwdah <u>alone</u>, who has the absolute authority of the *Promise* of Elohim. Ephraim, remove yourself from alignment with *Esau* (the enemy). It is your duty, Ephraim, to bring kol of your <u>Ten</u> parts of the family together in order for Yehuwdah (includes Benoni) to protect the family from Esau. It is inevitable that Yisra'el will eventually come back together, reconnecting as one; it is written. The Hebrews, and Yisra'el will reunite, each carrying out their Elohim appointed duties. Concurrently, kol Yisra'el must have our spiritual leaders, the Levites, carrying-out the sacraments of Elohim, that is: High Sacred days, such as: *Shabbath Day Feast*. However, there is a big but to this: the Hebrews cannot do anything until they have been collected in their own land again by TMH Elohim, those things <u>cannot</u> be done in captivity (She./Exo. 3:18). What has to be overstood is this: Esau has polluted the entire world against Yehuwdah, because Esau is quite aware of who Yehuwdah is, and has tried to destroy Yehuwdah from the time of *Aw-dawn* (Adam). Let us unite as the family The Most High created us to be, to fight against *Esau* (Hasatan), under the rules TMH gave us to lead the world in *spirituality.* Let not Esau keep us brainwashed against one another any longer; stop *THE WAR BETWEEN YEHUWDAH AND YISRA'EL (Ephraim).* To TMH Elohim be all of the honor and glory forevermore. Halleluia to HIS Wonderful Name. Selah.

Line upon line, and precept upon precept. We have looked at historical records on Hebrew enslavement from antiquity to modern times. Now let us look at the cooperation of *church* and *state*, in how to keep the brains of the enslaved empty of who they are. Religion is one of the most effective ways of controlling large populations of people. The Hebrews will serve "*<u>and there shall you serve other</u> **<u>gods</u>**</u>".

We will now let the historical record inform us on how the Hebrews became partakers of the worship practices of the enemy.

# THE HEBREW AND CHRISTIANITY

*In this section of our study, is some of the most revealing information of Christianity in the Americas, from its early inception unto this day. Governmental Instructions written for the cause of infiltrating so-called freedom of religion into a people, to the benefit of White Supremacy Racism, for one main cause: The Hebrews were <u>disobedient</u> to Elohim repeatedly, leading to the captivity the Hebrews are in unto this day. Under the banner of the White Man's Christianity many Hebrews lives have been destroyed. This forcing of Christianity was invented by the Elite Class to give honor to their god, and not to the honor Elohim. The following information is available for anyone to use, as long as the initial credits listed below are included in your research article or teaching sessions. With that said, I have taken every effort to make sure any comments I make are clearly indicated as my words, and are not part of the Article itself; therefore, the Article is directly quoted as published; with the sections written by me presented in italic. I have used <u>underlining</u> and **bold print** to point out specific instructions of the Architects of the Article, the Official Document provided to the British people of the Americas, with regard to their enslaved Hebrew property. This document alone is enough to make anyone of humanity, living today, cringe in their <u>**ruach**</u> (spirit), no matter what color their skin is.*

*THE CHRISTIAN NEGRO:*

"The Religious Instruction of the Negroes. In the United States: Electronic Edition.

Jones, Charles Colcock, 1804-1863

Funding from the Library of Congress/Ameritech National Digital Library Competition supported the electronic publication of this title.

Text scanned (OCR) by Richard Musselwhite
Images scanned by Richard Musselwhite
Text encoded by ill Kuhn
First edition, 1999
ca. 560K
Academic Affairs Library, UNC-CH
University of North Carolina at Chapel Hill,
1999.

© This work is the property of the University of North Carolina at Chapel Hill. It may be used freely by individuals for research, teaching and personal use as long as this statement of availability is included in the text.

**Source Description:**
The Religious Instruction of the Negroes. In the United States.
Charles C. ones
277 p.
Savannah: Published by Thomas Purse, 1842.
Call number LC2751 .7 (Rare Book Collection, University of North Carolina at Chapel Hill)

The electronic edition is a part of the UNC-CH digitization project, *Documenting the American South.*
Any hyphens occurring in line breaks have been removed, and the trailing part of a word has been joined to the preceding line.
All quotation marks, em dashes and ampersand have been transcribed as entity references.
All double right and left quotation marks are encoded as "and" respectively.
All single right and left quotation marks are encoded as 'and' respectively.
All em dashes are encoded as --

Indentation in lines has not been preserved.

Running titles have not been preserved.

Spell-check and verification made against printed text using Author/
Editor (SoftQuad) and Microsoft Word spell check programs.

*Library of Congress Subject Headings, 21ˢᵗ edition, 1998*
Languages Used:
* English

LC Subject Headings:
* African Americans -- Religion -- History.
* African Americans -- Missions -- History.
* African Americans -- Education -- History.
* African Americans -- Education -- History.
* Church and education -- United States -- History.
* Christian education -- United States -- History.
* Slavery and the Church -- United States – History.

Revision History:
* 1999-11-16,
  Celine Noel and Wanda Gunther
  revised TEIHeader and created catalog record for the electronic
  edition.
* 1999-11-05,
  ill Kuhn, project manager,
  finished TEI-conformant encoding and final proofing.
* 1999-11-05,
  ill Kuhn
  finished TEI/SGML encoding
* 1999-10-27,
  Richard Musselwhite
  finished scanning (OCR) and proofing.

# THE
# RELIGIOUS INSTRUCTION
# OF THE
# NEGROES.
# IN THE UNITED STATES

BY

CHARLES C. JONES
SAVANNAH:
PUBLISHED BY THOMAS PURSE
1842.

Page verso

**ENTERED according to the Act of Congress, in
the year eighteen hundred and forty-two:
BY C. C. JONES,
In the Office of the Clerk of the District Court of the
United States for the District of GEORGIA.**

**THOMAS PURSE, PRINTER,**

**SAVANNAH.**

"The **Bishop** of London's Letter to the **Masters and
Mistresses** of Families in the English Plantations abroad;
exhorting them to encourage and promote the **Instruction
of their Negroes in the Christian Faith**. London, 1727."

*As you can clearly see from these opening statements and credits, these
instructions are written to the White slave owners, men and women. These
instructions clearly come from the Heads of the Church, and are totally
accepted by the U.S. Government; and were approved by the Leadership
of the British Imperial Government. Listen-up, my brothers and sisters:
black, white, or brown skin; information has been hidden from us for*

*a long time, but is now available for all to see. As long as we continue in ignorance of what has been done to all of us, there will always be rhetoric of mistrust, hate, and race superiority. The fact is, we have all been controlled by THE GOVERNMENT; THE CHURCH; THE PLUTOCRATS (WEALTHY); THE OLIGARCHS (POWERFUL), AND THE ILLUMINATI. Until we realize what has been done to us: black, white, or brown skin; the brainwashing, divisiveness and superiority rhetoric will continue. Interestingly enough, note the date the Article was published: 1842. That date is important and will be discussed thoroughly in this study. However, briefly, that date is important because the Hebrews have been enslaved since 1619, and then 223 years later comes the forcing of this religion upon the enslaved Hebrews. What that should signify to the Hebrew (Negro) Christian of today is, you are a Christian today because great, great, great, great grandma "nem"back in 1727 began to have this foul religion called Christianity brutally inflicted upon "nem." This Article speaks loudly to the effect of mentally, physically, emotionally, and spiritually inserting the god of the oppressor into every dimension of the mind-set of the oppressed. If grandma "nem," many generations ago were not forced into Christianity, you Hebrew man, Hebrew woman, would almost assuredly not be a Christian today.*

*We will begin the Instructions to the "Masters" as follows:*

"Page 20

If it be said that no time can be **spared from the daily labor and employment of the Negroes, to instruct them in the Christian religion**; this is in effect to say that no consideration of propagating the Gospel of God, or saving the souls of men, is to make the *least abatement* from the **temporal profit** of the masters; and that God cannot or will not make up the little they may lose in that way, by blessing and **prospering their undertakings by sea and land, as a just reward** of their zeal for his glory and the salvation of **men's souls**. In this case, I may well reason as St. Paul does in a case not unlike it, that if they make you partakers of their temporal things, (of their strength and spirits, **and** even of their offspring,) you ought to make them partakers of **your spiritual things**, though it **should abate somewhat from the profit** which you might otherwise receive from **their labors**. And considering the ***greatness* of the profit that is received from their labors**, it might be hoped that all **Christian masters**, those especially who are possessed of considerable numbers, should also be at some small *expense* in providing for the **instruction of these poor creatures**, and that others, whose numbers are less, and who dwell in the same neighborhood, should join in the **expense** of **a common teacher for the Negroes belonging to them**. The Society for **Propagating the Gospel** in Foreign Parts, are sufficiently sensible of the great importance and necessity of such an established and **regular provision for the instruction of the Negroes**, and"

*The above entire opening reading of the Article, is of the most moronic readings in all of the research I have done. How can anyone think or believe the word "__employment__" can in any way be equated to the status of someone forced into servitude? Moreover, how is it that forcing the belief system of one group onto another group is of The Most High Elohim? And while it is true, it is because the Hebrews brought it upon themselves in disobedience. Elohim will remove this curse for any Hebrew, who returns to serving HIM only. Folks, I have repeatedly stated that: Christianity is the worship of another god; the captor and the captive do not serve the same god. The god of the captor is not the Elohim of the Hebrews. The god of the Elite Class is Hasatan, who grants the "__Masters__" the cruel mind-set to gain power, wealth, and superiority above all other peoples. Their mind-set is the same desire Hasatan had in Shamayim.*

*The above writing is contradictory on many levels, and the contradictions are intensely moronic: "__men's souls__" versus "__poor creatures__" versus "__Negroes belonging to them__." What the under world kind of evil is that? How in their twisted minds did they consider the enslaved to be <u>men</u> worthy of salvation by their Christian doctrine and god; and in the next breath see the enslaved as "__creatures__" and __property__ "__belonging to them__"? Their thoughts on the Hebrew are mind boggling; they want* it both ways: creatures do not have souls; therefore, in one breath the enslaved is human, and in the next breath an animal. What has actually been described in their contradictory statements is: they have unknowingly described themselves: some of them, Caucasoids, are the descendants of the fallen angels (Anglo Saxon), and are hybrid Beings of human flesh and spirit. These writings are of the most heinous practices in all of inhumanity. Look at the built-in superiority of the white race in the Article: and how they prosper off of the free labor of the enslaved; from the enslaved adults, to their children, and from generation to generation. Do you get the picture? This entire Article is about **wealth**; it has nothing to do with leading anyone to heaven. Additionally, after forcing this Christian religion onto grandma "nem," two generations later, those who are now grandma "nem," pass this vile religion on freely to their children and forward, it has become accepted into the Hebrew psyche. Now, if you don't go to Christian church, grandma "nem" might beat you senseless. This Article is against the very Scriptures the powers that be state they are upholding. Moreover, these writings assuredly disclose that Christianity is the religion of the white race: THE OPPRESSORS, WHO DILIGENTLY SERVE THEIR god, the god OF OPPRESSION, WHO HAS THE NEED FOR WEALTH, AND POWER, AND SUPERIORTY.

The Europeans forcibly, deceitfully, and cunningly applied their god upon the people everywhere in the world they invaded; particularly in the **Americas** (Turtle Island). The Scriptures make it perfectly clear that; even the servant (enslaved) is to be treated with humanity. In fact, in reading VaYikra/Lev. 25:10, in the **Law of the Yowbel** (Yubile) it expressly states that; **every fifty years**, slaves have the choice of freedom, or to remain as hired help to the end of their life; and above that, the enslaved, choosing to be set free, are to be restored to a decent level of material goods to get their life back on track in freedom. The Yowbel states matter-of-factually; those, who are working bond service or enslaved free labor, are to be restored to decent status in society. Now get this: the Yowbel is a set date on the Hebrew calendar; therefore, the time of Yowbel sets the person free whether they have worked one year or forty years as servants, the first day of the next fifty year segment, they are free.

*VaYikra/Lev. (AKJV) 25:8-14:*

'8 And you shall count seven Shabbaths of years unto you, seven times seven years; and the period of the seven Shabbaths of years shall be unto you forty and nine years. 9 Then shall you cause the trumpet to sound a broken blast on the tenth day of the seventh month, in the Day of Atonement shall you make the trumpet sound throughout all your land. 10 And you shall treat as hallow the fiftieth year, and **proclaim freedom throughout all the land** unto all the inhabitants thereof; it shall be a Yubilee unto you; and you **shall return every man unto the ancestral heritage** of his possession, and you shall return **every man unto his family**. 11 A Yubilee shall that fiftieth year be unto you; you shall not sow, neither reap that which grows of itself in it, nor gather the grapes in it of your untended vine, 12 For it is the Yubilee; it shall be sacred unto you; you shall eat the increase thereof out of the field. 13 In this year of Yubilee **you shall return every man unto his possession**. 14 And if you sell ought unto thy neighbor, or buys ought of your neighbor's hand, **you shall not take advantage of one another**.'

First of all these verses tell us straightforwardly that, the god of the Christian, and the Elohim of the Hebrew Yisra'elite, is not the same entity. The Yisra'elites are Commanded to release any person that has been in servitude at a specified Fifty Year mark. If the person in debt has been in debt 1 year or 49 years, they become free at the time of Yubilee: period. The Scriptures are clearly in diametrical opposition to the instructions of the Article to Christianize the Hebrews. Christianity holds the Negroes in perpetual enslavement, subservient to the slave owners. According to the Scriptures, the Hebrews are not only to release the person from servitude, the Hebrews are to also release any possessions that person has. In other words, the servant is to be completely restored or made whole again. The dictates and mind-set of those, who wrote the article, believe wholeheartedly in their completely antithetical bull-droppings. Here is the breakdown of their European thought processes: whatsoever the Hebrew has in his or her possession is not their property because Hebrews cannot own property, the

*Hebrew is property. In other words: property cannot own property, it all belongs to the "**Master**" or "**Mistress**" of the enslaved.*

*The Yubilee is time censored, meaning: it occurs every Fifty Years on the Hebrew calendar, so if someone has been a servant for only one year of a seven year debt, and the Yubilee occurs before that seven years is fulfilled, that person is to be restored debt free. Do you see that everything in the above portion of the British Government Article, is against the Word of Elohim? The Scriptures make it perfectly clear that, even in servitude, there is light at the end of the tunnel. There is not one Scripture that says, forced labor and enslavement or voluntary servitude is from generation to generation, or lifelong for the captive. The only time the Scriptures speak on generational curses is when the Hebrews apostatized from TMH Elohim. I am completely aware of the curses of Devarim/Deu. 28. Here is the point about Devarim 28 that has to be overstood: no Hebrew following The One and Only Great I AM is in bondage.*

*Folks, the Old Testament is not done away with, that is a lie from Hasatan, perpetrated upon the people by Hasatan and his demoniacs, under the dictates of Christianity. In the above readings from the Article did you catch what the Article says about the paid teacher for the Hebrews? Now I must speak boldly: in the days of the enslavement of the Hebrews, initially it pertained to paying a white minister to preach the messages; it then went into having a Hebrew to preach the slave mentality doctrine. I must admit, having a Hebrew to preach slave mentality sermons is the mind of a brilliant strategist. What more effective methodology can there be than to have a Hebrew, preaching that: THE god OF THE EUROPEAN OPPRESSORS IS THE god WHO APPOINTED THE CAUCASOID AS THE MASTERS OVER THE HEBREWS. In effect, having a Hebrew preacher causes the enslaved Hebrew to be more compliant to their subservient position in American society. Guess what? That same mentality, slave mind, indoctrinated foolery is still ongoing today. Did you notice how the collection of money was also encouraged in the Article? They were to collect the money for the preacher, who would deliver sermons that promote their doctrines of white superiority. This handpicked puppet, yes-man, "coon," sold out his people for the money. The pastor of your church today (most churches) have kept up this collecting of money for their benefit,*

*even more significantly important; <u>your pastor continues to preach the slave</u>*
*<u>mentality doctrines of this Article</u>.*

*The Most High Elohim is not pleased with the pastors, and that is*
*why Yeremiah, Chp. 22, speaks harshly against the pastors. Though this*
*collecting of money has nothing to do with tithing, tithing is also part of the*
*problem. The origin of <u>Tithing</u> had nothing to do with making the pastor*
*rich: tithing had to do with making sure the widows, and fatherless, and*
*even the stranger had sufficiency of food. The methodology of tithing today*
*is antithetical bull waste. You can clearly see in the above writing, the*
*collecting of the money is to pay preachers to deliver enslavement sermons,*
*and these greed filled preachers today: black, white, or brown skin, have*
*continued the evil collection of money for themselves. Many pastors today*
*continue spreading the <u>false doctrines of Christianity</u> because it is profitable*
*for them. And, indeed most of them don't believe what they preach, and*
*they know what they preach will not save anyone from hell. Having a Negro*
*Pastor is of significant importance with regard to:* "**a common teacher for**
**the Negroes belonging to them**." *If your treacher (teacher/preacher) is*
*presenting you Christian doctrine, he or she is the agent of Hasatan: period.*
*Did you notice in VaYikra/Lev. 25:14, it also says, not to "take advantage of*
*one another"? We Hebrews are supposed to support one another in our daily*
*lives. Our Abba, The Great I AM, is not pleased with us hurting and killing*
*one another. Folks, listen-up: the fix is easy, return to Torah and come out*
*of religion, and I assure you, your life will be vastly improved, no matter*
*what the enemy tries to do to you. Listen-up Yisra'el: the Scriptures of Torah*
*are written to the Hebrews (Yehuwdah), and to Ephraim (Yisra'el); the two*
*groups together are the Hebrew Yisra'elites under the Sir Name of Yisra'el.*
*Yisra'el as a whole is to practice Spirituality, not any religion of the pagans*
*and their pagan gods that allows a person to be kept in perpetual terror.*

"Page 21

earnestly wish and pray, that it may **please God** to put it
into the hearts of **good Christians**, to enable them to assist
in the work, by **seasonable contributions** for that end: but
at present their **fund** does scarce enable them to answer the

**many demands of missionaries**, for the performance of divine service in the **poorer settlements**, which are not in a condition to maintain them at their own charge."

*There is something in this portion of the Article that not many people will overstand in the casual reading of the Article. Part of the plan of the Elite Class was to make the poor whites feel they are still above other people of melanin skin. The preaching of enslavement doctrine sermons to mixed congregations, emboldens the whites to superiority. To make sure the right message(s) go out to the people there was always a white <u>overseer</u> in the congregation. Essentially, what the article is saying is: our trained missionaries will travel the world to spread our White Supremacy Racism, by way of Christianity. Everywhere we (Europeans) travel, we will deliver this doctrine, and in time, extend our empire to every land we travel. We, (Europeans) will eventually, concurring the Indigenous People of that land, will make them slaves to us and to our "god." Hear me now Hebrews, America, and world: black, brown, and white skin people; you don't even have to know history (which you do not because what they teach you in school is not the truth) to realize what is fact. Look at the map: everywhere the Europeans traveled, they conquered: Puerto Rico, and all of the Caribbean; Hawaii and much of the Pacific Islands; and most impressively: All of the Americas. Don't look at me like I'm stupid for saying this; I am fully aware that Haiti, Brazil, Mexico, and other countries are not U.S. Commonwealths or Territories, but believe this, those countries too have been greatly influenced by the U.S. Imperial Government, and the British Imperial Government, in one way or another; especially in the spreading of their Christian god. Haiti, in particular, unto this day is suffering the effects of U.S. Imperialism. <u>When Toussaint L'Ouverture and his army overthrew the French colonizers in November 1791, a pact was declared by the U.S. and European nations to assure Haiti would always be the poorest Nation in the Western Hemisphere.</u> (faculty.webster. edu/corbetre'haiti) . This is well documented by multiple credible sources, Britannica.com/biography/Toussaint-Louverture, being one such source. Other sources; however, provide greater detail than some of the more famous sources:*

*"After the revolution which concluded in January, 1804, Haiti became the second free country in the Western World (after the United States), and the first black republic. However, the United States was still a slave nation, as was England. While France had freed the Haitian slaves during the revolution, France and other European nations had slaves in Africa and Asia. The international community decided that Haiti's model of a nation of freed slaves was a dangerous precedent. An __international boycott of Haitian__ goods and commerce plunged the Haitian economy into chaos."*

*Faculty.webster.edu/corbetre'haiti*

Here is the main point that has to be taken from this information: *HAITI IS A CHRISTIAN NATION; THE U.S. IS A CHRISTIAN NATION; MOST OF EUROPE IS CHRISTIAN. All I can say is, this Christian Religion is filled with hate and violence that is beyond logical reasoning, and lacks all decency of humanity. Folks, Christianity is patently the most hypocritical sack of dung to effect this world in present times, that has plagued humanity for centuries. How in the world can your Christian values toward those of white skin be intensely fortified in togetherness, and equally as fortified in the disenfranchisement of the Haitians of melanin skin, when they both come under the banner of Christianity? Let us continue to build upon this religion that is akin to a double-edged sword.*

*Christianity: Hypocrisy at its best: look at the oxymoron, speaking out of both sides of one's mouth in this next section of the Article.*

"Page 23

The general law both of **humanity** and of **Christianity, is kindness, gentleness and compassion towards all mankind**, of what nation or condition soever they be; and therefore we are to make the exercise of those **amiable virtues** our choice and desire, and to have recourse to **severe and vigorous methods unwillingly** and only out of **necessity.** And of this necessity, you yourselves remain the judges, as much after they receive **baptism** as before;

so that you can be in no danger of suffering by the change; and as to them, the greatest hardships that the most **severe master can inflict upon them is not to be compared to the cruelty of keeping them in the state of heathenism** and depriving them of the tokens of **salvation** as reached forth to all mankind in the **Gospel of Christ**. And in truth one great reason why **severity is at all necessary to maintain governing** is the want of **religion** in those who are to be **governed,** and who therefore are not to be kept to their duty by any thing but **fear and terror**; than which there cannot be a more uneasy state, either to those who govern or those who are governed."

*In other words: these heathens (the enslaved Hebrews) must be taught about our god, by whatsoever means it takes to subdue them, even if it means, beating the heaven out of the enslaved person, to keep them in the torment of serving us. You read that correctly; though the enslaved are forced into Christianity, does not mean they have lost the Spiritual connection to the ancestors. While the enslaved externally has to present as Christian in order to avoid the most <u>heinous cruelty</u>, many of the enslaved pretended to be Christian. The Hebrew had to present externally to be Christian, that pretense had no bearing against their relationship to Abba. Many of the enslaved recognizing internally, they must keep their ruach attached to the Ruach Hakodesh (Sacred Spirit) in order to be pleasing to The Great I AM. Many of the enslaved, though forbidden to speak or practice anything of Hebraic tradition, when praying, were praying to Elohim, and not to the god of the oppressors. Whosoever is attached to the Ruach Hakodesh, no matter what is forced upon them, the Ruach will teach them what is right. The enslaved sensing that, he or she, has to remain tied to their spiritual beliefs, which would not be acceptable to their white captors would therefore, whenever possible, secretly pray to Elohim, in example: Kum bah yah or Kumbaya (come by here). For the enslaved to maintain their spiritual beliefs, the captors would view that as rebellion. Though the Hebrews were not allowed to speak their native tongue, some words they were able to speak because the word was pronounced similarly to an English word, in example: **<u>massa</u>**. The English took it as acknowledgment of their superior* *position, when in fact the Hebrew was saying something derogatory, such as: bandit, robber, or screw yourself. The instructions for making the Hebrew a Christian makes it implicitly clear, anything the Hebrew does that is not of Christianity, the master can take whatsoever action they feel is sufficient to tame the heathen. Therefore, if beating the Hebrew with whips, down to the bone is deemed as necessary, make it happen, and you will receive a reward from god, their god; the god of the oppressor. Additionally, in taming the heathen, the slave owner assures their ascent into heaven. You see, according to the dictates of this Article, the oppressor is saving his or her own soul, and the soul of the enslaved, which thing is pleasant to their god. Let me make this perfectly clear: Their god is not the Elohim of the Hebrew Yisra'elites. Do you overstand that the rhetoric of the Article makes it of no conscience to the offender to lash, brand, sodomize, or in anywise torture the heathen? There is no way for anyone with a conscience to do to the Hebrews what the Europeans did; the Euros are the most savage people on this planet. If someone has been taught from birth, they are superior, and others are inferior; and that god approves of, and commands them to brutalize the "heathen" leads to no conscience for the abusers. That lack of conscience equates to no big deal for the captors to maim; amputate body parts; cut a child out of a woman's womb; rape the enslaved women, children, <u>and the men</u>; burn at the stake; mutilate their genitals; and to lynch the "heathen" to keep them in their place. It takes a "fierce countenance" (Devarim/Deu. 28:49) to carry out such acts; not a conscious mind, or of giving honor to The Most High Elohim. The oppressor's mindset being: I want to be a pleasant vessel unto "god." You see, the brainwashing was not only on the enslaved, it was the people in general, in particular the poor whites, because even the poorest white is better than the enslaved Hebrew. Listen-up: the above excerpt of text is filled with all manner of inhumanity toward the Hebrew, and is contradictory on every level. The writing is filled with flaws beyond incomprehension to any rational, thinking, logical person. They have outright unwittingly admitted that "**humanity** and of **Christianity**" are not compatible, and are two separate entities. You see, it is impossible to be a humanitarian, and to simultaneously uphold the Christian values of the Euro devils, capable of :*

THE PLIGHT AND TRAVELS OF THE HEBREWS

**"severe and vigorous methods unwillingly ... the greatest hardships that the most severe master can inflict upon them is not to be compared to the cruelty of keeping them in the state of heathenism and depriving them of the tokens of salvation ... And in truth one great reason why severity is at all necessary to maintain governing is the want of religion in those who are to be governed ... their duty by any thing but fear and terror"**

All of the torture the Hebrews endured was supported by, and upheld by the U.S. IMPERIAL GOVERNMENT, THE BRITISH IMPERIAL GOVERNMENT, AND THE CHRISTIAN CHURCH PREACHING the "**Gospel of Christ**." This Christ is of European origin, and get this: hear me well; the Epithet "**Christ**" is the god of the Europeans, and has nothing to do with the Hebrew Yisra'elites: their god is not our Elohim. In fact, that word, Christ, is *not* found in the Old Testament, and only came into existence in the 1600's. Wake-up people, there is no way a "**Religion**" headed by someone called "the Christ" could be representative of **Ha Mashiach** (The Messenger) when that epithet has only been in existence above 400 years. I cannot emphasize strongly enough: THE WORD CHRIST IS NOT FOUND IN ONE SINGLE LINE OF THE OLD TESTAMENT; AND NEITHER ARE THE WORDS: YAH, TRINITY, JESUS, BAPTIST, BAPTISM, and BAPTIZE. I am not putting down anyone for their beliefs, I am simply pointing out the history of Christianity. The choice is yours, remain in the European teachings of Christianity or research your Hebrew roots. The "**amiable virtues**" of the European Christians are incompatible to humanity.

Feed the oppressor lines of rhetoric as below, and the result will be what occurred in all of the Americas, and elsewhere.

"Page 25

Gospel; to which if you add a **pious** endeavor and concern to see them duly instructed, you may become the instrument of saving many souls, and will not only **secure a blessing from God upon all your undertakings in this world,**

**but entitle yourselves to that distinguishing reward in the next** which will be given to all those who have been zealous in their endeavors to promote the **salvation of men and enlarge the kingdom of Christ**. And that you may be found in that number, at the **great day** of accounts, is the sincere desire and earnest prayer of your faithful friend.

EDM. LONDON."

*If you were fed such malarkey as this from the time you were in diapers, you would feel absolutely superior to anyone who does not look like you. This one paragraph is crucially important in Christian indoctrination, particularly of the Hebrews, because of the cruelty and suffrage the Hebrews endured in this land. However, the spreading of Christian doctrine has effected Africa, Asia, and many areas of the world. The teachers of this newly founded religion (circa 400 A.D.) have proscribed to its followers a* "**pious**" *approach to ensure their god is fully ingrained into the minds of their enslaved persons. In doing so, the enslavers have secured their own souls to heaven in their rightly god given role as kingdom builders for* "**Christ**". *In combining the above words with the previous readings in the document of instructions, one can easily see how beating, lynching, raping, and all of the heinous acts done to the Hebrews enslaved in this land, allowed such acts to be done without any consciousness of humanity. Anytime someone can do such acts, the one performing such atrocities is totally devoid of humanity, and is filled with evil. You don't get it; the teachings of Christianity is evil; Christianity is not of The Most High Elohim. Essentially, this writing is summed-up as this: beat Elohim out of your slaves until they succumb to our god, and in doing so, on that* great day of redemption, *you are secured unto Shamayim (heaven). But you know what? There is some* **Negropean** *somewhere, who will read the words the Europeans have written, and will stand in defense of the writing, and on top of that, is ready to strike off my ear for spreading the truth of the white mans' religion. I don't have words strong enough to denounce that slave mentality, of which the leaders of such foolery are the* **treachers** *(teachers/preachers) of the pulpit today. I'm not*

*presenting to you how or what to believe, I am presenting to you what the*
*Caucasoid has written about you, Hebrew man/woman.*

"6. The best form of Church Organization for the Negroes.
In the free States it is judged most advisable both by whites
and blacks, that the latter should have their own houses of
public worship and church organizations **independent of**
**the former**.

Page 274

But in the **slave States it is not advisable to separate the**
**black from the whites**. It is best that both classes worship
in the same building; that they be **incorporated** in the same
church, under the same pastor, having access to the same
**ordinances, baptism and the Lord's supper**, and at the
same time; and that they be subject to the same care and
discipline; the two classes forming one pastoral charge, one
church, one congregation.

Should circumstances beyond control require the Negroes to
meet in a separate building and have separate preaching, yet
they should be considered part and parcel of the white church.
Members should be admitted and excommunicated,[]and
ordinances administered in the presence of the united
congregations.

This mingling of the two classes in churches creates a greater
bond of union between them, and **kinder feelings; tends to**
**increase subordination**; and promotes in a higher degree
the improvement of the Negroes, in **piety and morality**.
The **reverse** is, in the general, true of **independent church**
**organizations of the Negroes**, in the slave States."

*There is a lot to this tactical approach to separating and or keeping*
*the two groups together. If the enslaved has been fully broken into their*
*subordinate position in society, let them be independent in SUN-day*
*worship of the god of the white race. Here is the thing though: In States of*

the North, States where slavery is not the main industry driver, the slaves are no threat because they have more freedom. But in the Southern States where slavery is the driving force of the economy, keep the slaves together with the whites. In other words: The Southern slaves, who have to endure harsh, grueling labor from sunup to sundown, the risk of them escaping is greater if the slaves are left independent of white supervision for too long period of time. Moreover, if the enslaved is not yet completely subdued into their subservient position, keep them with the whites to make sure control is maintained, and keeping them together thwarts any possibility for the enslaved to plot some plan of revolt. Once the "**heathen**" is fully ingrained into our religion, they will stay in their place; but even so, we have to have set rules for their independent worship service. The slaves must be "incorporated" under the rules of this Article. Question: Does the word "incorporated" sound familiar? It should because your church is most likely "incorporated" under the Governments 501c3 rules unto this day. You see, Government control of your church is _not_ new; it has been ongoing for centuries. The 501c3 is the dictate of your SUN-day sermons (sacrilege). I speak boldly: your pastor is one of the greatest offenders in the truth of Elohim. SUN-day after SUN-day, they preach from the same NT books over and again. Now let me throw you another nugget: THERE IS NO OLD TESTAMENT HEBREW SCRIPTURE OF SUPPORT, CHANGING THE DAY OF WORSHIP TO SUN-DAY. THE GREEK/ ROMAN CATHOLIC CHURCH WROTE AND MANUFACTURED THE FALSELY WRITTEN, SO-CALLED NEW TESTAMENT, commissioning SUN-day as the day of worship. The Hebrew Scriptures does not contain a new version of being in the Will of The Most High. In fact, the European writing of the New Testament is an attempt to overturn the Torah: (Bereshis/Gen., Shemot/Exo., VaYikra/Lev., Bamidbar/Num., and Devarim/Deu.). Stop, stop, stop, reading the blas-testament, and believing SUN-day worship is ordained of TMH Elohim; for it is not. SUN-day gathering of the congregation is blasphemy of the Fourth Commandment. I have to ask you another question: Where in the Scriptures do you find a wafer, and a cup of grape liquid as the ceremony of the Last Supper? Folks, it is not in there. The Last Supper was a fully cooked meal, with real wine. The truth of the matter is, there are seven holidays we are to observe each year (VaYikra/Lev. 23:15-16). The Last Supper, as recorded in the NT has nothing to do with the celebrations in honor of our Elohim, the Passover in particular, as outlined in the Torah. The following verse is from the NT: "For as often as you eat ..." (Kehillah Corinth I/1 Cor. 11:26)" Now here's the thing, do not totally discount the New Testament, but rather, read it with overstanding, letting the Ruach Hakodesh teach you what is contained in those Scriptures that is of TMH Elohim. Some portions of the NT are in alignment with the OT. One has to be acquainted with the content of both the OT and the NT in order to determine that which is truth from that of deception. The deceptive portions of the NT, written by the forces of evil, do not align with OT doctrine. The Elite Class scribes have cleverly given us a replacement, false narrative of what is required of us to be pleasing to our Elohim.

I would be totally remiss if I don't reinforce the following: there is no "**baptism and the Lord's supper**," in the Old Testament. I have to tell it like it is: all of that waste is of European origin, and is nothing more than a pile of trash. The easiest way to verify this is to do a word search of the AKJV of the Bible, using their own search engine, Bible Gateway. Baptism, and the Lord's Supper are make-believe, nonsensical garbage, invented from the minds of the workers of Hasatan. Now let me also say this, whether you agree or disagree, believe in the NT or not: Now think about this, I speak truth: the Scripture characters of the OT were not baptized with water, they were infiltrated by the Ruach Hakodesh. Do you get it? Those people were on the side of TMH Elohim, and are reserved in eternity with Elohim. Let me go a little farther with this: if you are a NT believer, check out Acts 10:44-48, it talks about the men hearing the preached word, and being filled with the Sacred Ruach. At that very instance they were saved, and they were _not_ baptized. Do you get it? It is being attached to the Ruach Hakodesh that saves; water _immersion_ is only an outward demonstration of your conversion. Hebrews, America, and world come out of _Egypt_ (captivity/bondage), freeing your minds to accept the truth, be no longer deceived. Listen-up: I tell you the truth, the vast portion of the New Testament is fictitious lies. While I am on a tangent, let me also say this: the story of _Lazarus_ is a giant lie from the pit of burning coals. When you research the name Lazarus, this is what you will find out: LAZARUS =

*IMAGINARY (Strong's 2976). I'm not saying that Strong's is all-knowing; however, Strong's does deserve credence in its accuracy.*

*As amazing as the reading of* "The Religious Instruction of the Negroes. In the United States." *has been, it gets even more revealing.*

> "The appointment of ***colored preachers* and *watchmen* (the latter acting as a kind of *elders,*)** *by the white churches, and under **their particular supervision,** in many districts of country has been attended with happy effects, and such **auxiliaries properly managed** may be of great advantage."

*In reflection of my days attending Christian church, and now being a Researcher of Scripture, and other Historical and or Ancient Documents, I can clearly see every element in the above paragraph in the Christian church today. As much as possible, I have avoided talking race in this book because race division is not the intent of this book. However, here, I must speak on race, not about Caucasian people; but rather, the so-called preachers standing in the pulpit, whose skin is filled with melanin. Hate me if you will but I will not spare the Word: Get ready, get ready, get ready! I'm coming full force in this segment. Until you UNDER-EDUCATED, NONE FACT SPEAKING BASTARDS (Heb. 12:8) OF THE PUPPET-PIT, LEARN NOT TO SPEAK THE BLASPHEMOUS TEACHINGS OF THE CHRISTIAN RELIGION, our Hebrew brothers and sisters will remain in chains, who have no clue they are being fed a bowl full of poop. You wretched preachers need to learn the truth of who the Hebrews are; what the role of the Hebrew is; and stop preaching that J-sus stench, that foul odor reaching to the lowest furnaces of fire. You "Black" Baptist preachers are agents of Hasatan. You "colored" pastors are worse than any white man or white woman enslaving the Hebrew Yisra'elite, because you are a traitor of the worse sort, treaching white "Jesus" to the detriment of your own people, either by ignorant default, not knowing the Scriptures; or possibly even worse by denying your own heritage, selling out for a morsel of bread and some lentiles (Ber./Gen. 25:34). Many of you "Black" preachers are simply mimics of what you have heard other dumb-downed Black preachers before you preach. Some of you have attended schools of Theology,* *where you were taught the foolery of what the above paragraph tells us: though the <u>overseer</u>, "**<u>watchmen</u>**," is not present in the congregation today to make sure you continue to preach enslavement mentality doctrine (Col. 3:22), that is exactly what you have continued to do. Here is the thing: though the "**<u>watchmen</u>**" and the "**<u>auxiliaries properly managed</u>**" are not physically present in the congregation today, the church is still governed under the same application, but has changed its method of operation. At this point we must discuss the 501c3, this is of such importance, it is necessary for the document to be presented in this segment of our study.*

> "*The **<u>State controls all aspects of an incorporated church</u>** through means of **<u>incorporation laws</u>** and are dictated also by **<u>state statutes</u>**. All paperwork must be sent into the State; the **<u>minutes of every meeting</u>** must be kept on file in case the State needs to see them. The State must know the **<u>names and addresses of anyone tithing over a certain amount of money</u>**, how a church advertises its meetings, how a church gains new members. The State regulates its day care, **<u>its religious instruction, the topics of sermons</u>**, its building additions, all its assets, its marriages, its deaths, and many more, and can close an incorporated church any time it pleases. It keeps the incorporated church in line with threats to revoke its incorporated and tax-exempt status: It can close an incorporated church for anything as small as **<u>picketing at a pro-life rally</u>** as a church group, for **<u>preaching a sermon it classifies as "propaganda"</u>**, or because a church supports anyone who runs for state or federal office. It can close an incorporated church for any violation of fire, health, safety, and educational rules and regulations; like because it feels the Church has too many people in the services, or because it **<u>doesn't like the Church curriculum</u>**.*"

*iahushua.com/WOI/control.htm*

Have you made the connection? Both the official document of instruction for the Hebrew to become a Christian, and the 501c3, are the Government's means of keeping the Hebrews in servitude. The bottom-line to both documents is this: In the one document <u>the enslaved is the money</u>, and in the other document is <u>the means to obtain your money</u>. In the one document where you are at all times is closely <u>monitored</u>, and in the other document you are <u>monitored</u> by the church (government) keeping track of what you do. Lastly, on this topic, before digging deeper into the flesh of those reprehensible deceivers of the puppet-pit: Elohim is not pleased with you, and you need to get out of the pulpit, preaching the doctrines of devils.

The following paragraph speaks expressly on behalf of the Government for the control of the Hebrew Yisra'elites of <u>Turtle Island</u> (America).

> "Such are the **means and plans for promoting and securing the religious instruction of the Negroes, in the United States**, and of those in the **Southern States in particular**, which experience and observation have suggested to my own mind. And having brought this part of the subject to a close, I have reached, in the good providence of God, the **end of my undertaking**."

Oh my gosh, there is really <u>no more</u> to this end that I need to add; however, I will. The greatest enemy of the Hebrews today, are the religious leaders of the church. Many use the words: "sell out," to indicate when someone turns away from their own kind. The Negro Pastors preaching the Blas-Testament (<u>suffrage in cheerfulness; the smiling, happy Negro</u>) are instruments of Hasatan, and of the Government (501c3), and are the main cause of the Hebrew remaining in bondage unto this day (I am quite aware of the curses of VaYikra/Lev. 26 and Devarim/Deu 28). Some of the Negro Pastors of the past knew the truth, and they lost their lives for revealing the truth. We must not allow fear to keep us from the truth of Biblical History, no matter the consequence; we have to overstand the enemy will come to fight against the truth tellers to preserve their power and riches on <u>ha'aretz</u> (the earth). The other submissive pastors of today, gained status as the leaders of "Black People." They were pawns for the U.S. Government, and still are unto this day, signing onto the white establishment naming us degrading terms; such as: "Black" and "African American." Those names are of no consequence to OUR ABORIGINAL (<u>meaning: no one lived here prior</u>

*to the Hebrews) NATIONALITY TO TURTLE ISLAND (America). In fact, under U.S. Law, anyone classed as "Black" or "African American" is not a legal Citizen of the U.S.A.. Not to get too far off of topic, but a short excerpt is beneficial here to support this opinion:*

> *"In March of 1857, the United States Supreme Court, led by Chief Justice Roger B. Taney, declared that all blacks -- slaves as well as free -- **were not and could never become citizens of the United States**. The court also declared the 1820 Missouri Compromise unconstitutional, thus permitting slavery in all of the country's territories."*
>
> *Pbs.org/wgbh/aia/part4/4h2933*

*Essentially, beyond the outright declaration that no "Blacks" are and can never be U.S. Citizens is this: This Supreme Court ruling has never been reversed. The Thirteenth Amendment did not free Hebrews from slavery, it changed the methodology of slavery by way of incarceration laws; such as, Jim Crow, and Sundown Laws. In fact the Supreme Court ruling goes on to tell us something that most Americans were never taught, but the Elite Class are fully aware exist, and that is:*

> *"The words "people of the United States" and "citizens" are synonymous terms, and mean the same thing. They both describe the political body who ... **form** the sovereignty, and who hold the power and conduct the Government through their representatives.... The question before us is, whether the class of persons described in the plea in abatement [**people of African ancestry**] compose a portion of this people, and are constituent members of this sovereignty? We think they are not, **and that they are not included, and were not intended to be included, under the word "citizens" in the Constitution**, and can therefore claim none of the rights and privileges which that instrument provides for and secures to citizens of the United States."*
>
> *Pbs.org/wgbh/aia/part4/4h2933*

*A picture should be forming in your mind about the true history of the Negro in our own land at this point. At any rate, here is the truth of all of these writings. The invaders/colonizers came into this land, and in time overthrowing the Hebrews, took possession of our land, and gave us their "Jesus" religion. In time, as they created laws another phenomenon was also occurring. The Hebrews were given epithets that their laws banned as being Citizens: Colored, Black American, and African American. At this point you should have a better overstanding of why over the many decades, the Elite Class has given us new epithets, all with no right to Citizenship.*

*It is time for New Leadership to emerge from the Hebrew Community: new, forward thinking leaders, not controlled by external forces. The "old heads" need to move aside, and "new heads" need to emerge. That old slavery mentality doctrine: the preaching of "Jesus" needs to die. The orchestrators of Christianity have well documented what they did; their reasoning for what they did; how they accomplished the indoctrination of Christianity into the Hebrew; and most importantly, how to keep the Hebrew under control for centuries. People of conscience: My black skin, brown skin, white skin people, come out of Christianity, the only hope we have is to unite, coming into the Sacred Covenant of The Most High Elohim. In doing so, the true enemy is defeated (the spirit of Esau), and victory is established in Elohim. My friends, let not evil suggest to you, that you are better than or less than anyone else; as humanity, we are one. May Elohim bless the goodness of your countenance always. Selah.*

*In my lifetime, the name given to the people, the Hebrews, in this land has changed many times. In my childhood, we were called <u>Negro</u>; which is the race of the Hebrew people of United States of America; and the Hebrews in Africa, and everywhere in the world the Hebrews have been scattered. After being called Negro, we were then called "<u>Colored</u>." The truth of the matter is, ninety (90) percent of the earth's population are people of varying levels of melanin skin. There is no other Race, whose heritage has been designated or relegated to a none identifiable class such as "Colored." The purpose in changing the epithet of the Negro Hebrew to Colored was to, in my opinion, declassify the Hebrew to none human status, as those in power, the Elite Class, knew the Negro and the Hebrew is one and the same. The use of "Colored" to designate a Race is offensive and* demeaning, and has <u>no legal</u> standing in a U.S. Court of Law. Listen-up very closely: the <u>Laws</u> of the U.S. Government are written to specifically keep anyone born under titles; such as: Colored, Black American, and African American, that does not include the words Native American, can never be a Citizen of the U.S.A.. Now get this: Hebrews born in the U.S. and its Imperial Territories does not make one a Citizen under such titles as, Black American, African American, and Colored. The Caucasian establishment gave us those demeaning epithets, with concomitant Laws to exclude anyone under those epithets from being Citizens in this land. There has never been one law in this land granting citizenship to the Negro. Do you get it? They created Laws that ban those specific epithets from citizenship, and then very scrupulously, set-up so-called leaders for those epithets to call themselves names of non-citizenry. Talk about an oxymoron; we were duped beyond logic. Talk about a sell-out. That trash tops the charts. I don't know if the so-called leadership were "coons" are themselves victims. Which ever does not matter, either way, the Hebrews gained no ground. After being labeled "Colored" for years, some civic minded leaders of the Negro Community, thought rather ignorantly, under the influence of the Elite Class powers that be, the name "Black American" was more appropriate. That spurred a long period of the: "I'm Black and proud" movement. This too was as absurd a name for the Hebrew people as any label could be. Black is a color, a classification of colors; not a race. The term "Black American" is as oxymoronic a term as the phrase: Dung don't stink. Hebrews come in a variety of differing skin hues from copper, to caramel, to deep dark chocolate, all brown, with red undertones. The human race is basically made-up of four groups: <u>the Negroid, the Caucasoid, the Mongoloid, and the Hamites</u>. There are however, many ethnicities and cultures; those groups derive from the customs of their family, and the region of the world they live in. Furthermore, many of those groups are the result of mixing. If you believe the Scriptures, all people on <u>ha'aretz</u> (the earth) today came from Noah, Ham, Shem, and Yepheth. Let me break this down for you: Noah was chosen to survive the flood because he was not polluted by the bloodline of the <u>Annunaki</u> (Fallen angels). Those fallen angels mated with the human females producing the <u>Nephilim</u> (giants; Ber./Gen. 6:4). The Annunaki, who retained all of the power and knowledge they had in

*Shamayim (heaven), realizing Elohim's plan to destroy the Nephilim in the flood, developed their own plan of how they would return after the flood, to continue their bloodline. The Annunaki entered into Ham, and after the flood caused Ham to do evil; resulting in the curse of Canaan. That curse resulted in the dark races, the Hamites, suffering under many types of plagues, and eventual colonization by the evil bloodline of the fallen angels.*

*Note: Do not confuse the curse of Ham with the curse of the Annunaki (Esau). The Hamites are not the evil spirit of Esau, the curse of Ham was a generational curse, that can be lifted by serving the True Elohim. The Annunaki are different in that they are forever cursed, and banned from Shamayim. Think about this: at some time long ago, each race has had a generational curse upon them, but even so, the only group that cannot be redeemed is the spirit of Esau. Selah.*

*After being "Black American", we became "African American". That too, was a misnomer of great disinformation. The Hebrews of the Americas are not African; that label further fostered the stereotypical, unsubstantiated belief that, all Hebrews are African, and thus heathens, and are not capable of the same intellect as other people. The use of the word "heathen" in context to the word "African" is not to offend African people; the word "heathen" is actually what the Scriptures use to describe the enemies of the Hebrews. The fact of the matter is, the First humans did originate in Africa, somewhere around the area of Ethiopia. However, the Negro, the Hebrew people, had already moved to Asia (which is also Northeast Africa, Yisra'el), and had been there many millennia before coming into their own as the Hebrew Yisra'elites. I have to say this, there has been so much bashing of Africans by some claiming to be Hebrew, the bashing of Africans is absurd to entertain. Look folks, not every melanized person living in Africa are Hamites, many are Negro. Not every melanized American is Negro, some are Hamites. Then there are those of melanized skin, Hebrews and Hamites, who are indistinguishable. Let this sink into your brain: the biggest difference between those captured and put onto slave ships is: Where the boat stopped to drop off its cargo. Let me clean this up for you: There were Hebrews in Africa, particularly South Africa, Nigeria, and much of West Africa, who were captured and brought to the U.S., and other U.S., French, Spanish, and British Imperial Territories. Also there were Africans brought to the*

*U.S., the Caribbean Islands, and South America. Many of the Hamites were dropped off in the Caribbean, Haiti in particular, and Southern America. Jamaica, however, those captured and enslaved there were mainly Hebrews. Jamaicans and Haitians are diametrically distinguishable peoples. Haitians are clearly Hamitic people, while Jamaicans are Hebrews, twins to the Hebrews in the U.S.A.. I have to emphasize this point for the Hebrews: in our scattering we were already in this land, and on every continent before any Europeans came here. In observation of the physical attributes of Hebrews and Hamites, anyone with an awareness and discerning ruach (spirit) can see with the natural eye, Hebrews and Hamites do not have the same physical make-up. However, there are those in between because of breeding by the slave masters. The truth of the matter is, listen-up Hebrews, many people living in Africa are our brothers and sisters. You are bashing them out of ignorance of the Scriptures, and pseudo (false), European history given to us by the Elite Class. Hebrews branding all Africans as Hamites are out of order. Moreover, and very importantly, the only people on this planet disqualified from serving The Most High Elohim, The Great I AM, are those of the bloodline of the fallen angels. The possessors of the spirit of Esau (Esau is not the Caucasoid, Esau is the spirit of evil) are the Elite Class, whose kingdom is the earth. It is those of the Elite Class, the one (1) percent, who control the power, the wealth, and push white supremacy racism.*

*At this point, I believe it to be appropriate to insert a volume of information on the history of humanity, and how people evolved depending on where their particular families settled on ha'aretz (the earth). Don't get the word evolved twisted and confused with evolution; I am only referring to exterior changes that occur per the environment; such as, more body hair growing in colder climates, eye color changes as the melanin fades from the body, and so forth. So don't accuse me of being an evolutionist.*

> "*Ham* (ham, persons, hot). 1. The youngest son of Noah, born probably about 96 years before the Flood; and one of eight persons to live *through the Flood. He became the progenitor of the dark races; **not the Negroes**, but the Egyptians, Etiopians, Libyans and Canaanites (Gen. 10:6-20).*

> His indecency, when his father lay drunken brought a curse
> upon Canaan (Gen.9:25)"

Zondervan Bible Dictionary

*The Hebrews are a completely separate entity from all other people, even our cousins, the Ephraimites. Our other cousins, **Yepheth became the Gentiles** (Bereshis/Gen. 10:1-5). Look at the following information from African Diaspora II:*

> *"40,000 – 10,000 BC Late Stone Age; Rise of **brown-skinned** Homo Sapiens, spreading to **all major regions** of the world and adapting to variations in **climate and environment**; Development of bow and arrow; evidence of rock paintings; Hunter gathering lifestyle; Arrival of the **Grimaldian Negroid in Europe**"*

African Diaspora II International Migration

*The most revealing information from the above paragraph is the "**Grimaldian Negroid in Europe**" Listen-up Hebrews, America, and world, hear me well: what has been intentionally left out of the miseducation system in America is that: THE FIRST OCCUPANTS OF THE WHOLE OF EUROPE WERE PEOPLE OF MELANIN SKIN. What this Biblical and Historical data reveals to us is that, from Yepheth came the greatest enemy to the Negro Hebrews, the Caucasoid. This opinion is not rendered from the mind of a biased, bigoted, racist; it is derived from the hisotry records, written by the Caucasoids themselves. The Caucasoids have always known the Hebrews are the Hebrews, the Chosen of Elohim.*

*Now let us look at Shem:*

*Shem became the Hebrews. The family-line of Shem, to Aram, to Arphaxad, to **Eber** (synonym: Iberia). The name Eber is the **etymological** name from which came the name Hebrew (etymonline.com). Abraham was the **first** to be called Hebrew (Bereshis/Gen. 14:13). Nahor, Abraham's brother became the Syrians (Bereshis/Gen. 24:15-47). The Syrians and all of the people of the Middle World are Mongoloid. What we have seen in* *the above sentences thus far, in the origins of people are the Hamites, the Mongolians, and the Hebrews. There is one group missing: the Caucasoids. Now for the skeptics out there who believe that, there is no difference in the Hebrews and the Hamites because we all came from two people: If that is the case, how then do we have the four races afore mentioned? Do you get it? Elohim separated the offspring of Aw-dawn and Chavvah, according to how events from humans unfolded, making whole other races of people from those already in existence to serve a new purpose for HIM. Each race has a specificity: the Hebrews to serve HIM only in bringing spirituality to the world; the Caucasoid, to torment the Hebrews, who turned their backs on HIM. The above information explains the Caucasoids emergence into a race: The Africans, over many hundreds of thousands of years in the <u>African Diaspora</u>, in traveling East, reached the coldest habitable lands on the planet. Over the thousands of years of living in Europe, with little sun, and cold weather, the skin of the Africans began to fade out from a lack of hot temperatures and bright sun light. That caused the body's <u>melanin</u> production, which is promoted by sunshine, to decrease, and over many thousands of years, their Darker Skin lightened to <u>Brown Skin</u> (Grimaldian), eventually becoming what we call White Skin today. Not only did the lack of sun/melanin cause changes in the skin, it changed the external characteristics of the people. Oh yes, some of you really will not like what I am about to present to you; however, I will only present to you the truth: WHITE PEOPLE ARE AFRICANS. White people are of the family line of Yepheth. Don't be angry with me for telling you the truth; I did not write the Scriptures, or the history books, or the scientific data, so stop looking at me all stupid. Not only is this written in the Scriptures, True History bears it out; the first inhabitants of Europe were the <u>Moors,</u> the very same dark-skinned Hamites of Africa.*

*Note: Ibrahim, Hebrew, Iberia, Eber, Ibrim, and Ibriyyim, are all synonyms of Abraham. <u>Iberia,</u> in particular, is very important to overstand because that name was given to the Southwest most region of Europe, across from North Africa, called the <u>Iberian Peninsula</u>. That means it is likely the Iberian Peninsula is named for the Hebrews, and it could be representative of Hebrews having lived there at some time in Geographical History, as recorded by none other than the Caucasoids themselves.*

*You can find the picture of the appearance of the first Europeans online at images.search.yahoo.com. The caption to the bust reads as follows:*

> *"Forensic bust of the first European created by Richard Neave, one of Britain's leading forensic scientists. Using fossilized fragments of skull and jawbone, carbon-dated to between 34,000 and 36,000 years ago, that were found in a cave in the Carpathian Mountains of Romania"*

*No need to elaborate on this one, the caption says it all. However, and listen well to this: the Diasporal information on the brown-skinned Grimaldian Negroid, combined with the scientific information above cannot be disputed. Believe me, the Privileged, Elite Class Caucasians, know this information, and have worked tirelessly to keep this information hidden. This kind of well-founded information destroys all aspects of White Supremacy Racism. If it were not for the good ruachs of the true historians, scientists, paleontologists, geographers, and theologians, this information would not be available on the internet today. Additionally, books that were written in antiquity; such as, "How To Make a Negro Christian" would still be hidden. I want to encourage every good ruach, to research the internet, and to explore or incorporate reading old books into your study, and not only reading the Blas-Testament. Whenever something in your ruach does not feel right about history, research it. Everything in history has been written down somewhere: books, videos, documents, and Bibles. You can go online to multiple sites, type into the search engine: 10th century Moorish king of Croatia. The image of the king clearly showed him to be of Hamitic, African heritage.*

*Wow America and world, what we don't know? What has been hidden? This figure of a Royal from Croatia, a Black-A-Moor, distinctively Hamitic, is a treasure chest of information. The internet has provided us great access to information previously kept secret or hidden. In another search of the web type in: The Moors Who Conquered Spain, or Moorish Conquest of Spain. The image that will appear is Djabal Tarik, a Black-A-Moor, whom the Rock of Gibraltar is named. In 711 A.D. Tarik lead his army* of 10,000 men from Africa to the Iberian Peninsula, where they defeated the Spaniards living there.

America, have you ever heard this bit of history? Spain was conquered by African Moors. America and world, you have been duped. Folks, this information is not new; it has been hidden. The powers of this world are losing ground thanks to the internet, and by the Will of The Most High Elohim. Did you observe the name "Iberian"? This information lends more credence to the Hebrews having lived there at some point in antiquity.

Have you ever heard of Eadgyth of Britain? I speculate that most reading this book have not. The early royals of Britain were Negroes, and were the cream of the crop. This information is available from the British themselves:

> "The remains of Alfred the Great's granddaughter, Eadgyth - a Saxon Queen and one of the oldest members of the English royal family were unearthed in a tomb in Germany ... Eadgyth was married off to Otto I, the Great, in AD 929 by her half brother Athelstan, who was the first king to rule all of England."

Daily Mail.com

Now you see why those of White Supremacy Racism would hide so much true history from the public. How can you push your Elite Class, racist agenda against Africans and Hebrews, when both groups, in all likelihood, preceded the White race by many millennia, both in intellect and civil living? Some of you reading this will refuse this information, presented by Caucasian Historians because it goes against everything you were taught. The fact of the matter is, this data reveals something else that most Caucasoids will not accept as truth: The Royals of Britain are the distant posterity of melanized people, they have been whited-out by centuries of living in cold, dim, Europe. Now ain't that blip!

With all of that said, here is what has to be overstood most: It is time out for pastors preaching the sermons dictated by the mandates of the Article "The Religious Instruction of the Negroes. In the United States." This must stop! Folks, and I speak boldly: Pastors are the enemy of the people. I *don't care what color skin you wear, you have been deceived by the powers that be. Read and research for yourself, and you will find that the history of humanity has been recorded accurately somewhere; and the history you have been taught, does not match what has been hidden from the general population. The Negro is not less than anyone else; the Caucasian is not better than anyone else. The truth of the matter is, according to DNA Research, most Caucasians having their blood tested, in the era of DNA, have become angry that African origin is found in their heritage (Democracy Dies in Darkness; The Washington Post, February 6, 2018).*

*The role of the Hebrew is one role only: TO LEAD THE WORLD IN SPIRITUALITY FOR THE MOST HIGH ELOHIM. The creation of the Negro Hebrew Yisra'elites was for one purpose only, to educate the world about the True Supreme Elohim, because people were worshiping Baal, Molech, Ashtoreth, and other demigods; whose leader is Hasatan. I must speak boldly: Caucasian people, don't get angry with me for telling you the truth; direct your anger toward those, who have deceived and defrauded you into believing, the White Race is above all other peoples on ha'aretz (the earth).*

*Now to an issue that burns deep into the very fiber of my Being: "The skin color of Jesus does not matter". Well, it sure as heck does. The reason this matters is multi-faceted: the Europeans took the original drawings of Ha Mashiach, and made new paintings with Him having white skin. Making new copies of articles from antiquity is not new. Such methods are essential as part of their brainwashing technique to indoctrinate white privilege, and white supremacy to the world. There are several very important doctrines built into the Article, of which, is the god of the Caucasian cannot obviously be the Elohim of the enslaved. And, there is a designed plan of U.S. Expansionism built into the Article. You see, Manifest Destiny gives the Caucasian Race the right to go into any land, and by god commanded right, to take over the land, spreading out from border to border, and suppressing, and oppressing the indigenous people of the land. Any person of melanized skin, who believes the creation of a white god to be of no consequence, is totally devoid of how that white god influence has dominated and suppressed people of melanin skin in Africa, the Americas, the Philippines,* the Caribbean Islands, and Hawaiian Islands, but most of all the Hebrews in America.

> "Manifest Destiny was also a key slogan deployed in the United States Imperial ventures in the 1890's, and early years of the twentieth century that led to U.S. possession or control of the Philippines and the Hawaiian Islands. But Manifest Destiny was not simply a cloak for American Imperialism, and a rationale for America's territorial ambitions."

nationalhumanitiescenter.org

You do know the U.S. is an Imperial Government? When the image of Ha Mashiach was changed to a Caucasian by what is referred to as iconography, that imagery alone has enough power to manipulate the world into the doctrine of white supremacy racism. I must make a disclaimer about images of the Hashilush Hakadosh: Such imagery is prohibited by decree of The Most High Elohim (She./Exo. 20:4). With the establishment of "Jesus" as the "Savior" of the world, all Manifest Destiny, superiority of the Caucasian; the inferiority of the Negro; all of the power over the world; all of the wealth of the world; now rightfully belongs to the Caucasian people. Moreover, Ha Mashiach being a Hebrew means, He was Negro, and His teachings were Hebrew teachings of the Law. Do you get it? Ha Mashiach did not teach Christianity. Christianity is a plague upon the earth that gives all authority to the Caucasoid, and their white god: "Jesus". Therefore, when the Hebrews say, the color of Ha Mashiach's skin does not matter, it is in my opinion, the most ignorant statement ever made. The image of a white "savior" has done more damage to humanity than any hydrogen bomb has ever done. Therefore, my plea is that all people accept the fact that Ha Mashiach, of the family line of Abraham, will research for themselves, and see the truth: Ha Mashiach was a Negro, of the Negro Shevet (Tribe) of Yehuwdah.

Inasmuch, for a Negro to say that, "The skin color of Jesus does not matter," How then, how then, does taking the Brown Skin Mashiach, changing His image into a Caucasian; changing the Spiritual Practice of the Hebrew into that of Christianity; using Manifest Destiny; Drawing up

*Articles of Dominance; not make the statement of the most absurd saying any Negro could ever make?*

*The book:* "The Religious Instruction of the Negroes. In the United States" *is one of the most revealing documents in the world about the difference between the Caucasian and the Negro; Christianity and Hebrew Spirituality; Superiority of the White Race, and the false narrative of the inferiority of the Negro Hebrew. And very importantly, the realism that the Caucasian and the Negro, do not serve the same god. Whenever the attitude of a group is dominance, supremacy, greed, wealth, and power, that group is capable of the most heinous atrocities in all of inhumanity. The instructions for the Negro to become a Christian is one of the grossest demonstrations of demonism. The Article of itself is proof that the Hebrews are the true children of Devarim 28. Those, who hold the Hebrews captive in America are those from a land far away, from the end of the eretz, whose language the Hebrews knew not, and whose countenance is fierce (Dev./ Deu. 28:49:50).*

*Clearly, anyone adhering to the instruction book for the Negro to become a Christian, has in their mind that, no matter what torture they inflict upon the assumed inferior Negro, that such punishment is in giving honor to their god. Therefore, if the captor has to beat, maim, torture, dismember, or in anywise mutilate the so-called inferior Negro, to bring them into Christianity, let it be done. In carrying out such discipline, not only has the brutal slave "master" brought a soul to god, which is a gross contradiction of belief; the oppressor has brought reward to their own soul as well. HEAR ME NOW: how can you save the soul of a creature not considered to be human, as the Article clearly views the enslaved as "**poor creatures**"? The fact of the matter is, in researching the history of the Scriptures, one will find that, Hebrews are a different specie than the contaminated offspring of the Annunaki. From the time of Abraham the Hebrew is a new race of people. This new people are the uncontaminated portion of humanity. In other words, it is the Negro Hebrew who is pure human, made in the image and likeness of the Hashilush Hakadosh (Ber./Gen. 1:26). It is those, who control the world that are hybrid creatures and are not completely human. They are part fallen angel; they are the offspring of the Annunaki. You see, the seed of the fallen angels have an attitude reflective of their conscious awareness of* *who the Hebrews are, and of who they are. The ideal of the Hebrews being labeled as "__poor creatures__" meaning the Negro Hebrews are not human, it is akin to <u>reverse psychology</u>. Now think on this question: Do animals have souls? It is the language of speaking out of both sides of one's mouth. Not only has the enslaver saved a lost Negro soul by torture, he or she have secured their own soul to <u>Shamayim</u> (heaven), and as a result of converting the Negro to Christianity, the Christian will receive a monetary reward for their service on <u>ha'aretz</u> (the earth), and in Shamayim. The mind-set of the oppressors is truly reflected in Devarim/Deu. 28:50, a people of a "fierce countenance" and Bereshis/Gen. 6:4, tells us of their contaminated status.*

*The instruction book for the Negro to become a Christian, reflects the attitude of the most racists mind-sets anyone could ever possess, an attitude totally supported by the <u>Ekklesia</u> (Church); the U.S. Imperial Government, and the British Imperial Government. Additionally, as is proof negative of unanimous support of the Article, is the District Court of the United Stated affixed their signatures upon the Article, giving it all legitimacy of United States Law. This is all found in the prelude to the instructions. A preponderance of the Article is this:*

> *CHRISTIANS THINK ON THIS- THE CHURCH, THE CHRISTIAN CHURCH, WROTE A BOOK OF TORTURE, AGAINST THE NEGRO HEBREWS SUPPOSEDLY TO SAVE THE SOULS OF A SOULLESS CREATURE. A RELIGION THAT SIMULTANEOUSLY SUPPOSEDLY PROMOTES LOVE OF ALL PEOPLE. THEREFORE, THE CREATURE BEING SOULLESS, WHEREIN THEN LIES THE STRENGTH IN THE ARTICLE? HOW CAN SAID ARTICLE GOVERN OVER A CREATURE THAT HAS NO SOUL? MOREOVER, THE SOULLESS NEGRO CANNOT BE CONVERTED TO CHRISTIANITY BECAUSE THE NEGRO IS NOT HUMAN, AND THEREFORE IS NOT A CANDIDATE FOR THE CHRISTIAN RELIGION.*

*Folks, the Article is one of the grossest hypocritical documents ever written. Anyone reading this Article has to know, the Article is simply, white supremacy racism of the highest order, written by the church of the Elite Class, who control this planet.*

*Note: By "proof negative" I mean, these presents are damnable heresy against The True Creator: The Elohim of the Hebrews. All praise to The Most High Elohim, The Great I AM THAT I AM.*

*In all that is contained in the Article, the points that have to be overstood, beyond the punishments incorporated into the Article is this: the practice of Christianity is not about saving souls; Christianity is about control, wealth, superiority, and power. The most influential and powerful people on this planet control religion, which controls the people; which in-turn controls the wealth and the power. The bottom-line is that, yes, race has also been part of the greatest blasphemy in religion. However, race superiority is far superceded by the wealth and power generated in keeping the people under control. In feeding the people white supremacy and Christianity, is control of the people: white, black, or green skin. Christianity is false theology which is headed-up by Hasatan.*

*Negro Hebrews, America, and world wake-up: If there is anything which can prove to you that we have all been brainwashed, it should be this Article:* "The Religious Instruction of the Negroes. In the United States." *Those of conscience will be sickened in reading the Article; while those of evil countenance will uphold the horrid document, and in all sincerity, hope to return to the ways outlined in the Article. The time for said Article to end is soon coming to a close. Listen, the reason the Article is still in effect is this: Though the chains and shackles are no longer in place, slavery has not ended, it only evolved into a court and prison system of laws that assures slavery for Hebrews will continue. In the end, the fate of the people will depend on the ruach each person carries in their soul: the hatov (good) or the harah (evil), determines the next phase of existence upon death of the natural body.*

After such a long break and insertion of historical and scientific data, let us now return to Devarim/Deuteronomy, Chapter 28.

Devarim/Deu. 28:36; 41; 43-44;48; 68:

'The HASHEM shall bring you, and your king which you shall set over you, unto a nation which neither you nor your fathers

*have known; <u>and there shall you serve other **gods**, **wood and***
*<u>stone</u>. 41 <u>You shall beget sons and daughters</u>, but you shall not*
*comfort them; <u>for they shall go into **captivity**</u>. 43 The **stranger***
*that is within you shall get <u>up above you</u> **very high**; and you*
*shall come down **very low**. 44 He shall **lend** to you, and you*
***shall not lend** to him: he shall be the **head**, and you shall be*
*the **tail**. 48 therefore shall you **<u>serve your enemies</u>** which the*
*HASHEM shall **<u>send against you</u>**, in **<u>hunger</u>**, and in **thirst**,*
*and in **nakedness**, and in want of **all** things: and he shall*
*put a **yoke of iron upon your neck**, until he have destroyed*
*you. 68 And the HASHEM shall bring you into Mitzrayim*
*(bondage) again with **ships**, by the way whereof I spake unto*
*you, You shall see it no more again: and there you shall be **<u>sold</u>***
***<u>unto your enemies</u>** for bondmen and bondwomen, and **<u>no</u>***
***<u>man shall buy you</u>**.'*

Now let us look at what the Hebrews must do to correct the curses of Devarim/Deu., Chapter 28. The Hebrews are told again in Dev./Deu., Chapter 29, that any Hebrew man or woman, **who serves the gods of the enemy**, of any nation is cursed (29:18). The scriptures then go on to say: the Hebrew found guilty of such will have their name removed from the book of life (29:20), and that he or she for not keeping the *Law*, will be tossed into a dry land of brimstone, and salt, and great heat (29:23-29). Hebrews, here is the cure for all of the plight, and travel of the Hebrews, the Chosen People of Elohim. THIS PROPHESY, THE PROSHESY OF MOSHEH UPON THE HEBREW YISRA'ELITES: THE WARNINGS, THE BLESSINGS OF OBEDIENCE, THE CURSES OF DISOBEDIENCE: THE PLIGHT AND TRAVELS BROUGHT UPON THE HEBREWS THEN, AND NOW, SELF-INFLICTED: HEBREWS COME OUT OF HER. TO ELOHIM BE ALL PRAISES. SELAH!

The leadership of Yisra'el must lead the people. Yehuwdah is the appointed leader over all of the Shevets of Yisra'el (Ber./Gen. 49:8-12). Ephraim is to encourage all of the Twelve Shevets to work together (Ber./Gen.48:19-20). Yehuwdah, Ephraim, The Prophet has charged you to guide all of these people in the Commandments of Elohim. No man shall buy you because you will be taken violently taken away by force, and iron not only put upon your necks, but also shackles on your hands and feet, and muzzles upon your mouth. You will be taken into **_Egypt_** (bondage) again by ship represents the Hebrews, who escaped the *Babylonian Exile* into Africa, will be hunted down by the enemy and loaded onto ships, taken to lands where you will be enslaved, Egypt again.

Devarim/Deu. 30: 1-3:

> *'And **it shall** come to pass, when all these things are come upon you, **the blessing and the curse**, which I have set before you, and you shall call them to mind among **all the nations**, where the HASHEM your Elohim has **driven you**, 2 and shall **return** unto the HASHEM your Elohim, and shall **obey** HIS voice according to **all** that I Command you this day, you and your children, with all your heart, and with **all your soul**; 3 that then the HASHEM your Elohim will **turn your captivity**, and have compassion upon you, and will **return and gather you from all the nations**, where the HASHEM your Elohim **had scattered you**.'*

Mosheh had gathered all of Yisra'el together to deliver his last address to all of the Hebrews. Mosheh makes it perfectly clear, his words will both bless and curse, both being conditional predicaments. The Hebrews are about to cross over into the *Promised Land*. Once in the land of promise, the Hebrews in compliance to the Commandments of Elohim will have all of their needs fulfilled. This is important to overstand: What is hidden in these verses is this, there have been scattering of the shevets many times prior to the Hebrews reaching the Promised Land. But here, in the Promised Land, if you allow other god worship, I (Elohim) will put you out of the land, and scatter you to different lands. The inference being: The Babylonians will come upon you, and in history the event will be called: *The Babylonian Exile of Yisra'el*. Line and precept, moving forward. There is good news in this for the Hebrews of today.

Devarim/Deu. 30:7-8:

'*7 And the HASHEM your Elohim will put **all these curses upon your enemies**, and on them that **hate** you, which **persecuted** you. 8 And you shall return and **obey** the voice of the HASHEM, and do all HIS Commandments which I Command you this day. 9 And the HASHEM your Elohim will **make you plenteous in every work** of your hand, in the fruit of your body, and in the fruit of your cattle, and in the fruit of your land, for good: for the HASHEM will again delight over you for good, as HE delighted over your fathers:*'

Hebrews, in returning to the Commandments of Elohim, all that the enemy has done to the Hebrews will be put upon the enemy. The first thing Hebrews of today have to overstand is this: Negro man, Negro woman, you are the Hebrews of Scripture. Come out of the worship of other gods. Come out of *cognitive dissonance*, allow your reading comprehension to connect what you read, to the meaning(s) or message(s) in full context. Negro man, Negro woman, in reading this book, if you have read to this point, you have to overstand that you are Hebrew. Also you should be aware that not every person of melanin skin is Hebrew, there are billions of people, who have melanin skin, but they are not Negro. Let me state this as emphatically as possible: It is only the Negro who is Hebrew. Hebrews you have to overstand that serving other gods can be your **car**, or following the religion(s) of other people. You have to overstand that you, Hebrew man, Hebrew woman are a set-apart people that should not intermingle with other people in marriage and production of children, those marriages have always led to the Hebrews worshiping other gods, Shelomoh is a prime example. Shelomoh married heathen women causing him to build houses of worship for their gods (2 Kings 23:13). Mosheh's next message to the Hebrews is very poignant.

Devarim/Deu. 30:15:

'*See, I have set before you this day **life and good, and death and evil**,*'

Here Mosheh has said more than a mouthful. He told the Hebrews that in <u>obedience</u>, you have life, and life abundantly, with all of the good of Elohim; however, if you <u>disobey</u>, death will follow for the evil you have done. This does not mean, you will die immediately, it means: You will suffer at the hands of captors, all of the evil tactics described in: "*The Religious Instruction of the Negroes. In the United States*", and all of the aspects involved in "*Manifest Destiny*", and the enemy taking the place of the Hebrews, claiming Hebrew heritage as their own, will come upon you. Hebrews today, there is a saying that many have been using: *Wake-up Hebrews!* Come out of those religions that are the noose around your neck. Those religions are the Negroes laying in the streets dead or dying with a knee on their neck. Those religions are the cause of Negro parents stressing and distressing when their child, in particular, their male child leaves the house, the parents worry about whether their child will return home safely. Here is the fix, Hebrews!

Devarim/Deu. 30:16:

'*in that I Command you this day to love the HASHEM your Elohim, to walk in HIS ways, and to keep HIS **Commandments** and HIS **statutes** and HIS **rulings**, that you may live and multiply: and the HASHEM your Elohim shall bless you in the **land where you go to possess it**.*'

This is not a difficult thing to accomplish. I realize there are 613 rules the Hebrews have to follow, but there is a caveat that must be pointed out: Until the Hebrews have complied to: having no other Elohim, keeping the Shabbath Day, honoring parents, not to kill, not to steal, not to commit adultery, not to lie against anyone, and not to take by force, that which does not belong to you. These ten (10) rules have to come first. Without being in compliance to these ten (10) rules, the

Hebrews will not have their own homeland. Those other rules cannot be completely upheld because the Hebrews are not collected into their own land, where they will grow their own vegetables, and raise their own herds, and so on. Once the Hebrews awaken to who they are, and return to following *The Ten Commandments*, all that they lost will be restored to them. Watch this, line and precept.

Devarim 30:17-19:

*'But if your heart turn away, so that you will not hear, but shall be drawn away, **and worship other gods**, and serve them; 18 I denounce unto you this day, that you shall surely **perish**, and that you shall not prolong your days upon the land, when you pass over Yarden to go to possess it. 19 I call heaven and earth to record this day against you, that I have set before you life and death, blessing and cursing: **therefore choose life**, that both you and your seed may live.'*

The message hidden in these verses is this: When the Hebrews return to worshiping Elohim only, and comply with the Commandments of Elohim, wherever the Hebrews have been scattered, they will be collected from all corners of the globe, and their Sovereignty restored. Passing over the Yarden is symbolic of when the Hebrews have passed into the Promised Land, apostatized from Elohim, and then after realizing their errors, are now ready to cross the Yarden for the last time. Hebrews, the only way to be healed is in Elohim. I would suggest to the Hebrews individually, while the family is still in exile, if you are in recognition of who you are, comply to the Laws of Elohim; teach the truth of Elohim, and of Hebrewism. Many Negroes will deny who they are in the lies that have been ingrained into their brains for many millennia by the enemy. Not all Hebrews will awaken, and will continue in the ways of the heathens, but you individually, teaching in truth, walking in truth, have reserved your own soul in Elohim. Halleluia to the King! Selah!

# THE BOOK IN REVIEW

We have taken a panoramic view of History, Science, and Scripture in the *Plight And Travels Of The Hebrews*. All of the information covered in this work are supported by information written in the following documents: *The Authorized King James Bible*, *The Book of Enoch*, *The Cabala/Talmud*, *The Septuagint*, *The Book of Yashar*, *The Orthodox Jewish Bible*, *History Manuals*, *Science Manuals*, and various *World Institutions*, such as: *The U.S. Geological Service; National Geographic; The Smithsonian; Vatican City; The British Museum; The Russian Museum; Archaeological Museums, and of Artifacts from Ancient Mitzrayim (Egypt)*.

We have viewed information on time periods before the earth formed into what it is today; covering the *Triassic Period: The Mesozoic, Permian, Tertiary, and Cenozoic* eras, to *Pangaea/Pangea*, in ancient days to the present. During the time of *Pangaea/Pangea* all of *Africa, Australia, Madagascar, Antarctica, India*, and all of the countries below the equator, including *South America, are referred to as: Gondwanaland/Gondwana*. We have discussed the world map being drawn top-side down, as presented by several institutions on how the earth formed in ancient days. In studying world formation, clearly the maps are drawn in reverse orientation, meaning: What we have known as South is North, and vise versa. Information about Gondwanaland tells us of the *Tethys Sea*, the route that would eventually become the route from *Gondwanaland* to *Laurasia* in the *African Diaspora*. In looking at the history of the earth's formation, we came to the time of the first life forms that existed in the time after the *Jurassic* and *Cretaceous Periods*. The first life would be the animal kingdom, which included the *homo erectus*, pre-human creatures more like an ape than a human. All of the information involving the formation of the earth's plates comes from *Geological* and *Paleontological Sciences*. Over millions of years the earth's *tectonic* plates separated more and more until there were four (4) continents as we have today. According to the *U.S. Geological Institute*, and other geological institutions, this planet is at minimum 200 million years old.

After going through the many creations periods of the *Triassic Era*, our focus turned to the days of creation from the Biblical perspective. In that discussion, we ventured into the War in Shamayim, and the *Malachs (__Angels__)* "*which __kept not their first estate__, but left their __own habitation__*,". Those fallen angels, the *Annunaki*, contaminated the *Pre-Aw-dawnics*, and other animals with their wild and extreme sexual prowess. Those *Pre-Aw-dawnic* creatures were not completely human; they were a cross between the animal world, and the humans yet to come; those creatures are referred to as *homo erectus*. From discussioning the homo erectus, we introduced some books not commonly known to the vast portion of society, books, such as: *The Book of Enoch, The Midrash Rabbah, The Babylonian Talmud, The Cabala Talumd, The Septuagint, and The Orthodox Jewish Bible*. Those books introduced us to stories not detailed in the *Authorized King James Bible*; such as: the curse of *Ham*; the first female recorded in the Scriptures, *Lillith*, and what actually transpired in the *Garden of Eden*.

After venturing into the beginning stories of humanity, we examined the words of Bereshis/Genesis, Chapters 1 and 2, examining the differences in the stories: Bereshis 1:27: '*created male and female*' simultaneously, is not the same creation as Bereshis 2:22: '*made from the rib of the man*'. These are two separate births or *genesis*. The Scriptures then go on to varify the difference in the stories in its use of the word: *__Replenish__*, in Bereshis 1:28.

In examining multiple books of Scripture, we looked at the fallen malachs, and the Watchers, and what their role was in the War in Shamayim; what their punishment is; where the fallen ones are today; and their influence on humanity. Furthermore, we lookded at the difference between the good Malachs: *__Michael__ and __Gabriel__, __Raphael__, __Suryal__, and __Uriel__*; and the evil malachs: *__Samyaza, Armen, Basasael, Turyal__, and their leader, __Azazyel__*."

As we continued through the history of Gondwanaland, and the fallen malchs, we approached *The African Diaspora*. That brought us to the people spreading out to all corners of the earth, and how people have warred, and conquered, and been conquered, leading to the *Arab Slave Trade, The Trans Atlantic Slave Trade*, and the *The Babylonian Exile of Yisra'el*. The movement of people brought us to the inhabitors of Europe, and discussion of the *Grimaldian Negroid in Europe*. The African Diaspora led to multiple languages. That inturn brought us to the formation of a new language referred to as *The Lingua Franca*, a combination language of the following languages: *Italian, French, Arabic, Spanish, and Greek*. The variation in languages then brouht us to word etymology, and names of people and lands that are synonymous. The following names are all synonyms of Yisra'el; these names relate to the forefather of Yisra'el: *Ibrahim, Hebrew, Iberia, Eber, Ibrim, Ibriyyim*, and all of them trace back to the name *Abraham*. What was discovered in the synonyms for Abraham is the word *Iberia*. That information led to research of Iberia, which is the *Iberian Peninsula*, a short distance from Africa across the *Straight of Gibralta*, in the *Mediterranean Sea*.

After visiting historical and scientific data the focus of our attention then went into the Scriptures once again to explore what occured in the Garden of Eden. Afterward visiting Cain and Able, Seth, and what it means to be "**beguiled**"? What is the seed of Hasatan and the woman? What is it to be the "**likeness**" and "**image**" of Elohim? And what is "**daughters of men, and the sons of Elohim**"? Those are topics of great value because the answers to those questions is explained in a condition known as *Hetero-paternal super-fecundation*: To be pregnant with twins by two different men.

We also discussed the role of mythology in history: characters, such as: *Enki, Heru, Osiris, Poseidon, Zeus*, and *Hades*. And also there is this: *The word **dog** is word play for the word **god**? The word dog goes back to Ancient Mitzrayim, and is representative of the god of the afterlife, **Anubis**. "This god, Anubis, a dog; hence (by euphemism) a **male prostitute**"*. History tells us the use of the word dog is symnonomous with the word god.

*Another important topic we covered in our reading is the importance of melanin, its function, and why melanin plays a vital part in world* history. *Melanin provides us information that relates directly to the African Diaspora. Melanin is also important in healing diseases and or preventing disease. One of the greatest benefits of melanin is it protects the skin from the sun. Several Scriptures were pulled together showing exactly how melanin tells us, the outer appearance of people seven millennia ago. To substantiate the effects of melanin, science by way of deoxyribonucleic acid (DNA) has proven the importance of melanin.*

In honor of Elohim, the Hebrews are to hold specified celebrations each year, at the same date every year, perpetually. The celebration of *The Passover* is a *Sacred Convocation* which involves the *Feast of Unleavened Bread, The Festival of Wine, The Feast of Weeks, and The Feast of Tabernacles.* The dates of these celebrations are of the Hebrew calendar, not the *Gregorian* calendar. The Passover takes place in the month *Abib,* which marks the *Hebrew New Year.* Another important day for the Hebrews to observe and keep is the *Shabbath Day,* the Seventh Day of the week.

In visiting the historical and scriptural data on where the Hebrews lived, and their disobedience to Elohim, the Hebrews were ousted from the land. The Hebrews failure to remain obedient to Elohim led to the **_Ashkenaz_** and **_Sephardim_** peoples being the possessors of the land because Elohim was angry with HIS Chosen people. The Scriptures make it expressly clear, the Hebrews of **_Samaria_** (Yisra'el) were replaced by *Askenazim, and Sephardic* people. Those people did not serve the Elohim of the Hebrews, they served *Adrammelech* and *Anammelech,* their gods. In seeing the Hebrews were pushed-out of their homeland, we then discussed several maps showing the location of Samaria, Mt. Hor, and Yerushalayim.

*We also looked at historical records on the writing of the First King James Bible. That bible, the first 1611 publication contains no "J" words because the letter "J" had not been invented at the time of publication. The name "James" was spelled "Iames", as the letter "J" was created from the letter "I". In the section of this book discussing when the AKJV of Scripture was written, a photo of the cover of that bible cleary shows the kings name as "Iames".*

*One of the most cloaked aspects of Scripture involves sex, sexuality,*

334

*and things associated with reproduction. The Scriptures discuss topics such as: Not* having sex with a woman on her period, homosexuality, and bestiality. Those, who don't read from OT Scriptures miss-out on valuable information such as; Bamidbar/Num. 31:17: *'Now therefore* **kill every male** *among the* **little ones**, *and* **kill every woman** *that has* **had sex with man** *by* **lying with him**'. The Scriptures also discuss venereal disease.

We also discussed parts of speech and writing, breakingdown how some words in the bible are not Hebrew in origin, and should not be used by Hebrews in reference to Elohim: god, lord, and holy. In researching the etymology of those words, is where the *pleonasm* and *dative* come into play: **Pleonasm**: redundancy. **Dative**: represents something already in existence, a person, place or thing. The redundancy in a *pleonasm* is: *The* **lady**, **she** *said*; rather than: The **lady said**. The *dative* is where in Scripture word usage significantly changes the story. A *dative* represents something already in existence, a person, place or thing that has been given a new name, and what was represented previously, has been replaced by another person, place or thing.

In all of the King James bible, almost every word used is in English, and very few of the original Hebrew names for the people and the names of cities were left intact. However, the words *"Eli, Eli Lama Sabachthani?"*, which is Hebrew was left intact. Why would the transcribers leave those Hebrew words in the NT, an actual *transliteration*, and not a *translation*? As discussed, the sons of Eli did evil, and was "Jesus" calling on Elohim or his god? We know Ha Mashiach could not have been the Messenger of Elohim because their can never be any place in B.C., any person or place spelled with the letter *"J"*. Who was tortured an hung on that tree is written of in *The Cabala Talmud*. Furthermore, the punishment of being hung is the most dishonorable death in all of humanity.

We also looked at the *History of the Moors*, and the *British Royals*. From historical records we looked at who those people were, and how the secrets of their identity was kept from public view. Those truths were kept in secret places; such as: *The Smithsonian; Vatican City; The British Museum; The Russian Museum; Archaeological Museums, and of Artifacts Museums of Ancient Mitzrayim (Egypt)*.

We have discussed history from many official documents. Some of the Laws written againt Hebrew rights and humanity were: *The Thirteenth Amendment, Jim Crow, and Sundown Laws.* Those laws were applied strictly to the Negroes in the Southern States of the United States of America. Those laws involved tenants of heinous intent; such as: *amalgamation* and *acculturation,* and then *Assimilation.* However, assimilation is where the Hebrew outwardly is given the facade of being equal to the enemy, but inwardly, is ostracized into an inferior lifestyle, unable to bridge out of intersectionalism. Other documents that support the subordinate position of the Hebrew is the *Star-Spangled Banner,* and *The Religious Instruction of The Negroes. In The United States.* *The Thirteenth Amendment* clearly says, if a person (Negro) commits any crime, the Hebrew can be put into slavery again for the smallest infraction of Jim Crow. The instructions to make a Negro Christian, clearly comes from the *Heads of the Church,* and are totally accepted by the *U.S. Government*; and was approved by the *Leadership of the British Imperial Government.* What all of these documents represent was not unkown to many spokespersons of the Negroes. Dr. Martin L. King Jr., made acknowledgement of the inequities in his "*I Have a Dream Speech*", in the march on Washington. Another tenant of the Hebrews in America is also well documented in *Manifest Destiny.*

*The Plight And Travels Of The Hebrews* will end when the Hebrews awaken to who they are, and return to their roots in Elohim. Selah..

# REFERENCES

Africans and Negroes Are Not the Same People (Youtube)
African Diaspora II International Migration
Ancient.eu/Anubis
Ancient.eu/Indra
Andrew Fazekas, For National Geographic News; Sep 9, 2012
Archives.gov/files/press:pg.1
Bbc.co.uk/worldsevice/africa/features/storyof
Biblearchaeology.org/research/exodus-egypt4012
Cambridge English Dictionary
Cone, James H., GOD of the OPPRESSED, Orbis Books, Mary Knoll,
     NY 1054500308, ISBN: 978-1-57075-158-5, 1997, pages 10-11
Daily Mail.com
Democracy Dies in Darkness; The Washington Post, February 6, 2018
Dictionary.com
Etymonline.com
Faculty.webster.edu/corbetre'haiti
Greattimeline.com
Google.com
Iahushua.com/WOI/control.htm
Images.search.yahoo.com
Lyrics.com/track/508956
Mariobuildreps.com
Mationalgeographic.com/culture/2019/07/ancient-dna-reveal-
     philistine-origins/#close
Merriam-Webster.com
Midrash Rabbab
Nationalhumanitiescenter.org
Ncbi.nlm.nih.gov/pmc/articlespmc4269527

Newafricanmagaz.com/16616

Nps.gov/National Preserve Alaska

Nsf.gov/geo/opp/support/gondwana.jsp

Nhm.ac.uk/discover/when -did-dinosaurs

Orthodox Jewish Bible (OJB)

Quora.com

Pbs.org/wgbh/aia/part4/4h2933

Pubs.usgs.gov/piblications'text/historical

Sankofa.ch/Melanin.htm

Spanish-fiestas.com/history/moors

Stanford Encyclopedia of Philosophy

Strong's Exhaustive Concordance of the Bible

The Babylonian Talmud

The Book of Enoch

The Book of Macaabees

The Book of Yashar

THE CABALA/TALMUD

Thedogplace.org

The Encyclopedia Americana

THE RELIGIOUS INSTRUCTION OF THE NEGROES. IN THE
    UNITED STATES    BY CHARLES C. JONES

Wiseconservatism.com/2011/01/06/35th-clause-in-the-constitution-
what-is-it-and-why-was-it-put-in/

Zondervan Bible Dictionary

Printed in the United States
by Bookmasters

Printed in the United States
By Bookmasters